Modern American Women

Modern American Women

A Documentary History

SECOND EDITION

Susan Ware

Radcliffe Institute for Advanced Study, Harvard University

Boston   Burr Ridge, IL   Dubuque, IA   Madison, WI   New York
San Francisco   St. Louis   Bangkok   Bogotá   Caracas   Kuala Lumpur
Lisbon   London   Madrid   Mexico City   Milan   Montreal   New Delhi
Santiago   Seoul   Singapore   Sydney   Taipei   Toronto

McGraw-Hill Higher Education &

A Division of The **McGraw-Hill** *Companies*

MODERN AMERICAN WOMEN
A Documentary History

Published by McGraw-Hill/Irwin, an imprint of The McGraw-Hill Companies, Inc., 1221 Avenue of the Americas, New York, NY 10020. Copyright © 2002, 1997 by The McGraw-Hill Companies, Inc. All rights reserved. No part of this publication may be reproduced or distributed in any form or by any means, or stored in a database or retrieval system, without the prior written permission of The McGraw-Hill Companies, Inc., including, but not limited to, in any network or other electronic storage or transmission, or broadcast for distance learning. Some ancillaries, including electronic and print components, may not be available to customers outside the United States.

This book is printed on acid-free paper.

1 2 3 4 5 6 7 8 9 0 DOC/DOC 0 9 8 7 6 5 4 3 2 1

ISBN 0-07-241820-6

Publisher: *Jane Karpacz*
Executive editor: *Lyn Uhl*
Developmental editor: *Kristen Mellitt*
Marketing manager: *Janise Fry*
Project manager: *Diane M. Folliard*
Production supervisor: *Lori Koetters*
Coordinator freelance design: *Mary Kazak*
Cover image: *©Corbis;™ 2001 Amelia Earhart CMG WorldWide under license authorized by CMG Worldwide, Inc., Indianapolis, Indiana, 46256 USA www.cmgww.com*
Cover and interior design: *Joanne Schopler*
Photo research coordinator: *Jeremy Cheshareck*
Photo researcher: *Catherine Nance*
Producer, Media technology: *Sean Crowley*
Compositor: *Graphic Arts Center*
Typeface: *10/12 Times Roman*
Printer: *R. R. Donnelley & Sons Company*

Library of Congress Cataloging-in-Publication Data

Modern American women: a documentary history / [compiled by] Susan Ware.—2nd ed.
     p.   cm.
  Includes bibliographical references.
  ISBN 0-07-241820-6 (alk. paper)
  1. Women—United States—History—20th century—Sources. 2. Feminism—United States—History—20th century—Sources. 3. Women social reformers—United States— History—Sources. I. Ware, Susan, 1950- II. Title.

HQ1410.M63 2002
305.4'0973—dc21

                                                                                                2001030910

www.mhhe.com

About the Author

SUSAN WARE specializes in twentieth-century U.S. history and the history of American women. She is the author of *Letter to the World: Seven Women Who Shaped the American Century* (1998); *Still Missing: Amelia Earhart and the Search for Modern Feminism* (1993); *Partner and I: Molly Dewson, Feminism, and New Deal Politics* (1987); *Holding Their Own: American Women in the 1930s* (1982); and *Beyond Suffrage: Women in the New Deal* (1981). From 1986 to 1995 she taught in the history department at New York University. She is currently affiliated with the Radcliffe Institute of Advanced Study at Harvard University, where she is editing the next volume of the biographical dictionary *Notable American Women*.

Preface

How does the world look through women's eyes? How have different women viewed that world? How does our perception of history change when women are placed at its center rather than on the margins? This anthology provides a woman-centered view of modern America. Every single document was written by a woman, including a Supreme Court decision—something that would have been impossible before Sandra Day O'Connor broke that barrier in 1981. In this book, history unfolds through the perspectives of the participants—women themselves—rather than through prescriptive literature designed to tell women what they ought to do and who they ought to be. When women tell their own stories, they emerge as actors and participants in a host of activities beyond home and family, providing strong evidence for the pioneer feminist historian Mary Beard's characterization of women as *force in history*.

In keeping with feminist scholarship and women's history methodology, no single female voice emerges from these documents, but rather a multiplicity of voices. There are intellectuals and housewives, seasoned political veterans and teenagers, radicals and antifeminists. Stories describe the despair of the unemployed in the 1930s and the anger of women on welfare in the 1960s, the exhilaration of learning to ride a bicycle in the 1890s and the challenge of experimenting with new feminist lifestyles in the 1920s. There are many women of courage in this anthology—settlement house leaders, civil rights activists, pioneer doctors, labor organizers, writers, and radicals, all of whom helped to shape the course of modern American history. There are also women whose courage was more private: women trying to feed their families during hard times, an anxious rural mother worrying that the doctor would not get there when her labor pains began, Japanese-American women coping with forced relocation during World War II, women living with disease or disabilities. The experiences of both the extraordinary women who shape public events and the ordinary women whose lives comprise the social history of the times find their places here.

This anthology is dedicated to documenting the diversity of American women's lives. There is much more to the story of American women in the twentieth century than the perspectives of the white, middle-class, urban, heterosexual women who have been its most visible actors. For every experience of a white woman, it is necessary to think how the lives of black women or Latinas or Native Americans might have been different, while also remembering the significant differences among minority women themselves. For every example from urban America, we need to recall the experiences of rural women, who were after all a majority until the 1920s and a significant minority ever since. And it is vitally important to contrast the lives of married women with their unmarried sisters, especially those who chose to remain single as an expression of a different sexual or affectional preference.

Two methodological tools are useful for highlighting and interpreting an even further diversity in women's lives. The first is the *life cycle:* that is, looking at women's experiences over the entire course of their lives. Women who choose to marry and have children can still spend a majority of their adult years working outside the home—in other words, once a homemaker, not necessarily always a homemaker. Women born and raised on farms might move *el rancho al barrio*— from rural area to the city—only to return late in life to the rural communities where they grew up. This life-cycle approach has the potential to capture the cumulative effects of small changes over time. It also can demonstrate how women's lives are shaped by outside events at the same time they are changing from within.

The other useful tool for understanding twentieth-century women's history is a *generational approach*. At any given historical moment, several generations of women are participating in events and interacting among themselves. A generational approach is especially well suited to understanding the 1920s and the 1980s and 1990s, two periods in which younger women inherited the victories of earlier feminist activism without having to fight for the gains themselves. A generational approach dramatically increases the complexity of the story historians are trying to tell, because at any given moment women of different age groups may be undergoing very different experiences. In conjunction with attention to the life cycle and minority perspectives, a generational approach reminds us that a host of factors simultaneously shape women's lives—ranging from class, ethnic, or racial identification to sexual preference, age, and geographical location. There can be no such thing as a "typical American woman"; instead there are stories of a multitude of American women.

New Content

A number of new documents have been added for this edition. For example, the chapter on female sexuality and the female body (Chapter 12) has been expanded to include an excerpt from Eve Ensler's "The Vagina Monologues." The final chapter on the state of the movement for women's equality has also been updated to include more documents about contemporary feminism and women's issues. Chapter 1 now offers a document on anti-lynching activism by Ida B. Wells, and new material on Indian relocation by Wilma Mankiller appears in Chapter 9. Other authors new to the collection include Katie Roiphe, Jennifer Baumgardner, and Amy Richards.

This anthology is divided into three parts, with its periodization designed to help structure and organize the past century of American women's history. Part One covers the period between 1890 and 1920, when women literally and figuratively left the nineteenth century behind and stepped into the modern era and into a period of reform that historians refer to as the Progressive era. Part Two traces women's lives in the postsuffrage era, situating their individual stories within periods of prosperity alternating with depression, world wars and their aftermaths, periods of conservatism and incipient political activism. Part Three focuses on the revival of feminism and its aftershocks, with 1963 chosen as a symbolic starting date because that year marked the publication of Betty Friedan's *The Feminine Mystique*. The new realities in women's lives are here to stay, although they continue to be the subject of ongoing public debate about their meaning and future.

Organization and Pedagogy

This volume also provides tools to help the student analyze the documents. Part-opening introductions, new to this edition, and chapter-opening introductions attempt to place the documents that follow in historical context and introduce key issues with which historians have been concerned. Headnotes to each document provide information about its author or origins, the reasons why it was written, and the intended audience. A photo essay is included in each part to give a visual history of the era under consideration, and Suggestions for Further Reading sections encourage further pursuit of the topics and events covered in each part.

The portrait that emerges from this collection of women's voices confirms the resourcefulness of American women and demonstrates their contributions to the shaping of the society at large. It captures women's hopes and aspirations for themselves, their families, and their communities, as well as their inevitable disappointments and setbacks. The history of the twentieth century, both its politics and everyday life, looks richer, fuller, and certainly more representative when the diverse stories of the nation's women occupy center stage. Here, then, is modern women's America.

Website

A new companion Website is also available. For additional information about and resources relevant to American women's history, visit www.mhhe.com/american-women.

Acknowledgments

Preparing another edition of this anthology has given me the chance to renew old acquaintances and make new friends as I decided which selections to keep and which to add. Just reviewing the new scholarship that has appeared since the first edition in 1989 confirms the vitality of women's history, a field of which I am proud to be a part.

Nancy Woloch has demonstrated unwavering belief in our linked anthologies, and I would like to thank her for her friendship, support, and good humor. David Follmer originally suggested the idea for the book, and I am grateful to him for sending me in this direction more than a decade ago. Stacy Braukman and Deborah Levine, my colleagues on the staff of *Notable American Women* at Radcliffe, served as sounding boards while I worked on this revision and also gave me suggestions of new sources. And I would like to acknowledge with gratitude the ongoing support of Joyce Antler, who has always been a big fan of this book and whose friendship means a great deal to me.

It is a pleasure to be associated with the College Division of McGraw-Hill, and I would like to thank Lyn Uhl and Kristen Mellitt for their editorial support. I am also grateful to reviewers of the previous edition who contributed their ideas and suggestions for improving this volume:

Elizabeth Clement, University of Utah
Nancy Gabin, Purdue University
Leah Halper, Gavilan College
Cynthia Harrison, George Washington University
Margaret Jacobs, New Mexico State University
Lisa Keller, Purchase College
Vicky Knickerbocker, Central Lakes College
Patricia Moore, Green Mountain College
Kathryn Tomasek, Wheaton College
Elizabeth Varon, Wellesley College

Finally, I would like to thank Radcliffe Institute for Advanced Study at Harvard University, and especially the staff of the Schlesinger Library, for providing such a congenial setting for the study of women's history.

SUSAN WARE

Contents

Part II
INDIVIDUAL CHOICES,
COLLECTIVE PROGRESS, 1920–1963   117

Part III
THE PERSONAL BECOMES POLITICAL,
1963 TO THE PRESENT   233

Modern American Women

PART ONE

Modern Women in the Making

1890–1920

*H*istorians usually refer to the period between 1890 and 1920 as the Progressive era. During this cycle of reform and activism, the United States began to confront the problems raised by its recent industrialization, the massive immigration under way, its new role as an international power, and the increasing concentration of population in urban areas. Although no one strand unifies Progressive era historiography, the period certainly looks different when women are included. Instead of just hearing about efficiency, regulation, and scientific management (the dominant interpretations of men's participation), the women's perspective directs attention toward humanitarian and social reform: concern for child labor, unhealthy conditions in city neighborhoods, and long hours and low pay in factories or sweatshops. What had long been women's province through voluntary associations and charitable benevolence was increasingly defined as a proper scope for public policy.

As women claimed these new roles, they played a major part in shaping the course of the Progressive era and women's history. Besides being central to the reform movement, women joined unions, battled racial discrimination, entered the professions, organized for birth control, and waged a successful campaign for the vote. In areas such as fertility, wage-force participation, and political activity, their lives were, tentatively, beginning to prefigure patterns that resemble women's lives today. And yet alongside the excitement about new opportunities for women went a continuation of old attitudes and ideas that still relegated women to an unequal status. While visions of the "new woman" held out the promise for a fuller life, her freedom remained incomplete.

This section shows the "new" and the "old" coexisting—and sometimes competing—in women's lives between 1890 and 1920. Daring journalists such as Nellie Bly travel around the world, and women homesteaders stake claims in the West. Rural women talk about the burdens of their lives, and domestic servants and industrial workers document harsh conditions on the job. College-educated women struggle to find meaningful work in a society that still expects them to

1

marry and bear children, and recent immigrants try to reconcile values from the Old World with the possibilities that America holds, especially for its daughters. And women come together in women's organizations—in unions, in suffrage groups, in anti-lynching societies—entering the public sphere and actively participating in all aspects of public life.

CHAPTER 1

Visions of the New Woman

By the 1890s, a new woman had appeared on the American scene in education, athletics, reform, and the job market. One way to capture what was "new" about the new woman is to examine how she was dressed. Rather than encumbered in yards of material, heavy corsets, and petticoats like her mother and grandmother wore, the new woman was dressed comfortably in tailored suits or long dark skirts worn with simple blouses. Artist Charles Dana Gibson popularized this image of women with his magazine illustrations of "Gibson girls." The new styles were more than just a change in fashion. Not only did these women look self-reliant, but they also acted that way. Style changes allowed more freedom of movement, increased athleticism, and more physicality on the part of women who were no longer confined by corsets and hoopskirts. As such, the new style symbolized the freedom and opportunity available to the new woman of the 1890s.

The new woman was one product of the vast changes under way in American society due to the maturation of the economy and the growing urban orientation of the country. The increase in opportunity for higher education for women in the late 19th century and the corresponding growth in professional careers provided avenues for gainful employment and a viable alternative to marriage. In many ways, the late 19th century was a golden age for single women: such women as settlement pioneer Jane Addams were widely revered for their contributions to public life. Approximately 10 percent of the cohort of women born between 1860 and 1880 remained single—one of the highest rates recorded. Choosing not to marry did not mean, however, giving up a fulfilling emotional life, for many of these new professional women chose to share their lives with other women in life-long relationships.

In addition to these changes for single women, there were also important changes in the lives of married women, especially the white, middle-class home-makers who lived in urban areas. Technological changes began to free women from some of the hardest toil associated with housekeeping. Such improvements as central heating, electricity, indoor plumbing, and kitchen appliances lightened their chores; so too did the availability of store-bought goods and food, such as commercially baked bread or men's ready-to-wear clothing. The family was completing a long-term shift from a unit of production to one of consumption. In a related trend, as more families settled in urban areas rather than rural, the economic rewards of large families diminished. The birthrate had declined steadily through-out the 19th century, and by 1900, women were having an average of 3.5 children, half the level in 1800.

The lessened time that middle-class women devoted to housekeeping and child rearing helped pave the way for women's increased activism beyond the four walls of their homes. One striking characteristic of American society by the 1890s was the proliferation of women's organizations. The key to understanding this development lies in the way that women extended the values they prized in their families and domestic sphere to the broader body politic. Historian Mary Beard described how this progression worked in a 1915 study of women's work in municipalities:

> Woman's historic function having been along the line of cleanliness, her in-stinct when she looks forth from her own clean windows is toward public cleanliness. Her indoor battle has been against the dirt that blew in from out-side, against the dust and ashes of the streets, and the particles of germ-laden matter carried in from neglected refuse piles. Ultimately she begins to take an interest in that portion of municipal dusting and sweeping assigned to men: namely street cleaning.

This ideology is often called *municipal housekeeping.*

Middle-class women, black and white, did not lack institutional or organiza-tional bodies with which to influence public policy. Starting with the women's club movement in the post-Civil War period, women strove to fuse politics with their domestic ideals. Such an ideology also helped the final push for suffrage. The responsibilities that instruments of government increasingly took on for im-proving the social welfare of citizens testify to women's impact. Women's activi-ties also show how fluid and porous the supposed separation of the public and private spheres had become by the early 20th century.

Many of these developments were limited to the members of the middle and upper classes who had the option of taking advantage of these new opportunities. Very few recent immigrants from Italy or Poland were sending their daughters off to Wellesley in the 1890s, nor were immigrant families who were crowded in the nation's cities able to enjoy the advantages of the new housekeeping technologies. But the nation's working-class women were far from passive, downtrodden vic-tims. They, especially the younger women, were actors in shaping a new destiny for themselves in the urban environment of factory, shop, department store, and dance hall. Women of different classes and racial and ethnic backgrounds did feel a stirring, an awakening to the possibilities that the "new woman" represented.

"Girl Reporter Derring-Do"

Nellie Bly

Perhaps there is no better image of the open-ended possibilities for Ameri-can women at the end of the 19th century than that of the plucky journalist

Nellie Bly setting off to travel around the world on her own in 1889. Her inspiration, as she pitched the idea to her editor at *The World,* was to beat the record of the fictional Phileas Fogg in Jules Verne's *Around the World in Eighty Days* (1873) and share the story of her travel adventures with readers back home. As this selection from her book chronicling her journey describes, her editor was reluctant to send a young woman off alone (she was then 25 years old, although she cut three years off her age to heighten her youthfulness). He was also worried that a female traveler would insist on taking dozens of trunks. Nellie Bly proved him wrong on both counts, safely traveling the world by commercial transportation in 72 days, 6 hours, and 11 minutes. Her luggage? The traveling dress and cape she wore, plus the contents of a small gripsack. So much for female vanity!

Nellie Bly was the name Elizabeth Cochrane adopted when she became a reporter—it came from a popular Stephen Foster song. Born in 1864 in a small Pennsylvania town, she entered journalism at age 20 when her spirited response to an anti-feminist article in a Pittsburgh paper so captured an editor's attention that he offered her a byline. Much of her journalistic output, including her trip around the world, was what has been called detective or stunt journalism—she would conceal her identity (she once feigned insanity to write about conditions within an asylum) or put herself in an unusual situation and then write about it for audiences. The often crusading nature of these pieces foreshadowed the muckraking journalism of the early 20th century.

Nellie Bly's around-the-world trip was a commercial and financial success. *The World* saw its circulation soar, and more than 300,000 readers participated in a contest to guess the exact time of her return. (The winner, who got a free trip to Europe, was only off by two-fifths of a second.) Bly found herself in great demand as a lecturer and author, and her image was commercialized on games, cards, and other collectors' items. However, she left *The World,* and the public eye, soon after. In 1895 she married a 72-year-old New York businessperson named Robert L. Seaman and lived quietly in New York until his death in 1910. Bly tried to revive her journalism career but never regained her former celebrity. She died in 1922.

What gave me the idea?

It is sometimes difficult to tell exactly what gives birth to an idea. Ideas are the chief stock in trade of newspaper writers and generally they are the scarcest stock in market, but they do come occasionally.

This idea came to me one Sunday. I had spent a greater part of the day and half the night vainly trying to fasten on some idea for a newspaper article. It was my custom to think up ideas on Sunday and lay them before my editor for his approval or disapproval on Monday. But ideas did not come that day and three o'clock in the morning found me weary and with an aching head tossing about in my bed. At last tired and provoked at my slowness in finding a subject, something for the week's work, I thought fretfully.

Source: Nellie Bly, *Around the World in Seventy-Two Days* (New York: The Pictorial Weeklies Company, 1890), pp. 3–4, 5–6, 8–9, 10–11, 11–13, 14.

"I wish I was at the other end of the earth!"

"And why not?" the thought came: "I need a vacation; why not take a trip around the world?"

It is easy to see how one thought followed another. The idea of a trip around the world pleased me and I added: "If I could do it as quickly as Phileas Fogg did, I should go."

Then I wondered if it were possible to do the trip in eighty days and afterwards I went easily off to sleep with the determination to know before I saw my bed again if Phileas Fogg's record could be broken . . .

I approached my editor rather timidly on the subject. I was afraid that he would think the idea too wild and visionary . . .

To my dismay he told me that in the office they had thought of this same idea before, and the intention was to send a man. However he offered me the consolation that he would favor my going, and then we went to talk with the business manager about it.

"It is impossible for you to do it," was the terrible verdict. "In the first place you are a woman and would need a protector, and even if it were possible for you to travel alone you would need to carry so much baggage that it would detain you in making rapid changes. Besides you speak nothing but English, so there is no use talking about it; no one but a man can do this."

"Very well," I said angrily, "Start the man and I'll start the same day for some other newspaper and beat him."

"I believe you would," he said slowly. I would not say that this had any influence on their decision, but I do know that before we parted I was made happy by the promise that if any one was commissioned to make the trip, I should be that one . . .

I bought one hand-bag with the determination to confine my baggage to its limit.

That night there was nothing to do but write to my few friends a line of farewell and to pack the hand-bag.

Packing that bag was the most difficult undertaking of my life; there was so much to go into such little space.

I got everything in at last except the extra dress. Then the question resolved itself into this: I must either add a parcel to my baggage or go around the world in and with one dress. I always hated parcels so I sacrificed the dress, but I brought out a last summer's silk bodice and after considerable squeezing managed to crush it into the hand-bag . . .

The evening before I started I went to the office and was given £200 in English gold and Bank of England notes. The gold I carried in my pocket. The Bank of England notes were placed in a chamois-skin bag which I tied around my neck. Besides this I took some American gold and paper money to use at different ports as a test to see if American money was known outside of America.

Down in the bottom of my hand-bag was a special passport, number 247, signed by James G. Blaine, Secretary of State. Someone suggested that a revolver would be a good companion piece for the passport, but I had such a strong belief in the world's greeting me as I greeted it, that I refused to arm myself. I knew if my conduct was proper I should always find men ready to protect me, let them be Americans, English, French, German or anything else . . .

I have been asked very often since my return how many changes of clothing I took in my solitary hand-bag. Some have thought I took but one; others think I carried silk which occupies but little space, and others have asked if I did not buy what I needed at the different ports.

One never knows the capacity of an ordinary hand-satchel until dire necessity compels the exercise of all one's ingenuity to reduce every thing to the smallest possible compass. In mine I was able to pack two traveling caps, three veils, a pair of slippers, a complete outfit of toilet articles, ink-stand, pens, pencils, and copy-paper, pins, needles and thread, a dressing gown, a tennis blazer, a small flask and a drinking cup, several complete changes of underwear, a liberal supply of hand-kerchiefs and fresh ruchings and most bulky and uncompromising of all, a jar of cold cream to keep my face from chapping in the varied climates I should encounter.

That jar of cold cream was the bane of my existence. It seemed to take up more room than everything else in the bag and was always getting into just the place that would keep me from closing the satchel. Over my arm I carried a silk waterproof, the only provision I made against rainy weather. After-experience showed me that I had taken too much rather than too little baggage. At every port where I stopped at I could have bought anything from a ready-made dress down, except possibly at Aden, and as I did not visit the shops there I cannot speak from knowledge . . .

So much for my preparations. It will be seen that if one is traveling simply for the sake of traveling and not for the purpose of impressing one's fellow passengers, the problem of baggage becomes a very simple one. On one occasion—in Hong Kong, where I was asked to an official dinner—I regretted not having an evening dress with me, but the loss of that dinner was a very small matter when compared with the responsibilities and worries I escaped by not having a lot of trunks and boxes to look after.

⨉ The Fair Women, Chicago, 1893

Bertha Palmer

When the World's Columbian Exhibition opened in Chicago in May 1893, one of its most popular exhibits was the Woman's Building. Visitors had a chance to see women's art, sculpture, and handicrafts; visit a room devoted to women's organizations; and leave their children in a supervised child care facility. Many women were somewhat ambivalent about putting women's

Source: Address by Mrs. Potter Palmer, in The Congress of Women, ed. Mary Kavanaugh Oldham Eagle (Chicago: American Publishing House, 1894). Reprinted by Arno Press, New York, 1974, pp. 25, 26, 28–29.

contributions in a separate building; why not compete on an equal basis with men throughout the fair? The participants reasoned that the success of this pavilion (which consciously drew on the Women's Pavilion at the Philadelphia Centennial of 1876) would encourage women to be seen as human beings, and thus, the organizers argued, "women's buildings, women's exhibits, may safely become things of the past."

The Woman's Building was planned and executed by a Board of Lady Managers, headed by Bertha Honoré Palmer (1849–1918). This board confirmed the influence that women were wielding in urban life, especially in the expanding city of Chicago. The wife of Chicago financial leader Potter Palmer, Bertha Palmer had long been active both as an arts patron and as a participant in social-reform causes through such groups as the Chicago Woman's Club. Palmer presided over the opening ceremonies for the Woman's Building on May 1, 1893. This speech, whose rhetoric and style is symptomatic of women's public speaking at the time, conveys women's pride in female accomplishments around the world; at the same time, it suggests a tentative feminism critical of men for excluding women from activities in the public sphere. The speech demonstrates especially well the connection women saw between the advancement for their sex and the general uplift of humanity.

Members of the Board of Lady Managers and Friends:—The moment of fruition has arrived. Hopes which for more than two years have gradually been gaining strength and definiteness now become realities. Today the Exposition opens its gates. On this occasion of the formal opening of the Woman's Building, the Board of Lady Managers is singularly fortunate in having the honor to welcome distinguished official representatives of many of the able foreign committees and of the state boards, which have so effectively co-operated with it in accomplishing the results now to be disclosed to the world . . .

The theory which exists among the conservative people, that the sphere of woman is her home—that it is unfeminine, even monstrous, for her to wish to take a place beside or to compete with men in the various lucrative industries—tells heavily against her, for manufacturers and producers take advantage of it to disparage her work and obtain her services for a nominal price, thus profiting largely by the necessities and helplessness of their victim. That so many should cling to respectable occupations while starving in following them, and should refuse to yield to discouragement and despair, shows a high quality of steadfastness and principle. These are the real heroines of life, whose handiwork we are proud to install in the Exposition, because it has been produced in factories, workshops and studios under the most adverse conditions and with the most sublime patience and endurance.

Men of the finest and most chivalric type, who have poetic theories about the sanctity of the home and the refining, elevating influence of woman in it, theories inherited from the days of romance and chivalry, which we wish might prevail forever—these men have asked many times whether the Board of Lady Managers thinks it well to promote a sentiment which may tend to destroy the home

by encouraging occupations for women which take them out of it. We feel, therefore, obliged to state our belief that every woman, who is presiding over a happy
home, is fulfilling her highest and truest function, and could not be lured from it
by temptations offered by factories or studios. Would that the eyes of these ideal-
ists could be thoroughly opened, that they might see, not the fortunate few of a favored class, with whom they possibly are in daily contact, but the general status
of the labor market throughout the world and the relation to it of women. They
might be astonished to learn that the conditions under which the vast majority of
the "gentler sex" are living, are not so ideal as they assume; that each is not
"dwelling in a home of which she is the queen, with a manly and loving arm to
shield her from rough contact with life." Because of the impossibility of reconcil-
ing their theories with the stern facts, they might possibly consent to forgive the
offense of widows with dependent children and those wives of drunkards and
criminals who so far forget the high standard established for them as to attempt to
earn for themselves daily bread, lacking which they must perish. The necessity for
their work under present conditions is too evident and too urgent to be questioned.
They must work or they must starve.

We are forced, therefore, to turn from the realm of fancy to meet and deal
with existing facts. The absence of a just and general appreciation of the truth concerning the position and status of women has caused us to call special attention to
it and to make a point of attempting to create, by means of the Exposition, a well
defined public sentiment in regard to their rights and duties, and the propriety of
their becoming not only self-supporting, but able to assist in maintaining their
families when necessary. We hope that the statistics which the Board of Lady
Managers has been so earnestly attempting to secure may give a correct idea of
the number of women—not only those without natural protectors, or those thrown
suddenly upon their own resources, but the number of wives of mechanics, labor-
ers, artists, artisans and workmen of every degree—who are forced to work shoulder to shoulder with their husbands in order to maintain the family . . .

The board does not wish to be understood as placing an extravagant or sentimental value upon the work of any woman because of her sex. It willingly acknowledges that the industries, arts and commerce of the world have been for
centuries in the hands of men who have carefully trained themselves for the responsibilities devolving upon them, and who have, consequently, without question, contributed vastly more than women to the valuable thought, research,
invention, science, art and literature, which have become the rich heritage of the
human race. Notwithstanding their disadvantages, however, a few gifted women
have made their value felt, and have rendered exceptional service to the cause of
humanity.

Realizing that woman can never hope to receive the proper recompense for
her services until her usefulness and success are not only demonstrated but fully
understood and acknowledged, we have taken advantage of the opportunity presented by the Exposition to bring together such evidences of her skill in the various industries, arts and professions, as may convince the world that ability is not
a matter of sex. Urged by necessity, she has shown that her powers are the same

as her brothers', and that like encouragement and fostering care may develop her to an equal point of usefulness.

The fact that the Woman's Building is so small that it can hold only a tithe of the beautiful objects offered, has been a great disadvantage. The character of the exhibits and the high standard attained by most of them serve, therefore, only as an index of the quality and range of the material from which we have drawn. When our invitation asking co-operation was sent to foreign lands, the commissioners already appointed generally smiled doubtfully and explained that their women were doing nothing; that they would not feel inclined to help us, and, in many cases, stated that it was not the custom of their country for women to take part in any public effort, that they only attended to social duties. But as soon as these ladies received our message, sent in a brief and formal letter, the free masonry among women proved to be such that they needed no explanation; they understood at once the possibilities. Strong committees were immediately formed of women having large hearts and brains, women who cannot selfishly enjoy the ease of their own lives without giving a thought to their helpless and wretched sisters.

Our unbounded thanks are due to the exalted and influential personages who became, in their respective countries, patronesses and leaders of the movement inaugurated by us to represent what women are doing. They entered with appreciation into our work for the Exposition because they saw an opportunity, which they gracefully and delicately veiled behind the magnificent laces forming the central objects in their superb collections, to aid their women by opening new markets for their industries.

The Exposition will thus benefit women, not alone by means of the material objects brought together, but there will be a more lasting and permanent result through the interchange of thought and sympathy among influential and leading women of all countries now for the first time working together with a common purpose and an established means of communication. Government recognition and sanction give to these committees of women official character and dignity. Their work has been magnificently successful, and the reports which will be made of the conditions found to exist will be placed on record as public documents among the archives of every country. Realizing the needs and responsibilities of the hour, and that this will be the first official utterance of women on behalf of women, we shall weigh well our words, words which should be so judicious and convincing that hereafter they may be treasured among the happy influences which made possible new and better conditions.

We rejoice in the possession of this beautiful building, in which we meet today, in its delicacy, symmetry and strength. We honor our architect and the artists who have given not only their hands but their hearts and their genius to its decoration. For it[s] women in every part of the world have been exerting their efforts and talents, for it[s] looms have wrought their most delicate fabrics, the needle has flashed in the hands of maidens under tropical suns, the lacemaker has bent over her cushion weaving her most artful web, the brush and chisel have sought to give form and reality to the visions haunting the brain of the artist—all have wrought with the thought of making our building worthy to serve its great end. We thank them all for their successful efforts.

The eloquent President of the Commission last October dedicated the great Exposition buildings to humanity. We now dedicate the Woman's Building to an elevated womanhood—knowing that by so doing we shall best serve the cause of humanity.

✣ *Black Women Plan to Lead Their Race*

Anna J. Cooper

Black women matched white women in organizational talent in the late 19th and early 20th centuries. Like their white sisters, they set an ambitious agenda that included not only larger roles for women but also general uplift for the race. The two were integrally related. As Anna J. Cooper said in 1892, "only the BLACK WOMAN can say 'when and where I enter in the quiet, undisputed dignity of my womanhood, without violence and without suing or special patronage, then and there the whole NEGRO RACE ENTERS WITH ME.' "

Much of the organizational energy of black women occurred within the club movement, which owing to the prevailing racism of the times ran on a separate but parallel track to the white women's club movement. Often groups came into existence to work for educational or social welfare goals in local communities; this commitment necessarily engendered a strong emphasis on race pride and racial advancement. By the 1890s, black women's clubs and organizations had coalesced into a national movement. When the National Association of Colored Women was founded in 1896 (Mary Church Terrell served as its first president), it counted 100 member organizations; by 1914, the NACW represented 50,000 women in 1,000 clubs.

Anna J. Cooper (1858–1964) represents the values and consciousness of these black organizational women at the turn of the century. Her book, *A Voice from the South* (1892), recognizes the unique situation of black women to reflect on both the woman question and the race problem. This excerpt from her chapter on the status of women in America calls on black women to take on wider social responsibilities in their communities as a way of uplifting both themselves and the entire black population. Such a dual consciousness has often characterized African-American women from the 19th century through the present.

The colored woman of to-day occupies, one may say, a unique position in this country. In a period of itself transitional and unsettled, her status seems one of the least ascertainable and definitive of all the forces which make for our civilization. She is confronted by both a woman question and a race problem, and is as yet an

Source: Anna J. Cooper, *A Voice from the South, By a Black Woman of the South* (Xenia, OH: The Aldine Printing House, 1892), pp. 134–137, 142–145.

unknown or an unacknowledged factor in both. While the women of the white race can with calm assurance enter upon the work they feel by nature appointed to do, while their men give loyal support and appreciative countenance to their efforts, recognizing in most avenues of usefulness the propriety and the need of woman's distinctive co-operation, the colored woman too often finds herself hampered and shamed by a less liberal sentiment and a more conservative attitude on the part of those for whose opinion she cares most. That this is not universally true I am glad to admit. There are to be found both intensely conservative white men and exceedingly liberal colored men. But as far as my experience goes the average man of our race is less frequently ready to admit the actual need among the sturdier forces of the world for woman's help or influence. That great social and economic questions await her interference, that she could throw any light on problems of national import, that her intermeddling could improve the management of school systems, or elevate the tone of public institutions, or humanize and sanctify the far reaching influence of prisons and reformatories and improve the treatment of lunatics and imbeciles—that she has a word worth hearing on mooted questions in political economy, that she could contribute a suggestion on the relations of labor and capital, or offer a thought on honest money and honorable trade, I fear the majority of "Americans of the colored variety" are not yet prepared to concede. It may be that they do not yet see these questions in their right perspective, being absorbed in the immediate needs of their own political complications. A good deal depends on where we put the emphasis in this world; and our men are not perhaps to blame if they see everything colored by the light of those agitations in the midst of which they live and move and have their being. The part they have had to play in American history during the last twenty-five or thirty years has tended rather to exaggerate the importance of mere political advantage, as well as to set a fictitious valuation on those able to secure such advantage. It is the astute politician, the manager who can gain preferment for himself and his favorites, the demagogue known to stand in with the powers at the White House and consulted on the bestowal of government plums, whom we set in high places and denominate great. It is they who receive the hosannas of the multitude and are regarded as leaders of the people. The thinker and the doer, the man who solves the problem by enriching his country with an invention worth thousands or by a thought inestimable and precious is given neither bread nor a stone. He is too often left to die in obscurity and neglect even if spared in his life the bitterness of fanatical jealousies and detraction.

And yet politics, and surely American politics, is hardly a school for great minds. Sharpening rather than deepening, it develops the faculty of taking advantage of present emergencies rather than the insight to distinguish between the true and the false, the lasting and the ephemeral advantage. Highly cultivated selfishness rather than consecrated benevolence is its passport to success. Its votaries are never seers. At best they are but manipulators—often only jugglers. It is conducive neither to profound statesmanship nor to the higher type of manhood. Altruism is its *mauvais succes,* and naturally enough it is indifferent to any factor which cannot be worked into its own immediate aims and purposes. As woman's influence as a political element is as yet nil in most of the commonwealths of our republic, it is not surprising that with those who place the emphasis on mere political capital she may yet seem almost a nonentity so far as it concerns the solution of great national or even racial perplexities . . .

Fifty years ago woman's activity according to orthodox definitions was on a pretty clearly cut "sphere," including primarily the kitchen and the nursery, and rescued from the barrenness of prison bars by the womanly mania for adorning every discoverable bit of china or canvass with forlorn looking cranes balanced idiotically on one foot. The woman of to-day finds herself in the presence of responsibilities which ramify through the profoundest and most varied interests of her country and race. Not one of the issues of this plodding, toiling, sinning, repenting, falling, aspiring humanity can afford to shut her out, or can deny the reality of her influence. No plan for renovating society, no scheme for purifying politics, no reform in church or in state, no moral, social, or economic question, no movement upward or downward in the human plane is lost on her. A man once said when told his house was afire: "Go tell my wife; I never meddle with household affairs." But no woman can possibly put herself or her sex outside any of the interests that affect humanity. All departments in the new era are to be hers, in the sense that her interests are in all and through all; and it is incumbent on her to keep intelligently and sympathetically *en rapport* with all the great movements of her time, that she may know on which side to throw the weight of her influence. She stands now at the gateway of this new era of American civilization. In her hands must be moulded the strength, the wit, the statesmanship, the morality, all the psychic force, the social and economic intercourse of that era. To be alive at such an epoch is a privilege, to be a woman then is sublime.

In this last decade of our century, changes of such moment are in progress, such new and alluring vistas are opening out before us, such original and radical suggestions for the adjustment of labor and capital, of government and the governed, of the family, the church and the state, that to be a possible factor though an infinitesimal one in such a movement is pregnant with hope and weighty with responsibility. To be a woman in such an age carries with it a privilege and an opportunity never implied before. But to be a woman of the Negro race in America, and to be able to grasp the deep significance of the possibilities of the crisis, is to have a heritage, it seems to me, unique in the ages. In the first place, the race is young and full of the elasticity and hopefulness of youth. All its achievements are before it. It does not look on the masterly triumphs of nineteenth century civilization with that *blasé* world-weary look which characterizes the old washed out and worn out races which have already, so to speak, seen their best days.

Said a European writer recently: "Except the Sclavonic, the Negro is the only original and distinctive genius which has yet to come to growth—and the feeling is to cherish and develop it."

Everything to this race is new and strange and inspiring. There is a quickening of its pulses and a glowing of its self-consciousness. Aha, I can rival that! I can aspire to that! I can honor my name and vindicate my race! Something like this, it strikes me, is the enthusiasm which stirs the genius of young Africa in

America; and the memory of past oppression and the fact of present attempted repression only serve to gather momentum for its irrepressible powers. Then again,
a race in such a stage of growth is peculiarly sensitive to impressions. Not the
photographer's sensitized plate is more delicately impressionable to outer influences than is this high strung people here on the threshold of a career.

What a responsibility then to have the sole management of the primal lights
and shadows! Such is the colored woman's office. She must stamp weal or woe on
the coming history of this people. May she see her opportunity and vindicate her
high prerogative.

Speaking Out Against Lynching

Ida B. Wells

Ida B. Wells (1862–1931) took Anna Cooper's call for black women's activism to new heights with her impassioned crusade against lynching. Already an outspoken opponent of discrimination (she had unsuccessfully sued
the Chesapeake & Ohio railroad in the 1880s over its policy of forcing all
black passengers to travel in segregated cars), her personal epiphany over
lynching came in Memphis in 1892, when three male acquaintances were
lynched. Part owner of a newspaper called the *Memphis Free Speech,* Wells
used that forum to expose the lynchings as an attempt to remove the economic challenge that black men posed to white shopkeepers, rather than retribution for supposed rapes of white women. As she later wrote in her
autobiography, *Crusade for Justice,* "This is what opened my eyes to what
lynching really was. An excuse to get rid of Negroes who were acquiring
wealth and prosperity and thus keep the race terrorized and 'keep the nigger
down.' " For her outspoken public criticism, her office was trashed and her
life threatened, forcing her to leave Memphis for New York.

Ida B. Wells's one-woman crusade against lynching took her throughout
the United States and to England. In 1895 she published *A Red Record,* an
analysis of recent lynchings with a preface by noted abolitionist Frederick
Douglass. In this selection, Wells lays out her argument that the notion of
protecting white Southern women from sexual assault by black men falsely
assumes that no white woman would ever engage in voluntary sexual relations with a black man.

In 1895 Wells married widower Ferdinand Lee Barnett, a Chicago
lawyer, and had four children between 1896 and 1904. Lynching was but one
of the many crusades for justice that Ida B. Wells-Barnett (as she was now
known) undertook in her lifetime. In 1890 she had challenged temperance
leader Frances Willard of the Women's Christian Temperance Union for her
racist depictions of black men's moral character, and in 1893 she had

Source: Ida B. Wells, *A Red Record: Tabulated Statistics and Alleged Causes of Lynchings in the
United States, 1892–1893–1894* (Chicago: Donohue & Henneberry, 1895), reprinted in Ida B. Wells-
Barnett, *On Lynchings: Southern Horrors; A Red Record; Mob Rule in New Orleans* (New York: Arno
Press, 1969), pp. 10–13.

protested black women's exclusion from the World's Columbian Exhibition in Chicago. In 1913 she organized one of the first black woman suffrage organizations, the Alpha Suffrage Club of Chicago, although she sometimes spent as much time fighting the racism of the white suffrage movement as she did battling for the vote. In a 1913 suffrage parade in Washington, D.C., timed to coincide with the inauguration of President Woodrow Wilson, Wells-Barnett was originally told that her delegation would have to march separately so as not to offend white Southerners. Undaunted, she marched alongside white suffragists, refusing to be deemed a second-class citizen in a movement dedicated to winning women their rights.

Humanity abhors the assailant of womanhood, and this charge upon the Negro at once placed him beyond the pale of human sympathy. With such unanimity, earnestness and apparent candor was this charge made and reiterated that the world has accepted the story that the Negro is a monster which the Southern white man has painted him. And to-day, the Christian world feels, that while lynching is a crime, and lawlessness and anarchy the certain precursors of a nation's fall, it can not by word or deed, extend sympathy or help to a race of outlaws, who might mistake their plea for justice and deem it an excuse for their continued wrongs.

The Negro has suffered much and is willing to suffer more. He recognizes that the wrongs of two centuries can not be righted in a day, and he tries to bear his burden with patience for to-day and be hopeful for to-morrow. But there comes a time when the veriest worm will turn, and the Negro feels to-day that after all the work he has done, all the sacrifices he has made, and all the suffering he has endured, if he did not, now, defend his name and manhood from this vile accusation, he would be unworthy even of the contempt of mankind. It is to this charge he now feels he must make answer.

If the Southern people in defense of their lawlessness, would tell the truth and admit that colored men and women are lynched for almost any offense, from murder to a misdemeanor, there would not now be the necessity for this defense. But when they intentionally, maliciously and constantly belie the record and bolster up these falsehoods by the words of legislators, preachers, governors and bishops, then the Negro must give to the world his side of the awful story.

A word as to the charge itself. In considering the third reason assigned by the Southern white people for the butchery of blacks, the question must be asked, what the white man means when he charges the black man with rape. Does he mean the crime which the statutes of the civilized states describe as such? Not by any means. With the Southern white man, any mesalliance existing between a white woman and a colored man is a sufficient foundation for the charge of rape. The Southern white man says that it is impossible for a voluntary alliance to exist between a white woman and a colored man, and therefore, the fact of an alliance is a proof of force. In numerous instances where colored men have been lynched on the charge of rape, it was positively known at the time of lynching, and indisputably proven after the victim's death, that the relationship sustained between the man and woman was voluntary and clandestine, and that in no court of law could even the charge of assault have been successfully maintained.

It was for the assertion of this fact, in the defense of her own race, that the writer hereof became an exile; her property destroyed and her return to her home forbidden under penalty of death, for writing the following editorial which was printed in her paper, the Free Speech, in Memphis, Tenn., May 21, 1892:

"Eight Negroes lynched since last issue of the 'Free Speech' one at Little Rock, Ark., last Saturday morning where the citizens broke (?) into the penitentiary and got their man; three near Anniston, Ala., one near New Orleans; and three at Clarksville, Ga., the last three for killing a white man, and five on the same old racket—the new alarm about raping white women. The same programme of hanging, then shooting bullets into the lifeless bodies was carried out to the letter. Nobody in this section of the country believes the old threadbare lie that Negro men rape white women. If Southern white men are not careful, they will over-reach themselves and public sentiment will have a reaction; a conclusion will then be reached which will be very damaging to the moral reputation of their women."

But threats cannot suppress the truth, and while the Negro suffers the soul deformity, resultant from two and a half centuries of slavery, he is no more guilty of this vilest of all vile charges than the white man who would blacken his name.

During all the years of slavery, no such charge was ever made, not even during the dark days of the rebellion, when the white man, following the fortunes of war went to do battle for the maintenance of slavery. While the master was away fighting to forge the fetters upon the slave, he left his wife and children with no protectors save the Negroes themselves. And yet during those years of trust and peril, no Negro proved recreant to his trust and no white man returned to a home that had been despoiled.

Likewise during the period of alleged "insurrection," and alarming "race riots," it never occurred to the white man, that his wife and children were in danger of assault. Nor in the Reconstruction era, when the hue and cry was against "Negro Domination," was there ever a thought that the domination would ever contaminate a fireside or strike to death the virtue of womanhood. It must appear strange indeed, to every thoughtful and candid man, that more than a quarter of a century elapsed before the Negro began to show signs of such infamous degeneration.

In his remarkable apology for lynching, Bishop Haygood, of Georgia, says: "No race, not the most savage, tolerates the rape of woman, but it may be said without reflection upon any other people that the Southern people are now and always have been most sensitive concerning the honor of their women—their mothers, wives, sisters and daughters." It is not the purpose of this defense to say one word against the white women of the South. Such need not be said, but it is their misfortune that the chivalrous white men of that section, in order to escape the deserved execration of the civilized world, should shield themselves by their cowardly and infamously false excuse, and call into question that very honor about which their distinguished priestly apologist claims they are most sensitive. To justify their own barbarism they assume a chivalry which they do not possess. True chivalry respects all womanhood, and no one who reads the record, as it is written in the faces of the million mulattoes in the South, will for a minute conceive that the Southern white man had a very chivalrous regard for the honor due the women of this own race or respect for the womanhood which circumstances placed in his power. That chivalry which is "most sensitive concerning the honor of women" can hope for but little respect from the civilized world, when it confines itself entirely to the women who happen to be white. Virtue knows no color line, and the chivalry which depends upon complexion of skin and texture of hair can command no honest respect.

Frances Willard Equates Learning to Ride a Bicycle with Opening New Frontiers for Women

[handwritten marginalia: metaphor for independence]

[handwritten marginalia: interested in well-being of women, goal was to protect women]

Frances Willard (1839–1898) was the indefatigable leader of the Women's Christian Temperance Union (WCTU). After serving as head of the Methodist-run Evanston College for Ladies in the 1870s, Willard shifted her attention to the temperance issue then gaining force in the United States, especially among Protestant women. Her rise to national prominence was swift: in 1879, she was elected the national president of the WCTU, a position she held for the next 20 years. Although the WCTU made prohibition of the use of liquor its top priority (Willard coined the "home protection" rallying cry and promoted the white ribbon as a symbol of the purity of the home), under Willard's leadership the WCTU embraced a wide host of reforms, including woman suffrage, social hygiene, labor unions, and even participation in politics. Willard's motto was succinct: "Do Everything!"

A tomboy as a youth, Frances Willard called herself Frank and bemoaned the day she had to put on long skirts and pin up her hair. Not until she was in her 50s did she learn to ride a bicycle. In the 1890s, approximately 30,000 women were experiencing the freedom of mobility and exercise bicycles provided. Willard methodically set out to master the physical skill of riding the bike in the same way that she proposed women make contributions to the wider world. So enamored was Willard of the experience (she gave her bicycle the name of Gladys!) that she wrote an entire book about it, *A Wheel within a Wheel; How I Learned to Ride the Bicycle* (1895), from which these selections are drawn.

From my earliest recollections, and up to the ripe age of fifty-three, I had been an active and diligent worker in the world. This sounds absurd; but having almost no toys except such as I could manufacture, my first plays were but the outdoor work of active men and women on a small scale. Born with an inveterate opposition to staying in the house, I very early learned to use a carpenter's kit and a gardener's

Source: Frances Willard, *A Wheel within a Wheel; How I Learned to Ride the Bicycle,* 1895. Found in Stephanie Twin, *Out of the Bleachers* (Old Westbury, NY: Feminist Press, 1979), pp. 104–105, 112–114.

tools, and followed in my mimic way the occupations of the poulterer and the farmer, working my little field with a wooden plow of my own making, and felling saplings with an ax rigged up from the old iron of the wagon-shop. Living in the country, far from the artificial restraints and conventions by which most girls are hedged from the activities that would develop a good physique, and endowed with the companionship of a mother who let me have my own sweet will, I "ran wild" until my sixteenth birthday, when the hampering long skirts were brought, with their accompanying corset and high heels; my hair was clubbed up with pins, and I remember writing in my journal, in the first heartbreak of a young human colt taken from its pleasant pasture, "Altogether, I recognize that my occupation is gone."

From that time on I always realized and was obedient to the limitations thus imposed, though in my heart of hearts I felt their unwisdom even more than their injustice. My work then changed from my beloved and breezy outdoor world to the indoor realm of study, teaching, writing, speaking, and went on almost without a break or pain until my fifty-third year, when the loss of my mother accentuated the strain of this long period in which mental and physical life were out of balance, and I fell into a mild form of what is called nerve-wear by the patient and nervous prostration by the lookers-on. Thus ruthlessly thrown out of the usual lines of reaction on my environment, and sighing for new worlds to conquer, I determined that I would learn the bicycle . . .

Let me remark to any young woman who reads this page that for her to tumble off her bike is inexcusable. The lightsome elasticity of every muscle, the quickness of the eye, the agility of motion, ought to preserve her from such a catastrophe. I have had [only one] fall . . . I have proceeded on a basis of the utmost caution, and aside from . . . one pitiful performance the bicycle has cost me hardly a single bruise.

They that know nothing fear nothing. Away back in 1886 my alert young friend, Miss Anna Gordon, and my ingenious young niece, Miss Katherine Willard, took to the tricycle as naturally as ducks take to water . . . Remembering my country bringing-up and various exploits in running, climbing, horseback-riding, to say nothing of my tame heifer that I trained for a Bucephalus, I said to myself, "If those girls can ride without learning so can I!" Taking out my watch I timed them as they, at my suggestion, set out to make a record in going round the square. Two and a half minutes was the result. I then started with all my forces well in hand, and flew around in two and a quarter minutes. Not contented with this, but puffed up with foolish vanity, I declared that I would go around in two minutes; and, encouraged by their cheers, away I went without a fear till the third turning-post was reached, when the left hand played me false, and turning at an acute angle, away I went sidelong, machine and all, into the gutter, falling on my right elbow, which felt like a glassful of chopped ice, and I knew that for the first time in a life full of vicissitudes I had been really hurt. Anna Gordon's white face as she ran toward me caused me to wave my uninjured hand and call out, "Never mind!" and with her help I rose and walked into the house, wishing above all things to go straight to my own room and lie on my own bed, and thinking as I did so how pathetic is that instinct that makes "the stricken deer go weep," the harmed hare seek the covert.

Two physicians were soon at my side, and my mother, then over eighty years of age, came in with much controlled agitation and seated herself beside my bed, taking my hand and saying, "O Frank! you were always too adventurous."

If I am asked to explain why I learned the bicycle I should say I did it as an act of grace, if not of actual religion. The cardinal doctrine laid down by my physician was, "Live out of doors and take congenial exercise"; but from the day when, at sixteen years of age, I was enwrapped in the long skirts that impeded every footstep, I have detested walking and felt with a certain noble disdain that the conventions of life had cut me off from what in the freedom of my prairie home had been one of life's sweetest joys. Driving is not real exercise; it does not renovate the river of blood that flows so sluggishly in the veins of those who from any cause have lost the natural adjustment of brain to brawn. Horseback-riding, which does promise vigorous exercise, is expensive. The bicycle meets all the conditions and will ere long come within the reach of all. Therefore, in obedience to the laws of health, I learned to ride. I also wanted to help women to a wider world, for I hold that the more interests women and men can have in common, in thought, word, and deed, the happier will it be for the home. Besides, there was a special value to women in the conquest of the bicycle by a woman in her fifty-third year, and one who had so many comrades in the white-ribbon army[1] that her action would be widely influential . . . *say herself as a Role Model to other women.*

It is needless to say that a bicycling costume was a prerequisite. This consisted of a skirt and blouse of tweed, with belt, rolling collar, and loose cravat, the skirt three inches from the ground; a round straw hat; and walking-shoes with gaiters. It was a simple, modest suit, to which no person of common sense could take exception.

As nearly as I can make out, reducing the problem to actual figures, it took me about three months, with an average of fifteen minutes' practice daily, to learn, first, to pedal; second, to turn; third, to dismount; and fourth, to mount independently this most mysterious animal. January 20th will always be a red-letter bicycle day, because although I had already mounted several times with no hand on the rudder, some good friend had always stood by to lend moral support; but summoning all my force, and, most forcible of all, what Sir Benjamin Ward Richardson declares to be the two essential elements—decision and precision—I mounted and started off alone. From that hour the spell was broken; Gladys was no more a mystery: I had learned all her kinks, had put a bridle in her teeth, and touched her smartly with the whip of victory. Consider, ye who are of a considerable chronology: in about thirteen hundred minutes, or, to put it more mildly, in twenty-two hours, or, to put it most mildly of all, in less than a single day as the almanac reckons time—but practically in two days of actual practice—amid the delightful surroundings of the great outdoors, and inspired by the bird-songs, the color and fragrance of an English posy-garden, in the company of devoted and pleasant

[1]Women who belonged to the Women's Christian Temperance Union.

comrades, I had made myself master of the most remarkable, ingenious, and inspiring motor ever yet devised upon this planet.

Moral: *Go thou and do likewise!*

An Immigrant Daughter Awakens to the Possibilities of the New World

Anzia Yezierska

Anzia Yezierska (1880?–1970) is best known for her chronicles of Jewish
immigrant life on New York's Lower East Side. Her writings were often autobiographical, drawing on her family's experience of emigrating from
Poland to New York City at the turn of the century. A collection of her short
stories called *Hungry Hearts* (1920) caught the attention of Hollywood producer Samuel Goldwyn, who offered her $10,000 to write a screenplay of the
stories. But Yezierska found it impossible to write the kind of stories she
knew best in the conspicuous and flamboyant Hollywood atmosphere, and
she returned to New York soon after. By the 1930s she (like much of the rest
of the country) had fallen on hard times. A short stint on the Federal Writers'
Project, about which she wrote engagingly in her last autobiographical
novel, *Red Ribbon on a White Horse* (1950), restored her spirits.

Yezierska's stories often featured strong-willed and independent female
characters who took advantage of the possibilities that turn-of-the-century
America could offer to such immigrant daughters: education, satisfying
work, and the option to choose one's own marriage partner rather than being forced to submit to an arranged match. *Bread Givers* (1925) is one of
Yezierska's most powerful books. Its subtitle, "A struggle between a father
of the Old World and a daughter of the New," anticipates its major theme of
the conflict between heroine Sara Smolinsky (modeled on Yezierska) and her
father, a Talmudic scholar who dominates his family's destiny once they are
in America. In Reb Smolinsky's view, women are to be the servants of men,
and that applies to daughters as well as wives. Sara's three sisters let their father rule their lives with disastrous results, especially in matrimonial choices,
but Sara refuses to go along. In this scene, the 17-year-old protagonist de-
cides to leave home after an argument with her father in a small grocery store
the family has opened. She consciously equates America with independence
and autonomy for women, a stark contrast to the restrictions of the Old
World.

In the rest of the novel, Yezierska follows Sara Smolinsky through a variety of jobs and finally to school, confirming the importance of education
for immigrant girls as well as boys. After college, she becomes a teacher, an
inspiring feat of upward mobility for a young woman on her own. At the end
of the novel, however, Sara realizes that she too has roots in the Old World,

and she reconciles with her family and with many of their customs and values. Such an ending reflects the ambivalence with which immigrant daughters found themselves "between two worlds."

While Father was preaching Mother back into her place, a girl came in for a pound of rice. When she went to pay, she had only ten cents.

"The rice is twelve cents," I told her.

"Can I have it now? I just live next door and I'll bring back the two cents later."

I handed Father the ten cents, saying it was for a pound of rice.

"Crazy! Where was your head? Don't you know yet, rice is twelve cents?"

"I trusted her the two cents—"

"Without asking me? I'm the one to decide who is to be trusted."

"But you're never here. You're away praying most of the time."

"Hold your mouth! You're talking too much."

"Why do you make such a holler on me over two cents, when you, yourself, gave away four hundred dollars to a crook for empty shelves?"

"Blood-and-iron! How dare you question your father his business? What's the world coming to in this wild America? No respect for fathers. No fear of God." His eyes flamed as he shook his fist at me. "Only dare open your mouth to me again! Here I struggle to work up a business and she gives away all the profits of my goods. No heart. No conscience. Two cents here and two cents there. That's how all my hard-earned dollars bleed away."

Oh, God! *Two cents!* My gall burst in me! For seventeen years I had stood his preaching and his bullying. But now all the hammering hell that I had to listen to since I was born cracked my brain. His heartlessness to Mother, his pitiless driving away Bessie's only chance to love, bargaining away Fania to a gambler and Mashah to a diamond-faker—when they each had the luck to win lovers of their own—all these tyrannies crashed over me. Should I let him crush me as he crushed them? No. This is America, where children are people.

"I can't stand it! I can't!" I cried, rushing to the back of the store. "Two cents! Two cents! All that cursing and thundering over two cents!"

Blindly, I grabbed my things together into a bundle. I didn't care where I was going or what would become of me. Only to break away from my black life. Only not to hear Father's preaching voice again.

As I put on my hat and coat, I saw Mother, clutching at her heart in helplessness, her sorrowful eyes gazing at me. All the suffering of her years was in the dumb look she turned on me. Bending over, she took out from her stocking the red handkerchief with the knot that held her saved-up rent money. And without a word, she pushed it into my hand.

As I came through the door with my bundle, Father caught sight of me. "What's this?" he asked. "Where are you going?"

"I'm going back to work, in New York."

"What? Wild-head! Without asking, without consulting your father, you get yourself ready to go? Do you yet know that I want you to work in New York?

Let's first count out your carfare to come home every night. Maybe it will cost so much there wouldn't be anything left from your wages."

"But I'm not coming home!"

"What? A daughter of mine, only seventeen years old, not home at night?"

"I'll go to Bessie or Mashah."

"Mashah is starving poor, and you know how crowded it is by Bessie."

"If there's no place for me by my sisters, I'll find a place by strangers."

"A young girl, alone, among strangers? Do you know what's going on in the world? No girl can live without a father or a husband to look out for her. It says in the Torah, only through a man has a woman an existence. Only through a man can a woman enter Heaven."

"I'm smart enough to look out for myself. It's a new life now. In America, women don't need men to boss them."

"*Blut-und-Eisen!* They ought to put you in a madhouse till you're cured of your crazy nonsense!"

Always before, when Father began the drum, drum of his preaching on me, my will was squelched. But now he saw the stony hardness of my eyes. And suddenly his whole face saddened with the hurt of a wounded martyr, suffering for his righteousness.

"Is this your thanks for all your father did for you?" he pleaded, with the gentle patience of a holy one. "Where do you find a poor father who has done for his children as much as I? I didn't cripple you. I didn't give you consumption. I didn't send you to work at the age of six like some poor fathers do. You didn't start work till you were over ten. Now, when I begin to have a little use from you, you want to run away and live for yourself?"

"I've got to live my own life. It's enough that Mother and the others lived for you."

"*Chzufeh!* You brazen one! The crime of crimes against God—daring your will against your father's will. In olden times the whole city would have stoned you!"

"Thank God, I'm not living in olden times. Thank God, I'm living in America! You made the lives of the other children! I'm going to make my own life!"

"You hard heart! You soul of stone! You're the curse from all my children. They all honoured and obeyed their father."

"And what's their end? Look at them now! You think I'll slave for you till my braids grow gray—wait till you find me another fish-peddler to sell me out in marriage! You think I'm a fool like Bessie! No! No!"

Wild with all that was choked in me since I was born, my eyes burned into my father's eyes. "My will is as strong as yours. I'm going to live my own life. Nobody can stop me. I'm not from the old country. I'm American!"

"You blasphemer!" His hand flung out and struck my cheek. "Denier of God! I'll teach you respect for the law!"

I leaped back and dashed for the door. The Old World had struck its last on me.

A Woman Homesteader

Edith Eudora Ammons

The New Woman who traveled the globe, rode a bicycle, or defied her father had a Western "sister"—the female homesteader. While many of our images of the West are male, women were always part of the westward migration and settlement. A surprising number went as homesteaders, taking advantage of the Homestead Act of 1862 promising 160 acres of land to anyone who kept up residence and made improvements for five years. The law did not discriminate against women: All a settler had to be was the head of a household and over 21. According to figures cited by historian Glenda Riley, women made up 11.9 percent of homestead entrants in Lamar, Colorado, and Douglas, Wyoming, in 1887, 1891, 1907, and 1908. And women were more tenacious at sticking with their claims, with 43 percent of women "proving up" their claims as against 37 percent of men.

Like men who staked claims, there was no single reason why women decided to homestead. For an unmarried woman, it could be a good investment, a way to look for a husband, or a statement of independence; for a widowed or divorced woman, it could be a way to make a living for her family. But all homesteaders had to have some sense of adventure and courage, because staking a claim was hard, hard work, not something to be undertaken lightly.

This is the story of two unmarried sisters, Edith Eudora Ammons and Ida Mary Ammons, who bought a semi-improved claim in South Dakota in 1907. Since their initial costs for land, a shack, supplies, and fuel were probably only around $300, the sisters saw this as a good investment, but they also were lured by what Edith called the "wild adventure" of homesteading. This selection describes their disillusioning first view of the piece of land they had just bought. The next year they tried another piece, but just as they were able to finalize the claim, a fire caused by a severe drought raged over the prairie and burned them out.

Edith and Ida Ammons exemplify the independence that is often associated with women in the West. Although their lives were tough and physical, Edith concluded that a woman "had more independence here than in any other part of the world," noting that the hardships "were more than compensated for by its unshackled freedom . . . The opportunities for a full and active life were infinitely greater here." And, yes, even though this was not their original intention, both sisters did marry.

Oddly enough, we had never questioned the impulse which led two young city girls to go alone into unsettled land, homesteading. Our people had been pioneers, always among those who pushed back the frontier. The Ammonses had come up

Source: Pages 5–6, 7–9, 10–13 from *Land of the Burnt Thigh* by Edith Eudora Kohl. Copyright © 1928 by Funk and Wagnalls. Reprinted by permission of Harper Collins Publishers, Inc.

from Tennessee into Illinois in the early days and cleared the timberland along the Mississippi Valley some forty miles out of St. Louis. They built their houses of the hand-hewn logs and became land and stock owners. They were not sturdy pioneers, but they were tenacious.

Some of them went on into what Grandma Ammons called the Santa Fe Bottoms, a low marshy country along the river, where they became wealthy—or well-to-do, at least—by fattening droves of hogs on acorns. Generally speaking, my mother's family ran to professions, and my father's family to land. Though there was father's cousin, Jack Hunter, who had been west and when he came to visit us now and then told wild tales about the frontier to which my sister and I as little children listened wide-eyed. He wove glowing accounts of the range country where he was going to make a million dollars raising cattle. Cousin Jack always talked big.

It was from his highly colored yarns that we had learned all we knew of the West—and from the western magazines which pictured it as an exciting place where people were mostly engaged in shooting one another.

While Ida Mary and I were still very young our mother died, and after that we divided our time between our father's home—he had married again and had a second family to take care of—and the home of his sister. As a result my sister and I came to depend on ourselves and on each other more than two girls of our age usually do.

By the time we were old enough to see that things were not going well financially at home, we knew we must make our own way. Some of the girls we knew talked about "going homesteading" as a wild adventure. They boasted of friends or relatives who had gone to live on a claim as though they had gone lion-hunting in Africa or gold-hunting in Alaska. A homestead. At first thought the idea was absurd. We were both very young; both unusually slight, anything but hardy pioneers; and neither of us had the slightest knowledge of homesteading conditions, or experience extending beyond the conventional, sheltered life of the normal city girl in the first decade of the century.

We were wholly unfitted for the frontier. We had neither training nor physical stamina for roughing it. When I tried to explain to an uncle of mine that I wanted to go west, to make something of myself, he retorted that "it was a hell of a place to do it." In spite of the discussion which our decision occasioned, we made our plans, deciding to risk the hazards of a raw country alone, cutting ourselves off from the world of everyone and everything we had ever known. And with little money to provide against hardships and emergencies . . .

How did one go about homesteading? we asked. Well, all you had to do to get a deed to a quarter-section—160 acres of land—was to file on it at the nearest Land Office, live on it eight months, pay the government $1.25 an acre—and the land was yours. Easy as falling off a log!

The only improvement required by the government was some sort of abode as proof that one had made the land his bona-fide residence for the full eight months.

What would that cost? And the whole undertaking? It depended partly on what kind of shack one built and whether he did it himself or hired it done. A shack cost all the way from $25 to $100 or more. Some of those who had families and intended to stay, built cheap two- and three-room houses.

Of course, it cost women who had to hire things done more to homestead. But with grub, fuel and other necessities we figured it would cost not more than $500 all told.

Then we learned of this quarter-section with a shack already built, bunk and all. It had been filed on and the owner had left before proving-up time so that the claim, shack and all, had reverted to the government. We had about $300 saved up, and this was enough, we decided, to cover homesteading expenses, inasmuch as the shack was provided. So we had all but the final payment of $200 to the government, which would be due when we had "made proof."

We decided to let the money for that final payment take care of itself. The thing to do was to get hold of a piece of land before it was all gone. To hear people talk, it was the last day of grace to apply for a claim. They talked like that for ten years. We did not know there were several million acres lying out there between the Missouri and the Pacific waiting to be settled. We would have all winter to figure out how to prove up. And we found that one could get $1000 to $1500 for a raw claim after getting a deed to it.

The claim with the shack on it was in South Dakota; thirty miles from a town called Pierre. We looked that up in the geography to make sure it really existed. But when we tried to get detailed information, facts and figures to help us prepare for what was to come, we got only printed pamphlets of rules and regulations which were of no real help at all. Land Offices were so busy in those days that all they could do was to send out a package of printed information that no one could understand.

Armed with our meager array of facts, we talked to our father—as though the information we gave him so glibly had any real bearing on this precarious undertaking of his two young daughters. Whatever his doubts and hesitations, he let us decide for ourselves; it was only when we boarded the old Bald Eagle at St. Louis one summer day in 1907, bound up the river, that he clung to our hands as though unable to let us go, saying, "I'm afraid you are making a mistake. Take care of yourselves."

"It will be all right," Ida Mary told him cheerfully. "It is only for eight months. Nothing can happen in eight months . . ."

Section 18, Range 77W—about thirty miles from Pierre. It seemed more real now. The hotel proprietor promised to find us a claim locator to whom that cryptic number made sense.

The next morning at sun-up we were on our way. At that hour the little homestead town of Ft. Pierre lay quiet. Other homesteaders were ready to start out: a farmer and his wife from Wisconsin, who were busy sandwiching their four children into a wagon already filled with immigrant goods, a cow and horse tied on behind.

At a long table in the fly-specked hotel dining room we ate flapjacks and fried potatoes and drank strong coffee in big heavy cups. Then, at long last, perched on the seat of the claim locator's high spring wagon, we jolted out of town, swerving to let a stagecoach loaded with passengers whip past us, waiting while a team of buffalo ambled past, and finally jogged along the beaten road through the bad lands outside of town.

Beyond the rough bad lands we came upon the prairie. We traveled for miles along a narrow, rutted road crossed now and then by dim trails leading nowhere, it seemed. Our own road dwindled to a rough trail, and the spring wagon lurched over it while we clung to the sides to ease the constant jolting, letting go to pull our hats over our eyes which ached with the glare, or over the back of our necks which were blistered from the sun.

Our frantic haste to arrive while the land lasted seemed absurd now. There was land enough for all who wanted it, and few enough to claim it. All that weary day we saw no people save in the distance a few homesteaders mowing strips of the short dry grass for hay. Now and then we passed a few head of horses and a cow grazing. Here and there over the hot, dusty plain we saw shacks and makeshift houses surrounded by patches of corn or flax or dried-up garden. Why were the houses so scattered, looking as though they had been thrown down at random? "They had to be set on the claims," our locator said dryly.

About noon we stopped at a deserted ranch house, surrounded by corrals—a camp, our driver explained, where some stockman held his cattle overnight in driving them to market. Here we ate a lunch and the locator fed and watered the team, refilling the jars from an old well with its long wooden water troughs.

There the trail ended. Now we struck out over a trackless land that grew rougher the farther we went. To look for a quarter-section here was like looking for a needle in a haystack. It was late summer and the sun beat down on the hot prairie grass and upon our heads. We had driven all day without sign of shade— and save for that brief interval at noon, without sight of water. Our faces and hands were blistered, our throats parched from the hot wind.

This was not the West as I had dreamed of it, not the West even of banditry and violent action. It was a desolate, forgotten land, without vegetation save for the dry, crackling grass, without visible tokens of fertility. Drab and gray and empty. Stubborn, resisting land. Heroics wouldn't count for much here. It would take slow, back-breaking labor, and time, and the action of the seasons to make the prairie bloom. People had said this was no place for two girls. It began to seem that they were right.

And this was the goal of our long journey—the tar-paper shack. We pushed the trunk over in front of the door which had no lock, piled the chairs and suit-cases on top of the trunk; spread a comforter over the criss-cross rope bed and threw ourselves across it without undressing. We had no gun or other weapon for protection and were not brave enough to use one had we possessed it.

The little cellar windows which stood halfway between the low ceiling and the floor were nailed shut. But we needed neither window nor door, so far as air was concerned. It poured through the wide cracks like water through a sieve.

While we tossed, too tired and sick at heart to sleep, I asked: "What became of the young man who built this shack?"

"He lived here only a few weeks and abandoned it," Ida Mary explained. "The claim reverted to the government, shack, bunk and all. He couldn't stick it out."

Homestead act
- 21, maintain land for 5 yrs
- head of household
- make improvements

CHAPTER 2

Expanding Horizons for Educated Women

One of the most far-reaching changes in the post-Civil War period was the expansion of higher education for women. In the late 19th century, educating daughters still remained controversial. In 1873, a Harvard physician named Edward Clarke published a book called *Sex in Education,* which argued that if women used their "limited energy" on studying, it would harm the "female apparatus." Doctors such as Mary Putnam Jacobi soon produced scientific studies demonstrating that women college students could think and menstruate at the same time, but Clarke's impact lingered. Not until several generations of college women had shown that higher education did not in fact unsex them did such fears disappear.

The expansion of women's education took several routes. The most widely known experiments were the Eastern women's colleges such as Vassar (1865), Wellesley and Smith (1875), and Bryn Mawr (1884). But as early as the 1870s, a majority of women were enrolled in coeducational schools rather than single-sex institutions. Some private universities in the East, such as Boston University and Cornell, opened their doors to women in the 1870s, but much of the progress came in the large state universities of the Midwest and West, such as Wisconsin (1867), Michigan, and California (1870). A third route was the establishment of coordinate colleges, such as Radcliffe (1884) to Harvard and Barnard (1889) to Columbia. In almost all cases, it took the determined efforts of women, and a few male allies, to win these breakthroughs in higher education.

While still limited to a tiny minority of American women, the numbers of college women grew steadily after 1870, as did their proportion of total students. By 1900, 85,000 women were enrolled in colleges and universities, comprising almost 37 percent of all students; just 20 years later, 283,000 women made up 47.3 percent of enrollments. In fact, some schools such as Stanford and the University of Chicago became alarmed at what they perceived as the feminization of higher education and took steps (unsuccessfully) to limit women's enrollment. This response suggests a certain uneasiness about how far American society should go in providing a college education for its women.

Female students enjoyed the stimulation of intellectual work, strenuous physical education (to counter Dr. Clarke), and a myriad of extracurricular activities. But on graduation came the difficult question of "after college, what?" Many women, especially the first generation of college graduates from the 1870s and 1880s, felt in limbo; they had been educated to be useful and productive, but there were few outlets to put their education to use. More options for professional work, stimulating reform or volunteer activities, or graduate study greeted the next generation, those graduating in the 1890s and early 1900s, but the transition from college student to educated, adult woman was rarely easy.

The question of marriage was always uppermost. Parents had been reassured that a college education would not cause daughters to be unfit for marriage. Despite popular fears that unmarried college women were causing "race suicide," they did marry, but at a somewhat lower rate than noncollege women and at a later age. Most of the women who married did not intend to combine marriage with career: For women of these early generations, this decision operated as an either/or choice. By the early 20th century, some professional women were beginning to juggle the two, but such pioneers were still unusual. One group that did consistently combine professional work with marriage was African-American women teachers, reflecting the much higher wage-force participation rate of African-American women than their white counterparts.

One of the greatest benefits of a college education was that it provided a way for women who chose not to marry to support themselves, rather than remaining a superfluous unmarried daughter at home. By the 1890s, middle-class women could find paid employment that allowed them to establish households of their own. Often, they chose to share their lives with other like-minded professional women. Such long-term relationships won approval from family and society alike as an alternative to what was perceived as lonely spinsterhood.

Educated women took advantage of expanding opportunities when they entered the professions, but they never enjoyed anywhere near as wide options as did men with comparable education and training. Men were applauded for ambition, decisiveness, and drive for success (the very personality traits necessary for professional achievement); such traits in women were viewed as unfeminine, undesirable, and highly suspect. As a result, women were often marginalized in professional life, segregated to fields dominated by women (like teaching, social work, and librarianship) or consigned to lesser ranks with no hopes of advancement in others (like science). Women were always paid less than men. A further characteristic of women's professional activity was that it was often interpreted as an extension of women's traditional responsibilities in the home, hence the term *helping professions.*

Despite such a discouraging outlook for professional advancement, women college graduates in the early 20th century felt like pioneers, as indeed they were. The ability to contemplate useful, interesting work outside the home (which could apply to volunteer work on the part of married women as well) was a definite expansion of options over earlier times. These college-educated women provided many of the recruits who fueled Progressive reform.

Molly Dewson's Letters Home
from Wellesley

"When I was seventeen, I told my father I 'ached' to know more and wanted to go to college. I had never consciously met a woman college graduate but I had chanced on a Bryn Mawr catalogue." Instead of Bryn Mawr, Mary W. (Molly) Dewson (1874–1962) ended up as a member of the class of 1897 at Wellesley College, closer to her childhood home of Quincy, Massachusetts. Living on campus, she wrote regular letters home, mainly addressed to her mother but meant to be shared with the whole family. In these selections, she talks about the insecurities of first-semester exams, dorm parties and college rituals, her courses, and she even makes fun of one of her professors. In other words, not all that different from letters home from college students today, except that hers were penned in ink instead of e-mailed.

The fact that Wellesley was (and is) a women's college did not stop female college students in the 1890s from having an active social life. On more than several occasions, Molly Dewson dressed as a man for college events, seeing nothing odd about such behavior, as evidenced by the matter-of-fact way she shared these events with her family. There is no mention, however, of the phenomenon known as "smashing," when two young women fell violently in love and formed intense bonds expressed in explicitly passionate language. Such relationships were a recognized and accepted part of women's emotional lives in the late 19th century, but Molly Dewson had no "particular" friend at college. She never married, however, and instead chose to spend her life in partnership with a woman named Polly Porter, whom she met in 1909. The Porter-Dewsons, as they called themselves, spent the next 52 years together, sharing homes in Massachusetts, New York City, and Castine, Maine.

Molly Dewson's yearbook predicted that one day she would serve as President Dewson of the United States, just as she had served as President Dewson of the class of 1897. The prediction was not far off the mark. Dewson never ran for political office, but she did serve as a trusted adviser to President Franklin D. Roosevelt in the 1930s and a confidante of first lady Eleanor Roosevelt. Not all women went from Wellesley to the White House, but for many pioneering college graduates, access to higher education opened new opportunities for personal and professional growth.

January 17, 1894

I am just out of history and never in my life did I ever feel such a load off my shoulders, I know I must have passed. I shall be very much surprised if I did not, but alas! alack! I walked all over my toes in two questions so did not do my self proud. (Well if I am through I wont kick about how far through I got.) I could screech I am so glad I can forget a little of the mess I have been shoving in since Saturday noon. Before exam I thought my head would walk off in space, it felt so

Source: Reprinted by permission of Virginia S. Bourne.

like a balloon. So I took a brisk run down to Stone Hall back over Norumbega Hill and felt as fresh as a daisy after it. This morning too the French notice is up that all have passed who are not notified so I am safe there. We had English yesterday, a terribly lengthy and equally (to its length) easy paper. From what Miss Hart said I do not worry over that for my theme work carried me through any way. There is now only Bible and Math. left, and they are not enough to send me home if my other things are as I hope. So I am quite jubilant. The lake is frozen and I am going to have a good skate and then with an hour or so this p.m. and all tomorrow for Bible and in evening and morning for Math. I shall be well enough off.

late January 1894

The mid-years being over we are having quite a fit of spreads. One I went to was just a crowd of Phi Sigma girls, and an impromptu affair. The hostesses made "chocolate anna" and pepermints over the lamp. They were fine and we had a jolly time. The other was very swell. Cards were sent out. At home, Room 129, 8.45 to 9.20 "Eating". (It was Fan Hoyt's birthday and we felt called upon for an extra effort.) Elaborate toilets were made. Evy, Edith, and I with two Juniors represented the masculine element. There was no flaw in us, except that my trousers were too tight to sit down. There was one Indian chief there too. The girl has short hair with the fever (?) curl still in it, and little knots of these curls were tied together with feathers from some convenient duster stuck in at all angles. A striped blanket added to this produced a truly weird effect. The ladies wore very most superb evening toilets, and swelldom was well represented. (It was truly a feast for the Gods.) First we began with pate-de-fois-gras cracker sandwiches, then jam and jelly and more crackers of many kinds. Then all chocolate-cakes and some other kinds of cake beside eclairs. Salted almonds, French molasses-candy and marsh-mallows. On the whole the most sumptuous affair I ever attended. We were invited to stay only until 9.20, silent time, but were enjoying ourselves so much concluded to stay through. We were upon the fourth floor and people on the second could hear us, and we had already been informed that as no one could study anywhere near we must be quieter. This, however, did not dampen our enthusiasm and the guilty kept on until ten.

April 29, 1894

Here it is Sunday again and I have been too busy to write during the whole week. Unusually so, for I spent Tuesday in bed not feeling xxx well, and then I have been reading about five hours a day in the library, which fills out these brief days pretty easily. Today is too heavenly to stay in, with such woods and water within reach, but I felt you might be alarmed if you did not hear for two weeks, and so I consented to boxing myself up. I have so much to say, I am going to begin with Monday, and keep on until I am tired.

I came out on the train with Evy, and we reached #73 to find it turned into an impromptu dress-making establishment. Blanche Rhodes and Fan Hoyt, Ed.'s and Ev.'s great friends, were dressing and helping dress and the confusion was immense. However, at last we got Blanche shaken into her six tarltan skirts, and

Ed. and Ev. as fairs of morning and night, into their flowing robes, and I myself converted into quite a gallant youth. I took Blanche into the fairy circle and they were so convulsed at my appearance that they forgot to flutter and dance greetings on their toes, in regulation style. The girls looked simply dear, and I never should have thought short-skirts could have been so becoming to any one. The colors were very effective and every dress showed enough work to turn my hair gray. The Gym was hung with portieres over the rib-walls and screens and the girls potted ferns and palms took off the bare effect. Around the walls were numbered seats and we took our places by the numbers, on the wands tipped either with a star or moon, which were given us. I danced with Dennison Wilt, the vice-president of our class. After the favor and flower figures, we had just single dances, and it was just too jolly and pretty. (I would like to have you see some of the things gotten up here, they go away ahead of anything you would think possible.) I was the only one in regular men's clothing, although there was a Mephistopheles and several fairy pages. One girl was a fairy bumble-bee in gold and brown, it was the neatest costumes I have seen for some time. In the evening I kept on my suit, and walked with one of the girls to call at Stone Hall. We met several people, but they thought I was a real man, which was all the more amuzing (sic). I felt rather queer out-of-door in that rig without even a macintosh. The girls took innumerable kodachs of us, but since it was about dusk, they probably will not come out. We were over the lakeside porch and the fairies dropped themselves over the balustrade and me in the most interesting manner. I do not feel in the mood for writing so I cannot make it interesting.

October 1895

Wednesday, no it was Thursday last, I had laboratory work. The chemistry people devoted the whole time to letting the girls make up back experiments which they had been told to repeat. I had had mine all right, and I was up to date, so I told the assistant who is a young woman, Miss Wiggins, and quite a brick to me always. I asked her if she had any work she would like to have me do, thinking she would give me the time off and I could play golf as a reward of merit for being good. She said that she knew Miss Roberts would be pleased if I would do an experiment we omited. It was really in Quantitative Analysis with a curve to plot at the end, having taken 2nd Math I know how of course. So down trotted Miss W. to Prof. Roberts and got a lot of watch glass crystals, beakers, etc. which Miss R sent up with her compliments. Well I toiled manfully. I weighed and I boiled and I tested and weighed again, evaporated and weighed again, keeping all the little things separate. Miss W. was so interested that she stayed over her time a whole period. I was so hot and weary and fussed up with all my little messes I thought I should expire and then another assistant who is a lecturer beside just hooted at us and said she had never seen that experiment come out with an ordinary laboratory equipment. It was rather discouraging, and especially when the two of them went into a gale of giggle over my little row of glasses cooling away. I was bound I would go thro with it anyway tho' I had burned the inside of my forefinger to a blister— N.B. Nell, its all well now—by picking up by graduate which Miss W. had been carefully toasting while my back was turned. I didn't swear or say a word nor again when at a critical point one of my dishes was broken in the melee and they tho' I was pretty patient in my sufferings I guess for as I went downstairs, Miss W. had gone down ahead of me—having left me to clean up my dishes and make the last calculations—Prof. Roberts beckoned me to come into her study. There she was eating grapes with Miss W. off chemistry glasses fine as you please. They sat weary me down in a big rocking chair, gave me grapes and treated me like a queen generally. In the mean time I plotted my curve with Lady Roberts help—Miss W. had run off early so that she wouldn't have to show she did not know how. And what do you think after all our fussing, the curve was the right one. Miss W. and I sang in high glee, and we are going to tell Miss Parker she has seen the experiment done after all. Dr. Roberts is a star. She is jolly and full of the old boy. She lives with Profs. Bates and Coman. She is coming to see me play tennis tomorrow. She thinks my chem. apron is a beauty. I had a great time that p.m. All the other girls were quite envious.

June (1896?)

Friday was Tree Day. '97 represented the Coming of Proserpina back to Earth again. All the flowers bloomed on that momentous occasion, or something happened being exceedingly poorly read in the classics I'm in the dark as to exactly what. At any rate, we followed our President, Proserpina for the time, in the guise of different flowers. I was a daffodil, walking on my head, tho' if in another sense had I been doing that I should have been growing in the customary direction. My little cap was my green calyx and terribly cunning with a little stem from the top of it. Then came my green color and from that burst the yellow corolla. I was the long tube part and then fastened to my collar were long yellow paper petals like the below. Reverse the page and you will see the daffodil very clearly. It was a heap of bother but I felt bound to dress this year at any rate. The '98s were the exit of domestic service work, there being squads of office girls, sweeping girls, cleaners of tables, waiters + the department girls. The languages carried flags. The Chem girls wore their holey aprons and carried Laboratory bottles etc. The Mineralogy girls trays with minerals etc. Most touching of all (to me) were four girls in white dresses leghorn hats parasols etc. with Pol. Econ. as a label. They were showing up the snap of domestic work in that department. I happen to be the sole worker so I was quite honored. The 99's were the most gorgeous of all. They all wore very very full skirts and kept twirling and twisting them so that they looked mighty pretty. The colors were very effective on the green campus. We had a good time all day but the best was in the evening. Our class assembled in full at 8.15 by Crawfords arrayed in sheets and carrying joss sticks. We each brought our forensics throwing them in a bier. Then two by two we started, the spade bearers to the fore then the funeral oration and the bier with four bearers. Solemnly we marched off toward the West Woods passing thro' them, the oaks arching over our heads. Really as we filed along it was very impressive, the spades clanked on the gravelly path and everyone looked so weird. Coming out in the open a grave was dug the torches flaming above the bent forms cast more fearful shadows. We all stood

round in a circle sobbing at our parting friends. The grave dug, the bier was low-
ered, the diggers stood back leaning on their spades & forks, the torch was applied
and the funeral orator stood forth. Hers was the best speech of the day and as
"forensics necessary to a degree" turned to ashes the gods were thrown in amid
the heartbreaking moan of the mourners. Again we formed in line and filed back
the lovely wood chanting a Latin dirge. No ceremony could be more impressive.

November 1896

Yesterday in chapel old Dean Stratton—the one I told you who giggled behind her
fan and is so self-important—gave out some notices and in one of them she said
at the 7.30 service Sunday night we will give prayer for Turkey. She was terribly
solemn and I don't know how it started—but it was the first service after Thanks-
giving and other tho'ts were fresh in our minds—and a suppressed giggle went
over the chapel like a flash. My wasn't the old lady mad. She had begun another
notice but she stopped short and just glared. I tho't she was going to descend and
pulverize some one on the spot. Poor little Ada Belfield in the front row of the
Seniors about four feet from the Dean was petrified. That made it funnier—i.e. to
see the Dean speechless with wrath—but fearing she would break a blood vessel
we stopped. The question, however, is still unsettled in my mind as to why the
prayer for Turkey and not Armenia. She must be wrapped up in the thought of future damnation and not the present agony.

Jane Addams Struggles with the Problem of "After College, What?"

Jane Addams (1860–1935) had a hard time finding her professional niche.
Addams graduated from Rockford Seminary in 1881 but spent the next
seven years aimlessly drifting as she tried to balance the "social claim" (her
interest in broader societal and economic questions raised by her education)
with the "family claim" (the tendency of families to regard daughters as
dependent possessions, rather than full individuals in their own right). The
solution to her dilemma came on an extended European trip with her step-
mother, as Addams later recounted it: "I gradually became convinced that it
would be a good thing to rent a house in a part of the city where many primitive and actual needs are found, in which young women who had been given
over too exclusively to study might restore a balance of activity along traditional lines and learn of life from life itself . . ." Thus did the settlement
house movement come to the United States, with Jane Addams and Hull
House (founded in 1889) quickly its most famous practitioners.

   The settlement house offered compensations both to its residents and
the surrounding neighborhood. The 19th ward in which Hull House was

Source: Jane Addams, *Twenty Years at Hull-House* (New York: Macmillan, 1910; Signet Classic
reprint, New American Library, 1960), pp. 75, 77–79, 87–89.

located was one of Chicago's poorest, containing 50,000 people, seven churches, no public schools, and 255 saloons. Hull House developed an extensive range of social services and recreational programs including day care, health and hygiene, language classes, crafts, poetry readings, and the like. This selection from Addams's autobiography, *Twenty Years at Hull-House* (1910), describes the first days at Hull House and introduces some of the neighbors who visited the settlement house.

Settlement house residents, primarily college-educated women from the middle classes, also reaped rewards. They found useful roles that allowed them to move beyond charity work in the "Lady Bountiful" tradition to the scientific investigation that characterized Progressive era reform. They lived together in an atmosphere that resembled a college dorm, an especially congenial setting for women who chose not to marry. Hull House residents included Julia Lathrop, Alice Hamilton, and Grace and Edith Abbott, all noted Progressive era reformers. In addition, the institution drew on the support of women's groups in Chicago, including the Chicago Woman's Club, which had been influential in building support for the Woman's Building at the 1893 Columbian Exhibition.

At age 33, in 1893, Jane Addams remarked, "I find that I am considered quite the grandmother of American settlements." During the Progressive era, she was the most admired woman in America, a symbol of women's new roles in public life.

The next January found Miss Starr[1] and myself in Chicago, searching for a neighborhood in which we might put our plans into execution . . . We decided upon a location somewhere near the junction of Blue Island Avenue, Halsted Street, and Harrison Street. I was surprised and overjoyed on the very first day of our search for quarters to come upon the hospitable old house, the quest for which I had so recently abandoned. The house was of course rented, the lower part of it used for offices and storerooms in connection with a factory that stood back of it. However, after some difficulties were overcome, it proved to be possible to sublet the second floor and what had been the large drawing-room on the first floor . . .

The fine old house responded kindly to repairs, its wide hall and open fireplaces always insuring it a gracious aspect. Its generous owner, Miss Helen Culver, in the following spring gave us a free leasehold of the entire house. Her kindness has continued through the years until the group of thirteen buildings, which at present comprises our equipment, is built largely upon land which Miss Culver has put at the service of the Settlement which bears Mr. Hull's name. In those days the house stood between an undertaking establishment and a saloon. "Knight, Death, and the Devil," the three were called by a Chicago wit, and yet any mock heroics which might be implied by comparing the Settlement to a knight quickly dropped away under the genuine kindness and hearty welcome extended to us by the families living up and down the street.

[1]Ellen Gates Starr (1859–1940), a classmate of Jane Addams at Rockford Seminary, was a cofounder of Hull House. However, the venture was always publicly identified with the more famous Jane Addams.

We furnished the house as we would have furnished it were it in another part of the city, with the photographs and other impedimenta we had collected in Europe, and with a few bits of family mahogany. While all the new furniture which was bought was enduring in quality, we were careful to keep it in character with the fine old residence. Probably no young matron ever placed her own things in her own house with more pleasure than that with which we first furnished Hull-House. We believed that the Settlement may logically bring to its aid all those adjuncts which the cultivated man regards as good and suggestive of the best life of the past.

On the 18th of September, 1889, Miss Starr and I moved into it, with Miss Mary Keyser, who began by performing the housework, but who quickly developed into a very important factor in the life of the vicinity as well as in that of the household, and whose death five years later was most sincerely mourned by hundreds of our neighbors. In our enthusiasm over "settling," the first night we forgot not only to lock but to close a side door opening on Polk Street, and were much pleased in the morning to find that we possessed a fine illustration of the honesty and kindliness of our new neighbors . . .

In those early days we were often asked why we had come to live on Halsted Street when we could afford to live somewhere else. I remember one man who used to shake his head and say it was "the strangest thing he had met in his experience," but who was finally convinced that it was "not strange but natural." In time it came to seem natural to all of us that the Settlement should be there. If it is natural to feed the hungry and care for the sick, it is certainly natural to give pleasure to the young, comfort to the aged, and to minister to the deep-seated craving for social intercourse that all men feel. Whoever does it is rewarded by something which, if not gratitude, is at least spontaneous and vital and lacks that irksome sense of obligation with which a substantial benefit is too often acknowledged.

In addition to the neighbors who responded to the receptions and classes, we found those who were too battered and oppressed to care for them. To these, however, was left that susceptibility to the bare offices of humanity which raises such offices into a bond of fellowship.

From the first it seemed understood that we were ready to perform the humblest neighborhood services. We were asked to wash the newborn babies, and to prepare the dead for burial, to nurse the sick, and to "mind the children."

Occasionally these neighborly offices unexpectedly uncovered ugly human traits. For six weeks after an operation we kept in one of our three bedrooms a forlorn little baby who, because he was born with a cleft palate, was most unwelcome even to his mother, and we were horrified when he died of neglect a week after he was returned to his home; a little Italian bride of fifteen sought shelter with us one November evening, to escape her husband who had beaten her every night for a week when he returned home from work, because she had lost her wedding ring; two of us officiated quite alone at the birth of an illegitimate child because the doctor was late in arriving, and none of the honest Irish matrons would "touch the likes of her"; we ministered at the deathbed of a young man, who during a long illness of tuberculosis had received so many bottles of whisky through the mistaken kindness of his friends, that the cumulative effect produced wild periods of exultation, in one of which he died.

We were also early impressed with the curious isolation of many of the immigrants; an Italian woman once expressed her pleasure in the red roses that she saw at one of our receptions in surprise that they had been "brought so fresh all the way from Italy." She would not believe for an instant that they had been grown in America. She said that she had lived in Chicago for six years and had never seen any roses, whereas in Italy she had seen them every summer in great profusion. During all that time, of course, the woman had lived within ten blocks of a florist's window; she had not been more than a five-cent car ride away from the public parks; but she had never dreamed of faring forth for herself, and no one had taken her. Her conception of America had been the untidy street in which she lived and had made her long struggle to adapt herself to American ways.

But in spite of some untoward experiences, we were constantly impressed with the uniform kindness and courtesy we received. Perhaps these first days laid the simple human foundations which are certainly essential for continuous living among the poor: first, genuine preference for residence in an industrial quarter to any other part of the city, because it is interesting and makes the human appeal; and second, the conviction, in the words of Canon Barnett, that the things which make men alike are finer and better than the things that keep them apart, and that these basic likenesses, if they are properly accentuated, easily transcend the less essential differences of race, language, creed, and tradition.

Perhaps even in those first days we made a beginning toward that object which was afterward stated in our charter: "To provide a center for a higher civic and social life; to institute and maintain educational and philanthropic enterprises; and to investigate and improve the conditions in the industrial districts of Chicago."

Alice Hamilton Explores the Dangerous Trades

One of the most appealing careers for educated women in the late 19th century was that of physician. Around 1900, as many as one in five doctors were women, a percentage that would not be reached again until the 1970s. One such physician was Hull House resident Alice Hamilton (1869–1970), an 1893 graduate of the University of Michigan medical school. In her autobiography *Exploring the Dangerous Trades* (1943), she explained why she had settled on that career: "I chose medicine, not because I was scientifically minded, for I was deeply ignorant of science. I chose it because as a doctor I could go anywhere I pleased—to far-off lands or to city slums—and be quite sure that I could be of use anywhere. I should meet all sorts and conditions of men, I should not be tied down to a school or college as a teacher is, or have to work under a superior, as a nurse must do." Hamilton became a pioneer in the field of industrial medicine, that is, the investigation of the workplace effects of poisons and chemicals on employees. She was especially well known for her pioneering studies of lead.

Alice Hamilton was no narrow-minded scientific investigator; this selection from her autobiography describes her methods of investigation and her sympathy and sensitivity for the victims. Hamilton's almost single-handed development of the field of industrial medicine led to her appointment to the Harvard Medical School faculty in 1919, the first woman appointed. (It would be World War II before Harvard would admit women students to its medical school.) She limited her teaching to one semester a year in order to spend the rest of her time traveling or at Hull House. Thus did she blend professional achievement with personal satisfaction in a way characteristic of the early generations of college graduates and professional women.

It was pioneering, exploration of an unknown field. No young doctor nowadays can hope for work as exciting and rewarding. Everything I discovered was new and most of it was really valuable. I knew nothing of manufacturing processes, but I learned them on the spot, and before long every detail of the Old Dutch Process and the Carter Process of white-lead production was familiar to me, also the roasting of red lead and litharge and the smelting of lead ore and refining of lead scrap. From the first I became convinced that what I must look for was lead dust and lead fumes, that men were poisoned by breathing poisoned air; not by handling their food with unwashed hands. Nowadays that fact has been so strongly established by experimental proof that nobody would think of disputing it. But in 1910 and for many years after, the firm (and comforting) belief of foremen and employers was that if a man was poisoned by lead it was because he did not wash his hands and scrub his nails, although a little intelligent observation would have been enough to show its absurdity. . . .

Here are four histories, picked at random, from my notes of 1910.

A Bohemian, an enameler of bathtubs, had worked eighteen months at his trade, without apparently becoming poisoned, though his health had suffered. One day, while at the furnace, he fainted away and for four days he lay in coma, then passed into delirium during which it was found that both forearms and both ankles were palsied. He made a partial recovery during the following six months but when he left for his home in Bohemia he was still partly paralyzed.

A Hungarian, thirty-six years old, worked for seven years grinding lead paint. During this time he had three attacks of colic, with vomiting and headache. I saw him in the hospital, a skeleton of a man, looking almost twice his age, his limbs soft and flabby, his muscles wasted. He was extremely emaciated, his color was a dirty grayish yellow, his eyes dull and expressionless. He lay in an apathetic condition, rousing when spoken to and answering rationally but slowly, with often an appreciable delay, then sinking back into apathy.

A Polish laborer worked only three weeks in a very dusty white-lead plant at an unusually dusty emergency job, at the end of which he was sent to the hospital with severe lead colic and palsy of both wrists.

A young Italian, who spoke no English, worked for a month in a white-lead plant but without any idea that the harmless-looking stuff was poisonous. There was a great deal of dust in his work. One day he was seized with an agonizing pain in his head which came on him so suddenly that he fell to the ground. He was sent to the hospital, semiconscious, with convulsive attacks, and was there for two weeks; when he came home, he had a relapse and had to go back to the hospital. Three months later he was still in poor health and could not do a full day's work . . .

Life at Hull-House had accustomed me to going straight to the homes of people about whom I wished to learn something and talking to them in their own surroundings, where they have courage to speak out what is in their minds. They were almost always foreigners, Bulgarians, Serbs, Poles, Italians, Hungarians, who had come to this country in the search for a better life for themselves and their children. Sometimes they thought they had found it, then when sickness struck down the father things grew very black and there were no old friends and neighbors and cousins to fall back on as there had been in the old country. Often it was an agent of a steamship company who had coaxed them over with promises of a land flowing with jobs and high wages. Six hundred Bulgarians had been induced to leave their villages by these super-salesmen, and to come to Chicago. Of course they took the first job they could find and if it proved to be one that weakened and crippled them—well, that was their bad luck!

It sometimes seemed to me that industry was exploiting the finest and best in these men—their love of their children, their sense of family responsibility. I think of an enameler of bathtubs whom I traced to his squalid little cottage. He was a young Slav who used to be so strong he could run up the hill on which his cottage stood and spend all the evening digging in his garden. Now, he told me, he climbed up like an old man and sank exhausted in a chair, he was so weary, and if he tried to hoe or rake he had to give it up. His digestion had failed, he had a foul mouth, he couldn't eat, he had lost much weight. He had had many attacks of colic and the doctor told him if he did not quit he would soon be a wreck. "Why did you keep on," I asked, "when you knew the lead was getting you?" "Well, there were the payments on the house," he said, "and the two kids." The house was a bare, ugly, frame shack, the children were little, underfed things, badly in need of a handkerchief, but for them a man had sacrificed his health and his joy in life. When employers tell me they prefer married men, and encourage their men to have homes of their own, because it makes them so much steadier, I wonder if they have any idea of all that that implies.

African-American Women Enter the Teaching Profession

Mamie Garvin Fields

Teaching has always been a profession dominated by women. For black women, the choice of a teaching career often involved an element of racial self-consciousness, because teaching future generations was seen as a concrete way to improve conditions in the black community. It is no coincidence that many African-American leaders, among them Fannie Jackson Coppin, Charlotte Hawkins Brown, and Mary McLeod Bethune, all taught at some point during their lives.

The segregated school systems of the South and the northern cities created a steady demand for black teachers, a by-product of the publicly supported system of segregation in force in the United States until the 1950s. In 1910, there were 17,266 black women teaching in the South, comprising 1 percent of all the black women workers, Like white teachers, blacks tended to be young and single, although black teachers were far more likely to be married than whites. Yet black teachers faced special handicaps: their contracts and budgets were at the mercy of white administrators; their pay, averaging $25 to $30 a month, was less than half their white counterparts, while their classes were twice as large; and they often could not count on full-time or year-round employment because black schools sometimes ran for as little as three months a year.

The career of Mamie Garvin Fields shows the importance black women attached to teaching as well as the handicaps under which they labored. Born in 1888 in Charleston, South Carolina, Fields's commitment to uplifting the black community through teaching comes through clearly in this excerpt from her 1983 memoir, *Lemon Swamp and Other Places*. A graduate of Claflin University, Fields's first jobs were in poor rural areas of South Carolina, where two teachers could have upwards of 100 students in a single room. After her marriage, Mamie Garvin Fields alternated teaching with volunteer and civic contributions in Charleston.

The first school I ever taught in was the Pine Wood School, Pine Wood, South Carolina, in what we call the "Sand Hills." The Sand Hills of Sumter County is a belt of sandy land that crosses the state in the south central portion. It's the poorest part of the state. The women there did two types of work. They would "muddy" for eels or mullet, and they would fish for cats in the Pee Dee River and its creeks. ("Muddying" meant that they would hike their dresses up and wade in, taking up the fish in baskets or nets.) The men went to nearby mills or into the forest to cut crossties for the railroad. My sister Hattie and I taught there in 1908–1909.

The people of Pine Wood were the poorest people I had ever seen. The whites there were poor too, but at least they had a six-month school for their children, and the building was on the main street in town. There was no school building for Negro children. But some of the Negro people had a lodge hall, a queer building designed like a train coach, long and narrow. When they found out that they would be given a teacher, they decided to use this building. They made benches and a table for the teacher, and they painted blackboards.

Over a hundred children came in November, when Hattie was to start teaching, so she asked for an assistant. The trustee said that if they divided the hall through the center, they would be given another teacher, which is how Sister sent for me in December. We were to have a three-month school that year, and I would teach for one month. (However, parents in the School House Meeting raised the money so that I could stay another month.) By the time they got the hall divided, we had 5 feet apiece, half the width of the hall. When we finished putting the benches end to end for about 30 feet length, very little space was left to pass in front of the children. If you were on one end, you couldn't see the children on the other, so you had to move up and down this narrow space. They put a door in the partition so that my principal and I could communicate. Believe me, we really had to work together, because you could hear the children on the other side. If Sister was doing something noisy and I wasn't, it would ruin my lesson, and so forth. Now I wonder how we did it . . .

In 1909 I landed a school on John's Island, a coveted venture, because very few of the black graduates were getting jobs. All the schools were taught by white women, mainly the wives of trustees. But even the old rebel Department of Education became convinced that the Negro graduates should be given a chance. But since white people taught in the city schools, you had to try to go in the county. The way to get in Charleston County was to know a cook or maid or butler who came in touch with the powers that be. You had to get your job through the kitchen, through any of those who worked for the "aristocrats" below Broad Street. However, I said to myself, "You mean to tell me I got my education and still have to go through the kitchen? Never!" That was one of my words, "never!" My old aunts and uncles of the early days had race pride. Although slaves, they stood up. It must have been those ancestors, working through me, when I chose not to go to the kitchen for an appointment, after spending all my life so far in school and graduating with honors.

I went down to the superintendent's office and knocked. He said, "Come in," but when he saw I was a Negro, he bent back over his work as though I wasn't there. After ten minutes passed, he looked up and said, "Well?" I answered, "Mr. Waring, I brought my diploma to show you, as I want to teach in Charleston County." He said, "I have 100 ahead of you." I answered, "Please put me down 101. I have prepared to teach at home and have nowhere else to go." He took my diploma and copied my name and my degree, "Licentiate of Instruction," given to those who took special work in pedagogy. He reached for a red pencil and marked an "X" by my name. I thought then that I was doomed. On my way out, I met Reverend John Green, who taught on James Island and was one of our Methodist preachers. When Reverend Green got in, the superintendent asked if the reverend knew me. Reverend Green said he did and paid quite a tribute to me. The superintendent: "Do you know where she lives? Go by and tell her she will teach at our Humbert Wood Elementary on John's Island, with another Claflinite, Miss Rosalee Brown."

Well! When I began teaching on John's Island, eyebrows were raised by the Sam Fabers and by people who wanted to teach. "How did *she* get it?" they wanted to know. "Who gave it to her?" I opened many a person's eyes to the possibility of using their own brain. Then, strange to say, everybody came to me to see if I could get them a job. I told them to go down to the powers that be, as I did: don't wait for a go-between. In fact, even the go-betweens came to see how I did it: they wanted to know who helped me. But that system of going to go-betweens didn't break up for a long time. It gave some colored people power over the rest . . .

John's Island was wild then, with great, thick woods of pine and live oak, with Spanish moss hanging from the branches, black all around you. You could hear forest noises and the wagon wheels. You could hear the horse. But that was all. You couldn't see anything. Our host didn't do much talking. Rosalee and I about held our breath. On the way we came to a gully that separated us from the people we were to stay with, our future home. They had a log across the divide to walk on. Rosalee, who lived all her life on James Island, crossed this log with success, but I slipped and fell down in the gully, in the big old deep gully with the frogs and everything. Lord, I almost died! I went screaming, for I knew I was visiting the realm of snakes, lizards, spiders, and what-have-you. Although I could see none of them, the pitch black made me "see" all of them! Fortunately, though, no water was in the gully. My host pulled me out, dirty and frightened to death . . .

You couldn't find the school for the weeds growing around it. It just looked God-forsaken. I must have had a look on my face, because the children said, "Well, you know, we going to clean the ya'd." I know for sure that I had a look when we got in the door. Lord have mercy, everything was inside! I thought about snakes, and the children told me, "You know, last year when the teacher sit over there, snake come right down on the teacher!" Telling stories to scare me! But it looked so bad I thought it might be true, so we all looked, and we found several snakes, here and there. The children killed them—as I looked on from afar. By the time we got through killing snakes, I was worried about Rosalee. In the time she took, nowadays she could have gone to New York. She finally returned from the trustee's house about noon. Why so late? She said the ox decided to stop pulling and lie down in the road. They had to wait until he could be coaxed to get up.

The school was just an old wooden house with two rooms. The benches inside had no backs. Next day we told the children not to put on their school clothes, to come on down and let's rake out the yard and clean up the house. Bring your hoe and rake. The children even had to bring brooms, because the county didn't give you a thing. I said, "No blackboard?" "No, don't have no blackboard." "You have crayon?" "Crayon! Ee ain't got no crayon." The county gave you a big old brass bell with a black handle, the only pretty thing they had. Our school equipment was the bell and the rollbook.

We started with about sixty or seventy children between the two of us, and before long we got to a hundred and some. Before us, they had been taught by a white teacher, the trustee's wife. She let us know that we needn't bother much: the children didn't come to school. Well, the white folks didn't much care if our children came to school or didn't, but we tried hard to get them to come. But goodness, they had every type of reason for not coming. Some had no pants, no shoes, or no sweater to wear when it was cold. If it rained, they would say the road was too muddy to pass, or else they couldn't get the school clothes dry. Some children told me they had nobody to come with; and if they came alone, the bigger children would "fight me in the road, and no kin to take up for me." Certain mothers would say, "Mr. so-and-so [a white farmer] want us to work, so nobody to dress 'em, nobody to comb the hair." Many of the reasons for absence had to do with poverty, one way or the other. But some had to do with custom. If the mother and dad went to a funeral, the children would stay home "out of respect." But the biggest reason was that the parents weren't trained to send their children to school regularly. The teacher could have a lot to do with that. Rosalee and I couldn't just stand in the school and wait for the children to come. We had to help the parents to get the clothes or whatever was needed. And of course, we wanted to work with the children. The teacher before Rosalee and me hardly cared if they came or not. We tried to bring in all the children of school age.

Women and Progressive Politics

Mary Ritter Beard

One of the most striking aspects of American life in the Progressive era is the prominent role played by women reformers. Undaunted by the lack of the vote, women reformers moved far beyond their earlier charitable and philanthropic work to boldly enter the public arena, often participating in local and state politics to achieve their goals.

Mary Ritter Beard (1876–1958) was both a participant in and chronicler of women's urban activism. Active in both the woman suffrage and trade union movements, her pathbreaking 1915 book, *Women's Work in Municipalities,* chronicled the scope and variety of women's activities in cities and towns across the country. Her goal was to show that women were participating equally with men in confronting the great social forces of the day. As she documented women's contributions, Beard discovered "in the making, before our very eyes, a conscious national womanhood."

Source: Mary Ritter Beard, *Women's Work in Municipalities* (New York: D. Appleton-Century-Crofts, 1915), pp. 59–63.

This selection, about the campaign for pure milk stations, is typical of the tactics that Progressive women employed to force municipalities to deal with issues that they felt strongly about as women and mothers. They consciously linked the issue of contaminated milk with broader social issues such as infant mortality, conditions of women's industrial employment, and political corruption; the result, as Mary Beard forcefully demonstrates, is that "babies' milk thus becomes essentially a social-economic problem." The crusade for pure milk occurred in most major cities across the country, primarily spearheaded by women.

As far back as 1915, Mary Beard recognized women's contributions to the Progressive era, an insight historians are now mining for its implications both for women's history and the history of Progressive reform. In her later years, Beard turned more to writing than activism; she achieved her widest recognition as the coauthor (with her historian husband Charles Beard) of *The Rise of American Civilization* (1927). Beard's *Woman As Force in History* (1946), arguably her most original book, demonstrates her ongoing commitment to feminist scholarship.

In the education of public opinion on the question of reducing infant mortality, it is inevitable that great attention should be given to the matter of pure milk. One cannot think of a baby without thinking of milk, so that the effort to provide pure milk is directly associated with every effort to reduce infant mortality and make children strong. The problem of milk is twofold: to supply the best possible grade for bottle-fed babies, on the one hand, and on the other to provide the mother of the breast-fed baby with necessary conditions for nursing her infant properly. There is no dispute as to the greater importance of the latter phase of the problem.

The milk station to supply pure milk to the poor at low cost is an outgrowth of the knowledge that the greater part of infant mortality comes in summer months from the feeding of babies upon unsatisfactory milk. The risk of death among such babies is far greater than it is among breast-fed babies so that emphasis has perhaps naturally been placed there to an undue degree. Knowing that bottle babies were subject to such danger, the first thought was to minimize the peril for such babies. As Miss Lathrop[1] points out, however, in harmony with the best scientific teaching: "There may be and in some places there have been certain attending dangers where the furnishing of milk has been the only thing attempted. On this account in many, if not most, milk stations, positive proof is required that the mother either cannot or ought not to nurse her baby before she can get the pure milk, and this precaution has been found necessary in order to prevent an increase in bottle feeding in the community as a result of the feeling of greater safety which the pure-milk station gives to mothers who, while perfectly able to nurse their children, would prefer, for insufficient reasons, not to do so. It is never intended that there should be less insistence upon the duty of breast feeding because of the milk station, for while the death rate among the bottle-fed is reduced by

[1]Julia Lathrop (1858–1932) was head of the Children's Bureau within the federal Department of Commerce and Labor from 1912 to 1921.

pure milk, the death rate among the bottle-fed from the purest milk possible is still much higher than the death rate among the breast-fed, and if there is any perceptible increase in bottle feeding as against breast feeding because of the milk station the latter might thus become an agency to increase rather than decrease infant mortality."

Dr. S. Josephine Baker of the Bureau of Child Hygiene of the New York Health Department also has a large perspective in dealing with this problem. She says: "The evolution of the infants' milk station is essential. Pure milk, however desirable, will never alone solve the infant-mortality problem. Under our system of home visiting to instruct mothers in the care of babies we have demonstrated that babies may be kept under continuous supervision at the cost of 60 cents per month per baby, and the death rate among babies so cared for by us has been 1.4 per cent. The death rate among babies under the care of milk stations has been 2.5 per cent, and the cost $2 per month per baby. Without overlooking the value of pure milk, I believe this problem must primarily be solved by educational measures. In other words, the solution of the problem of infant mortality is 20 per cent pure milk and 80 per cent training of the mothers. The infants' milk stations will serve their wider usefulness when they become educational centers for prenatal instruction and the encouragement of breast feeding and teaching better hygiene, with the mother instructed to buy the proper grade of milk at a place most convenient to her home."

Here, as in medical prescriptions, it is futile to insist that a mother who is physically able shall nurse her baby if she is so poor that she must work under conditions that weaken her and thus reduce the grade and quality of her milk or that preclude leisure in which to nourish the infant. The question of poverty, that skeleton in every social closet, looms up here with an insistency that nothing will banish. No kind of philanthropy will solve the requirements of infant welfare when poverty or labor conditions are the root of the problem.

Babies' milk thus becomes essentially a social-economic problem. It is so recognized by many women and is becoming more and more recognized as such by those who work along baby-saving lines. No one sees this fact more clearly perhaps than Miss Lathrop who joins in the ever-growing cry for a "war on poverty." Mothers' pensions, and every attempt to increase the wage of the husband or of the wife before the child-bearing experience has entered into her life, that she may lay by a sum for that function, reaches infant mortality more fundamentally and directly than do milk stations. In spite of this truth, milk stations are a useful supplementary social service and the value of pure milk where mothers cannot nurse their offspring or secure a competent wet-nurse must not be underestimated. The milk station, too, for one thing, affords an acceptable avenue through which to reach mothers and instruct them in the care of infants, to assist them with a nurse in times of trouble or crisis, and to prepare them for the hour when milk from the stations becomes a necessity.

In most cases women now recognize the milk station not as a private but as a public responsibility. They first demonstrated the wisdom and practicability of the enterprise as direct health activity, then urged the municipalities to incorporate the plans into their regular health department program. Cities have accepted the lesson readily, although there are still places like our national capital, where the death rate among infants is disgracefully high and where no provision is made by the commissioners, during even the hot summer months, to care for babies in this way.

The superiority of breast feeding is so well known that the provision of wet-nurses is recognized as a social advantage. The examination, registration, pay and care of wet-nurses are matters of increasing interest to women health workers and the Women's Municipal League of Boston is attempting to deal seriously with this social mother.

No more interesting story of women's help on the problem of general milk supply is to be found than comes from the Oranges, although it is fairly typical of the way women have viewed their responsibility elsewhere. In the spring of 1913, the Civic Committee of the Woman's Club of Orange, New Jersey, offered, for the summer, the services of its secretary to the Orange Board of Health in order that a more thorough study of the milk supply might be made than was possible with the limited official staff alone. "Through the courtesy of the Board, Miss Hall was made a temporary special milk inspector in June, 1913, and has enjoyed the use of the department's laboratory in assisting in the test of over 600 samples on which conclusions are based as to the quality of the milk furnished in the Oranges." Those conclusions are published in a report by the aforesaid club in order to give the consumer a better knowledge of the production and supply of milk "in the hope of arousing citizen interest in a union of effort among the four municipalities, toward a more efficient control."

The joint effort of the Woman's Club and of the Department of Health led to their common support of certain proposals dealing with the milk situation in the four Oranges. In this case, after a careful and detailed study of all the elements that enter into the provision of milk for these communities, the women determined upon a citizen support of the health officers that, among other proposals, they might obtain better appropriations for the work of inspection. Their publications and general agitation have been marked by exact information.

From New York on the eastern seaboard to Portland on the western come countless reports of the activities of organized groups of women in behalf of pure milk. The "Portland Pure Milk War" was graphically described by Stella Walker Durham in a recent number of *Good Housekeeping*. The struggle to secure the kind of milk they wanted meant a year's fight for the women who knew and proved that they knew the true conditions of their city's milk supply.

Didn't rely on the authorities —
- Saw a problem
- investigated it.
- did all the social science research.

CHAPTER 3

Women at Work

The post-Civil War period saw a dramatic expansion of women at work; by 1910, women comprised 20 percent of the workforce, up from 14 percent in 1870. The numbers of working women increased from 1.7 million to 7 million during that 40-year timespan. The typical woman worker was young (age 14 to 24), single, and usually the daughter of immigrants. She was unskilled and concentrated in a low-paying "women's job." She lived in an urban environment and usually saw her work as temporary until she married and established her own household.

The kinds of jobs that women held were shaped by the structural needs of the economy as well as by deeply ingrained patterns that divided the workplace into men's and women's jobs. Women worked primarily in jobs alongside other women; rarely did they work directly with men. It was also rare for women to displace men from jobs; many of the job opportunities that caused the spurt in women's employment in the late 19th century were created by industrialization, rather than being taken over from men. Although the largest employment category for women remained domestic service (which employed one-quarter of the urban female work force in 1900), the proportion of working women in service had by the 20th century entered a permanent decline in response to other, more desirable occupations. (To most working women, anything was preferable to domestic service.) Other areas where women were concentrated included the sewing trades, clerical work, teaching, laundry work, nursing, retail sales, and textile manufacturing.

Which jobs were taken by which women also varied in relation to class, racial, and ethnic patterns. The highest status jobs were usually reserved for the daughters of native-born Americans: clerical work (an expanding field that quickly came to be dominated by women), retail sales in the new department stores, and teaching. Although hours were long, working conditions tough (especially for saleswomen, who had to endure long stretches standing up), women would take these jobs over better-paying factory work precisely because of the status involved. Winning such a job was a measure of definite upward mobility for a woman from an immigrant background.

Other women could only aspire to such jobs. Young immigrant women were most likely concentrated in the expanding factory and sweatshop work, especially in such sectors as textiles and sewing, which were highly dependent on women's work. These workers were overwhelmingly single. It was quite rare for married women to work for wages outside the home, although many took in boarders in order to stretch the family income. Such work was not counted as employment in census tabulations, nor were women's contributions to farm labor, suggesting that statistics consistently underrepresent women's contributions to family income.

Black women faced the most restricted economic opportunities. Barred from industrial work, black women were heavily represented in domestic service, laundry work, and, in the rural areas where the vast majority of blacks still lived at the turn of the century, as agricultural workers. Because black women's income was crucial to family survival, they showed a wage-force participation rate twice as high as white women in 1900. The number of married black women who worked was especially high (25 percent) compared to white and immigrant groups (3 percent).

The conditions of life and work for the growing urban class of self-supporting women were harsh. A woman could expect to work at least 60 hours a week over six days, with only Sundays and Saturday afternoons off. Her wages would barely cover her expenses of lodging, food, and the most minimal clothing needs, even if she was working full time; seasonal layoffs and periodic unemployment increased the difficulties of her existence. A further hazard was industrial accidents. No wonder some urban women turned to prostitution, where wages were five times higher than what a working girl could make on the job.

These conditions were a cause of concern to reformers, especially during the Progressive era. Two possible routes to improve working conditions were available—through labor unions or through legislation to regulate hours, wages, and safety conditions. Although dramatic examples such as the Shirtwaist strike in New York in 1909–1910 (the so-called "uprising of 20,000") demonstrated that women could be successfully organized, unions were typically uninterested or hostile to women's interests. Union leaders, almost all men, saw working women as hard to organize because they planned to leave the work force when they married; such leaders also believed that women really belonged at home, not on the job, and that the goal of the labor movement was to win a decent family wage for the male breadwinner so that female family members did not need to work. Consequently, women made up only 2.2 percent of union members in 1900.

The other solution, protective labor legislation, was the one favored by many Progressive era reformers. Although attempts to regulate the working conditions of men had been ruled unconstitutional by the courts, middle-class reformers were able to win passage of state laws that limited working hours for women, regulated night work, set minimum wages, and imposed minimal safety conditions. Such legislation, sold in part on the premise that women were weaker than men and thus needed special protection, confirmed women's unequal status in the work force at the same time it gave them improvements in hours and wages.

By 1920, the self-supporting working girl was a totally accepted part of the urban economic landscape. No longer credible were the dire predictions of the 1870s and 1880s about urban women being swallowed up in prostitution rings or becoming unfit for future motherhood by their work. Women workers had proven themselves a crucial part of the economic structure, and such work was seen as a normal stage in women's lives before marriage.

There was a shift under way in the kinds of women working, however. The young, single, poor immigrant girl was being joined by a new woman worker: an older, often married woman, who was no longer desperately poor but working to improve her family's economic situation. With the declining birthrate and improvements in household technology, it was somewhat easier for married women to take on employment outside the home. An especially important factor was the decline in child labor after 1900, in large part because of legislation mandating school attendance and outlawing child labor. Attitudes about family roles were changing too. Increasingly, the supplemental family wage earner would be the mother rather than the child under 14. By 1920, therefore, the era of the working girl was beginning to give way to the era of the working mother, one of the most far-reaching changes of 20th-century women's lives.

The Burdens of Rural Women's Lives

In 1901, when this autobiographical piece was published in *The American Kitchen Magazine,* the majority of Americans still lived in rural areas. Not until 1920, according to the United States Census Bureau, would urbanites outnumber rural dwellers. Life in rural farm communities was rough no matter how you sliced it: sunrise to sundown labor, the vagaries of the weather, debt, crop failure, and isolation. Farm households worked longer hours than the nation's overworked industrial workers. Rural women had it especially hard. Not only did they have the full responsibility for bearing and raising children and maintaining their households, as did their urban counterparts, but they also actively participated in farm labor.

Farm women undertook these chores with precious little help from the conveniences increasingly available in urban areas. The lack of electricity was the most obvious deficit; as late as the 1930s, only 1 farm in 10 was electrified. Lack of electricity meant that all water had to be pumped by hand and then hauled to the household or barn. Since the average family used 200 gallons a day, that was a lot of hauling. If it was washday (and Monday was always washday on the farm), the farm wife had to fetch and heat large tubs of water for the washing, bleaching, and rinsing of a week's worth of farm clothes. Only rarely did a farm wife have the help of a hired girl; usually daughters were pressed into service, their own apprenticeship for their later lives on the farm. And yet farm women, such as this anonymous chronicler who took part in Cornell University's Reading Course for Farmers' Wives, rarely complained.

Source: Cornell Reading Course for Farmers' Wives, *The American Kitchen Magazine* XIV (October 1900–March 1901), quoted in *So Sweet to Labor: Rural Women in America, 1865–1895,* Norton Juster, ed. (New York: Viking Press, 1979), pp. 101–2.

Two things I have been taught in my long farm life: one is, that work never kills, and the other is, that we must calculate work beforehand in order to save steps and do a great amount of work. I am fifty-eight years old. Have been on a farm all my life until a year ago, when we built a new house on one end of our farm which opens on a public road and is retired from farm labor. My father was a farmer and a minister of the old school, who believed in no salary, but believed in working for a living. I learned to milk when seven years old, and always did my share while at home. I was sent to school, but at fourteen commenced to teach a district school on a third grade license. I soon received a second and then the first grade. I boarded around. I was married at nineteen, and then my farm life began in earnest. We always kept a dairy, from twelve to fourteen head. When we were married we did not own a foot of land. My husband and I bought thirty acres the day after we were married, joining the old homestead of his people with whom we lived. They owned fifty acres, but there was a mortgage of three hundred and fifty dollars on that. We took care of them until they died, paid the mortgage, bought enough more to make us two hundred acres. We had a sugar orchard and made from three to five hundred pounds of sugar and a great deal of sirup every year. We kept sheep and always worked up the wool, spun, wove, and made full cloth for men's wear and for flannel sheets. We knit our own socks and stockings. I would always rise in the morning at four or half past, winter and summer, and have built my own fires, milked from four to eight cows, prepared the breakfast and had it at six. Until about ten years ago we made butter, and since then have sent it to a factory. I always did my own churning, and many are the books of poems, histories, stories, and newspapers I have read through while churning. I am the mother of eight children, five of whom are living. The others died when small. The oldest living is thirty-six and the youngest is twelve. Three of them have graduated from high school and been a number of terms at an academy. One has been for five years at Cornell University. I have always done my own washing and weaving of carpets, as I have a large house and it is furnished with rag carpets. I make my own garden and have helped rake hay and husk corn. One fall, alone, I husked between five and six hundred bushels. I had one daughter and she was at home at that time; so I did no housework while husking, although I attended to the milk and butter, milked, and got breakfast. One summer I piled up one hundred cords of wood and did my own housework. You will say there was no call for this. We were married the first year of the Civil War. In '63 my husband was drafted, paid his three hundred dollars, and stayed at home. That had to be met in hard times for the farmer. Not many modern wives would think they could pull flax, cut corn, dig potatoes, and do all things on a farm that we used to do. All this time I had a hired girl only a year and a half. We made our own table linen and toweling, spinning and weaving it, and our flannel dresses. I have been with the sick a great deal, and always went to church and Sunday school, and attended societies which belonged to the church. To-day I can walk a mile or more as quickly as any one. At the present time I have two old people to care for; one of them is eighty-six and the other is eighty-three. There are five in our family, and I am doing all the work myself, and am going to take the teacher to board next year. So you see, work does not kill and there must have been some calculation to save steps. My husband says, "You helped earn and saved more than I did." The boys many times say, "If it had not been for your pushing and helping us to school, we never could have done so well." All this time I have kept up with the general reading of the day.

I never counted my steps but once and that was when I spun a skein of woolen yarn. I went a little over a mile.

Buffalobird Woman's Story

The agricultural practices of Indian women add another perspective on rural life at the turn of the century. In many tribes women owned the land and did most of the agricultural work using traditional farming methods passed down through mothers and grandmothers. By the late 19th century, however, the United States government had forced many Indian tribes onto reservations, where federal officials introduced changes in how agriculture was practiced. As this selection demonstrates, Native Americans were often reluctant to give up traditional food practices and tribal organization, with good reason.

The story of these changes is told by Maxi'diwiac, or Buffalobird Woman, a Hidatsa Indian who lived near the Missouri River in what is now North Dakota. The name Hidatsa is said to mean "willows" in the Sioux language, deriving from the promise of the god Itsikama'hidic that villagers would be as numerous as the willows that line the Missouri River. Buffalobird Woman was born around 1839, the daughter of Small Ankle, who was a leader of Hidatsas at the time they were being removed from their traditional land to the Fort Berthold reservation. According to her son Tsaka'kasakic, or Goodbird, his mother "knows more about old ways of raising corn and squashes than any one else on this reservation." Goodbird, who was educated at mission schools and became a congregational minister, served as interpreter for his mother, who did not speak English.

Buffalobird Woman's story was sought by Gilbert Livingston Wilson, a graduate student in anthropology at the University of Minnesota, who in 1911 wanted to study traditional agriculture, preferably from a woman's perspective. Buffalobird Woman's descriptions formed the basis for his doctoral thesis, and he collaborated on a book with Goodbird as well. Wilson offered Buffalobird Woman to readers in this spirit: "May the Indian woman's story of her toil be a plea for our better appreciation of her race." Or to put it in a slightly different way, may it be a plea for a better appreciation of the contributions that Indian women made to their people and to Western history.

The government has changed our old way of cultivating corn and our other vegetables, and has brought us seeds of many new vegetables and grains, and taught us their use. We Hidatsas and our friends, the Mandans, have also been removed

Source: Gilbert Livingston Wilson, "Agriculture of the Hidatsa Indians: An Indian Interpretation," *University of Minnesota Studies in the Social Sciences* 9 (November 1917), pp. 119–120.

from our village at Like-a-fishhook bend, and made to take our land in allotments; so that our old agriculture has in a measure fallen into disuse.

I was thirty-three years old when the government first plowed up fields for us; two big fields were broken, one between the village and the agency, and another on the farther side of the agency.

New kinds of seeds were issued to us, oats and wheat; and we were made to plant them in these newly plowed fields. Another field was plowed for us down in the bottom land along the Missouri; and here we were taught to plant potatoes. Each family was given a certain number of rows to plant and cultivate.

At first we Hidatsas did not like potatoes, because they smelled so strongly! Then we sometimes dug up our potatoes and took them into our earth lodges; and when cold weather came, the potatoes were frozen, and spoiled. For these reasons we did not take much interest in our potatoes, and often left them in the ground, not bothering to dig them.

Other seeds were issued to us, of watermelons, big squashes, onions, turnips, and other vegetables. Some of these we tried to eat, but did not like them very well; even the turnips and big squashes, we thought not so good as our own squashes and our wild prairie turnips. Moreover, we did not know how to dry these new vegetables for winter; so we often did not trouble even to harvest them.

The government was eager to teach the Indians to raise potatoes; and to get us women to cultivate them, paid as much as two dollars and a half a day for planting them in the plowed field. I remember I was paid that sum for planting them. After three or four years, finding the Indians did not have much taste for potatoes and rather seldom ate them, our agent made a big cache pit—a root cellar you say it was—and bought our potato crop of us. After this he would issue seed potatoes to us in the spring, and in the fall we would sell our crop to him. Thus, handling potatoes each year, we learned little by little to eat them.

The government also broke up big fields of prairie ground, and had us plant corn in them; but these fields on the prairie near the hills I do not think are so good as our old fields down in the timber lands along the Missouri. The prairie fields get dry easily and the soil is harder and more difficult to work.

Then I think our old way of raising corn is better than the new way taught us by white men. Last year, 1911, our agent held an agricultural fair on this reservation; and we Indians competed for prizes for the best corn. The corn which I sent to the fair took the first prize. I raised it on new ground; the ground had been plowed, but aside from that, I cultivated the corn exactly as in old times, with a hoe.

The Harsh Conditions of Domestic Service

Domestic service has always been a woman's job. As late as 1870, 7 out of 10 working women were employed as servants in other women's homes. Of the country's approximately one million domestic workers in 1900, 26 percent were native born, 19 percent were the daughters of immigrants, 28 percent were foreign born, and 27 percent were black. As the 20th century progressed, white women increasingly found jobs other than domestic service, especially in the expanding manufacturing, clerical, and sales sectors. Black women rarely had such options. Excluded from industrial and service jobs by discrimination, black women formed a steady pool of domestic servants, especially in the South. According to the 1890 census, 31 percent of employed black women were servants; the two other largest categories of occupations for them were agriculture (38 percent) and laundry work (15 percent).

This anonymous 1912 article titled "More Slavery at the South" confirms through one woman's eyes the intolerable conditions under which black women toiled. In many ways, such work was a continuation of slavery patterns, where blacks were expected to be servants first and allowed to lead their own lives only after hours. The surplus of potential black servants robbed any hope of improving working conditions or pay, which averaged 12 to 14 hours a day at wages of $4 to $8 a month. One key to getting by was the "service pan" of leftover food that southern servants took home every day, a custom that if stretched creatively could augment a meager income.

This anonymous black woman identifies herself as a nurse, but that label does not reflect a higher occupational status. In fact, there was little value placed on labor specialization within the home, and a nurse's chores would go beyond helping the sick and taking care of children to other tasks such as cleaning and gardening.

I am a negro woman, and I was born and reared in the South. I am now past forty years of age and am the mother of three children. My husband died nearly fifteen years ago, after we had been married about five years. For more than thirty years—or since I was ten years old—I have been a servant in one capacity or another in white families in a thriving Southern city, which has at present a population of more than 50,000. In my early years I was at first what might be called a "house-girl," or better, a "house-boy." I used to answer the doorbell, sweep the yard, go on errands, and do odd jobs. Later on I became a chambermaid and performed the usual duties of such a servant in a home. Still later I was graduated into a cook, in which position I served at different times for nearly eight years in all. During the last ten years I have been a nurse. I have worked for only four different families during all these thirty years. But, belonging to the servant class, which is the majority class among my race at the South, and associating only with servants, I have been able to become intimately acquainted not only with the lives of hundreds of household servants, but also with the lives of their employers. I can, therefore, speak with authority on the so-called servant question; and what I say is said out of an experience which covers many years.

Source: "More Slavery at the South" by a Negro Nurse, *The Independent* 72 (January 25, 1912), pp. 196–200.

To begin with, then, I should say that more than two-thirds of the negroes of the town where I live are menial servants of one kind or another, and besides that more than two-thirds of the negro women here, whether married or single, are compelled to work for a living,—as nurses, cooks, washerwomen, chambermaids, seamstresses, hucksters, janitresses, and the like. I will say, also, that the condition of this vast host of poor colored people is just as bad as, if not worse than, it was during the days of slavery. Though today we are enjoying nominal freedom, we are literally slaves. And, not to generalize, I will give you a sketch of the work I have to do—and I'm only one of many.

I frequently work from fourteen to sixteen hours a day. I am compelled by my contract, which is oral only, to sleep in the house. I am allowed to go home to my own children, the oldest of whom is a girl of 18 years, only once in two weeks, every other Sunday afternoon—even then I'm not permitted to stay all night. I not only have to nurse a little white child, now eleven months old, but I have to act as playmate or "handy-andy," not say governess, to three other children in the home, the oldest of whom is only nine years of age. I wash and dress the baby two or three times each day; I give it its meals, mainly from a bottle; I have to put it to bed each night; and, in addition, I have to get up and attend to its every call between midnight and morning. If the baby falls to sleep during the day, as it has been trained to do every day about eleven o'clock, I am not permitted to rest. It's "Mammy, do this," or "Mammy, do that," or "Mammy, do the other," from my mistress, all the time. So it is not strange to see "Mammy" watering the lawn in front with the garden hose, sweeping the sidewalk, mopping the porch and halls, dusting around the house, helping the cook, or darning stockings. Not only so, but I have to put the other three children to bed each night as well as the baby, and I have to wash them and dress them each morning. I don't know what it is to go to church; I don't know what it is to go to a lecture or entertainment or anything of the kind; I live a treadmill life; and I see my own children only when they happen to see me on the streets when I am out with the children, or when my children come to the "yard" to see me, which isn't often, because my white folks don't like to see their servants' children hanging around their premises. You might as well say that I'm on duty all the time—from sunrise to sunrise, every day in the week. I am the slave, body and soul, of this family. And what do I get for this work—this lifetime bondage? The pitiful sum of ten dollars a month! And what am I expected to do with these ten dollars? With this money I'm expected to pay my house rent, which is four dollars per month, for a little house of two rooms, just big enough to turn round in; and I'm expected, also to feed and clothe myself and three children. For two years my oldest child, it is true, has helped a little toward our support by taking in a little washing at home. She does the washing and ironing of two white families, with a total of five persons; one of these families pays her $1.00 per week, and the other 75 cents per week, and my daughter has to furnish her own soap and starch and wood. For six months my youngest child, a girl about thirteen years old, has been nursing, and she receives $1.50 per week but has no night work. When I think of the low rate of wages we poor colored people receive, and when I hear so much said about our unreliability, our untrustworthiness, and even our vices, I recall the story of the private soldier in a certain army who, once upon a time, being upbraided by the commanding officer because the heels of his shoes were not polished, is said to have replied: "Captain, do you expect all the virtues for $13 per month?"

Of course, nothing is being done to increase our wages, and the way things are going at present it would seem that nothing could be done to cause an increase in wages. We have no labor unions or organizations of any kind that could demand for us a uniform scale of wages for cooks, washerwomen, nurses, and the like; and, for another thing, if some negroes did here and there refuse to work for seven and eight and ten dollars a month, there would be hundreds of other negroes right on the spot ready to take their places and do the same work, or more, for the low wages that had been refused. So that, the truth is, we have to work for little or nothing or become vagrants! And that, of course, in this State would mean that we would be arrested, tried, and despatched to the "State Farm," where we would surely have to work for nothing or be beaten with many stripes! . . .

Another thing—it's a small indignity, it may be, but an indignity just the same. No white person, not even the little children just learning to talk, no white person at the South ever thinks of addressing any negro man or woman as Mr., or Mrs., or Miss. The women are called, "Cook," or "Nurse," or "Mammy," or "Mary Jane," or "Lou," or "Dilcey," as the case might be, and the men are called "Bob," or "Boy," or "Old Man," or "Uncle Bill," or "Pate." In many cases our white employers refer to us, and in our presence, too, as their "niggers." No matter what they call us—no matter what they teach their children to call us—we must tamely submit, and answer when we are called; we must enter no protest; if we did object, we should be driven out without the least ceremony, and, in applying for work at other places, we should find it very hard to procure another situation. In almost every case, when our intending employers would be looking up our record, the information would be given by telephone or otherwise that we were "impudent," "saucy," "dishonest," and "generally unreliable." In our town we have no such thing as an employment agency or intelligence bureau, and, therefore, when we want work, we have to get out on the street and go from place to place, always with hat in hand, hunting for it . . .

You hear a good deal nowadays about the "service pan." The "service pan" is the general term applied to "left-over" food, which in many a Southern home is freely placed at the disposal of the cook, or, whether so placed or not, it is usually disposed of by the cook. In my town, I know, and I guess in many other towns also, every night when the cook starts for her home she takes with her a pan or a plate of cold victuals. The same thing is true on Sunday afternoon after dinner—and most cooks have nearly every Sunday afternoon off. Well, I'll be frank with you, if it were not for the service pan, I don't know what the majority of our Southern colored families would do. The service pan is the mainstay in many a home. Good cooks in the South receive on an average $8 per month. Porters, butlers, coachmen, janitors, "office boys" and the like, receive on an average $16 per month. Few and far between are the colored men in the South who receive $1 or more per day. Some mechanics do; as, for example, carpenters, brick masons, wheelwrights, blacksmiths, and the like. The vast majority of negroes in my town are serving in menial capacities in homes, stores and offices. Now taking it for granted, for the sake of illustration, that the husband receives $16 per month and the wife $8. That would be $24 between the two. The chances are that they will have anywhere from five to thirteen children between them. Now, how far will $24 go toward housing and feeding and clothing ten or twelve persons for thirty days? And, I tell you, with all of us poor people the service pan is a great institution; it is a great help to us, as we wag along the weary way of life. And then most of the white folks expect their cooks to avail themselves of these perquisites; they allow it; they expect it. I do not deny that the cooks find opportunity to hide away at times, along with the cold "grub," a little sugar, a little flour, a little meal, or a little piece of soap; but I indignantly deny that we are thieves. We don't steal; we just "take" things—they are a part of the oral contract, expressed or implied. We understand it, and most of the white folks understand it. Others may denounce the service pan, and say that it is used only to support idle negroes, but many a time, when I was a cook, and had the responsibility of rearing my three children upon my lone shoulders, many a time I have had occasion to bless the Lord for the service pan!

Female Perspectives on the Great Migration

With conditions so limited in the South, it is no wonder that many African-Americans were lured by the promise of economic opportunities and greater social freedom in the North. Beginning in the 1910s but greatly hastened by opportunities opened by World War I, more than 500,000 blacks left the South between 1916 and 1919; close to a million more would follow in the 1920s. This exodus is called the "great migration."

Women migrated in fewer numbers than men and sometimes for different reasons and with different results. While both black men and women sought better economic opportunities, women faced greater economic discrimination and had fewer employment opportunities than men. Many found themselves still doing domestic work once they moved north, although at least for wages significantly higher than before. But economics cannot alone explain the pull of migration. Historians such as Darlene Clark Hine point to a desire for greater personal autonomy and an escape from sexual exploitation, especially at the hands of white Southern employers, as propelling reasons for the move.

More than any other city, Chicago represented the "promised land" for Southern migrants. The terminus of the Illinois Central railroad, which extended deep into the South, it was easily accessible by train. In addition, the *Chicago Defender,* a militantly pro-black newspaper founded in 1905 by

Source: "Letters of Negro Migrants of 1916–1918," *Journal of Negro History* IV, no. 3 (July 1919) and 4 (October 1919), pp. 317, 318–19, 332, 337–38, 339, 413.

Robert Abbott that counted two-thirds of its circulation from outside Chicago, played a key role in conveying information about opportunities to even the remotest corner of the South. The *Defender*'s articles, editorials, and advertisements all presented a picture of Chicago as a city with a vibrant and assertive black community, accompanied by ample opportunities for economic and personal advancement. The *Defender* actively promoted migration, and its pages served as an informal clearinghouse for jobs and other services to help migrants get settled.

Like the demographics of migration in general, fewer women wrote the *Defender* than men, but the letters selected here show some of the characteristics and motivations of women who decided to leave the South. The letters demonstrate the classic "push" and "pull" aspects of migration—the push out of the South because chances for advancement were so limited, and the pull of new opportunities, especially economic. The letters also show the enormous faith that Southern blacks had in the ability of the *Defender* to help them get settled in their new lives, a faith that was often not misplaced.

New Orleans, La., May 7, 1917.

Gentlemen: I read Defender every week and see so much good youre doing for the southern people & would like to know if you do the same for me as I am thinking of coming to Chicago about the first of June. and wants a position. I have very fine references if needed. I am a widow of 28. No children, not a relative living and I can do first class work as house maid and dining room or care for invalid ladies. I am honest and neat and refined with a fairly good education. I would like a position where I could live on places because its very trying for a good girl to be out in a large city by self among strangers is why I would like a good home with good people. Trusting to hear from you.

Jacksonville, Fla., April 28, 1917.

Kind Sir: We have several times read your noted paper and we are delighted with the same because it is a thorough Negro paper. There is a storm of our people toward the North and especially to your city. We have watched your want ad regularly and we are anxious for location with good families (white) where we can be cared for and do domestic work. We want to engage as cook, nurse and maid. We have had some educational advantages, as we have taught in rural schools for few years but our pay so poor we could not continue. We can furnish testimonial of our honesty and integrity and moral standing. Will you please assist us in securing places as we are anxious to come but want jobs before we leave. We want to do any kind of honest labor. Our chance here is so poor.

Mobile, Ala., April 25, 1917.

Sir: I was reading in theat paper about the Colored race and while reading it I seen in it where cars would be here for the 15 of May which is one month from to day. Will you be so kind as to let me know where they are coming to and I will be glad to know because I am a poor woman and have a husband and five children living and three dead one single and two twin girls six months old today and my husband can hardly make bread for them in Mobile. This is my native home but it is not fit to live in just as the Chicago Defender say it says the truth and my husband only get $1.50 a day and pays $7.50 a month for house rent and can hardly feed me and his self and children. I am the mother of 8 children 25 years old and I want to get out of this dog hold because I dont know what I am raising them up for in this place and I want to get to Chicago where I know they will be raised and my husband crazy to get there because he know he can get more to raise his children and will you please let me know where the cars is going to stop to so that he can come where he can take care of me and my children. He get there a while and then he can send for me. I heard they wasnt coming here so I sent to find out and he can go and meet them at the place they are going and go from there to Chicago. No more at present. hoping to hear from you soon from your needed and worried friend.

ATLANTA, GA., April 11, 1917.

Dear Sir: I am a reader of you paper and we are all crazy about it and take it every Saturday and we raise a great howl when we dont get it. Now since I see and feel that you are for the race and are willing to assist any one so I will ask you to please assist me in getting imployment and some place to stop with some good quiet people or with a family that would take some one to live with them. I will do any kind of work. I am a hair dresser but I will do any kind of work I can get to do I am a widow and have one child a little girl 6 years years old I dont know any body there so if you can assist me in any way will be greatly appreciated now this letter is personal please dont print it in your paper. I hope to hear from you soon.

KISSIMMEE, FLA., May 1, 1917.

Dear Sir: I am a subscriber for the Chicago Defender have read of the good work you are doing in employing help for your large factories and how you are striving to help get the better class of people to the north. I am a teacher and have been teaching five years successful, and as our school here has closed my cousin and I have decided to go north for the summer who is also a teacher of this county. I am writing you to secure for us a position that we could fit and one that would fit us, if there be any that is vacant.

We can furnish you with the best of reference. We would not like to advertise through a paper. Hoping to hear from you at an early date, I am

ALEXANDRIA, LA., June 6, 1917.

Dear Sirs: I am writeing to you all asking a favor of you all. I am a girl of seventeen. School has just closed I have been going to school for nine months and I now feel like I aught to go to work. And I would like very very well for you all to please forward me to a good job. but there isnt a thing here for me to do, the wages here is from a dollar and a half a week. What could I earn Nothing. I have a mother and father my father do all he can for me but it is so hard. A child with any respect about her self or his self wouldnt like to see there mother and father work so hard and earn nothing I feel it my duty to help. I would like for you all to get me a good job and as I havent any money to come on please send me a pass and I would work and pay every cent of it back and get me a good quite place to stay. My father have been getting the defender for three or four months but for the last two weeks we have failed to get it. I dont know why. I am tired of down hear in this——/ I am afraid to say. Father seem to care and then again dont seem to but Mother and I am tired tired of all of this I wrote to you all because I believe you will help I need your help hopeing to here from you all very soon.

The Story of a Glove Maker

Agnes Nestor

Working in factories was long, tedious work. Working women found that they were at the mercy of foremen, who had the right to hire and fire, speed up or slow down production, and take sexual advantage of working girls who desperately needed to hold on to their jobs. There were other minor, or not so minor, indignities on the job. Workers were often charged 50 cents a week for the power that ran their machines, so-called machine rent. They had to buy their own needles and machine oil. Their working hours were irregular, as was their pay. It was a rare factory that had a union to speak up for the women's demands.

Agnes Nestor's story of a day's work making gloves, written in Chicago around 1898, conveys the texture of working women's lives. Agnes Nestor (1880–1948) came from an Irish Roman Catholic family, never had more than an eighth-grade education, and she spent most of her working life in Chicago. To protest the conditions she describes in this article (especially the issue of machine rent), she impetuously led a walkout of her fellow glove makers. After 10 days of picketing, the women won all their demands, including the recognition of a glove makers' union. For the rest of her life, Nestor devoted herself to the International Glove Workers Union, serving in various national capacities. In addition to her union organizing, she was also a successful lobbyist for protective labor legislation, such as the eight-hour day, for women and children in Illinois.

The whistle blows at 7 A.M. but the piece workers have until 7.30 to come in to work. The penalty for coming late (after 7.30 A.M.) is the loss of a half day as the girls cannot then report to work until noon. This rule is enforced to induce the girls to come early but it often works a hardship on them when they are unavoidably delayed on account of the cars, etc. Stormy weather is the only excuse.

All the work in the sewing department is piece work so the wages depend upon the speed of the operator. The gloves are made by the dozen and each class of operators has a particular part of them to make. After they are cut they go to the

Source: Agnes Nestor, "A Day's Work Making Gloves" (1898) in Nestor, *Woman's Labor Leader* (Rockford, IL.: Bellevue Books Publishing Co., 1954), pp. 37–41.

silker, who does the fancy stitching on the backs; then to the closer, who sews in the thumbs and joins the pieces to the palms to form the backs; they then go to several operators each of whom does a small part of the banding; then the gloves come back to the closer to be closed around the fingers. This finishes most of the bandtop gloves but the gauntlets have to go to the binder or hemmer who finishes the tops. Nearly all of the gloves are finished on the wrong side and have to go to another department to be turned and layed off on a heated iron form; this is the finishing process. This is the making of the heavy working and driving gloves.

A few years ago most of the gloves were made throughout by one operator, but by degrees the manufacturers have divided the work into sections until now the closers and girls making the finer driving and fancy gauntlets are the only girls who really have a trade to learn. The other work is very straight and requires more speed than skill . . .

It is a curious sight to go through a factory and see in spaces between the windows and on the posts at certain distances apart, eighty-five-cent alarm clocks. The clocks are bought as the result of a collection, which means that each girl puts in five or ten cents.

I have heard and read criticisms of the men who work watching the clock, ready to drop their tools on the minute of quitting time. But the reason our girls buy and watch the clocks is not to see how soon they can quit work, but to see that they do not lose time. It is easy to lose a few minutes and not notice it until the end of the day when we count up our work and pay. Every girl knows just how long it takes her to make any part of the glove. We figure that we can make a pair in a certain number of minutes so we watch the clock to see that we will come out on time with our dozen.

When we begin our day's work we never know what our day's pay will be. We have to figure to make up for time we lose. Although it is not our fault it is at our expense. For instance: a dozen gloves may be cut from very heavy leather and very difficult to sew; or perhaps when we go to the desk for work we may have to stand waiting in line ten to twenty minutes; or the belt of our machine may break and we may have to walk around the factory two or three times before we find the belt boy who, perhaps, is hidden under a table fixing a belt, and then we have to wait our turn; or we go to another desk to get our supplies such as needles, thread, welt, etc. But what we dread most of all is the machine breaking down as we do not know how long it will take to repair it. For this work the machinist takes our name and again we have to wait our turn. The foreman is very willing to allow us to use another machine, but when a girl is accustomed to her own machine it is not an easy matter to sew on any other. For each kind of leather and style of glove we use a different color and number of thread and size of needle; each of these re-quires a certain tension so that in changing the thread, needles and machine for the various kinds of work again time is taken, our time. Each glove has to be stamped with the girl's number so that a glove can always be traced back to the maker and all "busters" brought to her to repair.

I remember a certain style of glove of which I found I could make a dozen in one hour and a half. There happened to be a large order for this work going through, so that I had a great amount of it. At the end of the day, nine and a half hours, I found that I had only five dozens made. The next day I watched the clock very closely to see where the two hours went the day before. I finished each dozen on "scheduled time" but at the end of this day I found I still had only my five dozens made. I tried this every day for a week, each day trying to work harder, only with the same result and to find myself completely tired out.

A great many employers give as their reason for preferring the piece-work system and establishing it as much as possible, that they are only paying for the work they receive and have more work turned out in a day. This no doubt is true; but it is too often at the expense of the girl. For she pays not only the loss of time but the loss of health too. I am one of the many who are very much against this system for I have seen too many awful results from it. We have a certain amount of strength and energy and if this is to be used up the first few years at the trade what is to become of the workers after that? This system, moreover, encourages a girl to do more than her physical strength will allow her to do continuously. Piece work is worry as well as work.

When I started in the trade and saw the girls working at that dreadful pace every minute, I wondered how they could keep up the speed. But it is not until you become one of them that you can understand. The younger girls are usually very anxious to operate a machine. I remember the first day that I sewed, making the heavy linings. The foreman came to me late in the day and asked how I liked the work. "Oh," I said, "I could never get tired sewing on this machine." But he had seen too many girls "get tired," so he said "Remember those words a few years from now if you stay," and I have.

At half-past nine the whistle blows again and we have five minutes for a light lunch. This time we have to make up so we work until 5:35 P.M. At noon we have only half an hour, which means that the girls have to bring cold lunches. The firm heats a large boiler of water so the girls can make tea or coffee. While half an hour seems a short time for lunch still a great many girls take ten or fifteen minutes of this to trim their gloves or whatever work they can do while the power is shut down. The girls all eat at their places, two or three grouping together. I believe a lunch-room should be provided where we could eat without the sight of gloves and the smell of leather.

There is a big army of foremen, forewomen, and others employed by the various manufacturers just to study and plan how they can save a few cents here and there for the firm. Their methods of saving too often result in a "cut" here and there. As these "cuts" continue to come one after another, the girls must work faster and faster to make up for them, until they have to give up, and then there are other girls ready to take their places in the race. They all have to compete with the "pacemaker." There is only one way of resisting this and that is through the united efforts of the workers in their trade union.

Employers frequently complain about the big expense of "breaking in so much help." If they spent some of this money to make the factory conditions better it would not be necessary to break in so many workers. I believe it would pay them in the end.

One of the valuable features of our trade union is that the workers have an opportunity to meet their employer. It is only by representatives of both employers and employed sitting around the table and talking matters over that they can both recognize and understand each other's rights and interests.

Working Women Write the Jewish Daily Forward

Another window on the struggles of young immigrant working women, this time on New York's Lower East Side, comes from a feature called "A Bintel Brief" in the popular Yiddish-language newspaper, the *Jewish Daily Forward*. Readers shared a variety of trivial, serious, comic, and tragic stories with the editor, who then offered advice or guidance. Especially in the early years after the Bintel Brief column was begun in 1906, many of the stories came from Jewish immigrants who had recently arrived in America and who were seeking help in making the transition from Old World to New. So popular and recognizable did the feature become that it entered the vernacular, with phrases like "It's just like a 'Bintel Brief' story!" often being used in conversations to convey an interesting or poignant story of family life on the Lower East Side.

Unlike the letters to the *Chicago Defender,* which were predominantly from men, women made up a much larger percentage of those who turned to the *Jewish Daily Forward* for help. Although many letter writers focused on family life and relations, working women also used the forum to seek help with job-related problems. The first selection from a 1907 shopgirl raised an issue that was far too familiar to many working women: sexual harassment at work. Speaking up or saying no to a boss's requests for sexual favors could have meant losing your job, and perhaps your family's livelihood, so most women either put up with it or switched jobs to avoid these unwelcome advances.

The second selection from 1914 tells a heartrending story about the hazards of industrial work. The event she refers to is notorious in history. On March 25, 1911, fire broke out at the Triangle Shirtwaist Factory, located just off Washington Square in lower Manhattan. To keep workers from leaving early, the doors had been kept locked, which prevented quick exit once the fire erupted. About 150 workers, mainly young immigrant women, either leaped to their deaths from windows or were burned to death inside. One concrete result of the Triangle Shirtwaist fire was the creation of the New York State Factory Commission in 1912 and the passage of legislation dealing with fire hazards, unsafe working conditions, and wages and hours. This was an important progressive reform but probably little consolation to this survivor, who lost the love of her life in the conflagration and wondered if she had a right to even think about being happy again.

Source: From Isaac Metzker, ed., *A Bintel Brief: Sixty Years of Letters from the Lower East Side to the Jewish Daily Forward,* pp. 72–73, 129–131. Copyright © 1971. Reprinted by permission.

1907

Dear Editor,

I am one of those unfortunate girls thrown by fate into a dark and dismal shop, and I need your counsel.

Along with my parents, sisters and brothers, I came from Russian Poland where I had been well educated. But because of the terrible things going on in Russia we were forced to emigrate to America. I am now seventeen years old, but I look younger and they say I am attractive.

A relative talked us into moving to Vineland, New Jersey, and here in this small town I went to work in a shop. In this shop there is a foreman who is an exploiter, and he sets prices on the work. He figures it out so that the wages are very low, he insults and reviles the workers, he fires them and then takes them back. And worse than all of this, in spite of the fact that he has a wife and several children, he often allows himself to "have fun" with some of the working girls. It was my bad luck to be one of the girls that he tried to make advances to. And woe to any girl who doesn't willingly accept them.

Though my few hard-earned dollars mean a lot to my family of eight souls, I didn't want to accept the foreman's vulgar advances. He started to pick on me, said my work was no good, and when I proved to him he was wrong, he started to shout at me in the vilest language. He insulted me in Yiddish and then in English, so the American workers could understand too. Then, as if the Devil were after me, I ran home.

I am left without a job. Can you imagine my circumstances and that of my parents who depend on my earnings? The girls in the shop were very upset over the foreman's vulgarity but they don't want him to throw them out, so they are afraid to be witnesses against him. What can be done about this? I beg you to answer me.

Respectfully,
A Shopgirl

ANSWER:

Such a scoundrel should be taught a lesson that could be an example to others. The girl is advised to bring out into the open the whole story about the foreman, because there in the small town it shouldn't be difficult to have him thrown out of the shop and for her to get her job back.

1914

Worthy Editor,

I am a girl twenty-two years of age, but I've already undergone a great deal in my life. When I was born I already had no father. He died four months before my birth. And when I was three weeks old my mother died too. Grandmother, my mother's mother, took me in and soon gave me away to a poor tailor's wife to suckle me.

I was brought up by the tailor and his wife, and got so used to them that I called them Mother and Father. When I grew up I learned from the tailor how to do hand sewing and machine sewing too.

When I was sixteen my grandmother died and left me her small dilapidated house. The rabbi of the town sold it for me for three hundred rubles and gave me the money.

In time one of the tailor's apprentices fell in love with me, and I didn't reject his love. He was a fine, honest, quiet young man and a good earner. He had a golden character and we became as one body and soul. When I turned seventeen my bridegroom came to me with a plan, that we should go to America, and I agreed.

It was hard for me to take leave of the tailor's good family, who had kept me as their own child, and oceans of tears were shed when we parted.

When we came to America my bridegroom immediately started to work and he supported me. He was faithful and devoted. I'll give you an example of his loyalty: once, during the summer in the terrible heat, I slept on the roof. But it started to rain in the middle of the night and I was soaked through to the bone. I got very sick and had to be taken to the hospital. I was so sick that the doctor said I could be saved only by a blood transfusion. My bridegroom said immediately that he was ready to give me his blood, and so, thanks to him, I recovered.

In time I went to work at the "famous" Triangle shop. Later my bridegroom also got a job there. Even at work he wanted to be with me. My bridegroom told me then, "We will both work hard for a while and then we'll get married. We will save every cent so we'll be able to set up a home and then you'll be a housewife and never go to work in the shop again."

Thus my good bridegroom mused about the golden future. Then there was that terrible fire that took one hundred and forty-seven young blossoming lives. When the fire broke out, the screaming, the yelling, the panic all bewildered me. I saw the angel of death before me and my voice was choked in my throat. Suddenly someone seized me with extraordinary strength and carried me out of the shop.

When I recovered I heard calming voices and saw my bridegroom near me. I was in the street, rescued, and saw my girl friends jumping out of the windows and falling to the ground. I clung to my bridegroom and rescuer, but he soon tore himself away from me. "I must save other girls," he said, and disappeared. I never saw him alive again. The next day I identified him, in the morgue, by his watch, which had my picture pasted under the cover. I fainted and they could hardly bring me to.

After that I lay in the hospital for five weeks, and came home shattered. This is the fourth year that I am alone and I still see before me the horrible scenes of the fire. I still see the good face of my dear bridegroom, also the black burned face in the morgue. I am weak and nervous, yet there is now a young man who wants to marry me. But I made a vow that I would never get married. Besides that, I'm afraid that I will never be able to love another man. But this young man doesn't want to leave me, and my friends try to persuade me to marry him and say everything will be all right. I don't believe it, because I think everything can be all right for me only in the grave.

I decided to write to you, because I want to hear your opinion.

Respectfully,
A Faithful Reader

ANSWER:

It is senseless for this girl to sacrifice her life in memory of her faithful bridegroom, since this would not bring him back to life. What the earth covers must be forgotten. She has suffered enough in her life already and is advised to take herself in hand and begin her life anew.

Photo Essay

FRANCES WILLARD LEARNS TO RIDE A BICYCLE "As a temperance reformer," Frances Willard wrote, "I always felt a strong attraction toward the bicycle, because it is the vehicle of so much harmless pleasure, and because the skill required in handling it obliges those who mount to keep clear heads and steady hands." But this photograph from the 1890s shows that women who wanted to learn to ride a bicycle had to grapple with the added impediment of cumbersome clothing, such as the heavy, floor-length suit worn by Willard. Even as women were discovering some of the joys of physical exercise, they had to maintain "proper" female attire.
(Credit: Courtesy of National Women's Christian Temperance Union)

IN THE COMPANY OF EDUCATED WOMEN Women college graduates went to great trouble to create rituals and ceremonies to help legitimize their pathbreaking decision to pursue higher education. Here graduating seniors in Mount Holyoke's Class of 1902 participate in the annual Ivy exercises. The women's white dresses (which suggest purity, virginity, and traditional womanhood) are kept very visible beneath their academic caps and gowns, which symbolize their new intellectual aspirations. The woman leading on the left is Frances Perkins, who became the first woman to serve in the cabinet when President Franklin D. Roosevelt named her Secretary of Labor in 1933.
(Credit: Mount Holyoke College Library/Archives)

EXPANDING HORIZONS OF WOMEN'S WORK Working in a
settlement house was exciting for the young college graduates who chose
to live in poor urban areas and provide services for the local neighborhood
residents. Some settlement houses such as Lillian Wald's Henry Street
Settlement in New York served as headquarters for a corps of visiting
nurses and public health workers who reached out to the poor in their
homes. Here a visiting nurse on her rounds (identifiable by her style of
dress and her black medical bag) takes a shortcut between two tenement
buildings.
(Credit: Museum of the City of New York)

SERVING WOMEN Domestic service was still the largest category of paid women's work in the early 20th century. Matrons had been complaining that "good help was hard to find" throughout the 19th century, and the demand for domestic servants often outstripped the supply. Domestic service was so associated with Irish women that the name *Brigit* practically became a generic term for a (usually hapless) Irish immigrant girl. This photograph of a group of household servants is from the early 20th century. If they were all employed in a single household, it was one of substantial wealth; most households employed only one, perhaps two servants. Their poses do suggest a level of specialization: the woman in the middle is possibly a nursemaid, the cook is front row right, the woman on the upper right seems to be a maid who serves at table, and the woman at the far left with broom and dustbin is probably the scullery maid, the lowest of the jobs on the occupational hierarchy.
(Credit: State Historical Society of Wisconsin)

TAKING WORK HOME This Italian immigrant woman has just picked up a bundle of clothing, which she will probably take home to finish. If she is a married woman with children (it is difficult to tell her age), she will likely have them help with some of the simpler tasks. Notice how dirty the street and sidewalk are. This photograph was taken on New York's Lower East Side in 1910 by Lewis Hine, a pioneer in the field of social documentary photography. The composition is striking, but somewhat misleading. Usually the streets of the Lower East Side were teeming with people and activity.
(Credit: Lewis Hine/Courtesy of George Eastman House)

WOMEN TYPEWRITERS The typical 19th-century office of clerks, stenographers, and accountants was an all-male preserve. But at the end of the century office work became feminized. A large factor was the introduction of the typewriter in the post-Civil War period. Since the typewriter was a new invention, without customary ties to workers of either sex, female typists did not have to overcome the prejudice that they were doing "men's work." These women are taking a Civil Service typing exam in Chicago in 1909 in the hope of finding employment in the expanding government bureaucracy. Winning such a job, with its expectations of neat dress and literacy in English, was a step upward for recent immigrants. (Credit: *Chicago Daily News*/Chicago Historical Society)

"DO YOU BELIEVE WHAT THEY ARE CHARGING FOR MEAT?!?" These women on the Lower East Side of New York are discussing the price of meat during one of the protests that periodically rocked immigrant communities in the early 20th century. The main instigators of such protests were usually married women in their 30s, the time in their life cycle when they would have the maximum number of children at home to clothe and feed. Some reformers tried to suggest that these women learn to substitute other vegetables and cuts of meat for those that had become so expensive, but, especially for Jewish immigrants, certain foods played central roles in religious observances and could not easily be given up.
(Credit: Library of Congress)

SUFFRAGISTS TAKE TO THE STREETS By the 1910s, the woman suffrage movement had mobilized a broad cross section of the American population. In an effort to win new converts to the cause, suffragists adopted the tactic of open-air parades. On the day that Woodrow Wilson arrived in Washington in 1913 for his inauguration, he asked where all the crowds were and was informed that they were watching the suffrage parade. This Philadelphia march, circa 1913, shows the interest of college students and recent graduates in the movement and their willingness to march publicly for the cause, dressed in their caps and gowns. Such parades not only won publicity but also bound women together in the camaraderie of collective displays of suffrage spirit.
(Credit: Courtesy of Wellesley College Archives)

CHAPTER 4

Feminists, Anarchists, and Other Rebel Girls

During the early 20th century, radicalism was a flourishing political and intellectual force in American life. Women such as Mother Jones, Emma Goldman, Kate Richards O'Hare, Elizabeth Gurley Flynn, and Margaret Sanger played prominent and visible roles on the Left, especially in such organizations as the Socialist Party, which was at the peak of its influence in the early 20th century. Of its 118,000 members in 1912, between 10 and 15 percent were women. No other political party in United States history has ever been as supportive of women's rights as the Socialist Party.

A concrete symbol of the Socialist commitment to women's emancipation was the 1908 formation of the Woman's National Committee, which served as a clearinghouse for women's issues within the party. Despite the prominence of this group, however, Socialist women still experienced problems when they tried to raise women's issues within the context of the class struggle. The usual response was that women's emancipation would occur automatically when class oppression ended, and that attention to women's issues deflected energies away from the more crucial (to male leaders' minds) question of working-class revolution. Socialist men, moreover, often had very traditional ideas about women's place in the home, which belied their public commitments to women's emancipation. Bourgeois women's organizations, on the other hand, were seen as too identified with the class interests of their members' husbands to be dependable allies, despite common ground on such issues as woman suffrage. Socialist women tried to balance feminist and class issues, but could only get so far. The Woman's National Committee was basically defunct by 1913.

While the Socialist Party was the focus for much leftist activity in the prewar period, other groups also absorbed radical energies. The Industrial Workers of the World (IWW), established in 1905, represented a new kind of union that sought to organize the working class along Socialist principles. It stressed militant industrial unionism through its chosen weapon of the general strike. One of its most prominent organizers was Elizabeth Gurley Flynn, who had joined the IWW in 1906 at the age of 16. A fiery speaker (she was called the "rebel girl" and later used that phrase as the title of her autobiography), Flynn organized workers, led free speech crusades, and participated in the Lawrence and Paterson general strikes.

New York's Greenwich Village was the center for a host of radicals, artists, socialists, writers, and otherwise generally interesting types before World War I. These self-described bohemians experimented with new forms of expression, both sexual (as in free love) and literary (poetry, drama, and the like). Women were at the center of the Greenwich Village scene, in many cases equal partners to the men. One group of women formed a club called Heterodoxy, which was, in the words of a member, for unorthodox women "who did things, and did them openly." Prominent members included Charlotte Perkins Gilman, journalists Inez Haynes Irwin and Mary Heaton Vorse, and future *Nation* editor Freda Kirchwey. In addition to their general commitment to socialism, these women added feminism to the agenda for the new world that would occur after the hoped-for cultural and political revolution.

Another manifestation of leftist organizing and action was in the fledgling trade union movement. Groups of radical women came together in what historian Meredith Tax has called "the united front of women"—a working coalition of socialists, trade unionists, and feminists who were prominent in such working-class struggles as the Shirtwaist strike in New York in 1909–1910 and the Lawrence textile strike in 1912. The Socialist Party played a central role here but was joined by other organizations such as the Industrial Workers of the World, the Women's Trade Union League, the International Ladies Garment Workers Union, and several bourgeois women's organizations.

This supportive leftist climate, much of it centered in major urban centers with large immigrant populations such as New York, Chicago, and Seattle, allowed for a broad range of individuals to promote their own versions of political and personal liberation. For example, working-class women in New York's Lower East Side neighborhoods organized spontaneous demonstrations to protest the rising cost of living, especially the price of food. Emma Goldman, who saw politics as cooperation with the capitalist state, developed her own strand of revolutionary anarchism in which women's emancipation was a central tenet. Activist Margaret Sanger started out within the Socialist fold, but by 1915 she was working full time on the fledgling birth control movement. Feminist theorist Charlotte Perkins Gilman identified herself as a socialist as she crisscrossed the country lecturing about women's economic independence. What all these intellectuals and activists shared was a hostility to capitalism and a desire to reconstruct industrial, social, and political life along more cooperative lines.

Such activists as Gilman, Sanger, and Goldman were also far to the left of middle-class women's organizations, especially the woman suffrage movement. Groups such as the Socialist Party and the IWW were more sympathetic to controversial issues relating to women's emancipation and sexuality (such as birth control) than reform movements like suffrage. Some suffragists, in fact, hoped to use the demands of radical women to their advantage. As one suffragist said to Charlotte Perkins Gilman, "What you ask is so much worse than what we ask, that they will grant our demand in order to escape yours."

The working-class activism and intellectual stirrings of the early 20th century were brought to an abrupt halt by America's entry into World War I. When the Socialist Party, the IWW, and other radical groups spoke out against the war, they were victims of a massive denial of civil liberties during wartime. Federal laws banned treasonous materials from the mails and allowed the government to arrest individuals who spoke out against government policies. During the war and the Red scare that immediately followed it, once-flourishing groups such as the IWW were decimated through arrests and deportations of leaders and followers. The supportive, questioning climate that had fostered discussions of women's emancipation, birth control, and a general critique of the dominant male power structure abruptly ended. Instead, the period closed with the winning of suffrage, a feminist reform with far less potential to change women's lives.

Mother Jones Supports Striking Coal Miners in Colorado

The life of labor organizer Mary Harris ("Mother") Jones spanned an entire century—she was born in 1830 and died seven months after her centennial in 1930—and many of the important, and often violent, labor struggles of the late 19th and early 20th centuries: the 1877 railroad strike; the Haymarket riot in 1886; the Pennsylvania anthracite coal strikes in 1900–1902; Ludlow, Colorado, in 1913–1914; and the 1919 steel strike. At times affiliated with the Knights of Labor or the United Mine Workers, she was just as likely to agitate on her own, rallying striking workers, organizing their wives and children, and winning national publicity for the shameful conditions under which many industrial workers labored in these years. Throughout her career she was especially identified with the struggles of coal miners.

Born in Cork, Ireland, her family emigrated to the United States as part of the wave of immigration that brought approximately 2 million Irish men and women to the United States before 1860. Working as a dressmaker and then teacher in Chicago and Memphis, she married a member of the Iron Molders' Union in 1861. Tragedy soon struck, as her husband and their four small children died in a yellow fever epidemic in 1867. She returned to Chicago, only to lose all her possessions in the devastating Chicago fire of 1871. For the rest of her life, she traded a settled life for the peripatetic existence of a labor organizer, going wherever she was needed and earning the reputation of the "mother of the laboring class." Here she describes going to Cripple Creek, Colorado, in 1903, where coal miners were striking to demand an eight-hour day, better ventilation in the mines, and a standard measure for the coal they extracted from the pits. The strikers held out over a harsh Colorado winter, but their strike was broken by company violence and intimidation the next summer. In western minefields, as in the East, the power of the mining companies, backed by state authorities, proved too much for the striking workers.

Mother Jones's philosophy is hard to categorize. She was always on the side of the underdog and felt that men, women, and children should be

Source: Mary Harris Jones, *The Autobiography of Mother Jones* (Publishing Co., Chicago, Charles H. Kerr & Company, 1996). Reprinted by permission.

protected from the abuses of modern industrial life. But she was so individ-ualistic and uncompromising that she often found it difficult to work con-structively within the labor movement. A good example of her sometimes unconventional ideology was her opposition to woman suffrage, which she dismissed as a hobby of the upper classes: "The plutocrats have organized their women. They keep them busy with suffrage and prohibition and char-ity." Her most enduring words of advice: "No matter what your fight, don't be ladylike!"

The state of Colorado belonged not to a republic but to the Colorado Fuel and Iron Company, the Victor Company and their dependencies. The governor was their agent. The militia under Bell did their bidding. Whenever the masters of the state told the governor to bark, he yelped for them like a mad hound. Whenever they told the military to bite, they bit.

The people of Colorado had voted overwhelmingly for an eight-hour day. The legislature passed an eight-hour law but the courts had declared it unconstitu-tional. Then when the measure was submitted directly to the people, they voted for it with 40,000 votes majority. But the next legislature, which was controlled by the mining interests, failed to pass the bill.

The miners saw that they could not get their demands through peaceful legis-lation. That they must fight. That they must strike. . .

I went immediately to Colorado, first to the office of The Western Federation of Miners where I heard the story of the industrial conflict. I then got myself an old calico dress, a sunbonnet, some pins and needles, elastic and tape and such sundries, and went down to the southern coal fields of the Colorado Fuel and Iron Company.

As a peddler, I went through the various coal camps, eating in the homes of the miners, staying all night with their families. I found the conditions under which they lived deplorable. They were in practical slavery to the company, who owned their houses, owned all the land, so that if a miner did own a house he must vacate whenever it pleased the land owners. They were paid in scrip instead of money so that they could not go away if dissatisfied. They must buy at company stores and at company prices. The coal they mined was weighed by an agent of the company and the miners could not have a check weighman to see that full credit was given them. The schools, the churches, the roads belonged to the Company. I felt, after listening to their stories, after witnessing their long patience that the time was ripe for revolt against such brutal conditions. . .

All civil law had broken down in the Cripple Creek strike. The militia under Colonel Verdeckberg said, "We are under orders only from God and Governor Peabody." Judge Advocate McClelland when accused of violating the constitution said, "To hell with the constitution!" There was a complete breakdown of all civil law. Habeas corpus proceedings were suspended. Free speech and assembly were forbidden. People spoke in whispers as in the days of the inquisition. Soldiers committed outrages. Strikers were arrested for vagrancy and worked in chain gangs on the street under brutal soldiers. Men, women, and tiny children were packed in the Bullpen at Cripple Creek. Miners were shot dead as they slept. They were ridden from the country, their families knowing not where they had gone, or whether they lived. . .

And why were these things done? Because a group of men had demanded an eight hour day, a check weighman and the abolition of the scrip system that kept them in serfdom to the mighty coal barons. That was all. Just that miners had refused to labor under these conditions. Just because miners wanted a better chance for their children, more of the sunlight, more freedom. And for this they suffered one whole year and for this they died.

A Feminist Challenge to the Privatized Home

Charlotte Perkins Gilman

Charlotte Perkins Stetson Gilman (1860–1935) was the leading intellectual of the women's movement in the early 20th century. Born into the prestigious Beecher family, she struggled through a lonely childhood and disastrous marriage, which caused a nervous breakdown. Her mental health returned once she separated from her husband (she gave him custody of their young daughter), moved to California, and threw herself into the heady reform climate of the 1890s. To support herself, she wrote poetry and short stories and lectured extensively. Her widely read book, *Women and Economics* (1898), argued for female economic independence, and she developed her iconoclastic views in later books and articles, including fiction. A second marriage in 1900, to her first cousin Houghton Gilman, gave her the personal stability she had been unable to find in her first marriage.

Gilman did not consider herself a feminist, preferring to call herself a sociologist because her vision was not for women alone. In Gilman's formulation, the interdependence of men and women was the most important result of human evolution. She was, therefore, highly critical of private institutions, such as families and marriage, that isolated women and prevented their participation in broader social developments. Not only did this stunt women's growth, but it also acted, in her understanding of hereditarian evolution, to retard the development of the human race as a whole.

Women and Economics, from which this selection is drawn, is a mix of evolution, polemics, common sense, and socialism. It is heavily indebted to Edward Bellamy's utopian novel *Looking Backward* (1889). Gilman's plans here for collectivist housekeeping show how she thought a socialist and feminist future might look. Such cooperative apartment houses would end women's isolation in individual homes, allow children to interact with others their own age in child care centers, and make housekeeping and cooking more efficient. Her desire to assign tasks that best utilized individual talents

Source: Charlotte Perkins Stetson (Gilman), *Women and Economics* (Boston: Small, Maynard, and Company, 1898; reprinted by Harper and Row, New York, 1966), pp. 242–47.

was in keeping with her deeply held conviction that all human work was en-
nobling, both to society and to the individuals who were performing it. But
notice how she assumes that women will choose occupations "compatible
with motherhood." Despite such a lapse into conventional thinking, Charlotte Perkins Gilman's vision of women and men emancipated from an outmoded private home still makes a compelling contribution to feminist
thought.

If there should be built and opened in any of our large cities to-day a commodious
and well-served apartment house for professional women with families, it would
be filled at once. The apartments would be without kitchens; but there would be a
kitchen belonging to the house from which meals could be served to the families
in their rooms or in a common dining-room, as preferred. It would be a home
where the cleaning was done by efficient workers, not hired separately by the
families, but engaged by the manager of the establishment; and a roof-garden, day
nursery, and kindergarten, under well-trained professional nurses and teachers,
would insure proper care of the children. The demand for such provision is increasing daily, and must soon be met, not by a boarding-house or a lodging-house,
a hotel, a restaurant, or any makeshift patching together of these; but by a permanent provision for the needs of women and children, of family privacy with collective advantage. This must be offered on a business basis to prove a substantial
business success; and it will so prove, for it is a growing social need.

There are hundreds of thousands of women in New York City alone who are
wage-earners, and who also have families; and the number increases. This is true
not only among the poor and unskilled, but more and more among business
women, professional women, scientific, artistic, literary women. Our school-
teachers, who form a numerous class, are not entirely without relatives. To board
does not satisfy the needs of a human soul. These women want homes, but they do
not want the clumsy tangle of rudimentary industries that are supposed to accompany the home. The strain under which such women labor is no longer necessary.
The privacy of the home could be as well maintained in such a building as described as in any house in a block, any room, flat, or apartment, under present
methods. The food would be better, and would cost less; and this would be true of
the service and of all common necessities.

In suburban homes this purpose could be accomplished much better by a
grouping of adjacent houses, each distinct and having its own yard, but all
kitchenless, and connected by covered ways with the eating-house. No detailed
prophecy can be made of the precise forms which would ultimately prove most
useful and pleasant; but the growing social need is for the specializing of the industries practised in the home and for the proper mechanical provision for them.

The cleaning required in each house would be much reduced by the removal
of the two chief elements of household dirt—grease and ashes.

Meals could of course be served in the house as long as desired; but, when
people become accustomed to pure, clean homes, where no steaming industry is
carried on, they will gradually prefer to go to their food instead of having it

brought to them. It is a perfectly natural process, and a healthful one, to go to one's food. And, after all, the changes between living in one room, and so having the cooking most absolutely convenient; going as far as the limits of a large house permit, to one's own dining-room; and going a little further to a dining room not in one's own house, but near by,—these differ but in degree. Families could go to eat together, just as they can go to bathe together or listen to music together; but, if it fell out that different individuals presumed to develope an appetite at different hours, they could meet it without interfering with other people's comfort or sacrificing their own. Any housewife knows the difficulty of always getting a family together at meals. Why try? Then arises sentiment, and asserts that family affection, family unity, the very existence of the family, depend on their being together at meals. A family unity which is only bound together with a table-cloth is of questionable value.

There are several professions involved in our clumsy method of housekeeping. A good cook is not necessarily a good manager, nor a good manager an accurate and thorough cleaner, nor a good cleaner a wise purchaser. Under the free development of these branches a woman could choose her position, train for it, and become a most valuable functionary in her special branch, all the while living in her own home; that is, she would live in it as a man lives in his home, spending certain hours of the day at work and others at home.

This division of the labor of housekeeping would require the service of fewer women for fewer hours a day. Where now twenty women in twenty homes work all the time, and insufficiently accomplish their varied duties, the same work in the hands of specialists could be done in less time by fewer people; and the others would be left free to do other work for which they were better fitted, thus increasing the productive power of the world. Attempts at cooperation so far have endeavored to lessen the existing labors of women without recognizing their need for other occupation, and this is one reason for their repeated failure.

It seems almost unnecessary to suggest that women as economic producers will naturally choose those professions which are compatible with motherhood, and there are many professions much more in harmony with that function than the household service. Motherhood is not a remote contingency, but the common duty and the common glory of womanhood. If women did choose professions unsuitable to maternity, Nature would quietly extinguish them by her unvarying process. Those mothers who persisted in being acrobats, horse-breakers, or sailors before the mast, would probably not produce vigorous and numerous children. If they did, it would simply prove that such work did not hurt them. There is no fear to be wasted on the danger of women's choosing wrong professions, when they are free to choose. Many women would continue to prefer the very kinds of work which they are doing now, in the new and higher methods of execution. Even cleaning, rightly understood and practised, is a useful, and therefore honorable, profession. It has been amusing heretofore to see how this least desirable of labors has been so innocently held to be women's natural duty. It is woman, the dainty, the beautiful, the beloved wife and revered mother, who has by common consent been expected to do the chamber-work and scullery work of the world. All that is basest and foulest she in the last instance must handle and remove. Grease, ashes, dust, foul linen, and sooty ironware,—among these her days must pass. As we socialize our functions, this passes from her hands into those of man. The city's cleaning is his work. And even in our houses the professional cleaner is more and more frequently a man.

The organization of household industries will simplify and centralize its cleaning processes, allowing of many mechanical conveniences and the application of scientific skill and thoroughness. We shall be cleaner than we ever were before. There will be less work to do, and far better means of doing it. The daily needs of a well-plumbed house could be met easily by each individual in his or her own room or by one who liked to do such work; and the labor less frequently required would be furnished by an expert, who would clean one home after another with the swift skill of training and experience. The home would cease to be to us a workshop or a museum, and would become far more the personal expression of its occupants—the place of peace and rest, of love and privacy—than it can be in its present condition of arrested industrial development. And woman will fill her place in those industries with far better results than are now provided by her ceaseless struggles, her conscientious devotion, her pathetic ignorance and inefficiency.

Wages for Housework

Josephine Conger-Kaneko

Wages for housework have been squarely on the feminist agenda since the 1970s, but that was not the first time the issue had been raised, as this spirited 1913 piece by Socialist writer Josephine Conger-Kaneko demonstrates. It appeared in *Progressive Woman,* the magazine that Conger-Kaneko had founded in 1907 under the original title of *Socialist Woman* with the help of her husband, prominent Japanese socialist Kiichi Kaneko. Starting with only 26 subscribers, she built circulation to 15,000 at its peak in 1912. Historian Mari Jo Buhle called this magazine and its editor the "single most important source of propaganda and news of the women's sector" for the entire Socialist movement.

Josephine Conger was born in Centralia, Missouri. While attending Ruskin College in Trenton, Missouri, she became an avid convert to socialism. She loved poetry and literature, but she loved journalism more. Building on her experience working for her brother's country newspaper, in 1903 she got a job on the editorial staff of the *Appeal,* the most popular Socialist newspaper in the United States at the time. Her column, which combined inspirational poetry, politics, and a belief in the moral imperative of traditional womanhood, was directed toward women. "A woman can understand anything if presented from a personal standpoint," she once stated.

Source: Josephine Conger-Kaneko, "Does a Woman Support the Husband's Employer?" *Progressive Woman,* 7.74 (August 1913).

Josephine Conger-Kaneko was always a strong believer in separate organizations for women within the wider Socialist movement. "There is a very great deal that women need to learn about themselves, about their history, and the traditions of their sex," she noted. "These things can best be learned, as a rule, in a separate organization, where the mind can be better centered upon the matter at hand." Her magazine—and her advocacy of women's issues—flourished in the heyday of women's activism from 1908 to 1913 but then fell on hard times when the Socialist movement shifted its priorities. *Progressive Woman* ceased publication in 1913.

Does a woman support her husband's employer?

Has anybody ever thought about a woman's part in her husband's contract for his wages?

Has anybody ever thought that when a man gets married he DOESN'T RECEIVE A PENNY MORE FOR HIS WORK THAN WHEN HE WAS SINGLE, AND THAT THEN HE GOT BARELY ENOUGH TO BOARD AND CLOTHE HIMSELF?

Evidently nobody has thought much about these things. And least of all the woman herself. So, let us see about it.

And you, madam, must see about it with us. It means something to you. It might mean that you are to have a new voile dress next spring, instead of making over that old thing again that you were married in ten years ago.

For that is just what it amounts to—your husband's employer getting the dimes and dollars that should be yours for a new dress and the other things you need so much to lead a normal, happy life.

Here is the situation. Your husband works eight or ten hours a day, and receives a cash return for his work. You work twelve or fifteen hours a day, AND NEVER SEE A CASH RETURN FOR YOUR WORK.

Your husband works to produce saleable goods for the man who employs him. YOU WORK TO KEEP A HOME AND FEED YOUR HUSBAND SO THAT HE CAN KEEP ON WORKING TO PRODUCE SALEABLE GOODS FOR THE MAN WHO EMPLOYS HIM.

Your husband, working for his employer, produces in a year, say $2,500 (the U.S. census statistics say the average worker produces this much in a year) and he gets back in wages $500 (census statistics also say that a man's average wage a year is $500).

Now, YOU make a home for your husband, cook his meals, wash his clothes and mend them; in fact, you keep him in trim and working order so he can produce $2,500 a year for his employer. Your husband gets back from what he makes $500.

WHAT DO YOU GET?

If you hired out to families to do the washing alone, you would get $2 a day and your car fare and lunch. If you went from family to family six days in the week, washing for them, you would get six free lunches and $12.

Working this way, your work is from 8 in the morning till 5 in the afternoon. After you are through with your work you have the evening to yourself, and $2 in your pocket.

When you work to keep your husband in good order for his employer you don't get through at 5 o'clock, and you don't have your evening for yourself. Nor do you have $2 in your purse at the end of the day.

No. Not exactly.

You work ALL HOURS, at BOARD WAGES. That is, you get a part of the food you cook, and live in the house you keep, and you can have a dress occasionally that you make, FOR WORKING ENDLESS HOURS THAT YOUR HUSBAND MAY BE AN EFFICIENT WORKER FOR HIS EMPLOYER.

And what does your husband's employer get out of it? Taking the U.S. census as a guide, he gets on the average $2,000 out of your husband's work. The employer gets $2,000, your husband gets $500, and YOU GET SOME OF THE FOOD YOU COOK, AND THE RIGHT TO LIVE IN THE HOUSE YOU KEEP.

It is a very nice arrangement—for the employer. Not so very nice for the husband, AND A SLAVE'S LIFE FOR YOU.

But a man needn't get married, someone says. The employer doesn't demand that he be married.

Oh, yes, workingmen have to get married. Not the individual man here and there, perhaps. But the masses of them. That is an undisputable fact, and we would not drag it into this except that some very short-sighted person will raise the question, and thinks he has shattered to star-dust our contention that a woman supports her husband's employer, by saying that A WORKINGMAN NEEDN'T GET MARRIED.

If he DOESN'T MARRY, whose children are going to do the world's work in the future? Not the employer's children. On the contrary, the employer WANTS his employees to marry, and raise up children to work for his heirs when THEY are grown.

So it is an indisputable fact that the workingman must get married. BUT IS IT AN ABSOLUTELY ESSENTIAL FACT THAT THE WOMAN MUST BE THE GOAT AND BEAR THE HARDEST, TOUGHEST, MOST SLAVISH END OF THE DEAL?

THAT IS WHAT SHE IS DOING TODAY!

When a man gets married, does he go to his employer and say: Now, Mr. Employer, I am going to take a partner to help me live as a decent man should live, and so increase my efficiency for my work with you. For her part in our three-cornered deal I think you had better allow me so-and-so.

Does Mr. Young-Man-About-to-Be-Married say that? No, he doesn't. If the boss hears that he is to be married he may unbend his dignity enough to say: "Well, Bill, old man, I hear you are going to hook up with a mighty nice girl. That's right. Every honest fellow should settle down and raise a family." And Bill—well, he just grins. That's all. It's real pathetic, that grin of Bill's. It stands so often for inefficiency. He just don't know what else to do. So when the boss unbends enough to "congratulate" him on the greatest event of his life he grins and feels that a great favor has been bestowed upon him.

But the new little wife! Heaven help her. Bill's grin won't coin into dollars; won't buy new dresses; won't buy baby clothes; won't pay the doctor's bill; won't hire any of the back-breaking work of the house done. The little wife has somehow got to manage to attend to all of these things herself, or go without. And keep Bill going besides, so he can produce saleable goods for the boss.

It's pathetic, but the wives have got to get at the problem themselves. The Bills DON'T KNOW HOW. Their ignorance and stupidity in some things is appalling.

So, next time your husband comes home with $10 in his pocket when he should have $20, ask him where YOUR share is. And don't be put off with the silly answer that you are getting your room and board out of HIS $10 for your share. Tell him you can go out and work by the week and bring home $12, AND YOU WANT TO KNOW WHAT IS GOING TO BE YOUR END OF THE DEAL BETWEEN HIM AND HIS EMPLOYER.

Time was when a man gave his slave men their board and clothes, AND GAVE THE WIVES OF THE SLAVE MEN THEIR BOARD AND CLOTHES ALSO. Today a wage slave gets the equivalent of HIS board and clothes in wages—and the wife of the wage slave gets nothing.

The employer thus gets off a whole lot easier than he did when he owned slaves and was responsible for the physical welfare of the whole family.

THE UNPAID AND GROSSLY EXPLOITED LABOR OF MARRIED WOMEN IN THEIR HOMES MAKES IT POSSIBLE FOR THE EMPLOYER TO PILE-UP IMMENSE PROFITS OUT OF HIS BUSINESS, WHICH, OF COURSE, IS HIGHLY SATISFACTORY TO HIM.

But is it to you, O Woman, who must pay the price?

Margaret Sanger's Epiphany over Birth Control

Birth control has a long history in America, but the name most closely associated with this cause is that of Margaret Sanger. One of the 20th century's most influential women, Sanger devoted her career to the promotion and legalization of birth control information.

Margaret Sanger (1879–1966) always had a publicists' flair for drawing lessons from the events of her life. The Sadie Sachs story recounted here proved very effective from the lecture podium and later in her autobiography. At the time the incident occurred, Sanger was a 29-year-old mother of three children, who was using her training as a public health nurse on New York's Lower East Side. Her specialty was obstetrical cases. Often women would ask her for the "secret" of birth control, and Sanger could only tell them of condoms and withdrawal, both methods that required the cooperation of men and thus were deemed unreliable by her clients. When Sadie Sachs died of the effects of a self-induced abortion, Sanger vowed to devote the rest of her life to making birth control widely available to all classes.

Source: Margaret Sanger, *An Autobiography* (New York: W. W. Norton, 1938; reprinted by Dover Publications, 1971), pp. 86–92. Reprinted by permission of Michael Sanger.

Sanger began her career as a birth control activist in the 1910s while associated with radical groups such as the Wobblies and the Socialist Party. She argued that family limitation would improve the lives of working-class people; concerned with increasing women's autonomy, she also wanted to separate intercourse from procreation in order to liberate women's sexuality. Birth control thus met both feminist and revolutionary goals. By 1915, however, Sanger began to concentrate on a strategy of legalization of the distribution of birth control information and devices through doctor-staffed clinics. (Under the Comstock Act of 1873, the dissemination of birth control information was illegal.) In the 1920s and 1930s, she won the right for doctors to dispense such information in clinics, and she successfully challenged federal laws that hindered the practice of birth control. Her organization, the American Birth Control League, became Planned Parenthood in 1942.

Although Margaret Sanger saw birth control as a feminist demand, the legalistic strategy she pursued after 1915 often played down its revolutionary demands for women's autonomy in favor of cooperation with the medical community, a conservative group dominated by men. By making birth control into a medical rather than a feminist issue, Sanger set the stage for the reasoning employed to legalize abortion in the 1973 Supreme Court case of *Roe* v. *Wade*.

During these years in New York trained nurses were in great demand. Few people wanted to enter hospitals; they were afraid they might be "practiced" upon, and consented to go only in desperate emergencies. Sentiment was especially vehement in the matter of having babies. A woman's own bedroom, no matter how inconveniently arranged, was the usual place for her lying-in. I was not sufficiently free from domestic duties to be a general nurse, but I could ordinarily manage obstetrical cases because I was notified far enough ahead to plan my schedule. And after serving my two weeks I could get home again.

Sometimes I was summoned to small apartments occupied by young clerks, insurance salesmen, or lawyers, just starting out, most of them under thirty and whose wives were having their first or second baby. They were always eager to know the best and latest method in infant care and feeding. In particular, Jewish patients, whose lives centered around the family, welcomed advice and followed it implicitly.

But more and more my calls began to come from the Lower East Side, as though I were being magnetically drawn there by some force outside my control. I hated the wretchedness and hopelessness of the poor, and never experienced that satisfaction in working among them that so many noble women have found. My concern for my patients was now quite different from my earlier hospital attitude. I could see that much was wrong with them which did not appear in the physiological or medical diagnosis. A woman in childbirth was not merely a woman in childbirth. My expanded outlook included a view of her background, her potentialities as a human being, the kind of children she was bearing, and what was going to happen to them.

The wives of small shopkeepers were my most frequent cases, but I had carpenters, truck drivers, dishwashers, and pushcart vendors. I admired intensely the consideration most of these people had for their own. Money to pay doctor and nurse had been carefully saved months in advance—parents-in-law, grandfathers, grandmothers, all contributing.

As soon as the neighbors learned that a nurse was in the building they came in a friendly way to visit, often carrying fruit, jellies, or gefüllter fish made after a cherished recipe. It was infinitely pathetic to me that they, so poor themselves, should bring me food. Later they drifted in again with the excuse of getting the plate, and sat down for a nice talk; there was no hurry. Always back of the little gift was the question, "I am pregnant (or my daughter, or my sister is). Tell me something to keep from having another baby. We cannot afford another yet."

I tried to explain the only two methods I had ever heard of among the middle classes, both of which were invariably brushed aside as unacceptable. They were of no certain avail to the wife because they placed the burden of responsibility solely upon the husband—a burden which he seldom assumed. What she was seeking was self-protection she could herself use, and there was none.

Below this stratum of society was one in truly desperate circumstances. The men were sullen and unskilled, picking up odd jobs now and then, but more often unemployed, lounging in and out of the house at all hours of the day and night. The women seemed to slink on their way to market and were without neighborliness. . .

Pregnancy was a chronic condition among the women of this class. Suggestions as to what to do for a girl who was "in trouble" or a married woman who was "caught" passed from mouth to mouth—herb teas, turpentine, steaming, rolling downstairs, inserting slippery elm, knitting needles, shoe-hooks. When they had word of a new remedy they hurried to the drugstore, and if the clerk were inclined to be friendly he might say, "Oh, that won't help you, but here's something that may." The younger druggists usually refused to give advice because, if it were to be known, they would come under the law; midwives were even more fearful. The doomed women implored me to reveal the "secret" rich people had, offering to pay me extra to tell them; many really believed I was holding back information for money. They asked everybody and tried anything, but nothing did them any good. On Saturday nights I have seen groups of from fifty to one-hundred with their shawls over their heads waiting outside the office of a five-dollar abortionist.

Each time I returned to this district, which was becoming a recurrent nightmare, I used to hear that Mrs. Cohen "had been carried to a hospital, but had never come back," or that Mrs. Kelly "had sent the children to a neighbor and had put her head into the gas oven." Day after day such tales were poured into my ears— a baby born dead, great relief—the death of an older child, sorrow but again relief of a sort—the story told a thousand times of death from abortion and children going into institutions. I shuddered with horror as I listened to the details and studied the reasons back of them—destitution linked with excessive childbearing. The waste of life seemed utterly senseless. One by one worried, sad, pensive, and aging faces marshaled themselves before me in my dreams, sometimes appealingly, sometimes accusingly.

These were not merely "unfortunate conditions among the poor" such as we read about. I knew the women personally. They were living, breathing, human beings, with hopes, fears, and aspirations like my own, yet their weary, misshapen bodies, "always ailing, never failing," were destined to be thrown on the scrap heap before they were thirty-five. I could not escape from the facts of their wretchedness; neither was I able to see any way out. My own cozy and comfortable family existence was becoming a reproach to me.

Then one stifling mid-July day of 1912 I was summoned to a Grand Street tenement. My patient was a small, slight Russian Jewess, about twenty-eight years old, of the special cast of feature to which suffering lends a madonna-like expression. The cramped three-room apartment was in a sorry state of turmoil. Jake Sachs, a truck driver scarcely older than his wife, had come home to find the three children crying and her unconscious from the effects of a self-induced abortion. He had called the nearest doctor, who in turn had sent for me. Jake's earnings were trifling, and most of them had gone to keep the none-too-strong children clean and properly fed. But his wife's ingenuity had helped them to save a little, and this he was glad to spend on a nurse rather than have her go to a hospital.

The doctor and I settled ourselves to the task of fighting the septicemia. Never had I worked so fast, never so concentratedly. The sultry days and nights were melted into a torpid inferno. It did not seem possible there could be such heat, and every bit of food, ice, and drugs had to be carried up three flights of stairs.

Jake was more kind and thoughtful than many of the husbands I had encountered. He loved his children, and had always helped his wife wash and dress them. He had brought water up and carried garbage down before he left in the morning, and did as much as he could for me while he anxiously watched her progress.

After a fortnight Mrs. Sachs' recovery was in sight. Neighbors, ordinarily fatalistic as to the results of abortion, were genuinely pleased that she had survived. She smiled wanly at all who came to see her and thanked them gently, but she could not respond to their hearty congratulations. She appeared to be more despondent and anxious than she should have been, and spent too much time in meditation.

At the end of three weeks, as I was preparing to leave the fragile patient to take up her difficult life once more, she finally voiced her fears, "Another baby will finish me, I suppose?"

"It's too early to talk about that," I temporized.

But when the doctor came to make his last call, I drew him aside. "Mrs. Sachs is terribly worried about having another baby."

"She well may be," replied the doctor, and then he stood before her and said, "Any more such capers, young woman, and there'll be no need to send for me."

"I know, doctor," she replied timidly, "but," and she hesitated as though it took all her courage to say it, "What can I do to prevent it?"

The doctor was a kindly man, and he had worked hard to save her, but such incidents had become so familiar to him that he had long since lost whatever delicacy he might once have had. He laughed good-naturedly. "You want to have your cake and eat it too, do you? Well, it can't be done."

Then picking up his hat and bag to depart he said, "Tell Jake to sleep on the roof."

I glanced quickly at Mrs. Sachs. Even through my sudden tears I could see stamped on her face an expression of absolute despair. We simply looked at each other, saying no word until the door had closed behind the doctor. Then she lifted her thin, blue-veined hands and clasped them beseechingly. "He can't understand. He's only a man. But you do, don't you? Please tell me the secret, and I'll never breathe it to a soul. *Please!"*

What was I to do? I could not speak the conventionally comforting phrases which would be of no comfort. Instead, I made her as physically easy as I could and promised to come back in a few days to talk with her again. A little later, when she slept, I tiptoed away.

Night after night the wistful image of Mrs. Sachs appeared before me. I made all sorts of excuses to myself for not going back. I was busy on other cases; I really did not know what to say to her or how to convince her of my own ignorance; I was helpless to avert such monstrous atrocities. Time rolled by and I did nothing.

The telephone rang one evening three months later, and Jake Sachs' agitated voice begged me to come at once; his wife was sick again and from the same cause. For a wild moment I thought of sending someone else, but actually, of course, I hurried into my uniform, caught up my bag, and started out. All the way I longed for a subway wreck, an explosion, anything to keep me from having to enter that home again. But nothing happened, even to delay me. I turned into the dingy doorway and climbed the familiar stairs once more. The children were there, young little things.

Mrs. Sachs was in a coma and died within ten minutes. I folded her still hands across her breast, remembering how they had pleaded with me, begging so humbly for the knowledge which was her right. I drew a sheet over her pallid face. Jake was sobbing, running his hands through his hair and pulling it out like an insane person. Over and over again he wailed, "My God! My God! My God!"

I left him pacing desperately back and forth, and for hours I myself walked and walked and walked through the hushed streets. When I finally arrived home and let myself quietly in, all the household was sleeping. I looked out my window and down upon the dimly lighted city. Its pains and griefs crowded in upon me, a moving picture rolled before my eyes with photographic clearness: women writhing in travail to bring forth little babies; the babies themselves naked and hungry, wrapped in newspapers to keep them from the cold; six-year-old children with pinched, pale, wrinkled faces, old in concentrated wretchedness, pushed into gray and fetid cellars, crouching on stone floors, their small scrawny hands scuttling through rags, making lamp shades, artificial flowers; white coffins, black coffins, coffins, coffins interminably passing in never-ending succession. The scenes piled one upon another on another. I could bear it no longer.

As I stood there the darkness faded. The sun came up and threw its reflection over the house tops. It was the dawn of a new day in my life also. The doubt and questioning, the experimenting and trying, were now to be put behind me. I knew I could not go back merely to keeping people alive.

I went to bed, knowing that no matter what it might cost, I was finished with palliatives and superficial cures; I was resolved to seek out the root of evil, to do something to change the destiny of mothers whose miseries were vast as the sky.

A Radical View of
Women's Emancipation

Emma Goldman

Although Margaret Sanger styled herself as the first advocate of birth control in America, the anarchist and feminist Emma Goldman (1869–1940) had already lectured widely on the subject. Goldman's life was a far cry from Sanger's. Born into a Jewish family in Lithuania, this strong-willed girl emigrated to America in 1885 at the age of 16. She found work in New York at the same time she found anarchism and a host of radical causes. She formed a liaison with Alexander Berkman, who spent 14 years in jail for his part in the attempted assassination of steel magnate Henry Clay Frick in 1892. Meanwhile, Emma Goldman was building a reputation as a revolutionary activist and a feminist committed to free love. (She had a deep capacity for friendships with men and women and had many lovers.) Goldman's speeches, pamphlets, and editorship of the monthly *Mother Earth* (1906–1917) provided forums for her unconventional views.

Like Mother Jones, Emma Goldman defies easy categorization. She was a totally liberated woman long before the word became fashionable; her revolutionary ideology of anarchism made her critical of all institutions. This selection, "The Tragedy of Women's Emancipation" (1911), criticized the superficial goals of the modern women's movement and provided Goldman's alternative view of women's liberation: "True emancipation begins neither at the polls nor in the courts. It begins in woman's soul."

Goldman's radical activities finally caused her deportation from the United States in 1919. She lived briefly in the Soviet Union, but quickly grew disillusioned with the Soviet experiment. Until her death in 1940, she lived in Europe and Canada, increasingly cut off from her radical roots. Writing her two-volume autobiography, *Living My Life* (1931), recaptured the excitement of those years and brought her unconventional lifestyle and ideas to new audiences.

Source: Emma Goldman, "The Tragedy of Women's Emancipation," in *Red Emma Speaks: Selected Writings and Speeches by Emma Goldman,* ed. Alix Kates Shulman, pp. 133–142. Copyright © 1972. Reprinted by permission.

Liberty and equality for woman! What hopes and aspirations these words awakened when they were first uttered by some of the noblest and bravest souls of
those days. The sun in all his light and glory was to rise upon a new world; in this
world woman was to be free to direct her own destiny—an aim certainly worthy
of the great enthusiasm, courage, perseverance, and ceaseless effort of the tremendous host of pioneer men and women, who staked everything against a world of
prejudice and ignorance.

My hopes also move towards that goal, but I hold that the emancipation of
woman, as interpreted and practically applied today, has failed to reach that great
end. Now, woman is confronted with the necessity of emancipating herself from
emancipation, if she really desires to be free. This may sound paradoxical, but is,
nevertheless, only too true.

What has she achieved through her emancipation? Equal suffrage in a few
States. Has that purified our political life, as many well-meaning advocates predicted? Certainly not. Incidentally, it is really time that persons with plain, sound
judgment should cease to talk about corruption in politics in a boarding-school
tone. Corruption of politics has nothing to do with the morals, or the laxity of
morals, of various political personalities. Its cause is altogether a material one.
Politics is the reflex of the business and industrial world, the mottos of which are:
"To take is more blessed than to give"; "buy cheap and sell dear"; "one soiled
hand washes the other." There is no hope even that woman, with her right to vote,
will ever purify politics.

Emancipation has brought woman economic equality with man; that is, she
can choose her own profession and trade; but as her past and present physical
training has not equipped her with the necessary strength to compete with man,
she is often compelled to exhaust all her energy, use up her vitality, and strain
every nerve in order to reach the market value. Very few ever succeed, for it is a
fact that women teachers, doctors, lawyers, architects, and engineers are neither
met with the same confidence as their male colleagues, nor receive equal re-
muneration. And those that do reach that enticing equality generally do so at the
expense of their physical and psychical well-being. As to the great mass of working girls and women, how much independence is gained if the narrowness and
lack of freedom of the home is exchanged for the narrowness and lack of freedom
of the factory, sweat-shop, department store, or office? In addition is the burden
which is laid on many women of looking after a "home, sweet home"—cold,
dreary, disorderly, uninviting—after a day's hard work. Glorious independence!
No wonder that hundreds of girls are so willing to accept the first offer of marriage; sick and tired of their "independence" behind the counter, at the sewing or
typewriting machine. They are just as ready to marry as girls of the middle class,
who long to throw off the yoke of parental supremacy. A so-called independence
which leads only to earning the merest subsistence is not so enticing, not so ideal,
that one could expect woman to sacrifice everything for it. Our highly praised independence is, after all, but a slow process of dulling and stifling woman's nature,
her love instinct, and her mother instinct.

Nevertheless, the position of the working girl is far more natural and human than that of her seemingly more fortunate sister in the more cultured professional walks of life—teachers, physicians, lawyers, engineers, etc., who have to make a dignified, proper appearance, while the inner life is growing empty and dead.

The narrowness of the existing conception of woman's independence and emancipation; the dread of love for a man who is not her social equal; the fear that love will rob her of her freedom and independence; the horror that love or the joy of motherhood will only hinder her in the full exercise of her profession—all these together make of the emancipated modern woman a compulsory vestal, before whom life, with its great clarifying sorrows and its deep, entrancing joys, rolls on without touching or gripping her soul.

Emancipation, as understood by the majority of its adherents and exponents, is of too narrow a scope to permit the boundless love and ecstasy contained in the deep emotion of the true woman, sweetheart, mother, in freedom.

The tragedy of the self-supporting or economically free woman does not lie in too many, but in too few experiences. True, she surpasses her sister of past generations in knowledge of the world and human nature; it is just because of this that she feels deeply the lack of life's essence, which alone can enrich the human soul, and without which the majority of women have become mere professional automatons. . .

The greatest shortcoming of the emancipation of the present day lies in its artificial stiffness and its narrow respectabilities, which produce an emptiness in woman's soul that will not let her drink from the fountain of life. I once remarked that there seemed to be a deeper relationship between the old-fashioned mother and hostess, ever on the alert for the happiness of her little ones and the comfort of those she loves, and the truly new woman, than between the latter and her average emancipated sister. The disciples of emancipation pure and simple declared me a heathen, fit only for the stake. Their blind zeal did not let them see that my comparison between the old and the new was merely to prove that a goodly number of our grandmothers had more blood in their veins, far more humor and wit, and certainly a greater amount of naturalness, kindheartedness, and simplicity, than the majority of our emancipated professional women who fill the colleges, halls of learning and various offices. This does not mean a wish to return to the past, nor does it condemn woman to her old sphere, the kitchen and the nursery.

Salvation lies in an energetic march onward towards a brighter and clearer future. We are in need of unhampered growth out of old traditions and habits. The movement for woman's emancipation has so far made but the first step in that direction. It is to be hoped that it will gather strength to make another. The right to vote, or equal civil rights, may be good demands, but true emancipation begins neither at the polls nor in courts. It begins in woman's soul. History tells us that every oppressed class gained true liberation from its masters through its own efforts. It is necessary that woman learn that lesson, that she realizes that her freedom will reach as far as her power to achieve her freedom reaches. It is, therefore, far more important for her to begin with her inner regeneration, to cut loose from the weight of prejudices, traditions, and customs. The demand for equal rights in every vocation of life is just and fair; but, after all, the most vital right is the right to love and be loved. Indeed, if partial emancipation is to become a complete and true emancipation of woman, it will have to do away with the ridiculous notion that to be loved, to be sweetheart and mother, is synonymous with being a slave or subordinate. It will have to do away with the absurd notion of the dualism of the sexes, or that man and woman represent two antagonistic worlds.

Pettiness separates; breadth unites. Let us be broad and big. Let us not overlook vital things because of the bulk of trifles confronting us. A true conception of the relation of the sexes will not admit of conqueror and conquered; it knows of but one great thing: to give of one's self boundlessly, in order to find one's self richer, deeper, better. That alone can fill the emptiness, and transform the tragedy of woman's emancipation into joy, limitless joy.

CHAPTER 5

The Final Push for Suffrage

The woman suffrage movement called on the energies and political skills of three generations of American women. Even as the movement melded into the mainstream of Progressive reform in the early 20th century, its success was never a foregone conclusion. A combination of factors, including women's patriotic contributions to the home front during World War I, helped to push the 19th Amendment over the top. On election day 1920, 26 million women were eligible to go to the polls as a result.

Dividing the suffrage movement into three distinct periods—1848–1869, 1869–1890, and 1890–1920—helps explain its shifting priorities and tactics over its more than seven decades of existence. The first period, from 1848 to 1869, began at the Seneca Falls convention, the first women's rights convention ever held in the world, where the Declaration of Sentiments included a controversial call for the ballot. Historian Ellen DuBois has pointed out how radical such a demand was in the mid-19th century, because it challenged the separation of the spheres into men's (public) and women's (private). The suffrage plank barely passed the assembled convention.

During the first 20 years of the women's rights movement, it was closely allied with abolitionism and the struggle to end slavery. Disagreements in the immediate post-Civil War period about the priorities of freed blacks versus women's rights led to a severing of this link. With the passage of the 13th, 14th, and 15th Amendments, black people won their freedom and black men won the right to vote. As feminists such as Elizabeth Cady Stanton and Susan B. Anthony pointed out, however, now that the word *male* was in the constitution as a definition of voting rights, it would take another constitutional amendment to enfranchise women.

By 1869, an independent woman suffrage movement had emerged in the United States. The period between 1869 and 1890 was not marked by any great breakthroughs for the cause. Only two territories allowed women the vote—Utah in 1869 and Wyoming in 1870. The suffrage movement on the national level split into two rival wings, mainly over whether to work on a state basis or the federal level. In 1890, the rival wings reunited as the National American Woman Suffrage Association (NAWSA).

By 1890, the suffrage movement was on the threshold of new activism and success. In part, the movement was more palatable because it was less radical. Instead of early demands by feminists such as Stanton for divorce and women's economic emancipation, the movement leaders now stuck very closely to the sole demand of the vote. And increasingly suffragists argued for the vote not as a challenge to conventional notions about women's proper sphere, but as an extension of that sphere. Women cited their domestic orientation as the reason they needed the vote: They could do for the country what they did for their homes and families. Suffragists also played up women's supposed moral superiority. This tactic of accepting conventional views of women and exploiting them was highly successful, especially as the Progressive reform spirit gathered strength.

As late as 1910, the woman suffrage movement had won the vote in only four states, but the tide was turning. New leadership, notably the NAWSA presidency of Carrie Chapman Catt from 1915 to 1920, revitalized the movement with a winning plan. Attention-grabbing tactics, such as suffrage parades and open-air meetings, won publicity. The movement also branched out into immigrant and working-class urban communities to mobilize support. Suffragists effectively pointed out the irony of fighting to make the world safe for democracy in World War I, while the female population remained disfranchised at home. Militant tactics, such as picketing the White House and conducting hunger strikes for the cause, won support.

But probably the main reason women finally won the vote in 1920 was that it was now a far less radical demand than it had been in 1848. Try to imagine how 19th century political history would have been revolutionized if women had actually received the vote around the time of the Civil War. Compare that to the small ripple that occurred when women were finally granted the vote in 1920. Women's roles had changed dramatically since the mid-19th century, with women actively participating in work, education, and voluntary organizations outside the home. The meaning of politics had also changed, so that the vote was less a potent symbol of political participation for men by 1920 than it had been at the height of the separate male political culture of the previous century.

Although granting the vote can be seen as a conservative measure that had little impact on women's equality, it is wrong to underestimate what the vote meant to the millions of women who campaigned so hard for its attainment. To the "new women" of the late 19th and early 20th centuries, it was an affront, a slap in the face, that they were not allowed this basic democratic right. Going to the polls would be confirmation of women's new roles as full citizens, the public equals of men. Of course, such sentiments were more likely held by white middle-class women, who shared most of the privileges of their class with men except the vote. But black women and working-class women also campaigned for the vote, seeing it as a tool that could be useful in broader political and economic struggles.

What made the suffrage movement so powerful was that it brought together a diverse range of individuals and organizations in a broad coalition dedicated to a common goal. To attain that goal, women's groups pioneered in innovative political tactics and legislative strategies that showed that women could work together effectively on common causes. While we may look back at the vote and see it as a fairly minor reform, women at the time had a far different perspective.

A Western Suffragist Talks to Her Eastern Sisters

Abigail Scott Duniway

The suffrage movement was made up of a variety of individuals and organizations—in many ways, that was its greatest strength. One of the most prominent voices in the Western states was that of Abigail Scott Duniway (1834–1915). Duniway is another representation of the Western pioneering spirit as it applied to women; reflecting her estimation of her place in history, she titled her autobiography *Path Breaking* (1914). Born in Illinois, she made the overland journey to Oregon with her family in 1851 at the age of 17. Married soon after, she lived the hard physical life of a young bride (and soon, young mother) on the Oregon frontier. An accident that disabled her husband prodded her to try a variety of jobs to earn money; the most satisfying was the newspaper she ran for 16 years called the *New Northwest*.

Of the causes that Duniway promoted in her newspaper and her frequent public speaking, none was more prominent than women's rights. Duniway quickly moved into a prominent role in the Oregon suffrage movement, but her outspoken and populist ideas were not always at one with the more conservative leaders of the suffrage movement in the East. This speech, titled "How to Win the Ballot" and given in 1899 to the National American Woman Suffrage Association national convention in Michigan, was—in Duniway's words—"the shortest way at my command for telling many truths that Eastern readers ought to read." Those "truths" included the reminder that the votes of men were needed to extend the franchise. What really comes through in this speech, however, is the incredible sense of sectional pride linked to the Western pioneering spirit.

Oregon women finally got the vote in 1912, and Abigail Scott Duniway became the state's first registered woman voter.

Coming as I do from the far Pacific, where the sun at night sinks into the sea, to greet a convocation of co-workers from the far Atlantic, where the sun at morn rises out of the sea; and standing here, upon the central swell of the Middle West, where the sun at high noon kisses the heaving bosom of the mighty inland sea that answers back to East and West the echoing song of liberty, I realize the importance of my desire to speak to the entire continent, such tempered words as shall help to further unite our common interests in the great work that convenes us.

The first fact to be considered, when working to win the ballot, is that there is but one way by which we may hope to obtain it, and that is by and through the

Source: Abigail Scott Duniway, *Path Breaking* (Portland, OR: James, Kerns, and Abbott, 1914; reprinted in 1971 by Schocken Books, New York), pp. 156–62.

affirmative votes of men. We may theorize, organize, appeal, argue, coax, cajole, and threaten men till doomsday; we may secure their pettings, praises, flattery, and every appearance of acquiescence in our demands; we may believe with all our hearts in the sincerity of their promises to vote as we dictate, but all of this will avail us nothing unless they deposit their affirmative votes in the ballot box.

Every man who stops to argue the case, as an opponent, tells us that he "loves women," and, while wondering much that he should consider such a declaration necessary, I have always admired the loyal spirit that prompts its utterance. But, gentlemen,—and I am proud indeed to see such a fine audience of you here tonight—there is another side to this expression of loyalty. Not only is our move-ment not instigated in a spirit of warfare between the sexes, but it is engendered, altogether, in the spirit of harmony, and inter-dependence between men and women, such as was the evident design of the great Creator when he placed fa-thers and mothers, brothers and sisters, in the same home and family. We are glad to be assured that you "love women," but we are doubly glad to be able, on proper occasions, and in every suitable way, to return the compliment. No good Equal Suffragist will any longer permit you to monopolize all the pretty speeches about the other sex. Every good woman in the world likes men a great deal better than she likes women, and there isn't a wise woman in all this goodly land who isn't proud to say so. We like you, gentlemen, and you cannot help it. We couldn't help it if we would; we wouldn't help it if we could. You like us, also, because you can-not help it. God made the sexes to match each other. Show me a woman who doesn't like men, and I will show you a sour-souled, vinegar-visaged specimen of unfortunate femininity, who owes the world an apology for living in it at all; and the very best thing she could do for her country, provided she had a country, would be to steal away and die, in the company of the man who doesn't like women. In order to gain the votes of men, so we can win the ballot, we must show them that we are inspired by the same patriotic motives that induce them to prize it. A home without a man in it, is only half a home. A government without women in it is only half a government. Man without a woman is like one-half of a pair of dislocated shears. Woman without man is like the other half of the same disabled implement. Male and female created He them, saith the Higher Law, and to them God gave dominion "over every living thing upon the earth"—except each other. . .

The fact that men, for the most part, contented themselves in those early days of the Suffrage Movement, with exhibitions of ridicule, I accepted as a good omen. If you wish to convince a man that your opinion is logical and just, you have conquered the outer citadel of his resentment when he throws back his head and opens his mouth to laugh. Show me a solemn-visaged voter, with a face as long as the Pentateuch, and I will show you a man with a soul so little that it would have ample room to dance inside of a hollow mustard seed. Having tickled your opponent with a little nonsense, that at first was necessary to arrest his at-tention, you must then be careful to hold the ground you have gained. Your next step must be to impress upon all men the fact that we are not intending to inter-fere, in any way, with their rights; and all we ask is to be allowed to decide, for ourselves, also as to what our rights should be. They will then, very naturally, ask what effect our enfranchisement will have upon their politics. Visions of riotous scenes in political conventions will arise, to fill them with apprehension, as the possibility occurs that women, if enfranchised, will only double the vote and augment the uproar. They will recall partisan banquets, at which men have tarried over cups and pipes until they rolled under the table, or were carried off to bed on shutters. Very naturally, men, everywhere, object to seeing reputable women, and especially their own wives, engaged in such excesses. But our mighty men of the Pacific Northwest are troubled very little by these vagaries. They realize, as they sleep off the results of their latest political banquet, that at every public function in which their wives participate, there is a notable absence of any sort of dissipation. They remember that in former times, before good women had joined them, in the mining camps, mountain towns, and on the bachelor farms, that such scenes as sometimes transpire today, at men's great gatherings, were once so common as to excite little comment. It was the advent of good women in the border territories that changed all this, and eliminated the bad woman from social life, just as the ballot will eventually eliminate the bad woman from political life, where she now reigns supreme among men, having everything her own way. By the very charm of good women's presence they brought these changes about on the Pacific Coast, in social life, till men began to wonder how they had endured the old conditions, before the women joined them. Now, quite naturally, they are learning to apply this rule to politics; and so our men of the Pacific Coast are not alarmed, as many men are in other states, lest women, if allowed to become equal with themselves before the law, will forget their natural duties and natural womanliness. If, however, any man grows timid, and exhibits symptoms of alarm, as they sometimes do (even in Oregon), lest the balloted woman will forsake the kitchen sink, at which she has always been "protected" (without wages), or abandon the cooking stove, the rolling pin, the wash tub and the ironing board, at which she has always been shielded (without salary), we remind him that housekeeping and homemaking are, like everything else, undergoing a complete process of evolution. We show him that there is no more reason why every loaf of bread should be baked in a different kitchen than there is why every bushel of wheat should be ground in a different mill. We show him that the laundry is destined, hereafter, to keep pace with the threshing machine; the creamery with the spinning jenny and power loom; the fruit cannery with the great flour mill; the dish washer with the steam-driven mangle, and the bakery with the ready-made clothing store.

When women have been voters long enough to have acquired recognition of their own equal property rights with men, the servant girl problem will settle itself. When that time comes there will be no more work left to do in the home than the wife and mother can perform with comfort to herself and household; and the servant girls of today will then find systematic employment in the great factories, where food and clothing are manufactured by rule. This evolution has already begun with the woman typewriter. You see her everywhere; pretty, tidy, rosy with a ribbon or flower at her throat, intent upon her work and sure to get her pay. Then can the mother, for the sake of herself, her husband, and children, preserve her health, her beauty, and her mental vigor. Then can she be an adviser in the home, the state, the church, and the school, remaining so to a ripe old age.

But women can never have the opportunity, or the power, to achieve these results, except in isolated cases, till they are voters and lawmakers; and never even then, till they have had time to secure, by legislation, the equal property rights that they have earned with men from the beginning.

Open-Air Meetings:
A New Suffrage Tactic

Florence Luscomb

Since the mid-19th century, the suffrage movement had relied on essentially the same tactics: lobbying state and national governments for suffrage bills, organizing women's suffrage organizations on the local, state, and national level, and trying to win publicity for women's cause. But decades of such agitation had seemingly brought the movement no closer to success, so about 1909 suffrage leaders in Massachusetts and other states developed new ways to reach voters and stimulate interest in their cause. Influenced by the tactics of militant British suffragists, Massachusetts women began holding open-air meetings and selling suffrage newspapers on streetcorners like newsboys. Brazenly discarding any lingering notions of protected Victorian womanhood, suffragists took to the streets in what must have been a liberating, if somewhat unsettling, experience.

Florence Luscomb (1887–1985) was one such pioneer. She was already active in the suffrage movement when she graduated from the Massachusetts Institute of Technology with a degree in architecture in 1909. For several years, she combined her architectural career with suffrage work, such as speaking at the open-air meetings described in this speech. In 1917, she took a full-time position as executive secretary of the Boston Equal Suffrage Association for Good Government. For the rest of her life, she was associated with progressive causes.

Such tactics as open-air meetings helped to turn the tide in favor of suffrage. What comes through the strongest in Luscomb's 1909 speech, however, is the sense of camaraderie and shared partnership that characterized the unique political movement that was suffrage.

Right here I want to tell you what outdoor speaking is *not* like. The majority of people who have never been to our open-air meetings have already decided what they are like, down to the minutest detail as to what variety of vegetable is thrown at the speaker. Although every one knows from experience that an American woman can stand in a hall and address American men with dignity and earnestness on her part, and courtesy and interest on theirs, yet, presto, remove the roof

Source: Florence Luscomb, unpublished speech, "Our Open-Air Campaign" (1909), in Woman's Rights Collection, Schlesinger Library, Radcliffe Institute for Advanced Study.

and the same woman must become a ranting fanatic, the same men are jeering hooligans. Now I have spoken at more than a score of sky-roofed meetings this summer, to audiences varying from twenty-five to two-thousand, at mill gates and at fashionable summer resorts, but have never seen anything which would disgrace an indoor meeting.

The open-air meetings promising so well, they were continued throughout the summer. It was found best to hold two meetings in nearby towns each Saturday; one at four o'clock and the other at seven-thirty. The time and strength required were but little more than one meeting consumed, and far less than would be needed to make two separate trips. Meetings were also held on Wednesday afternoons at various beaches. This being the marketman's day off, the seashore is almost as well attended on that day as on Saturday.

From the success of these meetings around Boston Mrs. Fitzgerald[1] gradually developed the idea of sending out a party which should spend the month of August touring the State and speaking in all the more important towns. The route as laid out went westerly through the Northern towns, swung around and returned through the Southern part of the State, taking in the Marshfield and Barnstable County Fairs. We aspired to go by automobile; we went by trolley. We spoke three times a day, generally in three separate towns, except as an entire day was devoted to such cities as Fall River and New Bedford. The party was made up of four ladies—Mrs. Fitzgerald, commander-in-chief and orator-in-chief, went for the whole month, as did also Miss Edith Haynes, a Boston lawyer. For the first half of the trip Mrs. Dennett (Mary Ware Dennett) and Miss Alfretta McClure accompanied them; and for the last two weeks Miss Katherine Tyng, Radcliffe '00, and I had the pleasure of being the other two members.

The paraphernalia of the trip consisted of one large yellow banner six feet long inscribed in black, "Votes for Women," a jointed flagstaff for the same made to fold in to three pieces, and a heavy, heavy suitcase of literature and buttons. Besides this, each member had her individual suitcase, and there was a bundle of umbrellas.

Picture our party unloading from a street-car in the central square of some little country town. This in itself is a lengthy operation. Then we make for the nearest drugstore, deposit all our luggage in one corner, and to compensate for its storage all of us are in duty bound to buy sodas. We have consumed innumerable soft drinks for the sake of the cause, and have become authorities upon the drugstores of Massachusetts. While we drink the drug clerk is cross-examined as to where the best audience can be collected, time of trolleys, hotel for the night, union or non-union, what they manufacture, and a few dozen other similar things. Meanwhile, if the town is large enough for us to require a permit to speak, Mrs. Fitzgerald has interviewed the police. Our leaflets are then unpacked, our flag erected, we borrow a Moxie box from the obliging drug clerk and proceed to the busiest corner of the town square. Our chief mounts the box, the banner over her

[1]Susan Walker Fitzgerald, a Bryn Mawr graduate and the wife of a wealthy Harvard-trained lawyer, was secretary of the Boston Equal Suffrage Association for Good Government (BESAGG).

shoulder, and starts talking to the air, three assorted dogs, six kids, and the two loafers in front of the grocery store just over the way. The rest of us give handbills to all the passersby and to all the nearby stores. Within ten minutes our audience has increased to from twenty-five to five-hundred, according to the time and place. We speak in turn for an hour or more, answer questions, sell buttons, and circulate the petition. Then we leave, generally in undignified haste, to catch our car for the next meeting. At New Bedford, all loaded down as we were, we fairly charged for a block down the middle of a street lined on either side by people waiting for their cars.

Such were the afternoon and evening meetings. The noon ones were slightly different in character. These were held at the mill gates in factory towns. If there were several mills in town, or several entrances to the same mill, our party was divided so that sometimes each of the four held an independent meeting. As the workers came out at noon we gave out the bills and announced speaking at half past. They returned early from dinner, and we had a half hour of speaking. These meetings were very interesting. The audience was there ready to be entertained, often sympathetic in advance; and I know some of us enjoyed the experience of being thrown on our own resources, with the entire subject to handle in that short time.

Ordinarily, of course, the arguments were divided up between us to prevent repetition and insure completeness.

During the speaking we circulated the petition as quietly as possible on the outskirts of the crowd. We found it best not to attempt to get many signatures during the speaking as it created too much disturbance. Whenever we had time to stop after the meeting we did canvas the audience pretty thoroughly, but this was not often. For this reason we averaged a smaller percentage of signatures on the trip than at the meetings carried on around Boston, where we were not so hurried.

The trip was by no means all hard work. The first week, while the party was passing through the Berkshires, meetings were far apart, and time for rest and meals scant. Later on, however, in the more thickly settled regions, travelling was not so hard although we never had much time to spare. The motto adopted to describe the trip was, "plain thinking, hard talking, any old kind of living." One other of our collection was, "Gather ye rosebuds while ye may," which being interpreted read, "Sit down every time you get a chance." Nevertheless it was a pleasant trip to travel in the fresh air through pleasant country and picturesque towns.

We were an inexhaustible source of wonder and interest to the small boy. He dogged our footsteps clamouring for literature; he audibly surmised whether we were Salvation Army or Anti-tuberculosis, and the climax of his joy was attained when we allowed him to carry our banner.

Our other constant admirers were the dogs. I feel hardly at home now at a meeting at which there is not at least one dog present, preferably yellow; and when there are a dozen dogs of assorted sizes, colors, and howls, oh, this is bliss! We even reveled in dog-fights; for, as our chief remarked while we were enjoying one such experience, "After all, there is nothing to draw a crowd like a dog-fight." . . .

Was our summer campaign successful? Did it pay? A few figures will answer. We have spoken to 24,900 people, and given literature to thousands of others. The expense of the trolley trip was about one hundred dollars a week, which includes fares and living expenses for four, cost of literature, press notices, and all other incidentals. We held sixty-eight meetings—fifteen of them at factories. Altogether this summer we have held 97 meetings at an average cost of $6.62 a meeting, with an average audience of 257, and have obtained over 2000 signatures to the National Petition. I think you will agree with me that it was a splendid success.

An Anti-Suffrage Monologue

Marie Jenny Howe

Opposition to woman suffrage was diffuse but potent. Liquor interests were afraid women would vote in prohibition, machine politicians feared women voters would turn them out of office, and manufacturers anticipated that newly enfranchised women would force protective legislation and child labor laws which would cut their profits. Conservative religious organizations like the Catholic church were hostile to larger political roles for women. Southerners feared woman suffrage might endanger white supremacy. Perhaps surprisingly, some of the most prominent "antis" were women themselves, who said they did not need or want the vote. The fact that many women, especially middle-class women, were not interested in their own suffrage was one of the most telling weapons that opponents had in their arsenal.

Anti-suffrage sentiment boiled down to the argument that voting, and by extension, exposure to the "muck and mire of politics," violated woman's essential nature, which should be confined to home, maternity, and domesticity. Women's entry into the public sphere, argued a Southern Congressional representative in a 1917 debate, would "disrupt the family, which is the unit of society, and when you disrupt the family, you destroy the home, which is the foundation of the Republic." Opponents of woman suffrage clung defiantly to traditional gender roles, despite the fact that women had already moved far beyond the confines of the home by the early 20th century. The heat of the debate was in part a reaction to how much had already changed in women's lives.

The suffragists found it fairly easy to punch holes in the often contradictory arguments put forward by the antis, as this satirical *Anti-Suffrage Monologue* by Marie Jenny Howe demonstrates. Howe is especially good at showing the contradictions of anti-suffrage propaganda by arranging her arguments in couplets: "if you don't like one you can take the other." When this pamphlet was published by the National American Woman Suffrage Association in 1913, victory was finally beginning to seem possible.

Source: Marie Jenny Howe, *An Anti-Suffrage Monologue* (New York: National American Woman Suffrage Association, 1913).

Please do not think of me as old-fashioned. I pride myself on being a modern up-to-date woman. I believe in all kinds of broad-mindedness, only I do not believe in woman suffrage because to do that would be to deny my sex.

Woman suffrage is the reform against nature. Look at these ladies sitting on the platform. Observe their physical inability, their mental disability, their spiritual instability, and general debility! Could they walk up to the ballot box, mark a ballot, and drop it in? Obviously not. Let us grant for the sake of argument that they could mark a ballot. But could they drop it in? Ah, no. All nature is against it. The laws of man cry out against it. The voice of God cries out against it—and so do I.

Enfranchisement is what makes man man. Disfranchisement is what makes woman woman. If women were enfranchised every man would be just like every woman and every woman would be just like every man. There would be no difference between them. And don't you think this would rob life of just a little of its poetry and romance?

Man must remain man. Woman must remain woman. If man goes over and tries to be like woman, if woman goes over and tries to be like man, it will become so very confusing and so difficult to explain to our children. Let us take a practical example. If a woman puts on a man's coat and trousers, takes a man's cane and hat and cigar, and goes out on the street, what will happen to her? She will be arrested and thrown into jail. Then why not stay at home?

I know you begin to see how strongly I *feel* on this subject, but I have some reasons as well. These reasons are based on logic. Of course I am not logical. I am a creature of impulse, instinct and intuition—and I glory in it. But I know that these reasons are based on logic because I have culled them from the men whom it is my privilege to know.

My first argument against suffrage is that the women would not use it if they had it. You couldn't drive them to the polls. My second argument is, if the women were enfranchised they would neglect their home, desert their families and spend all their time at the polls. You may tell me that the polls are only open once a year. But I know women. They are creatures of habit. If you let them go to the polls once a year, they will hang round the polls all the rest of the time.

I have arranged these arguments in couplets. They go together in such a way that if you don't like one you can take the other. This is my second anti-suffrage couplet. If the women were enfranchised they would vote exactly as their husbands do and only double the existing vote. Do you like that argument? If not, take this one. If the women were enfranchised they would vote against their own husbands, thus creating dissension, family quarrels, and divorce.

My third anti-suffrage couplet is—women are angels. Many men call me an angel and I have a strong instinct which tells me it is true; that is why I am an anti, because "I want to be an angel and with the angels stand." And if you don't like that argument take this one. Women are depraved. They would introduce into politics a vicious element which would ruin our national life.

Fourth anti-suffrage couplet: women cannot understand politics. Therefore there would be no use in giving women political power, because they would not know what to do with it. On the other hand, if the women were enfranchised, they would mount rapidly into power, take all the offices from all the men, and soon we would have women governors of all our states and dozens of women acting as President of the United States.

Fifth anti-suffrage couplet: women cannot band together. They are incapable of organization. No two women can even be friends. Women are cats. On the other hand, if women were enfranchised, we would have all the women banded together on one side and all the men banded together on the other side, and there would follow a sex war which might end in bloody revolution.

Just one more of my little couplets: the ballot is greatly over-estimated. It has never done anything for anybody. Lots of men tell me this. And the corresponding argument is—the ballot is what makes man man. It is what gives him all his dignity and all of his superiority to women. Therefore if we allow women to share this privilege, how could a woman look up to her own husband? Why, there would be nothing to look up to.

I have talked to many woman suffragists and I find them very unreasonable. I say to them: "Here I am, convince me." I ask for proof. Then they proceed to tell me of Australia and Colorado and other places where women have passed excellent laws to improve the condition of working women and children. But I say, "What of it?" These are facts. I don't care about facts. I ask for proof.

Then they quote the eight million women of the United States who are now supporting themselves, and the twenty-five-thousand married women in the City of New York who are self-supporting. But I say again, what of it? These are statistics. I don't believe in statistics. Facts and statistics are things which no truly womanly woman would ever use.

I wish to prove anti-suffrage in a womanly way—that is, by personal example. This is my method of persuasion. Once I saw a woman driving a horse, and the horse ran away with her. Isn't that just like a woman? Once I read in the newspapers about a woman whose house caught on fire, and she threw the children out of the window and carried the pillows downstairs. Does that show political acumen, or does it not? Besides, look at the hats that women wear! And have you ever known a successful woman governor of a state? Or have you ever known a really truly successful woman President of the United States? Well, if they haven't doesn't that show they couldn't? As for the militant suffragettes, they are all hyenas in petticoats. Now do you want to be a hyena and wear petticoats?

Now, I think I have proved anti-suffrage; and I have done it in a womanly way—that is, without stooping to the use of a single fact or argument or a single statistic.

I am the prophet of a new idea. No one has ever thought of it or heard of it before. I well remember when this great idea first came to me. It waked me in the middle of the night with a shock that gave me a headache. This is it: woman's place is in the home. Is it not beautiful as it is new, new as it is true? Take this idea away with you. You will find it very helpful in your daily lives. You may not grasp it just at first, but you will gradually grow into understanding of it.

I know the suffragists reply that all our activities have been taken out of the home. The baking, the washing, the weaving, the spinning are all long since taken out of the home. But I say, all the more reason that something should stay in the home. Let it be woman. Besides, think of the great modern invention, the telephone. That has been put into the home. Let woman stay at home and answer the telephone. . .

What ought these women to do with their lives? Each one ought to be devoting herself to the comfort of some man. You may say, they are not married. But I answer, let them try a little harder and they might find some kind of a man to devote themselves to. What does the Bible say on this subject? It says, "Seek and ye shall find." Besides, when I look around me at the men, I feel that God never meant us women to be too particular.

Let me speak one word to my sister women who are here today. Women, we don't need to vote in order to get our own way. Don't misunderstand me. Of course I want you to get your own way. That's what we're here for. But do it indirectly. If you want a thing, tease. If that doesn't work, nag. If that doesn't do, cry—crying always brings them around. Get what you want. Pound pillows. Make a scene. Make home a hell on earth, but do it in a womanly way. That is so much more dignified and refined than walking up to a ballot box and dropping in a piece of paper. Can't you see that?

Let us consider for a moment the effect of woman's enfranchisement on man. I think someone ought to consider the men. What makes a husband faithful and loving? The ballot, and the monopoly of that privilege. If women vote, what will become of men? They will all slink off drunk and disorderly. We antis understand men. If women were enfranchised, men would revert to their natural instincts such as regicide, matricide, patricide and race-suicide. Do you believe in race-suicide or do you not? Then, isn't it our duty to refrain from a thing that would lure men to destruction?

It comes down to this. Some one must wash the dishes. Now, would you expect man, man made in the image of God, to roll up his sleeves and wash the dishes? Why, it would be blasphemy. I know that I am but a rib and so I wash the dishes. Or I hire another rib to do it for me, which amounts to the same thing.

Let us consider the argument from the standpoint of religion. The Bible says, "Let the women keep silent in the churches." Paul says, "Let them keep their hats on for fear of the angels." My minister says, "Wives, obey your husbands." And my husband says that woman suffrage would rob the rose of its fragrance and the peach of its bloom. I think that is so sweet.

Besides did George Washington ever say, "Votes for women?" No. Did the Emperor Kaiser Wilhelm ever say, "Votes for women?" No. Did Elijah, Elisha, Micah, Hezekiah, Obadiah and Jeremiah ever say, "Votes for women?" No. Then that settles it.

I don't want to be misunderstood in my reference to woman's inability to vote. Of course she could get herself to the polls and lift a piece of paper. I don't doubt that. What I refer to is the pressure on the brain, the effect of this mental strain on woman's delicate nervous organization and on her highly wrought sensitive nature. Have you ever pictured to yourself Election Day with women voting? Can you imagine how women, having undergone this terrible ordeal, with their delicate systems all upset, will come out of the voting booths and be led away by policemen, and put into ambulances, while they are fainting and weeping, half laughing, half crying, and having fits upon the public highway? Don't you think that if a woman is going to have a fit, it is far better for her to have it in the privacy of her own home?

And how shall I picture to you the terrors of the day after election? Divorce and death will rage unchecked, crime and contagious disease will stalk unbridled through the land. Oh, friends, on this subject I feel—I feel, so strongly that I can—not think!

A Labor Organizer Speaks Out for Suffrage

Leonora O'Reilly

Although the suffrage movement remained predominantly a middle-class affair, working-class and immigrant women also found a place in its ranks, especially as the movement looked outward for new sources of support in the 20th century. (Black women, however, were not welcomed in white suffrage organizations and formed their own groups.) This testimony given by labor leader and reformer Leonora O'Reilly before a Joint Senate Committee in April 1912 effectively rebutted the criticisms that women did not want the vote or that the vote was irrelevant to the problems that working women faced in their lives. O'Reilly demolished the argument that women should stay at home by using her own experience to show that many women had no choice but to enter the work force, where they worked under terrible conditions with few weapons to redress their grievances. The vote would be one such weapon.

Leonora O'Reilly (1870–1927) knew what she was talking about. She was born into an Irish family on New York's Lower East Side and had started work not at 13, as she says in her testimony, but at 11. At 16, she showed her first interest in the trade union movement by joining the Knights of Labor. It was through organizing a working women's society that she came into contact with middle-class reformers such as Mary Dreier, Margaret Dreier Robins, Lillian Wald, and Grace Dodge. At first she pursued her reform and educational activities while still working in a shirtwaist factory, but Mary Dreier's 1909 gift of a lifetime annuity freed her to devote herself full time to activism on behalf of working women, much of it through the auspices of the Women's Trade Union League. As this testimony hints, Leonora O'Reilly was a charismatic speaker; since she wrote no books and few articles, such documents are all we have to recapture her passionate commitment to labor and women.

Source: Statement of Leonora O'Reilly (1912) before Joint Congressional Session of Congress, found in Anne F. Scott and Andrew Scott, *One Half the People* (Philadelphia: J. B. Lippincott, 1975), pp. 126–27.

Mr. Chairman and gentlemen of the committee: Yes; I have outdone the lady who went to work at 18 by five years. I have been a wage earner since I was a little over 13. I, too, know whereof I speak; that is the reason I do not want to play a bluff game with you any longer. You can not or will not make laws for us; we must make laws for ourselves. We working women need the ballot for self-protection; that is all there is to it. We have got to have it.

We work long, long hours and we do not get half enough to live on. We have got to keep decent, and if we go "the easy way" you men make the laws that will let you go free and send us into the gutter. [Applause.]

We can not believe in man-made laws any longer. We have gone from one assembly to another, from one State senator to another, and we have heard the same old story. You think only of output; there is not a soul among you who cares to save human beings. We have grown rich, as a nation, but we have grown very rotten. As a people—gentlemen, I use the term "rotten" advisedly—for, as far as the working women are concerned, the foundation we are building on is rotten. To purify the life of the Nation we women know we have got to do our part, political as well as industrial duty. Government, as a whole, rests on industry. You men say to us: "Go back to the home. Your place is in the home," yet as children we must come out of the home at 11, at 13, and at 15 years of age to earn a living; we have got to make good or starve.

"Pay your way" we are taught in school and in church—the greatest thing on earth is to be able to pay your way. Well, if any people on earth pay their way in life we working women do. The return we get is that most of us become physical wrecks along the roadside of life. When you gentlemen hear what it costs a working woman to "pay her way" in life, you sit back in your chairs, say "the story is terrible, but they manage to live somehow." Somehow—that is it, gentlemen. I want to make you realize the *somehow* of life to the hundreds of girls I have seen go down in the struggle. You men do not care. You want this country to get rich, and you do not know the only riches of a nation are its people. [Applause.]

We have gone before legislature after legislature making our pleas for justice. We have seen the game as you play it. What is it? We go there and we are told the same old tommyrot—let men do this for you. I tell you as a bit of business experience if you let anybody do a thing for you they will do you. That is business. [Applause.]

Now, while we have had the colleges opened to women, only one woman in a thousand goes to college, while modern industry claims one woman in every five to-day. It is industrial methods which are teaching the women the facts I am telling you. "Do the other fellow before he gets a chance to do you"—do him so hard that he can not stand up again; that is good business. We know that, and we women are sure that there must be some higher standard for life than business.

We are not getting a square deal; we go before legislature after legislature to tell our story, but they fail to help the women who are being speeded so high in the mills and in factories, from 54 hours to 72 hours in stores in New York, and 92 hours in one week in subcellar laundries. Who cares? Nobody! Nobody does; nobody cares about making laws so long as we get cheap and nasty things in the market. Working women come before you and tell you these things and think you will do something for them. Every man listening is convinced that the girls are telling the truth. It is only when you think of them as your own girls that you have the right to make laws for them. Every man listening wants to do the fair thing, but just as soon as our backs are turned, up comes the representative of the big interest and says, "Lad, you are dead politically if you do what those women ask." They know it is true, and we get nothing, because all the votes are owned.

Every vote you cast is owned, and it is the owned vote which has fought our women. Go before legislatures as you will, the only argument that you can bring in to the man in politics—he is there to go up the ladder, decently if he can, but he will go up anyhow, if he can—the only argument that you can bring to that man is the power of the ballot. When we can say to him, "Man, do this and we will return you so many million votes," he will listen and act.

This is what we want, because it is for the good of the women, because it is for the good of the whole people. It is for that reason that the working woman, facing the hard facts of life and having to fight her way, has come to the conclusion that you men in politics—I am not going to give you any taffy—you men in politics are not leaders, you follow what you think is the next step on the ladder. We want you to understand that the next step in politics, the next step in democracy, is to give to the women of your Nation a ballot. [Applause.]

The working women send me to you with the plain, honest truth; because, working beside you in the same mill or factory, we know you with your evening suit off and your tall hat in the box, or wherever it belongs; you are just a competitor with us there; we tell you the truth there, as I have come to tell you the truth here. Let women have the ballot, in order that you may once more throw the burden which you have carried, or thought you carried, onto them; that is the thing you have done since the beginning of time; when the load was too heavy for you you piled it onto Eve's back. [Applause.] You have got us in a devil of a mess, economic and political. It is so rank it smells to Heaven; but we will come in and help you clean house. We will start all over again, because we belong together shoulder to shoulder. We must get on to a better time. It is only because you will not, in your prejudice and your ignorance, let us into the political field with you that the situation is as bad as it is to-day.

We working women want the ballot, not as a privilege but as a right. You say you have only given the ballot as an expediency; you have never given it as a right; then we demand it as an expediency for the 8,000,000 working women. All other women ought to have it, but we working women must have it. [Applause.]

"Front Door Lobbying" for Suffrage

Maud Wood Park

The women who lobbied for suffrage faced an uphill battle: how as voteless citizens to convince elected representatives to grant them a new right without being able to promise retribution at the polls if their wishes were not taken seriously. Suffragists were determined to serve as a credit to their sex. They quickly earned the nickname of the "front door lobby," which Maud Wood Park remembered as "the half-humorous, half-kindly name given to our Congressional Committee in Washington by one of the press-gallery men there, because, as he explained, we never used backstairs methods."

Maud Wood Park (1871–1955) was the head of the Congressional Committee of the National American Woman Suffrage Association during Carrie Chapman Catt's presidency, and it was under Park's direction that much of the lobbying occurred that led to the final Congressional passage of the 19th Amendment in 1919. These instructions to her fellow lobbyists, and her recollections of the triumphs and setbacks they faced, suggest her skill as an efficient and pragmatic leader. They also show NAWSA's determination to be firm but above all *ladylike,* a sharp contrast to the militants who risked arrest for their public protests and picketing (see next document).

Maud Wood Park spent most of her life working to advance the cause of women in public life. An 1899 graduate of Radcliffe, she was a suffragist even in college and founded the College Equal Suffrage League soon after her graduation. Widowed after a short period of marriage in 1904, she continued an extensive round of suffrage activities in Massachusetts. Carrie Chapman Catt asked her to come to Washington in 1916 for the final stages in the assault on Congress. In 1919, with victory finally in sight, Park became the first president of the newly organized League of Women Voters, where she served until 1924. Her autobiography, appropriately titled *Front Door Lobby,* was published posthumously in 1960.

During January, 1917, our lobby, in addition to members of the Congressional Committee, consisted of twenty-nine women from sixteen different states, who stayed in Washington at their own expense for periods ranging from six days to four weeks. For their use we had our lobby rules drawn up in the following form:

Directions for Lobbyists

I. PREPARATION:

  1. Read our records of each member before calling on him. Also read biographical sketch in Congressional Directory. *Records must not be taken from the office.*

  2. Provide yourself with small directory. Your own representative is the best source of supply.

II. INTERVIEWING:

  1. If the member appears busy ask whether he would prefer to see you at some other time.

  2. Be courteous no matter what provocation you may seem to have to be otherwise.

  3. If possible learn the secretary's name and have a little talk with him or her. The secretary, if inclined to be interested, should be invited to headquarters.

Source: From *Front Door Lobby* by Maud Wood Park, pp. 38–41. Copyright © 1960 by Edna Lamprey Stantial. Reprinted by permission of Beacon Press, Boston.

4. If the member is known to be in favor *show that you realize that fact* and ask him for advice and help with the rest of the delegation. This point is *very important.*
5. Be sure to keep his *party* constantly in mind while talking with him.
6. Be a good listener. Don't interrupt.
7. Try to avoid prolonged or controversial argument. It is likely to confirm men in their own opinion.
8. Do not stay so long that the member has to give the signal for departure.
9. Take every possible means to prevent a member from *committing* himself definitely *against* the Federal Amendment. This is *most important.*
10. Leave the way open for another interview if you have failed to convince him.
11. If the member is inclined to be favorable invite him and his family to headquarters.
12. Remember to hold each interview confidential. Never quote what one member has said to you to another member. It is not safe to talk of your lobby experiences before outsiders or before servants. We can never know by what route our stories may get back to the member and injure our cause with him. We cannot be too cautious in this matter.

III. REPORTS:
1. Do not make notes in offices or halls.
2. Do find opportunity to make notes on one interview before starting another. If necessary, step into the "Ladies" dressing room to do this.
3. Write full report of your interview on the same day giving—
   a. Name and State of member.
   b. Date and hour of interview.
   c. Names of lobbyists and name of person making report.
   d. Member's argument in detail, especially with view to follow-up work.
   e. Any information you may glean about his family or friends that may be useful to the Washington Committee.
   f. Hand-written report to *Miss Bain,* not later than the day following the interview.
   g. Promptness in turning in reports is most important in order that lists and polls may be kept up to date.

When I was sufficiently familiar with the work to have a little sense of humor about it, I condensed those rules into a series of "don'ts":

Don't nag.
Don't boast.
Don't threaten.
Don't lose your temper.
Don't stay too long.
Don't talk about your work where you can be overheard.
Don't give the member interviewed an opportunity to declare himself against the amendment.
Don't do anything to close the door to the next advocate of suffrage.

The last "don't" was the one I dwelt on most in my talks with our workers, partly because it was the most difficult to follow. Knowing that the effect of our work in the case of doubtful members was cumulative, I used to say over and over again, "If we can't do any good, at least we must be sure that we don't do any harm."

Many of our lobby meetings were as entertaining as a good comedy. One of the women had the gift of ironic wit. Another was a capital mimic and gave us side-splitting imitations of some of the men whom she had interviewed. She was wise, too, for she cautioned us never to tell outside that any of our number had ventured to "take off" members of the Congress. I sometimes found it hard to stop my own laughter long enough to give out the next assignments.

Some of the written reports were funny, too. For example, this was turned in by one of our southern lobbyists after she had interviewed a Texas member:

> Polite but positive. Against woman suffrage—any phase of it. Declares that men represent women. When I suggested my being a widow and not having representation, he gallantly offered to represent me. The fact of his living in Texas and my residence being in Kentucky did not dismay him at all, but the proposition was most unsatisfactory to me. Against prohibition and against child labor bill. Has not seen any light at all in progressive legislation.

Another southern interview went into our record in these words:

> Invited us in—polite manner. Believes that woman dwells apart from man—in her nature. "She is different—Nature made it so—all history, science, and biology prove it! Look at the barnyard, the 'cockerel' protects the hen, etc. Woman is meant for the home, the hearth and to be sheltered by man." He acknowledged that there were some women outside the home, but men could protect them. The dirty mire of politics for women could not be thought of. He deplored the lack of woman's trust in men, and did not think women wanted to be called "suffragands" (the correlation of the word "brigand"). He is beyond the pale. We parted in a friendly way.

The shortest and most satisfactory report that I remember was of an interview with Hon. Fiorello La Guardia:

He said, "I'm with you; I'm for it, I'm going to vote for it. Now don't bother me," all in one breath.

Suffrage Militant Alice Paul
Goes to Jail

The suffrage movement was never monolithic; deep fissures split it over tactics, ideology, race, and even geography, as shown by Abigail Scott Duniway. There was no more emotional or far-reaching split than the one between the National American Woman Suffrage Association and the Congressional

Source: Alice Paul letters quoted in Doris Stevens, *Jailed for Freedom* (New York: Boni and Liveright, 1920; reprinted by Schocken Books, 1976), pp. 215–17, 220–23.

Union (CU), a group of militant suffragists led by the charismatic Quaker leader Alice Paul. Several points of conflict emerged: Should the suffragists endorse political candidates; should they support a federal amendment, or work for state by state gains; and did dramatic public confrontations, inspired by the example of British militants, help or hinder the suffrage cause?

The Congressional Union was determined to take militant action. In World War I, the CU broke with the more conservative NAWSA and refused to support American entry into the war. More pointedly, militants began picketing the White House protesting President Woodrow Wilson's lack of support for suffrage. Then they began more inflammatory acts, such as burning copies of Wilson's speeches or chaining themselves to the White House fence. Such actions earned them quick arrest for obstructing traffic, and they were sentenced to seven months in jail, an unusually harsh sentence.

Alice Paul (1885–1977) was the leader and inspiration of the jailed suffragists. She and Rose Winslow were the first two suffragists to undertake a hunger strike. Recounting her story in these letters to fellow militant Doris Stevens, Paul conveyed the terrible conditions under which the women suffered and their determination to make themselves into such troublemakers that they would have to be released. Emerging as martyrs, such sacrifices helped push the suffrage amendment to final victory. As Rose Winslow said, "God knows we don't want other women ever to have to do this over again."

It was late afternoon when we arrived at the jail. There we found the suffragists who had preceded us, locked in cells.

The first thing I remember was the distress of the prisoners about the lack of fresh air. Evening was approaching, every window was closed tight. The air in which we would be obliged to sleep was foul. There were about eighty negro and white prisoners crowded together, tier upon tier, frequently two in a cell. I went to a window and tried to open it. Instantly a group of men, prison guards, appeared; picked me up bodily, threw me into a cell and locked the door. Rose Winslow and the others were treated in the same way.

Determined to preserve our health and that of the other prisoners, we began a concerted fight for fresh air. The windows were about twenty feet distant from the cells, and two sets of iron bars intervened between us and the windows, but we instituted an attack upon them as best we could. Our tin drinking cups, the electric light bulbs, every available article of the meagre supply in each cell, including my treasured copy of Browning's poems which I had secretly taken in with me, was thrown through the windows. By this simultaneous attack from every cell, we succeeded in breaking one window before our supply of tiny weapons was exhausted. The fresh October air came in like an exhilarating gale. The broken window remained untouched throughout the entire stay of this group and all later groups of suffragists. Thus was won what the "regulars" in jail called the first breath of air in their time.

The next day we organized ourselves into a little group for the purpose of rebellion. We determined to make it impossible to keep us in jail. We determined, moreover, that as long as we were there we would keep up an unremitting fight for the rights of political prisoners.

One by one little points were conceded to quiet resistance. There was the practice of sweeping the corridors in such a way that the dust filled the cells. The prisoners would be choking to the gasping point, as they sat, helpless, locked in the cells, while a great cloud of dust enveloped them from tiers above and below. As soon as our tin drinking cups, which were sacrificed in our attack upon the windows, were restored to us, we instituted a campaign against the dust. Tin cup after tin cup was filled and its contents thrown out into the corridor from every cell, so that the water began to trickle down from tier to tier. The District Commissioners, the Board of Charities, and other officials were summoned by the prison authorities. Hurried consultations were held. Nameless officials passed by in review and looked upon the dampened floor. Thereafter the corridors were dampened and the sweeping into the cells ceased. And so another reform was won.

There is absolutely no privacy allowed a prisoner in a cell. You are suddenly peered at by curious strangers, who look in at you all hours of the day and night, by officials, by attendants, by interested philanthropic visitors, and by prison reformers, until one's sense of privacy is so outraged that one rises in rebellion. We set out to secure privacy, but we did not succeed, for, to allow privacy in prison, is against all institutional thought and habit. Our only available weapon was our blanket, which was no sooner put in front of our bars than it was forcibly taken down by Warden Zinkhan.

Our meals had consisted of a little almost raw salt pork, some sort of liquid— I am not sure whether it was coffee or soup—bread and occasionally molasses. How we cherished the bread and molasses! We saved it from meal to meal so as to try to distribute the nourishment over a longer period, as almost every one was unable to eat the raw pork. Lucy Branham, who was more valiant than the rest of us, called out from her cell, one day, "Shut your eyes tight, close your mouth over the pork and swallow it without chewing it. Then you can do it." This heroic practice kept Miss Branham in fairly good health, but to the rest it seemed impossible, even with our eyes closed, to crunch our teeth into the raw pork.

However gaily you start out in prison to keep up a rebellious protest, it is nevertheless a terribly difficult thing to do in the face of the constant cold and hunger of undernourishment. Bread and water, and occasional molasses, is not a diet destined to sustain rebellion long. And soon weakness overtook us.

At the end of two weeks of solitary confinement, without any exercise, without going outside of our cells, some of the prisoners were released, having finished their terms, but five of us were left serving seven months' sentences, and two, one month sentences. With our number thus diminished to seven, the authorities felt able to cope with us. The doors were unlocked and we were permitted to take exercise. Rose Winslow fainted as soon as she got into the yard, and was carried back to her cell. I was too weak to move from my bed. Rose and I were taken on stretchers that night to the hospital.

For one brief night we occupied beds in the same ward in the hospital. Here we decided upon the hunger strike, as the ultimate form of protest left us—the strongest weapon left with which to continue within the prison our battle against the Administration. . .

From the moment we undertook the hunger strike, a policy of unremitting intimidation began. One authority after another, high and low, in and out of prison, came to attempt to force me to break the hunger strike.

"You will be taken to a very unpleasant place if you don't stop this," was a favorite threat of the prison officials, as they would hint vaguely of the psycopathic ward, and St. Elizabeth's, the Government insane asylum. They alternately bullied and hinted. Another threat was "You will be forcibly fed immediately if you don't stop"—this from Dr. Gannon. There was nothing to do in the midst of these continuous threats, with always the "very unpleasant place" hanging over me, and so I lay perfectly silent on my bed.

After about three days of the hunger strike a man entered my room in the hospital and announced himself as Dr. White, the head of St. Elizabeth's. He said that he had been asked by District Commissioner Gardner to make an investigation. I later learned that he was Dr. William A. White, the eminent alienist.

Coming close to my bedside and addressing the attendant, who stood at a few respectful paces from him, Dr. White said: "Does this case talk?"

"Why wouldn't I talk?" I answered quickly.

"Oh, these cases frequently will not talk, you know," he continued in explanation.

"Indeed I'll talk," I said gaily, not having the faintest idea that this was an investigation of my sanity.

"Talking is our business," I continued, "we talk to any one on earth who is willing to listen to our suffrage speeches."

"Please talk," said Dr. White. "Tell me about suffrage; why you have opposed the President; the whole history of your campaign, why you picket, what you hope to accomplish by it. Just talk freely."

I drew myself together, sat upright in bed, propped myself up for a discourse of some length, and began to talk. The stenographer whom Dr. White brought with him took down in shorthand everything that was said.

I may say it was one of the best speeches I ever made. I recited the long history and struggle of the suffrage movement from its early beginning and narrated the political theory of our activities up to the present moment, outlining the status of the suffrage amendment in Congress at that time. In short, I told him everything. He listened attentively, interrupting only occasionally to say, "But, has not President Wilson treated you women very badly?" Whereupon, I, still unaware that I was being examined, launched forth into an explanation of Mr. Wilson's political situation and the difficulties he had confronting him. I continued to explain why we felt our relief lay with him; I cited his extraordinary power, his influence over his party, his undisputed leadership in the country, always painstakingly explaining that we opposed President Wilson merely because he happened to be President, not because he was President Wilson. Again came an interruption from Dr. White, "But isn't President Wilson directly responsible for the abuses and indignities which have been heaped upon you? You are suffering now as a result of his brutality, are you not?" Again I explained that it was impossible for us to know whether President Wilson was personally acquainted in any detail with the facts of our present condition, even though we knew that he had concurred in the early decision to arrest our women.

Presently Dr. White took out a small light and held it up to my eyes. Suddenly it dawned upon me that he was examining me personally; that his interest in the suffrage agitation and the jail conditions did not exist, and that he was merely interested in my reactions to the agitation and to jail. Even then I was reluctant to believe that I was the subject of mental investigation and I continued to talk.

But he continued in what I realized with a sudden shock, was an attempt to discover in me symptoms of the persecution mania. How simple he had apparently thought it would be, to prove that I had an obsession on the subject of President Wilson!

The day following he came again, this time bringing with him the District Commissioner, Mr. Gardner, to whom he asked me to repeat everything that had been said the day before. For the second time we went through the history of the suffrage movement, and again his inquiry suggested his persecution mania clue? [sic] When the narrative touched upon the President and his responsibility for the obstruction of the suffrage amendment, Dr. White would turn to his associate with the remark: "Note the reaction."

Then came another alienist, Dr. Hickling, attached to the psychopathic ward in the District Jail, with more threats and suggestions, if the hunger strike continued. Finally they departed, and I was left to wonder what would happen next. Doubtless my sense of humor helped me, but I confess I was not without fear of this mysterious place which they continued to threaten.

It appeared clear that it was their intention either to discredit me, as the leader of the agitation, by casting doubt upon my sanity, or else to intimidate us into retreating from the hunger strike.

After the examination by alienists, Commissioner Gardner, with whom I had previously discussed our demand for treatment as political prisoners, made another visit. "All these things you say about the prison conditions may be true," said Mr. Gardner. "I am a new Commissioner, and I do not know. You give an account of a very serious situation in the jail. The jail authorities give exactly the opposite. Now I promise you we will start an investigation at once to see who is right, you or they. If it is found you are right, we shall correct the conditions at once. If you will give up the hunger strike, we will start the investigation at once."

"Will you consent to treat the suffragists as political prisoners, in accordance with the demands laid before you?" I replied.

Commissioner Gardner refused, and I told him that the hunger strike would not be abandoned. But they had by no means exhausted every possible facility for breaking down our resistance. I overheard the Commissioner say to Dr. Gannon on leaving, "Go ahead, take her and feed her."

I was thereupon put upon a stretcher and carried into the psychopathic ward.

SUGGESTIONS FOR FURTHER READING

Anderson, Karen. *Changing Women: A History of Racial Ethnic Women in Modern America.*
New York, 1997.

Antler, Joyce. *Lucy Sprague Mitchell: The Making of a Modern Woman.* New Haven, 1987.

Armitage, Susan, and Elizabeth Jameson, eds. *Writing the Range: Race, Class, and Culture in the Women's West.* New York, 1997.

Blair, Karen J. *The Clubwoman as Feminist: True Womanhood Redefined, 1868–1914.* New York, 1980.

Buechler, Steven M. *The Transformation of the Woman Suffrage Movement: The Case of Illinois, 1850–1920.* New Brunswick, 1986.

Buhle, Mari Jo. *Women and American Socialism, 1870–1920.* Urbana, 1981.

Chesler, Ellen. *Woman of Valor: Margaret Sanger and the Birth Control Movement in America.* New York, 1992.

DuBois, Ellen Carol. *Harriet Stanton Blatch and the Winning of Woman Suffrage.* New Haven, 1997.

Dye, Nancy Schrom. *As Equals and As Sisters: The Labor Movement and the Women's Trade Union League of New York.* Columbia, MO, 1980.

Ewen, Elizabeth. *Immigrant Women in the Land of Dollars: Life and Culture on the Lower East Side, 1890–1925.* New York, 1985.

Faderman, Lillian. *Odd Girls and Twilight Lovers: A History of Lesbian Life in 20th Century America.* New York, 1991.

Fitzpatrick, Ellen. *Endless Crusade: Women Social Scientists and Progressive Reform.* New York, 1990.

Fowler, Robert Booth. *Carrie Catt: Feminist Politician.* Boston, 1986.

Frankel, Noralee, and Nancy S. Dye, eds. *Gender, Class, Race, and Reform in the Progressive Era.* Lexington, Kentucky, 1992.

Giddings, Paula. *When and Where I Enter: The Impact of Black Women on Race and Sex in America.* New York, 1984.

Glenn, Susan A. *Daughters of the Shtetl: Life and Labor in the Immigrant Generation.* Ithaca, 1990.

Gluck, Sherna B., ed. *From Parlor to Prison: Five American Suffragists Talk About Their Lives.* New York, 1986.

Gordon, Linda. *Woman's Body, Woman's Right: A Social History of Birth Control in America.* New York, 1976.

Gordon, Lynn D. *Gender and Higher Education in the Progressive Era.* New Haven, 1990.

Green, Elna. *Southern Strategies: Southern Women and the Woman Suffrage Question.* Chapel Hill, 1997.

Greenwald, Maurine Weiner. *Women, War, and Work: The Impact of World War I on Women Workers in the United States.* Westport, 1980.

Higginbotham, Evelyn Brooks. *Righteous Discontent: The Women's Movement in the Black Baptist Church, 1880–1920.* Cambridge, 1993.

Hine, Darlene Clark, ed. *Black Women in America: An Historical Encyclopedia.* New York, 1993.

Hine, Darlene Clark, and Kathleen Thompson. *A Shining Thread of Hope: The History of Black Women in America.* New York, 1998.

Jones, Jacqueline. *Labor of Love, Labor of Sorrow: Black Women, Work, and the Family from Slavery to the Present.* New York, 1985.

Kessler-Harris, Alice. *Out to Work: A History of Wage-Earning Women in America.* New York, 1982.

Kroeger, Brooke. *Nellie Bly.* New York, 1994.

Lane, Ann J. *To Herland and Beyond: The Life and Work of Charlotte Perkins Gilman.* New York, 1990.

Lunardini, Christine A. *From Equal Suffrage to Equal Rights: Alice Paul and the National Woman's Party, 1910–1918.* New York, 1986.

Meyerowitz, Joanne. *Women Adrift: Independent Female Wage Earners in Chicago, 1880–1930.* Chicago, 1988.

Morantz-Sanchez, Regina. *Sympathy and Science: Women Physicians in American Medicine.* New York, 1985.

Moynihan, Ruth Barnes. *Rebel for Rights: Abigail Scott Duniway.* New Haven, 1983.

Myres, Sandra L. *Westering Women: The Frontier Experience, 1800–1915.* Albuquerque, 1982.

Newman, Louise. *White Women's Rights: The Racial Origins of Feminism in the United States.* New York, 1999.

Orleck, Annelise. *Common Sense and a Little Fire: Women and Working Class Politics in the United States, 1900–1965.* Chapel Hill, 1995.

Palmieri, Patricia Ann. *In Adamless Eve: The Community of Women Faculty at Wellesley.* New Haven, 1995.

Peiss, Kathy. *Cheap Amusements: Working Women and Leisure in Turn-of-the-Century New York.* Philadelphia, 1986.

Riley, Glenda. *A Place to Grow: Women in the American West.* Arlington Heights, 1992.

Rosenberg, Rosalind. *Beyond Separate Spheres: Intellectual Roots of Modern Feminism.* New Haven, 1982.

Scharff, Virginia. *Taking the Wheel: Women and the Coming of the Motor Age.* New York, 1991.

Schlissel, Lillian, and Catherine Lavender. *The Western Women's Reader.* New York, 2000.

Schwarz, Judith. *The Radical Feminists of Heterodoxy.* Lebanon, 1982.

Scott, Anne F. *Natural Allies: Women's Associations in American History.* Urbana, 1992.

Sicherman, Barbara. *Alice Hamilton: A Life in Letters.* Cambridge, 1984.

Sklar, Kathryn Kish. *Florence Kelley and the Nation's Work: The Rise of Women's Political Culture, 1830–1900.* New Haven, 1995.

Solomon, Barbara Miller. *In the Company of Educated Women: A History of Women and Higher Education in America.* New Haven, 1985.

Stansell, Christine. *American Moderns: Bohemian New York and the Creation of a New Century.* New York, 2000.

Tax, Meredith. *The Rising of the Women: Feminist Solidarity and Class Conflict, 1880–1917.* New York, 1980.

Terborg-Penn, Rosalyn. *African-American Women in the Struggle for the Vote, 1850–1920.* Bloomington, 1998.

Weinberg, Sydney Stahl. *The World of Our Mothers: The Lives of Jewish Immigrant Women.* Chapel Hill, 1988.

Weiner, Lynn Y. *From Working Girl to Working Mother: The Female Labor Force in the United States, 1820–1980.* Chapel Hill, 1985.

Wexler, Alex. *Emma Goldman in America.* Boston, 1984.

Wheeler, Marjorie Spruill. *New Women of the New South: The Leaders of the Woman Suffrage Movement in the Southern States.* New York, 1993.

White, Deborah Gray. *Too Heavy a Load: Black Women in Defense of Themselves, 1894–1994.* New York, 1999.

PART TWO

Individual Choices, Collective Progress

1920–1963

"*T*he world broke in two in 1922 or thereabouts," observed writer Willa Cather. In many ways, the period beginning in the 1920s represented a new, more modern orientation to American life. The year 1920 definitely served as a watershed for the nation's women, as they secured the vote and embarked on full citizenship and political equality with men. In retrospect, the liberation and freedom women had gained was far from complete, but the 1920s still separate the emerging new woman of the late 19th century from her modern equivalent.

The lives of American women unfold within broader patterns in American society and culture, and their experiences often offer a different perspective on events. For example, the 1920s are often portrayed as a frivolous time when Americans were more concerned with bootleg gin and the stock market than with politics or activism. And yet when historians trace women's political mobilization pre- and postsuffrage, they see surprising continuities that fundamentally undercut the view of the 1920s as an apolitical era. Gender differences of another sort emerge in the Great Depression of the 1930s, when men found their self-esteem undermined by their inability to provide for their families while housewives saw their stature rise as they helped families cope with hard times. World War II is often seen primarily in terms of the men who went to war, but women's lives changed too, often as dramatically as men's. Women's previously overlooked activism in the civil rights, nuclear disarmament, and environmental movements in the 1950s revises the view of that supposedly complacent and domestic-bound decade in significant ways.

In a period without an active feminist movement, much of the progress for women came about through individual choices rather than collective solidarity, and this section documents a broad range of women's experiences between 1920 and 1963. Once again women across the political spectrum are represented: women for and against the Equal Rights Amendment, women in the Ku Klux Klan, women labor organizers in the 1930s, and activists in the 1950s who set the stage for the revival of feminism after 1963. Just as compelling are the voices of individual women as they struggle to hold their families together during the Great Depression or strike out as Rosie the Riveters during World War II. Experiences of black, Mexican-American, and Native American women offer counterpoints to those of white women whose stories often dominate historical narratives. The result is a more representative and "gendered" picture of American life in the middle years of the 20th century.

CHAPTER 6

New Dilemmas for Modern Women

The advent of modern times in the United States had as large an impact on the nation's women as its men. By the 1920s, the country had basically completed the process of industrialization and had taken on an increasingly urban orientation. Especially important in distinguishing modern times from earlier 19th-century patterns was the dramatic expansion of mass culture, which made it more likely that Americans (at least of the middle class) would share similar experiences throughout the nation. New instruments of mass media, such as radio and the movies, spread the message, as did the expansion of advertising. The automobile epitomized these new values of consumption, economic consolidation, and changing patterns of leisure.

The 1920s is noted for its booming economy, yet this prosperity was unequally distributed: more than 65 percent of households had incomes under $2,000 a year, which severely limited their ability to buy the new automobiles, vacuum cleaners, radios, toasters, and other consumer goods so central to the maintenance of prosperity in the 1920s. Consumer credit (which grew dramatically in the 1920s) could stretch family income only so far. The onset of the Great Depression in 1929 showed the underlying structural weaknesses of the economy.

Women were the focus of many of these broader developments—in the words of one historian, "In no other decade of the 20th century, until the 1970s, have women been so at the center of the major issues." The flapper, whose slim boyish figure and style of dress forms our visual image of women in the decade, served as the symbol of the new values of personal liberation, morality, and consumption. Despite the media's fascination with young women's new lifestyles, the goal for most women continued to be marriage and family life. Most of the advertising in the decade was geared toward accustoming women to that role, as were the movies. The growing acceptance of birth control made it possible for a more companionate ideal to reign in marital relations, and women increasingly turned to experts for help in running their homes or raising their children.

Despite the forces that were liberating women from the home, many cultural messages placed women squarely within the family domain, foreshadowing the "feminine mystique" of postwar America. Married women played vital economic roles as the primary consumers of household goods. Yet these new appliances hardly freed women from domestic toil: Often a washing machine or a vacuum cleaner just raised standards of cleanliness, making "more work for mother." Women still spent an average of 51 hours a week on household chores, little different from their mothers and grandmothers. And of course, these new appliances were only useful in urban areas where households had electricity. In rural America, few farms were electrified before the 1930s. For families on the fringes of the middle-class ideal promoted in advertising, magazines, and movies, the modern consumer economy of the 1920s had not yet arrived.

Paid employment occupied a central role in women's lives in the 1920s. The watchwords for many college-educated women were economic independence, but few women found unlimited economic opportunities. Women made up one-quarter of the workforce, but approximately 86 percent of women worked in only 10 occupations, with domestic and personal service leading the list. Women comprised only 3 percent of union members and received between 52 and 55 percent of men's earnings. Women in the professions continued to be concentrated in fields such as nursing, teaching, and social work. Despite the public attention to women's economic liberation that supposedly accompanied the vote, the largest influence on women's employment was the deeply rooted segmentation of the workforce.

One trend under way by the 1920s was the increase in married women who worked for pay outside the home. More than any other pattern, this change in women's economic roles shaped the modern era. By 1930, 11 percent of native-born white women, 10.2 percent of foreign-born women, and 37.5 percent of black women who were married were also employed. Professional women may have struggled on an individual basis to balance the demands of career and marriage in order to find personal fulfillment, but most women worked out of necessity. The rising expectations of the new consumer lifestyle propelled some married women into the workforce; black women's needs, however, were dictated by economic and family survival.

Equally central to assessing women's experiences in the 1920s is women's continued political activism. The 19th Amendment was treated as a major watershed, the culmination of seven decades of agitation and the beginning of new roles for women in politics and public life. The vote also fostered a false optimism that women were now men's equals as citizens and, by extension, in all other aspects of their lives. But contrary to popular wisdom, the winning of the vote did not cause the disbanding of the women's movement in the 1920s. Some women moved tentatively into the major political parties, but for the most part, women continued to use women's voluntary associations to influence public policy. Without denying the symbolic importance of the vote, historians now emphasize the continuities of women's postsuffrage behavior with the presuffrage patterns. As in the patterns of women's work, it is necessary to look at the long-range trends instead of getting sidetracked by the accomplishments or setbacks of individual decades.

New Voters

Carrie Chapman Catt

Once women won the vote, the organized women's movement stood at a crossroad. When the 19th Amendment removed the goal that had unified a fairly diverse set of organizations and individuals under the suffrage umbrella, women in public life turned their attention to a variety of causes. Many women continued the kind of political mobilization practiced in the 19th and early 20th centuries—that is, working through women's voluntary associations and networks on issue-oriented approaches to politics and social change.

One challenge posed by the winning of the vote was women's stance toward the political parties. For so long, women had influenced politics from the outside; should they now try to work their way into the inner sanctums of political power in the Democratic and Republican parties? Former suffrage leaders such as Carrie Chapman Catt (1859–1947) said yes. In this 1920 address to the newly created League of Women Voters, Catt emphatically argued that women must embrace partisan political activity as part of their new political roles.

Carrie Chapman Catt underestimated the difficulties of integration into the political system. While a few token appointments were made, it was not easy for women to move up the political ladder or exercise power in their own right. By the end of the decade, Emily Newell Blair, named the first woman vice chairman of the Democratic National Committee in 1924, was writing articles with such titles as "Discouraged Feminists in Politics." Catt's call for women to infiltrate the political parties remained an elusive goal in the 1920s and beyond.

Fellow suffragists, we have come to a turn of the road. For about sixty years we have been appealing to political parties to give up the vote, for there was no possible way of ever getting that vote until the political parties were willing that we should have it. I don't think we have ever won the vote in a single state, even by a state referendum, where one or both of the political parties have not tacitly given their consent that it should go through. Certainly ratification would not have been possible without their aid.

Well then, is it our intention to continue on the outside of those political parties where we have been for sixty years and to go on appealing for their favor as we have always been doing? Are we going to petition them as we have always done? Well, if so, what was the use of getting the vote? (Applause.)

It certainly was never any idea of the proposed League of Women Voters that we should remain out of the parties and appeal to them for the things that we wanted to do. The only way to get things in this country is to find them on the inside of the political party. (Applause.) More and more the political parties become

Source: Carrie Chapman Catt, "Political Parties and Women Voters," 1920 address to the League of Women Voters, Carrie Chapman Catt papers, Schlesinger Library, Radcliffe Institute for Advanced Study.

the power through which things are accomplished. One cannot get congressional action or legislative action unless the political parties represented there are willing, so powerful are they.

It is not a question of whether they ought to be powerful or ought not to be powerful; they are. It is the trend of the present political development and instead of appealing to them for the things you want, it is better to get on the inside and help yourself to the things you want. (Applause.) . . .

As I read the signs of the present political progress of women within the parties, you are going to have a continuation of the old familiar strife and it is just this: women must persuade men to respect and to have confidence in the capacities of women just as we have been doing for sixty odd years; and on the other hand, they must stimulate other women to forward movement and encourage them to increased self-respect. This is the same old struggle but in a new field. Because women have the vote, it doesn't follow that every man who is an election district ward or a county chairman has suddenly become convinced that women can do things as well as men. Many must be converted to that conclusion and converted by the actual political work of women.

Men will say that it is right for women to vote, but when it comes to administrative work within the party, that is still the exclusive man's business. The mass of women will be hesitant and timid and doubtful of themselves; they will be content to stand back and not use the power and the brains and the conscience that they have. They will be inclined to think that everything they find ready made in their hands is all right, no matter how wrong it may be. Women must not be content until they are as independent within the party as men are, which isn't saying much. (Laughter and applause.)

That struggle cannot be carried on from the outside. Success can only be found on the inside. For thirty years and a little more, I have worked with you in the first lap of this struggle toward woman's emancipation. I cannot lead or follow in the next lap. I do not wish to advise where I cannot follow. Younger and fresher women must do that work, and because I cannot advise and cannot follow, I only point to the fact that the battle is there, and that I hope you are not going to be such quitters as to stay on the outside and let all the reactionaries have their way on the inside. (Applause.) . . .

You won't be so welcome there, but that is the place to be. (Applause.) And if you stay there long enough and are active enough, you will see something else—the real thing in the center, with the door locked tight, and you will have a hard, long fight before you get behind that door, for there is the engine that moves the wheels of your party machinery. Nevertheless, it will be an interesting and thrilling struggle and well worth while. If you really want women's vote to count, make your way there.

Feminists Debate the Equal Rights Amendment

(Doris Stevens and Alice Hamilton)

One of the most divisive issues for political women in the immediate post-suffrage years was the Equal Rights Amendment, introduced in 1923 by Alice Paul on behalf of the National Woman's Party (NWP). The text of the proposed amendment was deceptively simple—"Equality of rights under the law shall not be denied or abridged by the United States or any State on the basis of sex"—but it caused a fundamental split between those who supported protective legislation for women workers and those who insisted that men and women be treated equally before the law.

The controversy concerned both ideology and tactics. Supporters of the amendment, primarily the National Woman's Party, which had grown out of the radical wing of the woman suffrage movement, decried any devices that artificially set women apart as a special class, such as labor legislation that limited the hours and conditions under which women could work. Women should be free, the NWP argued, to make their own choices with regard to employment and career, even at the cost of short-term losses for certain groups of women who had benefited from protective legislation through shorter hours and higher wages. Opponents of the amendment, primarily reform-minded women in groups such as the Women's Trade Union League, the National Consumers' League, and the League of Women Voters, saw legislative initiatives, especially protective legislation, as the best way to advance women's interests in industry and feared these gains would be lost under the so-called blanket amendment.

Both sides agreed that in an ideal world, men and women would enjoy such protection in the workplace, but few courts were likely to extend such benefits to men in the conservative judicial climate of the 1920s. In contrast, the Supreme Court had earlier upheld the constitutionality of an Oregon law mandating a 10-hour day for women workers in *Muller v. Oregon* (1908) on the grounds of women's supposed inequality and physical weakness due to maternity. Not exactly a stirring endorsement of women's emancipation, but to reformers half a loaf was better than none. Throughout the 1920s and 1930s, the two sides faced each other in an uneasy standoff.

In 1924, *The Forum* sponsored a debate on the issue. Doris Stevens, an Oberlin College graduate and veteran suffrage organizer, was the principal spokesperson for the National Woman's Party on this issue throughout the 1920s. In addition to her work for equal rights, she supported birth control and the right of married women to keep their own names. (She was married to political activist Dudley Field Malone.) Speaking against the amendment was Dr. Alice Hamilton, a pioneer in the field of industrial medicine and the first woman faculty member at Harvard (see Chapter 2). If you had picked up a copy of *The Forum* in 1924, which argument would you have found more convincing?

Source: "The 'Blanket' Amendment—A Debate," *The Forum* LXXII (August 1924), pp. 146–47, 152–54, 160.

I—SUFFRAGE DOES NOT GIVE EQUALITY

Doris Stevens

When women finally got the right to vote, after seventy-five years of agitation in the United States, many good citizens sighed with relief and said, "Now that's over. The woman problem is disposed of." But was it? Exactly what do women want now? Just this. They ask the same rights, in law and in custom, with which every man is now endowed through the accident of being born a male. Frail and inadequate as these rights may be, compared to those rights we would like to see enjoyed by all men, women are nevertheless still deprived of many of them. To establish equality between men and women in law and in custom is the task undertaken by the National Woman's Party, an organization composed of women diverse in political, religious, and economic faith, but united on the platform of improving the position of women.

There is not a single State in the Union in which men and women live under equal protection of the law. There is not a State which does not in some respects still reflect toward women the attitude of either the old English Common Law or the Napoleonic Code. Woman is still conceived to be in subjection to, and under the control of the husband, if married, or of the male members of the family, if unmarried. In most of the States the father and mother have been made equal guardians of their children, but many of these States still deny the mother equal rights to the earnings and services of the children. Among the poor this is often a serious handicap to the mother. In New York, fathers are preferred to mothers as controllers of the services, earnings, and real estate of the children. In two States the father can still will away the custody of the child from the mother. In two States the earnings of the wife outside the home belong to the husband. In forty States the husband owns the services of his wife in the home. In most of these States this means that the husband recovers the damages for the loss of these services, should the wife meet with an injury. A wife then cannot collect for her own suffering, for in the eyes of such laws, it is not the wife who is injured, but the husband is assumed to be injured through the loss of her services to him. More than half the States do not permit women to serve on juries. Some legislators oppose jury service for women because of "moral hazard" of deliberating in a room with men. Other legislators favor jury service for women, for it means extending to women a service which men are seldom willing to perform. In only a third of the States is prostitution a crime for the male as well as the female.

With the removal of all legal discriminations against women solely on account of sex, women will possess with men:

Equal control of their children   Equal opportunities in schools and
Equal control of their property   universities
Equal control of their earnings   Equal opportunities in government
Equal right to make contracts   service

Equal citizenship rights
Equal inheritance rights
Equal control of national, state,
  and local government

Equal opportunities in professions
  and industries
Equal pay for equal work

Of course, no law on earth can compel a woman to take her inheritance, for instance, if she prefers to give it to her brother or to some one else. But such an act would then become voluntary, not compulsory. No law can compel a woman to sit in the Cabinet or act as Ambassador if she does not wish to do so. But neither the law nor any other human-made restriction will, under a régime of equality, be able to prevent her from doing either of these things if she so chooses . . .

The National Woman's Party conceives women to be important, continuing, self-governing units of society. It conceives them to be possessed of talents and intelligences, of beauties and creative possibilities heretofore unfathomed. It proposes to do its uttermost to lift women from their present position of subjection and to put no human limits on the possibilities of their development.

To this end it seeks, as the next step, the equality of women in the law.

II—PROTECTION FOR WOMEN WORKERS

Alice Hamilton

There is a difference of opinion between two groups of women in this country with regard to the best way to secure for women freedom from discriminatory laws which hamper them as women and which survive as anachronisms in a modern society. The goal of all feminists is the same, the securing for women of as great a degree of self-determination as can be enjoyed in complex community life without detriment to others, and freedom from handicaps in the industrial struggle. The method whereby this is to be secured is the point of controversy. I belong to the group which holds that the right method is to repeal or alter one by one the laws that now hamper women or work injustice to them, and which opposes the constitutional amendment sponsored by the Woman's Party on the ground that it is too dangerously sweeping and all-inclusive. If no legislation is to be permitted except it apply to both sexes, we shall find it impossible to regulate by law the hours or wages or conditions of work of women and that would be, in my opinion, a harm far greater than the good that might be accomplished by removing certain antiquated abuses and injustices, which, bad as they are, do not injure nearly so many women as would be affected if all protective laws for working women were rendered unconstitutional.

It is a pity that words of general significance are used to describe this measure, for the result is a confusion which might be avoided by more precise terms. For instance, it is not really accurate to call this an amendment for "equal rights" for both sexes, when practically it forbids one sex to proceed along lines already tried and approved unless the other sex will come too. Organized working men in the United States long since adopted the policy of seeking improvement in hours, wages, and conditions of work through their unions and not by legislation. Women, whose labor organizations are young and feeble, have sought to secure reforms through legislation. This amendment would make it impossible for them to do so. The usual retort to that assertion is, that then the women must organize strongly, as men have done, but why? Trade unionism is a valuable weapon for the workers but it is not the only one. Women have never been strong in the trade union movement, not even in those industries which are overwhelmingly feminine, such, for instance, as the textile. Whatever be the reason for this, it is an indisputable fact, and it seems strange that women of the professional and leisure classes should wish to make it impossible for wage-earning women to use any method of procedure for their own betterment except one which they have shown themselves unable to use with any real power.

The advocates of the amendment quote in its favor working women who have lost their jobs because of laws prohibiting night work or overtime, and of course such cases do occur. Unfortunately there are always some individuals who lose out in any group action. The bitterest opponent of trade unionism is the highly skilled, exceptionally capable workman with an individualistic outlook on life, who resents any control from the group and wants to be let alone to work when and how he pleases. That his grievances are often real, nobody can deny, but if we are to live in a community, the greatest good to the greatest number must outweigh the rights of the individual. For every woman linotypist who wishes to take night work on a newspaper, there must be hundreds of textile mill operatives who suffer from the compulsion to work on the night shift. For one supervisor or forewoman who wishes to work overtime, there must be hundreds of saleswomen and telephone girls who long to be freed from the necessity of so doing. It would seem that the safer, if slower, way would be to work out exemptions, so far as possible, in such legislation, to provide for those women who really do wish for entire freedom in making their bargains and are entitled to it . . .

In Holland, I am told, the two sexes have recently been put on an equality in industry, not by taking privileges away from the women, but by extending them to the men. Holland is an old country, which has long been used to labor legislation. I cannot believe that we in the United States are nearing that point very fast, though I should like to think so. Meantime, until we reach it, I must, as a practical person, familiar with the great, inarticulate body of working women, reiterate my belief that they are largely helpless, that they have very special needs which unaided they cannot attain, and that it would be a crime for the country to pass legislation which would not only make it impossible to better their lot in the near future but would even deprive them of the small measure of protection they now enjoy.

Generational Conflicts

Dorothy Dunbar Bromley

One key to understanding the 1920s is a generational approach. Following the lead of social scientists from the 1920s such as Lorinne Pruette, it is possible to identify at least three generations of women, all of which coexisted (somewhat uneasily, as this selection suggests) in the decade. First, there were the old feminist pioneers, those activists whose lifelong struggle to increase women's options had (at least in the eyes of younger women) deeply embittered them toward men. Then came a middle generation, women in their 40s and 50s in the 1920s, who had struggled successfully for woman suffrage and women's professional advancement; while still "woman-identified," they were somewhat less strident in their antagonism toward men.

It was the third generation, the consciously modern women in their 20s and 30s, who captured the public imagination in the decade and have continued to intrigue historians ever since. Journalist Dorothy Dunbar Bromley's 1927 article, "Feminist—New Style," wittily captures the differing perspectives between old and young. Young women wanted little to do with the older generations, whom they characterized as too bitter toward men, lacking style, and generally unsuitable as role models. The new women of the 1920s had different agendas: instead of social reform, they looked to economic independence and professional advancement; instead of bonding with other women, they announced that they much preferred the company of men. Now a life that did not include marriage, children, and a career was seen as incomplete. The key to understanding this new woman (and these are only broad generalizations) is to recognize her highly individualistic approach to both personal and professional life. She would succeed and fail on her own; the women's movement was no longer necessary. Another characteristic of these new-style feminists was the relentlessly white and middle-class character of their self-images and goals; such lifestyles had scant relevance to immigrant, minority, or working-class women. Such personal and professional liberation remained an option only for a privileged elite.

The Queen is dead. Long live the Queen!

Is it not high time that we laid the ghost of the so-called feminist?

"Feminism" has become a term of opprobrium to the modern young woman. For the word suggests either the old school of fighting feminists who wore flat heels and had very little feminine charm, or the current species who antagonize men with their constant clamor about maiden names, equal rights, woman's place in the world, and many another cause . . . *ad infinitum*. Indeed, if a blundering male assumes that a young woman is a feminist simply because she happens to have a job or a profession of her own, she will be highly—and quite justifiably—insulted: for

Source: Dorothy Bromley, "Feminist—New Style," *Harper's* CLV (October 1927), pp. 552–60. Copyright © 1927 by *Harper's Magazine*. All rights reserved. Reproduced from the October issue by special permission.

the word evokes the antithesis of what she flatters herself to be. Yet she and her kind can hardly be dubbed "old-fashioned" women. What *are* they, then?

The pioneer feminists were hard-hitting individuals, and the modern young woman admires them for their courage—even while she judges them for their zealotry and their inartistic methods. Furthermore, she pays all honor to them, for they fought her battle. But *she* does not want to wear their mantle (indeed, she thinks they should have been buried in it), and she has to smile at those women who wear it to-day—with the battle-cry still on their lips. The worst of the fight is over, yet this second generation of feminists are still throwing hand grenades. They bear a grudge against men, either secretly or openly; they make an issue of little things as well as big; they exploit their sex for the sake of publicity; they rant about equality when they might better prove their ability. Yet it is these women— the ones who do more talking than acting—on whom the average man focuses his microscope when he sits down to dissect the "new woman." For like his less educated brethren, he labors under the delusion that there are only two types of women, the creature of instinct who is content to be a "home-maker" and the "sterile intellectual" who cares solely about "expressing herself"—home and children be damned.

But what of the constantly increasing group of young women in their twenties and thirties who are the truly modern ones, those who admit that a full life calls for marriage and children as well as a career? These women if they launch upon marriage are keen to make a success of it and an art of child-rearing. But *at the same time* they are moved by an inescapable inner compulsion to be individuals in their own right. And in this era of simplified housekeeping they see their opportunity, for it is obvious that a woman who plans intelligently can salvage some time for her own pursuits. Furthermore, they are convinced that they will be better wives and mothers for the breadth they gain from functioning outside the home. In short, they are highly conscious creatures who feel obliged to plumb their own resources to the very depths, despite the fact that they are under no delusions as to the present inferior status of their sex in most fields of endeavor.

Numbers of these honest, spirited young women have made themselves heard in article and story. But since men must have things pointed out to them in black and white, we beg leave to enunciate the tenets of the modern woman's credo. Let us call her "Feminist—New Style." . . .

In brief, Feminist—New Style reasons that if she is economically independent, and if she has, to boot, a vital interest in some work of her own she will have given as few hostages to Fate as it is humanly possible to give. Love may die, and children may grow up, but one's work goes on forever.

Third Tenet. She will not, however, live for her job alone, for she considers that a woman who talks and thinks only shop has just as narrow a horizon as the housewife who talks and thinks only husband and children—perhaps more so, for the latter may have a deeper understanding of human nature. She will therefore refuse to give up all of her personal interests, year in and year out, for the sake of her work. In this respect she no doubt will fall short of the masculine idea of commercial success, for the simple reason that she has never felt the economic compulsion which drives men on to build up fortunes for the sake of their growing families.

Yet she is not one of the many women who look upon their jobs as tolerable meal-tickets or as interesting pastimes to be dropped whenever they may wish. On the contrary, she takes great pride in becoming a vital factor in whatever enterprise she has chosen, and she therefore expects to work long hours when the occasion demands.

But rather than make the mistake that some women do of domesticating their jobs, *i.e.*, burying all of their affections and interests in them, or the mistake that many men make of milking their youth dry for the sake of building up a fortune to be spent in a fatigued middle-age, she will proceed on the principle that a person of intelligence and energy can attain a fair amount of success—perhaps even a high degree of success—by the very virtue of living a well-balanced life, as well as by working with concentration.

Fourth Tenet. Nor has she become hostile to the other sex in the course of her struggle to orient herself. On the contrary, she frankly likes men and is grateful to more than a few for the encouragement and help they have given her.

In the business and professional worlds, for instance, Feminist   New Style has observed that more and more men are coming to accord women as much responsibility as they show themselves able to carry. She and her generation have never found it necessary to bludgeon their way, and she is inclined to think that certain of the pioneers would have got farther if they had relied on their ability rather than on their militant methods. To tell the truth, she enjoys working with men, more than with women, for their methods are more direct and their view larger, and she finds that she can deal with them on a basis of frank comradeship.

When she meets men socially she is not inclined to air her knowledge and argue about woman's right to a place in the sun. On the contrary, she either talks with a man because he has ideas that interest her or because she finds it amusing to flirt with him—and she will naturally find it doubly amusing if the flirtation involves the swift interplay of wits. She will not waste many engagements on a dull-witted man, although it must be admitted that she finds fewer men with stagnant minds than she does women.

When all is said and done, most of the men of her world are such a decent likable lot that she is hard put to it to understand the sex antagonism which actuates certain "advanced" women who secretly look upon their husbands—and all men—as their natural enemies from whom they must wrest every privilege and advantage possible. Such tactics are a futile waste of energy; now that men have admitted that women can be valuable partners not only in the home, but also in business and civic life, the best thing for women to do is to prove their value.

Fifth Tenet. By the same corollary, Feminist—New Style professes no loyalty to women *en masse,* although she staunchly believes in individual women. Surveying her sex as a whole, she finds their actions petty, their range of interests narrow, their talk trivial and repetitious. As for those who set themselves up as leaders of the sex, they are either strident creatures of so little ability and balance that they have won no chance to "express themselves" (to use their own hackneyed phrase) in a manmade world; or they are brilliant, restless individuals who too often battle for women's rights for the sake of personal glory.

But when a woman in the professions or in public life proves herself really capable, Feminist—New Style will be the first to cheer, and to help her along still farther, by proffering her own support and co-operation. Indeed, she feels that there is to-day a stronger bond among thinking women than ever before . . .

Seventh Tenet. Empty slogans seem to Feminist—New Style just as bad taste as masculine dress and manners. They serve only to prolong the war between the sexes and to prevent women from learning to think straight. Take these, for instance, "Keep your maiden name." "Come out of the kitchen." "Never darn a sock." After all, what's in a name or in a sock? Madame Curie managed to become one of the world's geniuses even though she suffered the terrible handicap of bearing her husband's name, and it is altogether likely that she darned a sock or two of Monsieur Curie's when there was no servant at hand to do it.

"Keep your maiden name," the slogan which the members of the Lucy Stone League cry from the housetops so lustily, would seem the most inane of all. Will someone kindly tell us why these women don't prove their individuality—and their independence of their husbands—by some sort of real achievement? And would it not be more consistent for them to require that every member not only keep her maiden name but *that she support herself?* . . .

Finally, Feminist—New Style proclaims that men and children shall no longer circumscribe her world, although they may constitute a large part of it. She is intensely self-conscious whereas the feminists were intensely sex-conscious. Aware of possessing a mind, she takes a keen pleasure in using that mind for some definite purpose; and also in learning to think clearly and cogently against a background of historical and scientific knowledge. She aspires to understand the meaning of the 20th century as she sees it expressed in the skyscrapers, the rapid pace of city life, the expressionistic drama, the abstract conceptions of art, the new music, the Joycian novel. She is acutely conscious that she is being carried along in the current of these sweeping forces, that she and her sex are in the vanguard of change. She knows that it is her American, her twentieth-century birthright to emerge from a creature of instinct into a full-fledged individual who is capable of molding her own life. And in this respect she holds that she is becoming man's equal.

If this be treason, gentlemen, make the most of it.

Anxious Mothers Write the Children's Bureau

The reality of most women's lives in the 1920s was not shaped by the privilege of creating new feminist lifestyles or winning promotions in the world of business and the professions, but by a struggle to fulfill their roles as wives and mothers. This was no easy task. In addition to the problems generated by inadequate income and poverty, women faced very real fears about maternal and infant mortality. Between 1900 and 1930, approximately 60 white women and more than 100 black women died for every 10,000 live births; infant mortality was also unacceptably high.

After 1912, mothers had a new place to turn: the Children's Bureau of the Department of Labor. Created in response to pressure from settlement leader Lillian Wald and activist Florence Kelley, the Children's Bureau saw saving children as a form of social reform. Its widely read pamphlets, *Infant Care* (1913) and *Prenatal Care* (1914), offered mothers scientific information as well as commonsense advice on keeping themselves and their children healthy.

The Children's Bureau took on new responsibilities in the 1920s, when it administered the Sheppard-Towner Maternity and Infancy Protection Act. This pioneering piece of public health legislation supported the distribution of information on nutrition and hygiene, funded conferences, established well-baby clinics, and provided prenatal care for women in rural areas. The Children's Bureau boasted these programs saved 60,000 children before the program was allowed to lapse by a conservative Congress in 1929.

Individual women were just glad to know that a branch of the government was interested in their concerns and problems. Reflecting the modern tendency to look to experts for advice, women from diverse backgrounds wrote to the Children's Bureau with questions about child care, birth control (which the staff could not endorse for political reasons), infant hygiene, and other health-related issues. Letters such as the three included here offer a view of daily life in the 1920s, especially women's concerns about their own health and the health of their offspring.

Mrs. M. A., Minnesota
(October 19, 1921)

Dear Miss Lathrop:—

Two or three years ago, I wrote you for some pamphlets on "Care of the Baby" etc. I received them O.K. and found them very useful. But after my last Babe was two years old I gave away one or two of the pamphlets to a relative who has since gone away.

I'm to have another Babe in Jan. and I want very much a pamphlet of some kind containing instructions on the first things to do when the Baby arrives, the tying of naval cord etc. We are 7 1/2 miles from a Dr. and tho that isn't far in summer when cars are running, it's quite a distance in winter, when roads may be bad and one must depend on teams to get the Doctor when needed. I want to get some practical directions so that a woman could do all the necessary things if the Dr. was not in time. I thot you would have the latest and best information and would know just what to send me.

My last Baby was born during the War and a flu epidemic, and the two Doctors in our county were both out, miles away when we wanted them. Neither one got back to the office until our Babe was several hours old. I am usually sick just a short time, 3 1/2 hours only with our first boy. The Dr. arrived half an hour too late. The second boy received the Dr.'s attention as there was time, but not the 3rd.

Source: From Molly Ladd-Taylor, *Raising a Baby the Government Way: Mothers' Letters to the Children's Bureau 1915–1932*, pp. 55–56, 112–14, 175–79. Reprinted by permission.

Had no Dr. at all, but being a more experienced Mother and having my mother and a neighbor Lady with me, we got along fine. I have 3 boys.

I have been reading quite a bit about the work of the Children's Bureau. Naturally, I am much interested in the things being done for children. I consider them the Nations most important asset, tho I sadly fear that some of our politicians are blind to that fact. In the course of a few years the Babies of today will be directing affairs. How important that they should have some consideration. I wish to say that I appreciate your work very much, tho I am only one of the many commonplace "Ma's." I wish you the best of success, and hope that most of us will be able to profit by the needful information obtained thru your office. I'm too far away to "shake hands" so I'll close by signing myself

Sincerely Your Friend.

*   *   *

Mrs. W. M. (February 10, 1925)

Dear Friend:—

I am enclosing a stamp for an answer & am taking the liberty to ask you for advice. You have helped me before & told me I could write & ask your advice anytime.

I am pregnant a little over 6 months. I had a longing for strawberries for breakfast one day; I thought about them before I got up, and while in the bathroom com[b]ing my hair, I wiped out the corners of my eyes with my fingers. I thought, well, it doesn't matter even if I haven't eaten any strawberries yet. I asked a neighbor about it, & she told me I sure must of marked the baby. Is this possible? She told me if you have an appetite for anything & don't eat it, & you put your hand on your face, or scratch your face, that it will mark the baby sure. I'm just worried sick. Its on my mind all the time. I wake up nights & think of things to eat; it seems I just cant get that off my mind & what can you do when you long for watermelon or mush melon, or anything out of season? I cant get these things now. Can that mark or harm the baby in any way? Oh please tell me what to do. All these thoughts about marking the baby when you don't eat what you think of, or long for, just drive me frantic. I think of one thing, & then I think of something else, but I try to overcome these thoughts, & then I worry every time I wash or put my hand to my face that I'm marking the baby because I couldn't get or didn't eat what I longed for last. Does this come from worry? I never worried about these things the first few mo[n]ths, but her[e] of late I'm just sick from worry. I couldn't tell this to anyone else but you, as I have no mother, & no one else cares. I have kept it to myself, but I just had to go to some one. & I'm sure you will help me. I have your book on "Prenatal Care," but it doesn't say anything about longing for things to eat, so I just had to write and ask your advice. Thanking you very much. Please keep this confidentially. I am.

*   *   *

Mrs. A. E., Minnesota
(August 10, 1932)

Dear Sirs:

About six years ago I made the acquaintance of govt publications Infant Care, Prenatal Care etc. This book Infant Care did me more good than the Dr. I had at the time my baby was born. I did not have a great deal of money and the information in these booklets was [concise] and helpful. I just felt I should write and tell you how grateful I was that one can get even this little bit of free advice from our govt. We should be able to get more medical help and advice from our gov't regarding babies and child raising.

Our Gov't should have a check on doctors. We should be able to write to the Dept. of Labor and get a list of certified doctors who are capable and sincere about handling child birth. I feel that I should write of my experience. In these publications the advice is consult a reputable or family physician. I should like to ask you how one knows who *is* a reputable physician? What check other than public opinion is there on a doctor who is not reputable? Do you realize that doctors are so well organized and the profession has such ethics between themselves that it is almost impossible to check a doctor for malpractice? It requires money and is very hard to prove, so that medical men do about as they please. Is this the way it should be?

I was cared for when my son was born by Dr. B. He is supposed to be a reputable surgeon and qualified for maternity work. I was in the hospital two weeks at the time of his birth. I placed myself under his care about several months before he was born. He never advised a change of diet but I went from 110 lbs to 158 lbs the year he was born. I had a very hard birth, was torn and had three stitches, two surface and one deep tore the floor of the womb. When I left the hospital, Miss L., his head nurse, removed the stitches after they had been in two weeks. Then I went home. Dr. B. did not tell me to come back for further examination later but just let me go. I had milk fever while in the hospital and breast trouble. Then after I got home I was in bed for about two weeks with milk fever. Nothing was done about this . . .

Later we moved to St. Paul and a more competent doctor examined me. He said I had not been properly cared for after Child birth and that I was torn. He scraped my womb and took stitches. My health has improved [but] my nervous system is badly shattered. I am sore all through my back and shoulders and the back of my neck. I haven't slept real well for a long time. Now I will never be like I was if I had been properly cared for.

I graduated from a state teachers college and taught successfully four years. I had a very fine record. My son is now healthy and very intelligent, and it is hard for me to bring him up because of this trouble. I would have enjoyed raising him very much if I had stayed well. I came from a family of eight children, was the oldest girl, and helped to raise a family of intelligent brothers and sisters. I worked and saved very hard to get my education. My memory is impaired and my time sense seems to be gone, rendering my accuracy and ability a lot less than it used to be. I am carrying on doing the best that I can.

I want to say again that those government publications were a great consolation and help to me. I have told many about them. When one hasn't much money these things are greatly appreciated.

I have suffered endless torture and unnecessary worry and pain because of this doctors carelessness or ignorance, I don't know which. Life for me will never be as full. I have no come back on him. This same man had a verdict rendered against him on a malpractice case for bone setting some time ago. Now there seems to be nothing but public opinion to combat such practice. This Dr. B. I believe is in the blue book of surgeons.

Doctors all over our land are performing illegal operations too, and there seems to be no way of checking that. All it takes is ready cash for a woman or girl to relieve herself of the responsibility of a baby. This cheapens motherhood, ruins womanhood and encourages immorality. Operations of all kinds are emphasized because there is money in that, but maternity work is so neglected and a great many doctors know so little about baby raising that any old lady who has raised a family can give you better advice.

I have been wanting to put these facts before some body or organization with power and authority for a long time. I feel it my duty. Kindly read this and use your influence to better conditions in this respect. I think a gov't check on hospitals, doctors and operations is coming some day and it will be a good thing. Often times patients are unnecessarily held in hospitals after having operations for a longer period than necessary just to run up a bill. Every thing is done so underhanded and secretly among doctors and nurses that it is very hard for a patient to get a square deal.

This comes from the heart and soul of one who has suffered hell on earth because of carelessness and neglect by a doctor in the medical profession. I was an intelligent person seeking all the advice and knowledge I could get about babies and baby raising before my baby came. I was very pleased to get these government publications. I would have come out better, but your publications fail to tell how to detect a reputable physician, and I am marred for life because of this. The Gov't should have a list of qualified tried and true maternity doctors that a prospective mother could get by sending for it. This should go along with the publication. Please consider this suggestion.

Sincerely yours.

[P.S.] Kindly advise me what I can do in a case like this if there is no help for me. Please use your influence to prevent further ruination of mothers by such practice.

Women of the Ku Klux Klan

Anxiety of another kind fueled the revival of the Ku Klux Klan in the 1920s, anxiety over the threat that growing ethnic and racial pluralism posed to the traditional cultural domination of white Protestant Americans. From 1880 to 1920, more than 23 million people emigrated to the United States, many of them Jews and Catholics, most from peasant stock. Senator William Bruce

Source: Women of the Ku Klux Klan, (Md.) Records. Schlesinger Library, Radcliffe Institute, Harvard University. Reprinted by permission.

of Maryland called them "indigestible lumps" in the "national stomach," implying that the nation could never absorb their large numbers and different customs. Such nativist sentiments, which were widely shared, helped fuel the revival of the Ku Klux Klan. Unlike its earlier Reconstruction-era incarnation, the KKK of the 1920s did not limit its harassment to blacks—Catholics and Jews were targets as well. At its height in 1925, between 3 million and 4 million Americans belonged to the KKK.

Those membership figures included approximately 500,000 women who belonged to a separate but quite powerful organization called the Women of the Ku Klux Klan (WKKK), which was established in 1923. The group had its own creed (or Kreed, as the document spells it—the group liked alliteration), bylaws, membership standards, and penalties for not living up to WKKK standards. One perk of membership was that every member in good standing got a free white robe and helmet.

Women who joined the WKKK shared many similarities with male members, but they also pursued their own distinctive political agenda that combined racism and nativism with a commitment to equal rights for white Protestant women. Klan women used the organization to exercise political power and they knew how to get out the vote; more informally, they were not shy about organizing whispering campaigns against interlopers or outsiders in their communities. They also knew how to have a good time, and many later remembered the WKKK as a splendid opportunity for friendship and solidarity with like-minded women rather than as a racist, xenophobic organization. The WKKK was so well integrated into daily life in communities across the country that one member later recalled it as "just a celebration . . . a way of growing up."

The KKK of the 1920s attracted members in both urban and rural areas throughout the country. These documents are from Maryland and date from about 1927. By then the Klan was in decline, the victim of internal rivalries, much-publicized scandals, and an ebbing of nativist sentiment nationwide. The Ku Klux Klan reemerged in the 1950s and then again in the 1980s, but women played only minor roles.

KU KLUX KREED

(Original Kreed Revised)

We, the Order of the Women of the Ku Klux Klan, reverently acknowledge the majesty and supremacy of Almighty God and recognize His goodness and providence through Jesus Christ, Our Lord.

Recognizing our relation to the Government of the United States of America, the supremacy of its Constitution, the Union of States thereunder, and the Constitutional Laws thereof, we shall ever be devoted to the sublime principles of a pure Americanism, and valiant in the defense of its ideals and institutions.

We avow the distinction between the races of mankind as decreed by the Creator, and we shall ever be true to the maintenance of White Supremacy and strenuously oppose any compromise thereof.

We appreciate the value of practical, fraternal relationship among people of kindred thought, purpose and ideals and the benefits accruing therefrom; we shall faithfully devote ourselves to the practice of an honorable clannishness that the life of each may be a constant blessing to others.

"Non Silba Sed Anthar."

CONSTITUTION AND LAWS
OF THE
WOMEN OF THE KU KLUX KLAN
(INCORPORATED)

IMPERIAL HEADQUARTERS, INVISIBLE EMPIRE

Little Rock, Arkansas, U.S.A.

ARTICLE I.
APPELLATION AND GOVERNMENT

SECTION 1. To the name of the Society, Ku Klux Klan, has been prefixed the words "Women of the," and therefor forever hereafter this society shall be known as "WOMEN OF THE KU KLUX KLAN," and is hereinafter referred to as "This Order." It is and shall continue to be a Patriotic, Militaristic, Benevolent, Ritualistic, Social, Fraternal and Historical Order or Society.

SEC. 2. The government of this Order shall ever be military in character, especially in its executive management and control; and no legislative enactment or constitutional amendment hereafter shall encroach upon, affect or change this fundamental principle of the Invisible Empire.

SEC. 3. The government of this Order shall be vested primarily in the Imperial Commander, as Commander-in-Chief, who shall be supreme within the restrictions of this constitution, and as otherwise provided, and whose decisions, decrees, edicts, mandates, rulings and instructions shall be of full authority and unquestionably recognized and respected by each and every Woman of the Invisible Empire.

ARTICLE II.
OBJECTS AND PURPOSES

SECTION 1. The objects of this Order shall be to unite white female persons, native-born Gentile citizens of the United States of America, who owe no allegiance of any nature or degree to any foreign government, nation, institution, sect, ruler, person or people; whose morals are good; whose reputations and vocations are respectable; whose habits are exemplary; who are of sound minds and 18 years or more of age, under a common oath into a Sisterhood of strict regulation; to cultivate and promote patriotism toward our Civil Government; to practice an honorable clannishness toward each other; to exemplify a practical benevolence; to shield the sanctity of the home and the chastity of womanhood; to maintain forever white supremacy; to teach and faithfully inculcate a high spiritual philosophy through an exalted ritualism, and by a practical devotion to conserve, protect and maintain the distinctive institutions, rights, privileges, principles, traditions and ideals of a pure Americanism.

SEC. 2. To create and maintain an institution by which the present and succeeding generations shall commemorate the great sacrifice, chivalric service and imperishable achievements of the Ku Klux Klan and the Women of the Reconstruction period of American History, to the end that justice and honor be done the sacred memory of those who wrought through our mystic society during that period, and that their valiant accomplishments be not lost to posterity; to perpetuate their faithful courage, noble spirit, peerless principles and faultless ideals; to hold sacred and make effective their spiritual purpose in this and future generations, that they be rightly vindicated before the world by a revelation of the whole truth.

SEC. 3. This Order is an institution of Humanity, Justice and Patriotism, embodying in its genius and principles all that is noble in sentiment, generous in Womanhood, and patriotic in purpose. Its peculiar objects are:

First, to protect the weak, the innocent and the defenseless from the indignities, wrongs and outrages of the lawless, the violent and the brutal; to relieve the injured and the oppressed; to succor the suffering and unfortunate, especially widows and orphans.

Second, to protect and defend the Constitution of the United States of America, and all laws passed in conformity thereto, and to protect the states and the people thereof from all invasion of their rights by any agency whatsoever.

Third, to aid and assist in the execution of all constitutional laws, and to preserve the honor and dignity of the state by opposing tyranny, in any and every form or degree, from any and every source whatsoever, by a fearless and faithful administration of justice through due process of law; and to meet promptly and properly every behest of duty without fear and without reproach.

ARTICLE IV.

MEMBERSHIP

SECTION 1. The qualifications for membership in this Order shall be: An applicant must be a white female Gentile person, a native-born citizen of the United States of America who owes no allegiance of any nature or degree whatsoever to any foreign government, nation, institution, sect, ruler, prince, potentate, people or person; she must have attained the age of 18 years, be of sound mind, good character; of commendable reputation and respectable vocation, a believer in the tenets of the Christian Religion, and one whose allegiance, loyalty and devotion to the Government of the United States of America in all things is unquestionable. She must have been a resident within the jurisdiction of the Klan to which she applies for at least six months immediately preceding the date of her application for citizenship, provided, however, that special dispensation may be granted by the Realm Commander in organized Realms or by the Imperial Commander in unorganized Realms, to waive this condition.

SEC. 2. Applications for membership in this Order, before a charter is granted, must be on a regular charter petition by charter applicants of a Klan, and on a regular application blank after a Klan has been chartered. The applicant must state whether she has ever applied for membership in this Order, and such application made to a chartered Klan must be endorsed by at least two Klanswomen, or by a Kleagle, or by the Imperial Commander of this Order.

SEC. 3. The "Donation" is given by an applicant and accepted by this Order as a donation to its propagation and general fund and not in the sense of purchasing membership in this Order by the applicant, and this donation must accompany each application for citizenship. The Donation in the organization of Klans shall be Ten Dollars ($10.00). Upon naturalization, the applicant will be furnished one robe and helmet for her free use so long as she remains a member in good standing. Effective July 1, 1927.

SEC. 4. All women who were wives of men who served as members of the original Ku Klux Klan or rendered direct service thereto, or who were so connected with similar organizations during the Reconstruction period of American History, shall be admitted to full fellowship in this Order without payment of Donation or dues; provided, however, they individually qualify for membership under the requirements of Section 1 of this Article.

SEC. 5. An applicant's qualifications must be known before she is accepted for membership in this Order. Great care must be exercised on the part of a Kleagle or a Klan in ascertaining an applicant's qualifications under Section 1 of this Article.

ARTICLE XIX.
OFFENSES AND PENALTIES

SECTION 1. Offenses against this Order shall be divided into two classes—major offenses and minor offenses.

SEC. 2. *Major Offenses:* Major offenses shall consist of: (1) Treason against the United States of America; (2) Violating the oath of allegiance to this Order or any supplementary oath or obligation thereof; (3) Disrespect of virtuous womanhood; (4) Violation of the Constitution or the laws of this Order; conspiring against the interest and prosperity of this Order or any Klanswoman in any way or being a party thereto, or being a party to any move, conspiracy or organization whose existence is antagonistic or injurious to or is an imitation of this Order; whose name, style or title is a colorable imitation of this Order; swearing allegiance to or otherwise becoming a citizen or subject of any nation, government or institution of any nature or classification whatsoever, or any ruler or potentate, prince or person of any court whatever that is foreign to or is inimical to the government of the United States of America and its established institutions, or aiding or abetting such government, nation, institution, ruler, potentate, prince or person against the interest, well-being or dignity of the United States of America or the distinctive institutions of its government; violating the By-laws of a Klan of this Order; the habitual use of profane language or vulgarity during a Klonklave or during an assembly of Klanswomen just prior thereto; (5) Being responsible for the polluting of Caucasian blood through miscegenation, or the commission of any act unworthy of a Klanswoman; (6) The repeated commission of a minor offense shall in itself constitute a major offense.

SEC. 3. *Minor Offenses:* Minor offenses shall consist of use of profane language or vulgarity during a klonklave or in an assembly of Klanswomen just prior thereto, or committing any other act which might operate against the best interests of the Klan or Klanswomen; refusal or failure to obey the mandates, rules, edicts and orders of the Excellent Commander or the Klan, or the failure or refusal on the part of any Klanswoman, upon request of the Excellent Commander, to respond to any summons issued by her, unless she has a providential excuse; and failure or refusal to surrender her credentials when called for by the Excellent Commander.

The Harlem Renaissance

Nella Larsen

A different kind of cultural affirmation occurred in the black community of Harlem in the 1920s. The Harlem Renaissance was an artistic movement of young writers and artists who broke with the older, genteel traditions of black literature to champion racial pride and cultural identity in the midst of white society. It drew on the talents of both men and women: Claude McKay and Zora Neale Hurston, Langston Hughes and Jessie Fauset, Countee Cullen and Augusta Savage. In this group belongs Nella Larsen, best known for her novels *Quicksand* (1928) and *Passing* (1929).

In this excerpt from *Passing,* Larsen has just introduced her two protagonists, Irene Redfield and Clare Kendry, childhood acquaintances who meet again by chance on the rooftop of a Chicago hotel on a hot summer day. Clare is passing as a white woman, not just in social situations but in her marriage to a white man. Irene, who has also at times passed for white, is curious about how it feels. Their friendship rekindled, the novel shifts back to Harlem, ending when the defiant and unconventional Clare falls to her death in ambiguous circumstances while Irene stands by.

Nella Larsen was born in 1891 in Chicago to a Danish mother and black West Indian father who died when she was young. After an unsuccessful marriage, she studied nursing and later became a librarian in the children's division of the New York Public Library, which is when she began to write fiction. The success of Larsen's two novels won her a prestigious Guggenheim fellowship in 1930 to research a third novel set in Spain and France, but that book was never published. Around that time she was accused of plagiarizing a short story and her career never rebounded after the controversy. She returned to her nursing career at a Brooklyn hospital, where she worked until she retired. When she died in 1964, no obituaries marked her passing. With the revival of interest in the Harlem Renaissance caused by the civil

Source: From Nella Larsen, *Quicksand,* 1929, in Deborah E. McDowell, ed. *Quicksand and Passing,* 1986, pp. 157–60. Reprinted by permission.

rights and feminist movements of the 1960s and 1970s, Nella Larsen found
a new audience.

The truth was, she was curious. There were things that she wanted to ask Clare
Kendry. She wished to find out about this hazardous business of "passing," this
breaking away from all that was familiar and friendly to take one's chances in another environment, not entirely strange, perhaps, but certainly not entirely
friendly. What, for example, one did about background, how one accounted for
oneself. And how one felt when one came into contact with other Negroes. But
she couldn't. She was unable to think of a single question that in its context or its
phrasing was not too frankly curious, if not actually impertinent.

As if aware of her desire and her hesitation, Clare remarked, thoughtfully:
"You know, 'Rene, I've often wondered why more coloured girls, girls like you
and Margaret Hammer and Esther Dawson and—oh, lots of others—never
'passed' over. It's such a frightfully easy thing to do. If one's the type, all that's
needed is a little nerve."

"What about background? Family, I mean. Surely you can't just drop down on
people from nowhere and expect them to receive you with open arms, can you?"

"Almost," Clare asserted. "You'd be surprised, 'Rene, how much easier that
is with white people than with us. Maybe because there are so many more of
them, or maybe because they are secure and so don't have to bother. I've never
quite decided."

Irene was inclined to be incredulous. "You mean that you didn't have to explain where you came from? It seems impossible."

Clare cast a glance of repressed amusement across the table at her. "As a matter of fact, I didn't. Though I suppose under any other circumstances I might have
had to provide some plausible tale to account for myself. I've a good imagination,
so I'm sure I could have done it quite creditably, and credibly. But it wasn't necessary. There were my aunts, you see, respectable and authentic enough for anything or anybody."

"I see. They were 'passing' too."

"No. They weren't. They were white."

"Oh!" And in the next instant it came back to Irene that she had heard this
mentioned before; by her father, or, more likely, her mother. They were Bob
Kendry's aunts. He had been a son of their brother's, on the left hand. A wild oat.

"They were nice old ladies," Clare explained, "very religious and as poor as
church mice. That adored brother of theirs, my grandfather, got through every
penny they had after he'd finished his own little bit."

Clare paused in her narrative to light another cigarette. Her smile, her expression, Irene noticed, was faintly resentful.

"Being good Christians," she continued, "when dad came to his tipsy end,
they did their duty and gave me a home of sorts. I was, it was true, expected to
earn my keep by doing all the housework, and most of the washing. But do you
realize, 'Rene, that if it hadn't been for them, I shouldn't have had a home in the
world?"

Irene's nod and little murmur were comprehensive, understanding.

Clare made a small mischievous grimace and proceeded. "Besides, to their notion, hard labour was good for me. I had Negro blood and they belonged to the generation that had written and read long articles headed: 'Will the Blacks Work?' Too, they weren't quite sure that the good God hadn't intended the sons and daughters of Ham to sweat because he had poked fun at old man Noah once when he had taken a drop too much. I remember the aunts telling me that that old drunkard had cursed Ham and his sons for all time."

Irene laughed. But Clare remained quite serious.

"It was more than a joke, I assure you, 'Rene. It was a hard life for a girl of sixteen. Still, I had a roof over my head, and food, and clothes—such as they were. And there were the Scriptures, and talks on morals and thrift and industry and the loving-kindness of the good Lord."

"Have you ever stopped to think, Clare," Irene demanded, "how much unhappiness and downright cruelty are laid to the loving-kindness of the Lord? And always by His most ardent followers, it seems."

"Have I?" Clare exclaimed. "It, they, made me what I am today. For, of course, I was determined to get away, to be a person and not a charity or a problem, or even a daughter of the indiscreet Ham. Then, too, I wanted things. I knew I wasn't bad-looking and that I could 'pass.' You can't know, 'Rene, how, when I used to go over to the south side, I used almost to hate all of you. You had all the things I wanted and never had had. It made me all the more determined to get them, and others. Do you, can you understand what I felt?"

She looked up with a pointed and appealing effect, and, evidently finding the sympathetic expression on Irene's face sufficient answer, went on. "The aunts were queer. For all their Bibles and praying and ranting about honesty, they didn't want anyone to know that their darling brother had seduced—ruined, they called it—a Negro girl. They could excuse the ruin, but they couldn't forgive the tarbrush. They forbade me to mention Negroes to the neighbours, or even to mention the south side. You may be sure that I didn't. I'll bet they were good and sorry afterwards."

She laughed and the ringing bells in her laugh had a hard metallic sound.

"When the chance to get away came, that omission was of great value to me. When Jack, a schoolboy acquaintance of some people in the neighbourhood, turned up from South America with untold gold, there was no one to tell him that I was coloured, and many to tell him about the severity and the religiousness of Aunt Grace and Aunt Edna. You can guess the rest. After he came, I stopped slipping off to the south side and slipped off to meet him instead. I couldn't manage both. In the end I had no great difficulty in convincing him that it was useless to talk marriage to the aunts. So on the day that I was eighteen, we went off and were married. So that's that. Nothing could have been easier."

"Yes, I do see that for you it was easy enough. By the way! I wonder why they didn't tell father that you were married. He went over to find out about you when you stopped coming over to see us. I'm sure they didn't tell him. Not that you were married."

Clare Kendry's eyes were bright with tears that didn't fall. "Oh, how lovely! To have cared enough about me to do that. The dear sweet man! Well, they couldn't tell him because they didn't know it. I took care of that, for I couldn't be sure that those consciences of theirs wouldn't begin to work on them afterwards and make them let the cat out of the bag. The old things probably thought I was living in sin, wherever I was. And it would be about what they expected."

An amused smile lit the lovely face for the smallest fraction of a second. After a little silence she said soberly: "But I'm sorry if they told your father so. That was something I hadn't counted on."

"I'm not sure that they did," Irene told her. "He didn't say so, anyway."

"He wouldn't, 'Rene dear. Not your father."

"Thanks, I'm sure he wouldn't."

"But you've never answered my question. Tell me, honestly, haven't you ever thought of 'passing'?"

Irene answered promptly: "No. Why should I?" And so disdainful was her voice and manner that Clare's face flushed and her eyes glinted. Irene hastened to add: "You see, Clare, I've everything I want. Except, perhaps, a little more money."

At that Clare laughed, her spark of anger vanished as quickly as it had appeared. "Of course," she declared, "that's what everybody wants, just a little more money, even the people who have it. And I must say I don't blame them. Money's awfully nice to have. In fact, all things considered, I think, 'Rene, that it's even worth the price."

Women Face the Depression

More than any other factor, the Great Depression affected events and lives during the 1930s. Set in motion by the stock market crash in October 1929, the Depression reached its lowest point over the winter of 1932–1933. More than one-quarter of the work force was unemployed, and people were literally starving in the nation's cities. Not until the early 1940s did defense mobilization finally pull the economy out of the Depression.

The American political system responded to the economic crisis in unprecedented ways. President Herbert Hoover took the first steps to directly involve the federal government in the economy, but he balked at providing federal relief for the unemployed. When Franklin Delano Roosevelt was inaugurated in March of 1933, his New Deal administration accepted federal responsibility for relief, set up public works projects, and regulated the functioning of the stock market and the banks. When the initial measures of the early New Deal failed to end the Depression, Roosevelt embraced more far-reaching reforms, such as the Social Security Act of 1935, which set up old-age pensions; unemployment compensation; and the rudiments of the welfare system that lasted until the 1990s. FDR also put the force of the federal government behind workers' right to join unions by supporting the 1935 Wagner Labor Relations Act. The outpouring of New Deal legislation gave the country a sense of action and won Franklin D. Roosevelt and the Democratic Party a landslide victory in 1936. But the New Deal never solved the problem of the Depression.

Oral histories of Americans who lived through the Great Depression often betray what writer Caroline Bird called an *invisible scar.* Even when good times returned during World War II and after, these survivors of the 1930s still feared a return of the economic collapse. Of course, not everyone was devastated by the Depression: middle-class families were more cushioned from the impact, and some wealthy individuals even managed to increase their holdings during the decade. On the other end of the scale, for such groups as blacks and agricultural workers, the hard times of the 1930s were not all that different from normal times. As writer Langston Hughes observed, "The depression brought everybody down a peg or two. And Negroes had but few pegs to fall."

There is also strong evidence that men and women experienced the Depression differently, both in families and on the job. When a man lost his job, he lost his identification as the breadwinner for his family, the male role. But none of the nation's housewives lost their jobs; in fact, their roles in the home took on added significance when husbands were out of work. By substituting their own labor for goods previously purchased, housewives could stretch the family budget over periods of unemployment or cuts in pay. In a study of Muncie, Indiana, sociologists Robert and Helen Lynd saw this phenomenon at work: "The men, cut adrift from their usual routine, lost much of their sense of time and dawdled helplessly and dully about the streets; while in the homes the women's world remained largely intact and the round of cooking, housecleaning, and mending became if anything more absorbing." Yet few wives (or husbands) were comfortable with this affront to traditional gender roles. "We had no choice," one woman remembered. "We just did what had to be done one day at a time." Women's added burdens during the Great Depression solidified their identification with the home and laid the groundwork for the heightened emphasis on domesticity in the postwar period.

Another way that women helped their families in the Depression also challenged traditional gender roles: if husbands were unemployed, married women could take jobs. The number of married women in the paid work force increased 50 percent during the decade.

How could women get jobs in the midst of the Great Depression? The prevailing segmentation of the work force into primarily "men's" and "women's" jobs provided the mechanism. Men were concentrated in heavy industry, manufacturing, coal mining, and construction work—the very sectors that ground to a standstill during the Depression. Women's jobs in clerical work and domestic and personal service were less affected by the downturn; furthermore, since those occupations were typed as women's, unemployed men did not cross over into them. As one commentator observed, "Few of the people who oppose married women's employment seem to realize that a coal miner or steel worker cannot very well fill the jobs of nursemaids, cleaning women, or the factory and clerical jobs now filled by women." Such sex-stereotypes gave women a small measure of protection, but at the unfortunate cost of confirming their concentration in low-paying, low-status jobs. This gender advantage also benefited white women at the expense of minority women. To make ends meet, white women willingly took jobs usually held by minority women, such as domestic servants. White men also took jobs previously held by minority men.

The politics and government of the New Deal represent a final area where women made a difference in the 1930s. The dramatic expansion of social welfare programs provided jobs and opportunities for women reformers long active in the field. Women played an especially large role in the Works Projects Administration (WPA), the main relief agency, and in the administration of social security, fair labor standards, and welfare. Women also took on larger roles in the revitalized Democratic Party.

At the center of many of these developments for women in the New Deal stood First Lady Eleanor Roosevelt. Close by were Secretary of Labor Frances Perkins, the first woman to serve in the cabinet; social reformer-turned-politician Molly Dewson, head of the Women's Division of the Democratic National Committee; and a network of talented women who took on high-level positions throughout the New Deal bureaucracy. But Eleanor Roosevelt was by far the decade's most widely admired woman. Through her newspaper column, her wide-ranging travels, and her advocacy of such disadvantaged groups as blacks, youth, and women, she served as the conscience of the New Deal.

The Despair of Unemployed Women

Meridel LeSueur

In the 1930s, writer Meridel LeSueur chronicled forgotten women, the women who endured the Depression with a very privatized kind of despair. LeSueur's writings, which covered such subjects as strikes, unemployment, and the plight of the farmers, convey the human side of the Great Depression. As one historian observed, "Mass employment is both a statistic and an empty feeling in the stomach. To fully comprehend it, you have to both see the figures and feel the emptiness." Meridel LeSueur helps us to feel the emptiness.

LeSueur, who was born in Iowa in 1900, spent most of her life in the Midwest. Her family's radical roots—in socialism, the Industrial Workers of the World, populism, and farmer-labor organizing—combined with a stubborn frontier spirit to influence her political development, and in the 1920s she joined the Communist Party. In the 1930s, Meridel LeSueur was on the staff of the radical magazine *New Masses,* and also wrote for *The Daily Worker, Partisan Review,* and *The Nation.* She was blacklisted during the McCarthy era, only to be rediscovered in the 1960s and 1970s when her writings and speeches found new audiences.

When LeSueur submitted "Women on the Breadlines" to New Masses in December 1932, the editors chided her for her "defeatist attitude" and "her nonrevolutionary spirit," but published the piece nonetheless. The scene takes place in 1932, the worst year of the Depression. The situation—the waiting room of a women's employment bureau, populated by a ragged collection of women, young and old, single and married, who desperately need work—defies optimism. When these clients leave the employment agency at the end of the day, still jobless, they will continue their struggle to survive.

The problems of unemployed women (the Women's Bureau estimated their numbers at 2 million in 1931) were especially acute. The public image of the unemployed worker was a man; women were assumed (incorrectly) to have husbands, brothers, or fathers to take care of them, even though many were heads of households or responsible for dependents. Despite the title of LeSueur's piece, it was rare to see women in line for free food at the soup kitchens. New Deal programs, which did not go into effect until 1933, gave low priority to the needs of single women in cities. Even with LeSueur's haunting piece, these women remained practically invisible.

Source: Meridel LeSueur, "Women on the Breadlines," in Meridel LeSueur, Ripening: Selected Work, 1927–1980, ed., Elaine Hedges (New York: The Feminist Press at the City University of New York, 1982), pp. 137–143.

I am sitting in the city free employment bureau. It's the women's section. We have been sitting here now for four hours. We sit here every day, waiting for a job. There are no jobs. Most of us have had no breakfast. Some have had scant rations for over a year. Hunger makes a human being lapse into a state of lethargy, especially city hunger. Is there any place else in the world where a human being is supposed to go hungry amidst plenty without an outcry, without protest, where only the boldest steal or kill for bread, and the timid crawl the streets, hunger like the beak of a terrible bird at the vitals?

We sit looking at the floor. No one dares think of the coming winter. There are only a few more days of summer. Everyone is anxious to get work to lay up something for that long siege of bitter cold. But there is no work. Sitting in the room we all know it. That is why we don't talk much. We look at the floor dreading to see that knowledge in each other's eyes. There is a kind of humiliation in it. We look away from each other. We look at the floor. It's too terrible to see this animal terror in each other's eyes.

So we sit hour after hour, day after day, waiting for a job to come in. There are many women for a single job. A thin sharp woman sits inside a wire cage looking at a book. For four hours we have watched her looking at that book. She has a hard little eye. In the small bare room there are half a dozen women sitting on the benches waiting. Many come and go. Our faces are all familiar to each other, for we wait here every day.

This is a domestic employment bureau. Most of the women who come here are middle aged, some have families, some have raised their families and are now alone, some have men who are out of work. Hard times and the man leaves to hunt for work. He doesn't find it. He drifts on. The woman probably doesn't hear from him for a long time. She expects it. She isn't surprised. She struggles alone to feed the many mouths. Sometimes she gets help from the charities. If she's clever she can get herself a good living from the charities, if she's naturally a lick spittle, naturally a little docile and cunning. If she's proud then she starves silently, leaving her children to find work, coming home after a day's searching to wrestle with her house, her children.

Some such story is written on the faces of all these women. There are young girls too, fresh from the country. Some are made brazen too soon by the city. There is a great exodus of girls from the farms into the city now. Thousands of farms have been vacated completely in Minnesota. The girls are trying to get work. The prettier ones can get jobs in the stores when there are any, or waiting on table, but these jobs are only for the attractive and the adroit. The others, the real peasants, have a more difficult time.

Bernice sits next to me. She is a Polish woman of thirty-five . . . She lives alone in little rooms. She bought seven dollars' worth of second-hand furniture eight years ago. She rents a room for perhaps three dollars a month in an attic, sometimes in a cold house. Once the house where she stayed was condemned and everyone else moved out and she lived there all winter alone on the top floor. She spent only twenty-five dollars all winter.

She wants to get married but she sees what happens to her married friends, left with children to support, worn out before their time. So she stays single. She is virtuous. She is slightly deaf from hanging out clothes in winter. She had done people's washings and cooking for fifteen years and in that time saved thirty dollars. Now she hasn't worked steady for a year and she has spent the thirty dollars. She had dreamed of having a little house or a houseboat perhaps with a spot of ground for a few chickens. This dream she will never realize.

She has lost all her furniture now along with the dream. A married friend whose husband is gone gives her a bed for which she pays by doing a great deal of work for the woman. She comes here every day now sitting bewildered, her pudgy hands folded in her lap. She is hungry. Her great flesh has begun to hang in folds. She has been living on crackers. Sometimes a box of crackers lasts a week. She has a friend who's a baker and he sometimes steals the stale loaves and brings them to her.

A girl we have seen every day all summer went crazy yesterday at the Y.W. She went into hysterics, stamping her feet and screaming.

She hadn't had work for eight months. "You've got to give me something," she kept saying. The woman in charge flew into a rage that probably came from days and days of suffering on her part, because she is unable to give jobs, having none. She flew into a rage at the girl and there they were facing each other in a rage both helpless, helpless. This woman told me once that she could hardly bear the suffering she saw, hardly hear it, that she couldn't eat sometimes and had nightmares at night.

So they stood there, the two women, in a rage, the girl weeping and the woman shouting at her. In the eight months of unemployment she had gotten ragged, and the woman was shouting that she would not send her out like that. "Why don't you shine your shoes," she kept scolding the girl, and the girl kept sobbing and sobbing because she was starving . . .

A scrub woman whose hips are bent forward from stooping with hands gnarled like watersoaked branches clicks her tongue in disgust. No one saves their money, she says, a little money and these foolish young things buy a hat, a dollar for breakfast, a bright scarf. And they do. If you've ever been without money, or food, something very strange happens when you get a bit of money, a kind of madness. You don't care. You can't remember that you had no money before, that the money will be gone. You can remember nothing but that there is the money for which you have been suffering. Now here it is. A lust takes hold of you. You see food in the windows. In imagination you eat hugely; you taste a thousand meals. You look in windows. Colors are brighter; you buy something to dress up in. An excitement takes hold of you. You know it is suicide but you can't help it. You must have food, dainty, splendid food and a bright hat so once again you feel blithe, rid of that ratty gnawing shame.

"I guess she'll go on the street now," a thin woman says faintly, and no one takes the trouble to comment further. Like every commodity now the body is difficult to sell and the girls say you're lucky if you get fifty cents.

It's very difficult and humiliating to sell one's body . . .

It's one of the great mysteries of the city where women go when they are out of work and hungry. There are not many women in the bread line. There are no flop houses for women as there are for men, where a bed can be had for a quarter or less. You don't see women lying on the floor at the mission in the free flops. They obviously don't sleep in the jungle or under newspapers in the park. There is no law I suppose against their being in these places but the fact is they rarely are.

Yet there must be as many women out of jobs in cities and suffering extreme poverty as there are men. What happens to them? Where do they go? Try to get into the Y.W. without any money or looking down at heel. Charities take care of very few and only those that are called "deserving." The lone girl is under suspicion by the virgin women who dispense charity.

I've lived in cities for many months broke, without help, too timid to get in bread lines. I've known many women to live like this until they simply faint on the street from privations, without saying a word to anyone. A woman will shut herself up in a room until it is taken away from her, and eat a cracker a day and be as quiet as a mouse so there are no social statistics concerning her.

I don't know why it is, but a woman will do this unless she has dependents, will go for weeks verging on starvation, crawling in some hole, going through the streets ashamed, sitting in libraries, parks, going for days without speaking to a living soul like some exiled beast, keeping the runs mended in her stockings, shut up in terror in her own misery, until she becomes too super-sensitive and timid to even ask for a job . . .

Not one of them but looks forward to starvation for the coming winter. We are in a jungle and know it. We are beaten, entrapped. There is no way out. Even if there were a job, even if that thin acrid woman came and gave everyone in the room a job for a few days, a few hours, at thirty cents an hour, this would all be repeated tomorrow, the next day and the next.

Not one of these women but knows that despite years of labor there is only starvation, humiliation in front of them.

Mrs. Grey, sitting across from me, is a living spokesman for the futility of labor. She is a warning. Her hands are scarred with labor. Her body is a great puckered scar. She has given birth to six children, buried three, supported them all alive and dead, bearing them, burying them, feeding them. Bred in hunger they have been spare, susceptible to disease. For seven years she tried to save her boy's arm from amputation, diseased from tuberculosis of the bone. It is almost too suffocating to think of that long close horror of years of child-bearing, child-feeding, rearing, with the bare suffering of providing a meal and shelter.

Now she is fifty. Her children, economically insecure, are drifters. She never hears of them. She doesn't know if they are alive. She doesn't know if she is alive. Such subtleties of suffering are not for her. For her the brutality of hunger and cold. Not until these are done away with can those subtle feelings that make a human being be indulged.

She is lucky to have five dollars ahead of her. That is her security. She has a tumor that she will die of. She is thin as a worn dime with her tumor sticking out of her side. She is brittle and bitter. Her face is not the face of a human being. She has borne more than it is possible for a human being to bear. She is reduced to the least possible denominator of human feelings.

It is terrible to see her little bloodshot eyes like a beaten hound's, fearful in terror.

We cannot meet her eyes. When she looks at any of us we look away. She is like a woman drowning and we turn away. We must ignore those eyes that are surely the eyes of a person drowning, doomed. She doesn't cry out. She goes down decently. And we all look away.

The young ones know though. I don't want to marry. I don't want any children. So they all say. No children. No marriage. They arm themselves alone, keep up alone. The man is helpless now. He cannot provide. If he propagates he cannot take care of his young. The means are not in his hands. So they live alone. Get what fun they can. The life risk is too horrible now. Defeat is too clearly written on it.

So we sit in this room like cattle, waiting for a nonexistent job, willing to work to the farthest atom of energy, unable to work, unable to get food and lodging, unable to bear children—here we must sit in this shame looking at the floor, worse than beasts at a slaughter.

It is appalling to think that these women sitting so listless in the room may work as hard as it is possible for a human being to work, may labor night and day, like Mrs. Gray wash streetcars from midnight to dawn and offices in the early evening, scrub for fourteen and fifteen hours a day, sleep only five hours or so, do this their whole lives, and never earn one day of security, having always before them the pit of the future. The endless labor, the bending back, the water-soaked hands, earning never more than a week's wages, never having in their hands more life than that.

It's not the suffering of birth, death, love that the young reject, but the suffering of endless labor without dream, eating the spare bread in bitterness, being a slave without the security of a slave.

American Women Ask Eleanor Roosevelt for Help

Many Americans have always been poor, and for them the Great Depression of the 1930s meant hard times as usual. But there were quite a few Americans who had been getting by all right until 1929, and then, through no fault of their own, found themselves down and out. These "newly poor" were in many ways the most damaged by the depression experience.

Many Americans asked for help directly from the White House. Both Franklin and Eleanor Roosevelt encouraged ordinary citizens to write to them with their observations and troubles. People responded in unprecedented numbers; letters poured into the White House at a rate of 5,000 to 8,000 a day throughout the New Deal, all of which were answered or passed on to the appropriate government agency for action. People really felt that the Roosevelts cared about their problems and would try to correct injustices once they knew about them.

Source: From *Down & Out in the Great Depression: Letters from the Forgotten Man* by Robert S. McElvaine. Copyright ©1983 by the University of North Carolina Press. Used by permission of the publisher.

It was in that spirit that these women wrote to Eleanor Roosevelt with their problems. Although Eleanor Roosevelt's exact responses to these pleas are not known, she probably forwarded these requests to the appropriate relief authorities or local charities. When such requests came accompanied by a cover letter from the White House, they often got results.

Eureka, Calif.
June 14, 1934

Mrs. F. D. Roosevelt
Washington, D.C.

Dear Mrs. Roosevelt:

I know you are overburdened with requests for help and if my plea cannot be recognized, I'll understand it is because you have so many others, all of them worthy.

But I am not asking for myself alone. It is as a potential mother and as one woman to another.

My husband and I are a young couple of very simple, almost poor families. We married eight years ago on the proverbial shoe-string but with a wealth of love. We both wanted more than anything else to establish a home and maintain that home in a charming, quiet manner. I had a job in the County Court House before I married and my husband was, and is, a surveyor. I kept my job as it seemed the best and only way for us to pay for a home as quickly as we could. His work was not always permanent, as surveyors jobs seldom are, but we managed to build our home and furnish it comfortably. Perhaps we were foolish to put all our money into it but we felt it was not only a pleasure but a saving for the future.

Then came the depression. My work has continued and my salary alone has just been sufficient to make our monthly payments on the house and keep our bills paid. But with the exception of two and one-half months work with the U.S. Coast and Geodetic Survey under the C.W.A., my husband has not had work since August, 1932.

My salary could continue to keep us going, but—I am to have a baby. We wanted one before but felt we should have more assurance for the future before we deliberately took such a responsibility. But now that it has happened, I won't give it up! I'm willing to undergo any hardship for myself and I can get a leave of absence from my job for a year. But can't you, won't you do something so my husband can have a job, at least during that year? I realize there is going to be a lot of expense and we have absolutely nothing but our home which still carries a mortgage of $2000. We can't lose that because our baby will need it. And I can't wait until the depression is over to have a baby. I will be 31 in October and I'll soon be too old . . .

As I said before, if it were only ourselves, or if there were something we could do about it, we would never ask for help. We have always stood on our own feet and been proud and happy. But you are a mother and you'll understand this crisis.

Tommy is competent and dependable. He has a surveyor's license and was level man for the U.S. Coast and Geodetic work in this (Humboldt) county. He will go away from home for work, if necessary, but, dear Mrs. Roosevelt, will you see if you can arrange for a job for him? It sounds impossible, I know, but I am at a point where I *ask* the impossible. I have to be selfish now.

I shall hope and pray for a reply and tell myself that you are the busiest woman in America, if I don't receive it. I am going to continue to work as long as I can and then—an interval of waiting. God grant it will be serene and untroubled for my baby's sake.

Very sincerely yours,
Mrs. M. H. A.
Eureka,
Humboldt County,
California

*   *   *

Troy, N.Y.
Jan. 2, 1935.

Dear Mrs. Roosevelt,

About a month ago I wrote you asking if you would buy some baby clothes for me with the understanding that I was to repay you as soon as my husband got enough work. Several weeks later I received a reply to apply to a Welfare Association so I might receive the aid I needed. Do you remember?

Please Mrs. Roosevelt, I do not want charity, only a chance from someone who will trust me until we can get enough money to repay the amount spent for the things I need. As a proof that I really am sincere, I am sending you two of my dearest possessions to keep as security, a ring my husband gave me before we were married, and a ring my mother used to wear. Perhaps the actual value of them is not high, but they are worth a lot to me. If you will consider buying the baby clothes, please keep them (rings) until I send you the money you spent. It is very hard to face bearing a baby we cannot afford to have, and the fact that it is due to arrive soon, and still there is no money for the hospital or clothing, does not make it any easier. I have decided to stay home, keeping my 7 year old daughter from school to help with the smaller children when my husband has work. The oldest little girl is sick now, and has never been strong, so I would not depend on her. The 7 year old one is a good willing little worker and somehow we must manage—but without charity.

If you still feel you cannot trust me, it is allright and I can only say I donot blame you, but if you decide my word is worth anything with so small a security, here is a list of what I will need-but I will need it very soon.

2 shirts, silk and wool. size 2
3 pr. stockings, silk and wool, 4 1/2 or 4
3 straight flannel bands

2 slips—outing flannel

2 muslim dresses

1 sweater

1 wool bonnet

2 pr. wool booties

2 doz. diapers 30 × 30—or 27 × 27

1 large blanket (baby) about 45" or 50"

3 outing flannel nightgaowns

If you will get these for me I would rather no one knew about it. I promise to repay the cost of the layette as soon as possible. We will all be very grateful to you, and I will be more than happy.

Sincerely yours,
Mrs. H. E. C.

*   *   *

Tupelo. Miss
Feb. 4th 1935

Mr President and Wife

Im about to ask you A Question that I hate to trouble you with. but Ive tried hard to get by With out any assistance but Ive Nearly got to road end, I Just Cant make my way as I will explain. Now Mr President I owe Several different people that are compeling me to pay them They are Sending Squires an colectors To me every Week I hate not to pay them but I Just can not Ive a Job. but owing from 8 to 12 different ones It make it difficult To pay be Sides the fuel food House rent That has to be paid each week an fuel each Time it is ordered then Mr president the food is a Necessity We have to have that to keep going on our Jobs. every thing is very high in Tupelo but Im thankful To have a Job. Making Something but not nearly enough To pay those Bills I owe. Im not Writing Just because I can write for I have tried to borrow from the white people here and they say they have not got any money So I cannot get help from them as I used to. Now I am asking you please to help Me. Ive a little child 4 years a mother 62 years an She has ben Sick for 15 or 18 years Ive got along all right till the middle of last year up till now. It has been hard for 7 or 8 month doctor Bills Groceries coal Bill I do not ask for Money for foolish thing an I do not ask you to give it to me. I am only asking a loan an I will pay you as you desire Me to by the week or by the month only as you say. but please mr president keep This confidential as I would loose my Job. you See Mr President I can pay one person easier Than a lots of people. These Bill has got a head of me when I didnt have any work as they are demanding their pay please if It will not Trouble you to much help me I will appreciste it More than Any Thing. My bill Totals $150.00 that is for The Thing That I have Necessaraly needed not one bit of foolishness for I Tries to put every cent to good use please help me in the Name of the lord an I will pay you back. I have not got any thing for Security but my honor if you will Trust me Thank you

> *A Colored Friend down in Tupelo Miss*
> *G. T. [female]*
> *General delivery*

P.S. please answer direct to me

*   *   *

> Blacksburg S.C.
> January 19. [1934]

Dear Mrs. Roosevelt,

Mrs. Roosevelt will you send me and my sister, Ruth, a pair of ball bearing roller skates? Our friends have skates and we are not able to buy them. We sure will thank you if you will.

> *yours trully,*
> *L. L. [female]*

P.S. I am twelve years old and in the sixth grade at Blacksburg Grammar school. My friends at school have skates and laugh because I dont have some.

> *your's trully*
> *L.*

The Dust Bowl

Ann Marie Low

In addition to the ravages of the Great Depression, during the 1930s residents of the Great Plains endured the worst drought recorded in the climatological history of the United States. The "dirty thirties" saw crops wither and livestock die when the rains failed to materialize. Then the loosened soil was swirled into huge dust storms that descended on towns like tornadoes, turning day into night and enveloping residents in clouds of dirt, soot, and dust. Only in 1941 did the drought end, simultaneously with war mobilization, breaking the grip of the Depression.

Although the states of Oklahoma, Texas, and Arkansas were the hardest hit by the drought, the northern plains did not escape its impact. This memoir by Ann Marie Low, *Dust Bowl Diary,* describes her family's experience in the Badlands of southeastern North Dakota. Born in 1912, Ann Marie kept diaries from 1927 to 1937 that record both a young woman's coming of age

Source: Reprinted from *Dust Bowl Diary,* by Ann Marie Low, pp. 95–98, by permission of the University of Nebraska Press. Copyright 1984 by the University of Nebraska Press.

and the devastation wrecked by drought and depression on American agriculture.

The story that Ann Marie Low recorded in her diary reflected the frustrations of farm life for an ambitious young woman who nonetheless was devoted to her family and their commitment to keeping their farm going. The diary describes the daily struggle with the dust storms that invaded North Dakota, and it conveys the hard work (usually without benefit of electricity) that was the lot of women on the farm. One of three children, Ann Marie took teaching jobs to help out with family finances, especially to help pay for her siblings' educations. Although she acknowledges several marriage proposals, she saw matrimony as a threat to women's independence. The last entry in her diary, dated June 4, 1937, when she was 25 years old, records her frustration at her lost youth and the bleak prospects for the future: "This is a round that will go on forever. At least it will go on until my youth is gone. *Somehow, I've got to get out!!"*

April 25, 1934, Wednesday

Last weekend was the worst dust storm we ever had. We've been having quite a bit of blowing dirt every year since the drouth started, not only here, but all over the Great Plains. Many days this spring the air is just full of dirt coming, literally, for hundreds of miles. It sifts into everything. After we wash the dishes and put them away, so much dust sifts into the cupboards we must wash them again before the next meal. Clothes in the closets are covered with dust.

Last weekend no one was taking an automobile out for fear of ruining the motor. I rode Roany to Frank's place to return a gear. To find my way I had to ride right beside the fence, scarcely able to see from one fence post to the next.

Newspapers say the deaths of many babies and old people are attributed to breathing in so much dirt.

May 7, 1934, Monday

The dirt is still blowing. Last weekend Bud [her brother] and I helped with the cattle and had fun gathering weeds. Weeds give us greens for salad long before anything in the garden is ready. We use dandelions, lamb's quarter, and sheep sorrel. I like sheep sorrel best. Also, the leaves of sheep sorrel, pounded and boiled down to a paste, make a good salve.

Still no job. I'm trying to persuade Dad I should apply for rural school #3 out here where we went to school. I don't see a chance of getting a job in a high school when so many experienced teachers are out of work.

He argues that the pay is only $60.00 a month out here, while even in a grade school in town I might get $75.00. Extra expenses in town would probably eat up that extra $15.00. Miss Eston, the practice teaching supervisor, told me her salary has been cut to $75.00 after all the years she has been teaching in Jamestown. She wants to get married. School boards will not hire married women teachers in these hard times because they have husbands to support them. Her fiancé is the sole support of his widowed mother and can't support a wife, too. So she is just stuck in her job, hoping she won't get another salary cut because she can scarcely live on what she makes and dress the way she is expected to.

Dad argues the patrons always stir up so much trouble for a teacher at #3 some teachers have quit in mid-term. The teacher is also the janitor, so the hours are long.

I figure I can handle the work, kids, and patrons. My argument is that by teaching here I can work for my room and board at home, would not need new clothes, and so could send most of my pay to Ethel [her sister] and Bud.

In April, Ethel had quit college, saying she did not feel well.

May 21, 1934, Monday

Ethel has been having stomach trouble. Dad has been taking her to doctors though suspecting her trouble is the fact that she often goes on a diet that may affect her health. The local doctor said he thought it might be chronic appendicitis, so Mama took Ethel by train to Valley City last week to have a surgeon there remove her appendix.

Saturday Dad, Bud, and I planted an acre of potatoes. There was so much dirt in the air I couldn't see Bud only a few feet in front of me. Even the air in the house was just a haze. In the evening the wind died down, and Cap came to take me to the movie. We joked about how hard it is to get cleaned up enough to go anywhere.

The newspapers report that on May 10 there was such a strong wind the experts in Chicago estimated 12,000,000 tons of Plains soil was dumped on that city. By the next day the sun was obscured in Washington, D.C., and ships 300 miles out at sea reported dust settling on their decks.

Sunday the dust wasn't so bad. Dad and I drove cattle to the Big Pasture. Then I churned butter and baked a ham, bread, and cookies for the men, as no telling when Mama will be back.

May 30, 1934, Wednesday

Ethel got along fine, so Mama left her at the hospital and came to Jamestown by train Friday. Dad took us both home.

The mess was incredible! Dirt had blown into the house all week and lay inches deep on everything. Every towel and curtain was just black. There wasn't a clean dish or cooking utensil. There was no food. Oh, there were eggs and milk and one loaf left of the bread I baked the weekend before. I looked in the cooler box down the well (our refrigerator) and found a little ham and butter. It was late, so Mama and I cooked some ham and eggs for the men's supper because that was all we could fix in a hurry. It turned out they had been living on ham and eggs for two days.

Mama was very tired. After she had fixed starter for bread, I insisted she go to bed and I'd do all the dishes.

It took until 10 o'clock to wash all the dirty dishes. That's not wiping them— just washing them. The cupboards had to be washed out to have a clean place to put them.

Saturday was a busy day. Before starting breakfast I had to sweep and wash all the dirt off the kitchen and dining room floors, wash the stove, pancake griddle, and dining room table and chairs. There was cooking, baking, and churning to be done for those hungry men. Dad is 6 feet 4 inches tall, with a big frame. Bud is 6 feet 3 inches and almost as big-boned as Dad. We say feeding them is like filling a silo.

Mama couldn't make bread until I carried water to wash the bread mixer. I couldn't churn until the churn was washed and scalded. We just couldn't do anything until something was washed first. Every room had to have dirt almost shoveled out of it before we could wash floors and furniture.

We had no time to wash clothes, but it was necessary. I had to wash out the boiler, wash tubs, and the washing machine before we could use them. Then every towel, curtain, piece of bedding, and garment had to be taken outdoors to have as much dust as possible shaken out before washing. The cistern is dry, so I had to carry all the water we needed from the well.

That evening Cap came to take me to the movie, as usual. Ixnay. I'm sorry I snapped at Cap. It isn't his fault, or anyone's fault, but I was tired and cross. Life in what the newspapers call "the Dust Bowl" is becoming a gritty nightmare.

The Life Cycle of a White Southern Farm Woman

Margaret Jarman Hagood

The lives of white tenant farm women in the South shared certain similarities with the lives of rural women everywhere: harsh conditions, isolation, and unpredictable cash flow depending on the harvest. The agricultural system in the South was dominated by an overdependence on cash crops such as cotton or tobacco and by a sharecropping system where black and white farm families often worked land owned by white landowners. Gender roles were clearly defined. Women had full responsibility for running the household, while men oversaw farm duties. Wives also did field work during certain seasons, although husbands rarely (if ever) reciprocated by helping out with household chores. In addition, southern white women had a fertility rate (6.4 live births per married woman, excluding stillbirths and abortions), which was almost three times the national average.

Sociologist Margaret Jarman Hagood (1907–1963) first uncovered this high fertility rate while researching her doctoral dissertation in statistics at the University of North Carolina. Curious about the social and economic context, she embarked on 16 months of interviews with 254 white southern women. Since she herself was from Georgia, married, and the mother of a child, she found that women felt comfortable discussing intimate details (such as contraception and childbirth) with her. The results of her study were published in 1939 as *Mothers of the South.*

Hagood's chapter, "Of the Tenant Child as Mother to the Woman," utilizes the concept of *life cycle* to trace the experiences of Mollie Goodwin as she matures and marries. The life cycle approach captures the development of this individual over time and suggests how her life story interacts with broader themes such as farm tenancy, adolescence and education, work roles, marriage patterns, and fertility.

The story of the tenant child begins more than a quarter of a century ago. On Monday ten-year-old Mollie woke up when her mother lifted the stove lid and began making the fire. She slipped from underneath the cover easily, so as not to disturb her little brother, and took down her last year's red dress, which had been fleecy and warm, but now was slick and thin . . .

Mollie's plump arms stretched tight the seams of her outgrown dress, and as she leaned over to pick up fresh wood for the fire, she felt her dress split at the shoulder. She wondered what she would do the washing in if she couldn't get into the old dress next Monday or the one after that. Her father's rule was that her two new dresses of the same cotton fleece lined material, one red and one blue, must never be worn except for school or Sunday School. She had no sisters to hand down clothes to her, for the other four children were boys. Some girls she knew wore overalls for working, but her father would not allow that either. A wicked thought came to her mind—maybe if she had nothing to wear to wash in next Monday, she wouldn't have to wash and instead could go to school with her brothers. She could iron on Tuesday inside the house in her underwear—then a vision of her mother bending over the wash tubs, moaning with the pain in her back, made her put aside the daydream of a washless Monday.

After breakfast Mollie's older brother cut wood and started a fire under the wash pot while she and the brother next younger drew and carried water from the well. Then the boys left for the mile walk to the one-teacher school and Mollie started back for the house to get up the clothes. She lingered on the way, debating whether her father's overalls, stiff with a week's accumulation of winter mud and stable stains, were harder to wash than the baby's soiled diapers. They *were* harder, but the odor from the diapers made you feel you couldn't go on. It was a sensory symbol of babies, of her sick mother, of crying, little brothers, and now was vaguely mixed with her distaste for what two girl friends had told her at recess last week about how babies come. Mollie tried not to think about this and hoped she never had any babies.

The school bell's ringing interrupted her musing and reminded Mollie of how much she wanted to be there. Her dress was as new as any in school and its color still bright. The teacher had smiled approvingly at Mollie last week when the visiting preacher pinched her dimpled cheek and said, "Miss Grace, you have a fine looking bunch of little girls." Mollie thought now of having, when she was grown, a dress like Miss Grace's Sunday one. The bell stopped ringing and Mollie resolved to stop thinking and to work very hard and fast. Once before she had finished all the washing in time to go back with the boys after dinner. And so she scrubbed with all her force against the washboard and paid no attention to the pain from her knuckles scraped raw.

By dinner time all the clothes were on the line and the first ones out already frozen stiff. Mollie, numbed by cold and fatigue, ate peas, fat pork, and cornbread without joining in the family talk. When she got up from the table, her back ached—she wondered how many years of washing it would take to make it as bent over as her mother's. She changed to her new dress in time to set off for the afternoon session of school. She pulled herself together to respond to the teacher's beaming look of approval for having come to school that afternoon, and then relaxed into a lethargy from weariness and missed words she knew in the Third Reader and was spelled down quickly . . .

One stormy winter night three months before Mollie was twelve, she was put to bed early. Her father moved the trundle bed from the main room and all the children went to sleep in the kitchen—all but Mollie. She had a terrible feeling of impending disaster to her mother and herself. When she had asked her mother about babies not long before, her mother had told her she was going to have another and that something would happen to Mollie soon, too. From the front room Mollie heard groans and knew her mother was suffering. Her own body began to ache. Her mother's sounds grew louder and each time an anguished scream reached Mollie's ears, a shooting pain went through her. Hardly daring, Mollie reached down under the cover and felt that her legs were wet. All the boys were asleep and so she drew back the cover and in the moonlight saw black stains which had come from her body. Suddenly she thought she was having a baby. She tried to scream like her mother, but the terror of the realization paralyzed her. Fright overwhelmed her until she was no longer conscious of pain. She remained motionless for a long time, knowing and feeling nothing but a horrible fear of disgrace and dread. Then she became aware that the moaning in the next room had stopped and that someone had unlatched the kitchen door. Trembling, she eased out of bed and crept into her mother's room. There was a new baby lying on one side, but she slipped into the other side of the bed and nestled against her mother. The relaxing warmth and comfort of another's body released the inner tensions and Mollie melted into tears and weak, low sobs. Her mother stroked her but said nothing. She lay there for some minutes until the Negro "granny" said she must leave her mother and led her back to bed. Early in the morning she hid the soiled bedclothes in a corner until she could wash them secretly in the creek and found some cloths in her mother's drawer which she asked for without giving any reason. Not for two years, when a girl friend told her, did she have any instruction about how to fix and wear sanitary pads.

* * * * *

The summer Mollie was fourteen her mother persuaded Ben to buy her a silk dress. Mollie had worked so well that year that her father, in an appreciative mood, took her to town and let her select the material, which was a glamorous, changeable, rose and green taffeta. Mrs. Bynum helped her make it, and when her father consented to take the whole family to a Fourth of July celebration ten miles away, Mollie's cup overflowed with joy. She rolled up her hair in rags the night before. She helped bathe and dress the younger children two hours before leaving time so that she might extract the full delight from dressing leisurely in her new clothes for the first time. By eight o'clock in the morning, the family, now nine, piled into the wagon and set off. To keep from going through the county seat, they cut through a shorter, back road, which was rocky and went over steep hills. The boys got out and pushed on the worst places, but Mollie sat on the bench with her mother and father—accorded special privileges because of her new dress. The jolting and hot sun bearing down were unnoticed for the joy anticipated in being the most beautifully dressed girl at the celebration. Mollie was scarcely aware of her family in the wagon as she rode along with her head in the clouds.

They reached the tabernacle, where there were to be political speeches interspersed with hymn singing contests between churches. Mollie hopped down lightly and was about to run over to join a group of girls she knew when her mother, climbing over the edge of the wagon more slowly, called her back and took her a few steps away from the wagon.

"Your dress is ruined behind," she whispered to Mollie, "you'll have to set still over here by this tree all day." Excitement and the jolting had brought on her menstrual period early and the realization of this brought about a flush of hot shame which obliterated the festive scene of picnic tables and merry people. Mollie's heart seemed to close up and with it her capacity to perceive or respond. Passively she allowed herself to be led to a sheltered spot under an oak with protruding roots which afforded a seat. The loss of her life's triumph and the indescribable embarrassment kept her from comprehending meanings. She felt that she was dead and after awhile she leaned against the tree and slept. No one approached, for there seemed to be a tacit understanding of her plight. Late in the afternoon she rode home without speaking to her family. The next day she and her mother were unable to remove the stain from her dress and the beautiful taffeta was never worn. Her father never bought her another silk dress.

* * * * *

Two years later, Mollie finished the seventh grade at sixteen . . . That summer one of Mrs. Bynum's many nieces went to a town in another county to work in a tobacco factory and her sister reveled in telling Mollie about the money she made and spent. They planned what sort of things Mollie could buy if she were to go to work in town. After weeks of whispered plans, the sister in town arranged for Mollie to have a job weighing and wrapping cigarettes. Without telling even her mother, Mollie bundled up her clothes and left early one morning, just as the cotton picking season was beginning. A neighbor boy drove her to town and she went to a relative of Ben's to board.

For four months Mollie worked in the tobacco factory and exulted in making $20 a week. This was during the post-war boom period and labor was scarce. As fast as the money came in, she spent $15 for a coat, $11 for hightop shoes, $8 for a hat, and smaller amounts for slippers, dresses, beads, and brooches. There were five other women boarding in the same house and Mollie's greatest delight was in the just-before-bedtime lunches they shared. Each one chipped in a nickel every night for cheese, crackers, and fancy canned things. Mollie had never before eaten "store bought" food and had never had even one cent to spend on self-indulgence. After she had bought an entire outfit of new clothes, she went to a county fair with the women. A boy who worked in the cigarette factory asked her to go with him, but she thought she would have a better time with the other women. This boy always hung around Mollie in the factory and said things she thought were fresh, but the landlady wouldn't allow her to go out with him. Once in December he asked Mollie to marry him but she laughed and said, "Why should I marry and keep house and have babies when I've got such a good job and can buy myself such fine clothes?". . .

The following summer Mollie's mother gave birth to her ninth child. It was in the daytime and the baby came in a hurry. No one was in the house except Mollie and the sick brother in the back room. Ben had gone for a doctor but not soon enough and the doctor did not get there in time. The suffering woman begged for help but Mollie did not know what to do. She even pled with Mollie to kill her and put an end to her tortures. Finally the baby was born, but with the covers pulled up so that Mollie could not see. The mother wrapped the baby up and let it lie there until the doctor came and cut the cord.

* * * * *

With a sick brother, a sickly mother, and a new baby in the house, Mollie had a busy summer. About the only times she had off from household duties were when she spent the night with her cousins or with Mrs. Bynum's nieces. On one such night the young people all went to watch a Negro revival meeting. While they were standing on the outside listening to the shouting through the windows, a man who knew some of the boys came up and joined them. His name was Jim and he was ten years older than Mollie, but he "took a shine" to her from their first meeting. For the rest of the summer he rode his mule for nine miles to come to see her whenever she could spend a night away from home, as Ben was still adamant about no sports coming to his house.

In the fall the brother was better and the original plan for Mollie to go to school in town was feasible. Because Ben had no buggy of his own, and because he wished so much to have his favorite daughter at home on week-ends, he finally consented for Jim to drive her out on Fridays and back to town on Sundays. His mule was the fastest one for miles around, but walked very slowly when Jim was taking Mollie home. This was when they did their courting, for Jim was never permitted to linger after delivering Mollie to her parents. He pressed his suit with urgency, for he was nearly thirty and felt it was time for him to be getting married. Mollie wasn't enjoying going back to school after being out for a year, since she was older than the town girls in her grade and felt awkward with them. She liked Jim although she never felt gay or excited with him the way she did with younger boys. She still did not want to think of marrying and settling down to repeat her mother's life—ruining her health and looks with overwork and childbearing. She made one last appeal to her father to let her go back to work in the cigarette factory, for her one-time job has remained to this day a symbol of money for clothes and luxuries. Ben would not consent, however; he said that factories were no place for his womenfolks and that she could never go back. And so Mollie gave Jim a lukewarm "yes" and they planned to marry on Christmas Day . . .

Five years later Mollie was pregnant for the third time. She felt very hopeful because this was "the kickingest baby you ever felt." Her first child had been a girl, but a terrible disappointment to Mollie in looks. At four she was big, cumbersome, awkward, and slow moving, resembling her two-hundred-pound father so much that he was frequently told, "You couldn't deny that child if you wanted to!" The second baby was a boy, weakly and always crying just like the little brother Mollie used to sleep with and take care of. The alertness of the child she was now carrying promised better success.

Mollie showed more interest in everything that spring and summer. Jim's family had left them to go live and work in a cotton mill town and for the first time they were "tending" a farm and living in a house alone. Their family of four was the smallest she had ever cooked, cleaned, and washed for, and their tobacco crop looked good in July. She was glad Jim was raising tobacco instead of cotton because it meant more money in the fall. He was still kind about buying her one Sunday dress every year with the first tobacco money he got. Mollie was still pretty at twenty-three and during her nine months of pregnancy she often daydreamed of the child, who was to be a pert, attractive daughter whom she could dress daintily.

In midsummer when her time was nearing, the baby suddenly stopped moving one night, "right short like." Mollie knew that minute the baby was dead and alarmed she woke up Jim and told him about it. He reassured her, but on her insistence the next morning went to town and told the doctor about it. The doctor said there was nothing to do but wait, although it was eleven days before labor set in. The delivery was difficult for the dead fetus had begun disintegrating. The body was too much in pieces to be dressed for burial but they showed Mollie the face of her little girl and she thought it was the prettiest she had ever seen. Blood poison, complications, and a long illness afterwards made Mollie temporarily infertile and she had no more children for ten years.

* * * * *

At thirty-seven Mollie is again pregnant. She is not bitter about it, although she wishes doctors would tell you what to do when they say, "Now you shouldn't have any more children."...

Mollie doesn't worry too much about the child yet to be born. She is sorry about the trouble it will be, but she accepts the "Lord's will" here as she does when they have a bad crop year. She no longer expects to realize the goals of life herself, but has transferred her efforts to achieving them for her daughter. Last year she even chose to forego the Sunday dress in order to buy a fur-trimmed coat for her baby. And yet Mollie is cheerful, except when impatient with her two older children, and works routinely at her farm and housework without complaint.

A Mexican-American Childhood during the Depression

Carlotta Silvas Martin

The border is an apt metaphor for Mexican-American life, capturing the fluidity of crossing back and forth between two countries and two cultures. Carlotta Silvas Martin was born in 1917 in Superior, Arizona, a rural mining town. Her father, Miguel López Silvas, had been born in Mexico but often picked up work across the border. He met his future wife, Elena Amanda Romero, who was of Mexican heritage but had been born in Arizona, at the boardinghouse run by her mother for miners working at the Magma Copper Company in Superior. Many Mexican-American women, like immigrant women in Eastern cities, found that taking in boarders could add important cash to the family income. Even when men were employed, life was always hard in these mining towns.

Things got even worse during the Great Depression of the 1930s, as Carlotta Silvas Martin remembered. She was living with her grandmother, which was not unusual among Mexican-American families, when hard times struck. Her oral history documents how the community worked together to get by; her grandmother for a time had a relief job with the WPA, the main New Deal relief agency. But the depression was not on everybody's mind 24 hours a day. Life continued as usual for the teenaged Carlotta Silvas, a life shaped by religion, tradition, and community, plus new elements such as popular culture and movies.

After graduating from Superior High School, Carlotta Silvas attended Arizona State University and then returned to Superior, where she wrote a popular column called "Aqui y Alla" (Here and There) for the local newspaper. In 1955 she married Walter Martin, a mining engineer, and had two children. The family's decision to move to Mesa so their children could attend school was typical of the migration *el rancho al barrio* (from ranch, or rural area, to city) of many Mexican-Americans of her generation. But in a further migration, Carlotta Silvas Martin returned to Superior in the 1980s. The town had changed dramatically since the mine shut down in 1984. "It was a thriving town," she remembered, "and now it is barren, like a desert." The memories of women of her generation are increasingly our only windows on a world almost lost.

My mother had two small babies on her hands. When I became sickly, Grandmother Josefa took me home with her, and I never returned to my parents. From the time I can remember I was raised by my "Nani." In those years it was very common for grandmas to raise kids.

My grandmother worked very hard; I grew up during the Depression. My kids asked me why I can't ride a bike and I'd say, "That's the last thing I would ask for!" During the Depression my grandmother would give Armida, my Uncle Ernesto's wife, a dollar a day. With that she'd buy potatoes, lard, and beans. They had thirteen children, and she'd feed us all. That was the menu—*papas fritas, frijoles,* and *tortillas.* Aunt Armida made big piles of hot tortillas and we sat on those long benches and she gave them to us as she made them. Every once in a blue moon she bought a quarter's worth of hamburger and fried it with potatoes. That was a real treat!

During the Depression my grandmother sewed piecework for the WPA. I'd go by the building on my way to and from school and see her sitting at the sewing machine. My dad helped when he could, but the miners only made four dollars a day. Uncle Ernesto worked also. He used to dig graves.

My mother was very kind; she was known for her charity. She gave people food during the Depression. My dad used to buy one-hundred-pound sacks of sugar, flour, and potatoes, and my mother would portion it in little bags and give them to the people who were in need.

When my mother's father died, Doña Isabel, who never went out anywhere because she was partially paralyzed, went to my grandfather's wake. Mother asked her, "Ay, why are you coming out in this cold and windy weather?" "Because, Elena," she answered, "I owe you favors. If I owed you money, I would pay you, but I can only repay the kind favors that you have done for me by accompanying you in your grief." Many of the people in our little mining town were very ethical and high-class people in their own way.

Another young man was telling me the other day: "Carlotta, I never liked Superior because I suffered so much hunger there, but your parents were always very kind to us." "Yes," I told him. "They were kind to everybody."

The Depression years were very, very, hard. I remember seeing the people passing on the way to California from Oklahoma, Arkansas, and Missouri. At that time we lived on Queen Creek, and everyone went by there. It hurt me to see the people in their rickety old cars, their clothes in tatters, escaping from the drought and the dust bowls . . .

My early childhood years were spent playing in Queen Creek near my grandmother's home. It was so pretty—a green oasis shaded by huge cottonwood trees that made my playground a cool haven. Clean, clear water ran in the creek all the time. Sometimes, after a heavy rainstorm, the creek would flood as high as the bridge and then miraculously turn into a trickle the very next day. But now it's dirty, and there are no trees. My grandmother's house was located on the "American" side of town, but there was nothing they could do about it because she was there before anybody else and had staked her claim. Later on she sold the lot for five hundred dollars and moved the lumber and built another house on a lot she had on Heiner Street. I grew up playing with Anglo children and speaking English. Most of my friends were the Mahoneys, a big Irish family from Utah.

When it was time for me to go to school I was assigned to Harding School, which was the school for the non-English-speaking children on the Mexican side of town. We were segregated; there was a place called McKelveyville by Harding School, and those Anglo children were sent to Roosevelt School and the Mexican children who lived closer to Roosevelt had to go down to Harding. I'll admit, there was a lot of discrimination in those years. An ice plant located just below the present Hing's Market on Main Street seemed to be the unofficial boundary between the "American" side (we were all Americans!) and the "Mexican" side.

Superior's Mexican side of town could have been considered a barrio, but to me it was a lovely environment. The people were very united; they intermingled a lot. There was never a need to lock doors. I don't ever recall my seeing a key to any of the doors in either my parents' or grandmother's homes . . .

There was a strong feeling of community among the Mexican people of Superior. The fraternal organizations had socials and picnics as well as dances. When someone died, they all turned out in their uniforms and banners—all very formal.

We also celebrated Las Fiestas Patrias—el 16 de septiembre, el 5 de mayo, and also July 4. Some men in town knew a great deal about Mexican history and politics, and they were very involved in these celebrations. We'd have patriotic speeches, a queen and princesses, a parade with floats, a dance, and a picnic with races and pie contests. On September 16 they'd blow up some dynamite, and the blast would represent "El Grito de Dolores," which was the cry for independence from Spain by Miguel Hidalgo.

We had a theater at one time in Mexican town. It had a very nice stage and seated about three hundred people. It burned down and was never rebuilt. Touring stock companies came from Los Angeles and presented beautiful plays in Spanish—comedies, dramas, and musical reviews. You know who used to come here—Rita Hayworth! Her name was Rita Cansino then. She toured with her father. They sang together and she danced. That was in the early thirties.

I belonged to a women's group called "Las Mexicanitas." We did a lot of community service. We raised money for scholarships; we donated the altar and railing when they built the new St. Francis Church and raised money for the St. Mary's Community Center. We put on plays and skits and variety shows. One year I wrote a play in Spanish and English called "The Apparition of Our Lady of Guadalupe." Martin Fierro, the high school Spanish teacher, did the men's voices, and I did the women's voices. My husband, Walter, and I went up to the flats and collected manzanita bushes. Walter put them on stands, and we decorated them with paper roses. Then we blacked out the stage lights, and when the lights were turned on the Virgen de Guadalupe was standing there. Everyone said, "Ahhhh-hhh." It was so beautiful. It was such a big success we had to put it on twice.

The first movie theater was in American town. Later we also had a movie house in Mexican town that had movies in Spanish. That's about the only time my mother would go out. How she enjoyed those movies!

My father was a very honorable man; his word was his bond. He was a very hard worker and was respected. Some of the men didn't like to work with him because he was such a perfectionist at his job. At one time he was a contract miner and worked in a very lucrative spot. He was a good provider. But then, that's not all there is to life. He was in charge of the money, but my mother had to save for any of the extras. Sometimes he would just blow it away. When he retired in 1950 he had worked for the mining company forty-three years and had never been laid off. If he went out and drank, which he did do, he'd go to work the next day. People would tell time by him. He had a lunch pail with a canvas strip that he swung on his back. By six o'clock every morning, he was going up the hill on Pinal. People would say, "Ay, ya son las seis. Allí va el Mique Silvas." (Oh, it's six o'clock; there goes Mikey Silvas.) . . .

I married my husband, Walter Martin, in 1955. He is an Alaskan native and a mining engineer. We have two children, a son, Jonathan, and a daughter, Elena. I moved to Mesa for sixteen years so my children could attend school there. Our daughter is a music teacher at Lehi Elementary School in Mesa, and our son is a surveyor for Magma Copper Company.

I moved back to Superior three years ago, but so much has changed since the mine closed down in 1984. John Mitchell's was a beautiful department store with quality merchandise. There were appliance stores, two drugstores, and some nice restaurants. The Magma Hotel was a very nice place; the theater was going full blast. Every two weeks when the miners got paid, there was money flowing all over the place. It was a thriving town, and now it is barren, like the desert. Even the Kress' Dime Store has closed, and that was the meeting place for people.

I used to go and visit people that I have known since I was a little girl, but now so many of the people have gone away or died. I hardly go out anymore. To me that's one of life's sadnesses—to lose the people you've known all your life.

A lot of the children of the Mexican families from Superior have done very, very well. A lot of professional people have come out of our little mining community—doctors, lawyers, educators, and political leaders. A professor at ASU told me that young people from the mining towns always did well because they had support of their parents.

My sister's son, Aaron Kizer, is an attorney. I remember once when Aaron was a little boy he was singing "Anything you can do, I can do better." When my dad heard him singing that song, he asked me, "¿Que está cantando el muchacho?" I explained it to him. He got such a big kick out of that. He'd be so thrilled today if he knew how well our children have done.

Women and Labor Militancy

Genora Johnson Dollinger

The 1930s are rightly remembered as the decade when the labor movement became an institutionalized part of American life. This breakthrough occurred because of labor militancy engendered by the harsh conditions of the Depression as well as New Deal legislation such as the 1935 Labor Relations Act, which put the force of the federal government behind labor's right to

Source: From *Making Do: How Women Survived the '30s.* Copyright © 1976 by Jeane Eddy Westin.

organize. Women participated in this upsurge in labor organization, increasing their numbers in unions from barely 250,000 in 1929 to more than 800,000 just 10 years later.

The success of the Congress of Industrial Organizations (CIO) was a major factor in the growth of the labor movement in the 1930s. One of the earliest targets was the auto industry in Michigan. A successful 44-day sitdown strike against General Motors (where workers occupied the plants, but refused to work) led to recognition for the fledgling United Auto Workers union. Although women were only a fraction of autoworkers, they played a major role in the Flint sit-down strikes that led to the victory.

Genora Johnson Dollinger, a 23-year-old wife of a GM striker and mother of two small children, mobilized 500 women during the strike, mainly the wives, sisters, and girlfriends of the male strikers. These women called themselves the Women's Emergency Brigade and wore distinctive red berets and armbands. Their activities included responsibility for picket lines, staffing soup kitchens and first aid stations, and occasionally taking more militant action, such as breaking windows to protect strikers from tear gas. The women played a special role in deflecting the potential for violence and bloodshed, all in the name of protecting their men. As journalist Mary Heaton Vorse observed, "They were fearless and seemingly tireless. One and all were normal, sensible women who were doing this because they had come to the natural conclusion that it must be done if they and their children were to have a decent life."

The pride that these women felt in their contributions comes through in Genora Johnson Dollinger's story. So too does the hostility of the male union leaders, who quickly consigned the women back to the home once the emergency had passed.

I was raised in the city of Flint, Michigan. There are roads and streets in that city named for my family because they were among the early settlers there.

Actually, this was an advantage when the strike came. I could not successfully be labeled an outside union agitator brought in to cause trouble. My father was well-known and well-to-do—a portrait photographer who invested in real estate.

I was twenty-three years old on December 30, 1936, when the strike started. It lasted forty-four days, a very dramatic forty-four days, until February 11, 1937.

It was New Year's Eve when I realized women had to organize and join in the fight. I was on the picket lines when the men's wives came down. They didn't know why their husbands were sitting inside the plant. Living in a company town, you see, they got only company propaganda through the press and radio. So when they came down on New Year's Eve, many were threatening to divorce their striking husbands if they didn't quit and get back to work to bring home a paycheck.

I knew then that union women must organize on their own in order to talk with these wives.

At that time, I was a housewife myself with two sons, aged six and two. I had been exposed to socialist doctrine when I was very young . . . sixteen or seventeen, when I met my husband Kermit's father. He'd come from South Dakota bringing certain socialist ideas. So Carl Johnson, the father, and Kermit and I formed a socialist party branch in Flint. I knew what was going on within the AFL craft unions because our socialist party headquarters was in the Labor Temple where all their activities took place. Everybody knew me down there, and I had some pretty firm ideas about the responsibilities of industry to the factory worker.

So when the strike began, I already had many friends among the auto workers; and I was fairly well known by others in town, including the local newspaper, because of my father's position . . .

When the strike started, my mother—without my father's knowledge— agreed to take care of my two little boys, and other friends helped, as well. I was then relatively free, and immediately went to Roy Reuther and Robert Travis— those were the UAW organizers—and I volunteered to help. I was told to go to the kitchen and peel potatoes, but I said there were plenty of others who could do that, including some of the men. So they gave me a job setting up a press clipping bureau. I kept busy for a couple of days until I found out there was a person going over all the work I'd done. I decided anyone sitting with a pair of shears could handle that job, so I organized a sign painting department. We made signs and set up a children's picket line—and that's what the history books show. I remember one sign, my own little snow-suited two-year-old holding it high: "My daddy strikes for us little tykes." That picture went from one end of the nation to the other. Anyway, a professional sign painter friend of mine took that over, and that's when I got busy organizing the women.

Now remember, Chevrolet, A/C Sparkplug, and Buick were working—Fisher plants 1 and 2 were struck. On December 30, the police attempted to break the strike at Fisher 2. You see, the men were sitting-in on the second floor, and food was brought up to them by ladder—'cause the plant police had control of the bottom floor. On that night, the police decided to cut off the food, and the next thing we knew they started throwing tear gas at the plant to get the men out. That fight became famous as the Battle of Bull's Run and it went on into the long night. The street was barricaded on both sides by union men. The local GM-controlled radio was broadcasting that a riot—some people thought a revolution—had broken out in the city. People came to watch the police shooting us with rifle bullets, buckshot, and tear gas. We had nothing but rocks and car door hinges, but we picked up the tear gas bombs and heaved them back at the police before they exploded. Men were going down, and fourteen people were shot that night, one seriously. I saw blood flowing . . .

At this point Victor [Reuther] privately told some of us, "We may have lost this battle, but we're not losing the war." He seemed to be preparing us for defeat on this night. It was then I asked him: "Victor, can I speak to them?" And he replied, "We've got nothing to lose." He was a fine person, but still I could feel that he didn't think a woman could do much in this situation.

I got up on the sound car—I know it was an electrifying thing . . . a woman's voice calling to the people of Flint after so many hours of fighting . . . and I said, "I'm talking especially to you women out there. You didn't know that mothers"— I meant myself—"are being fired on by the police. The police are cowards enough to fire into the bellies of unarmed men. Aren't they also cowards to fire at mothers of little children? I'm asking you women out there behind the barricades to break through those police lines. Come down here and stand with your brothers, your sons, your sweethearts, your husbands and help us win this fight."

And so help me, I could hardly believe it—one woman started walking toward us. The police grabbed at her and she walked right out of her coat. She marched down, other women following her—the police didn't dare shoot all those women in the back. Then the union men broke through. The battle was over and the union had won.

The women had saved the day. It was then that I realized how much power women had, and I proceeded to organize the Women's Emergency Brigade.

This was an independent move. It was not under the direction of the union or its administrators—I just talked it over with a few women—the active ones—and told them this is what we had to do.

Women might, after all, be called upon to give their lives. That was exactly the appeal I made while we were forming the brigade—I told the women, "Don't sign up for this unless you are prepared. If you are prone to hysteria or anything like that you'd only be in our way." I told them they'd be linking arms and withstanding the onslaughts of the police and if one of our sisters went down shot in cold blood there'd be no time for hysteria.

Around 500 women answered that call. We bought red berets and made arm bands with the white letters "EB" for Emergency Brigade. It was a kind of military uniform, yes, but it was mainly identification. We wore them all the time so we'd know who to call on to give help in an emergency. I had five lieutenants—three were factory women. I chose them because they could be called out of bed at any hour, if necessary, or sleep on a cot at the union hall. Mothers with children couldn't answer calls like that—although they did sign up for the brigade. Even a few grandmothers became brigadiers and, I remember, one young girl only sixteen.

We had no communication system to speak of. Very few people had telephones so we had to call one woman who was responsible for getting the messages through to many others.

We organized a first aid station and child care center—the women who had small children to tend and couldn't join the EB took care of these jobs.

Listen, I met some of the finest women I have ever come across in my life. When the occasion demands it of a woman and once she understands that she's standing in defense of her family—well, God, *don't fool around with that woman then.*

The brigade developed in such a short period of time. Some of them we soon sent to Lansing, Pontiac, and other outlying automobile factory towns where the police were beating the heads of men attempting to organize a union. We went in carloads to give them courage. Women played important roles . . .

I saw women stand up under circumstances where big men ran around the corner and hid under a car. I have seen them rise up when I would not have believed they could.

I'd get up in the men's meetings and say, "Bring your wives down here." I'd tell them, "Your wives should come out and join us so they will understand what their husbands are fighting for." I explained it would make for closer companionship within the family.

Finally, you know, everything just came to a head. With so many workers' homes without sufficient food and heat in the freezing January temperatures, and powerful General Motors benefiting from the unequal contest . . . well, it came time for a major decision. Plant 4, the largest plant in the Chevrolet division of ten plants, produced all the motors for Chevrolet throughout the country. That plant became our target. We knew if we could close it down, profits would be cut and that would bring General Motors to the bargaining table. We also knew that 4 was the plant they guarded the most vigilantly—so what historians have called the finest labor strategy of the twentieth century was devised.

We pretended to strike one of the other Chevrolet plants, Plant 9, which was far removed on the other side of the whole complex and had that action drawing all the company police, city police, and Pinkerton agents . . . a diversionary tactic, you see. The Women's Emergency Brigade was there and they broke the windows to allow air to get in to the tear-gassed union men. Women just played a fantastic role over there at Plant 9.

Now, my husband Kermit's assignment was to shut down Plant 4, the target plant. But I dared not let the brigade know about it because it had to be such a tight secret. The whole union movement had been infiltrated with company spies. After the Plant 9 action, I sent the brigade back to headquarters and with my five lieutenants, walked around the city streets that paralleled the big Chevrolet compound—very leisurely, very casually—so that no one would notice us too much. The rest of the brigade marched back to the headquarters so our absence wasn't noticed.

We strolled over to Plant 4 which the union men were attempting to shut down. I was very nervous because I knew it was a life and death matter for my husband and the other men inside. By the time we got over there there was a great deal of confusion. It was a huge place—imagine a plant with 8,000 workers. They had to seal doors that were as big as the sides of houses—gondolas of steel parts had to be brought up in order to barricade some doors, while others were welded shut. They were having a helluva time.

The plant foreman and his hired agents were giving them trouble. There were fist fights breaking out all over the place. The men yelled to us, "My God, we're having an awful time. Don't let anybody come in through the front gate on Chevrolet Avenue." Naturally, that was a big order, so I sent one of my lieutenants to call headquarters. "Tell the brigade to come at once," I told her. And the five of us left strung ourselves across the front gate.

When the city police got word what was happening they came, seventy-five of them, and found us women on the gate. We defied them . . . told them they would have to go in over our dead bodies.

And we used psychology on them. Eighty percent had relatives working under those horrible conditions in the plants. "Look," I said, "if you worked in this plant, and you were being driven crazy, and your health was broken down, wouldn't you expect your wife to come down here to see what she could do?"

It threw them off their guard and they began answering my arguments, just long enough. By the time they got provoked and said, "Well, we've got a job to do," and started pushing us, at that point the brigade came down Chevrolet Avenue. There came hundreds of those red berets bobbing up and down with the American flag at their head, singing "Solidarity Forever." The sound of it, from all those voices, just flooded the whole area.

They quickly set up an oval picket line in front of the main gate. This meant the police would have to club and shoot these women, and they had no stomach for that. Then the truck arrived filled with union men, and God, it dawned on me, *we'd saved the gate.*

The union had closed the huge and valuable Plant 4 with another sit-down strike. Soon after, Governor Frank Murphy declared martial law and ordered negotiations started. On February 11th, an agreement was reached recognizing unions in GM plants across the nation. That was a much greater victory than our small, inexperienced union ever expected to win.

After the settlement, I was sent on a public speaking tour of the major unions on the Eastern coast for at least a month, and when I returned to Flint, I collapsed completely and I had to go into a sanatorium. Did I mention that I had TB during this time?

The union raised money to send me to a sanatorium in the Adirondacks. But when I came back, I found erosion had taken place. The brigade had been disbanded with the victory. Maybe it's a good thing I wasn't around during this period because the husbands began saying, "Well, you women did a wonderful job, but now your duty is back there getting those kids in school, getting the wash done, and regular meals again . . ."

Oh, the union had tremendous respect for us, but after the strike was over they said in effect, "Thank you, ladies, so much." And at the top level of the International Union they turned the women's group into a mockery that I couldn't even be a part of. They had courses in styling clothes, coiffure, and makeup—things which, of course, some women had an interest in—but that wasn't our whole interest nor did it represent our real concerns.

A few of the women tried to hang on, and they were meeting in homes and that sort of thing. But it was a phantom thing, and I decided I didn't want to carry on that way.

It's a measure of the strength of those women of the Red Berets that they could perform so courageously in an atmosphere that was often hostile to them. We organized on our own without the benefit of professional leadership, and yet, we played a role, second to none, in the birth of a union and in changing working families' lives forever.

"I Want You Women Up North to Know"

Tillie Olsen

Even with the labor legislation passed during the New Deal, many industrial workers continued to experience terrible conditions on the job—long hours, low pay, unsanitary working conditions. With the Depression still gripping the country, workers were often reluctant to organize or act for fear of losing their jobs. And yet many did speak out. For example, in Texas a woman named Felipe Ibarro filed a suit against local factory owners for exploitation of their mainly Chicana labor force. Writer Tillie Olsen took the facts contained in the indictment, including the names of workers, their ages, and their salaries, and wrote this poem, "I Want You Women Up North to Know." Published in the radical magazine *Partisan* in March 1934, the poem aimed to shock buyers about the sweatshop conditions under which garments had been made. The National Consumers' League, a middle-class organization, had tried a similar tactic earlier in the century with its publication of a "white list," which encouraged consumers to buy only goods manufactured under safe and sanitary conditions.

Like Meridel LeSueur, Tillie Lerner Olsen was a radical with roots in the Midwest. Born in Nebraska in 1913, she was profoundly affected by the radicalism of her parents, recent immigrants from Russia who had joined the Socialist Party when they arrived in this country. Forced to drop out of school in the early years of the Depression, she participated in various organizing drives and the San Francisco longshoreman strike of 1934. She also began to write, including a powerful novel called *Yonnondio: From the Thirties,* which was lost for many years and only published in 1974.

Tillie Olsen brought her radical perspective not just to politics and the labor movement but also to literature, specifically the ways in which circumstances such as class, race, and gender often conspired to inhibit the creative process. She knew from her personal experience as a wife and mother of four children: "In the twenty years I bore and raised my children, usually had to work on a paid job as well, the simplest circumstances for creation did not exist." That insight led to her pathbreaking book, *Silences* (1978), which joined *Yonnondio* and her 1962 novella *Tell Me A Riddle* as her contributions to breaking the silence of women writers.

I want you women up north to know
how those dainty children's dresses you buy
    at macy's, wannamakers, gimbels, marshall fields,
are dyed in blood, are stitched in wasting flesh,
down in San Antonio, "where sunshine spends the winter."

Source: Tillie Olsen, "I Want You Women Up North to Know," *Partisan,* (1934). Reprinted by permission.

I want you women up north to see
the obsequious smile, the salesladies trill
    "exquisite work, madame, exquisite pleats"
vanish into a bloated face, ordering more dresses,
    gouging the wages down,
dissolve into maria, ambrosa, catalina,
    stitching these dresses from dawn to night,
    in blood, in wasting flesh.

Catalina Rodriguez, 24,
    body shrivelled to a child's at twelve,
catalina rodriguez, last stages of consumption,
    works for three dollars a week from dawn to midnight.
A fog of pain thickens over her skull, the parching heat
    breaks over her body,
and the bright red blood embroiders the floor of her room.
    White rain stitching the night, the bourgeois poet would say.
    white gulls of hands, darting, veering,
    white lightning, threading the clouds,
this is the exquisite dance of her hands over the cloth,
and her cough, gay, quick, staccato,
    like skeleton's bones clattering,
is appropriate accompaniment for the esthetic dance
    of her fingers,
and the tremolo, tremolo when the hands tremble with pain.
Three dollars a week,
two fifty-five,
seventy cents a week,
no wonder two thousand eight hundred ladies of joy are spending
the winter with the sun after he goes down—for five cents (who
said this was a rich man's world?) you can
    get all the lovin you want
"clap and syph aint much worse than sore fingers, blind eyes, and
    t.b."

Maria Vasquez, spinster,
    for fifteen cents a dozen stitches garments for children she
    has never had,
Catalina Torres, mother of four,
    to keep the starved body starving, embroiders from dawn
    to night.
Mother of four, what does she think of,
    as the needle pocked fingers shift over the silk—
    of the stubble-coarse rags that stretch on her own brood,
    and jut with the bony ridge that marks hunger's landscape

of fat little prairie-roll bodies that will bulge in the
    silk she needles?
(Be not envious, Catalina Torres, look!
      on your own children's clothing, embroidery,
      more intricate than any a thousand hands could fashion,
      there where the cloth is ravelled, or darned,
designs, multitudinous, complex and handmade by Poverty
    herself.)
Ambrosa Espinoza trusts in god,
      "Todos es de dio, everything is from God,"
      through the dwindling night, the waxing day, she bolsters
    herself up with it—
but the pennies to keep god incarnate, from ambrosa,
and the pennies to keep the priest in wine, from ambrosa,
ambrosa clothes god and priest with hand-made children's dresses.

Her brother lies on an iron cot, all day and watches,
on a mattress of rags he lies.
For twenty-five years he worked for the railroad, then they
    laid him off.
    (racked days, searching for work; rebuffs; suspicious eyes of
    policmen.
    goodbye ambrosa, mebbe in dallas I find work; desperate
    swing for a freight
    surprised hands, clutching air, and the wheel goes over a
    leg,
    the railroad cuts it off, as it cut off twenty-five years of his
    life.)
She says that he prays and dreams of another world, as he lies
    there, a heaven (which he does not know was brought to
    earth in 1917 in Russia, by workers like him.)

Women up north, I want you to know
when you finger the exquisite hand-made dresses
what it means, this working from dawn to midnight, on what
strange feet the feverish dawn must come
    to maria, catalina, ambrosa,
how the malignant fingers twitching over the pallid faces jerk
them to work,
and the sun and the fever mount with the day—
    long plodding hours, the eyes burn like coals, heat jellies
    the flying fingers,
down comes the night like blindness.
    long hours more with the dim eye of the lamp, the breaking
    back,

weariness crawls in the flesh like worms, gigantic like earth's
in winter.
And for Catalina Rodriguez comes the night sweat and the blood
embroidering the darkness.
for Catalina Torres the pinched faces of four huddled
children,
the naked bodies of four bony children,
the chant of their chorale of hunger.
And for twenty eight hundred ladies of joy the grotesque act gone
over—the wink—the grimace—the "feeling like it baby?"
And for Maria Vasquez, spinster, emptiness, emptiness,
flaming with dresses for children she can never fondle.
And for Ambrosa Espinoza—the skeleton body of her brother on
his mattress of rags, boring twin holes in the dark with his eyes to
the image of christ, remembering a leg, and twenty five years cut
off from his life by the railroad.

Women up north, I want you to know,
I tell you this can't last forever.

I swear it won't.

EQUAL TIME FOR CHIVALRY

The independent woman of the 1920s felt herself to be man's equal, so why shouldn't she doff her hat to him as she passed him on the street? After all, men had been greeting women in that way for centuries. But notice that the hats being doffed in this photograph are decidedly stylish—in the cloche style—and that the women's hair underneath them is clearly bobbed because their necks are visible. This summer scene (the women's dresses, if not terribly stylish, are lightweight and comfortable) suggests the trappings of independence that women adopted in the decade.
(Credit: UPI)

THE AVIATOR AS FEMINIST HEROINE

For many Americans, Amelia Earhart (1897–1937) symbolized women's emancipation and modern roles. A former settlement house volunteer as well as a pioneer in the field of aviation, Earhart, in 1932, became the first woman to fly across the Atlantic alone. Her short, bobbed hair and appearance of easy self-assurance, plus a strong physical resemblance to aviator Charles Lindbergh, earned her the nickname *Lady Lindy.* She was presumed lost at sea somewhere in the Pacific in 1937 while attempting a round-the-world flight, although her plane was never recovered.
(Credit: UPI)

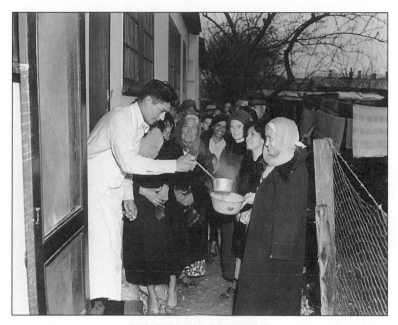

WOMEN IN A SOUP LINE

Although it was rare to see women on a breadline in the Great Depression, these Mexican-American women have gone around the back of a private agency called the International Institute in San Antonio, Texas, to receive a handout of free soup. The year is 1937, and the Depression still grips the nation. Although the federal government offered some assistance to San Antonians through the Works Progress Administration (WPA), it was never enough to assist all those who qualified, and many families were forced to rely on private agencies. The smiles on the faces of these women show their gratitude for this help, probably the difference between feeding their families and going to bed hungry that night.
(Credit: *San Antonio Light* Collection, University of Texas Institute of Texas Cultures, San Antonio)

STRIKING SOLIDARITY

Women from the United Auto Workers' Women's Auxiliary demonstrate their solidarity with their sisters from Flint during the sit-down strikes of 1937. If this picture had been in color, it would have shown the bright green caps of the Detroit women, which contrasted with the red berets worn by the Flint auxiliary. The nightsticks that the women carry suggest their vaguely paramilitary role, although one of their placards reminds the citizens of Flint "We Are against Violence." Another banner takes a stand for equal pay for equal work.
(Credit: Wayne State University Archives)

WARTIME WORKERS

When men went off to war, women moved into the jobs left behind in the defense industries. These women work in an aviation plant owned by Douglas Aircraft in Chicago in 1943. Note that most of the women are young, and all are white; black workers (if employed at all) would have been likely sent to other, less desirable jobs in the plant. Notice also that all the women are dressed in pants.
(Credit: UPI)

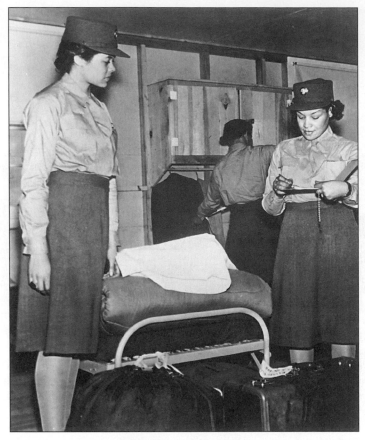

THE JIM CROW ARMY

These women are members of the 33rd Post Headquarters Company of the Women's Army Auxiliary Corps (WAACs), stationed at Fort Huachuca, Arizona, during World War II. Black women made up approximately 10 percent of the WAACs, although they were rigidly assigned (as were black men in the armed forces) to separate units. This barracks, into which the new recruit is settling, would have been segregated, and she would have eaten in an all-black mess hall and exercised at black-only recreational facilities. Also, it would have been highly unlikely that her unit would have seen duty overseas.
(Credit: Schomburg Center for Research in Black Culture, New York Public Library)

Women Want Homes Like This!

A FRIENDLY doorway that always says "Welcome!"...a lovely door-garden where sunshine and flowers suggest the happiness and contentment inside...not just a house, but a *home* where you have time to relax and enjoy life.

These are things we all want.

And in these days of tired bodies and troubled minds it's good for one to think about them now and then—about the new

kind of a home *you* will have after victory. Cooking, dishwashing, laundry and house-cleaning will still go on, of course; but they will be done the easy, efficient, electrical way without drudgery...there'll be time to fuss with flowers.

But just now new home things must wait—there's a war to win first. So put your money in war bonds—buy another and another and another. Each extra dollar does an extra bit

to speed victory. And each dollar you spend *after* victory will help provide jobs for the soldiers returning to peace-time industry.

Until the war is won General Electric will continue making only "tools of victory." But when that job is finished we will go back with added enthusiasm to the job we like best—making better electrical equipment for your home that will bring you better living at less cost.

GENERAL ELECTRIC

DELAYED DREAMS

Since so few consumer goods were manufactured during the war mobilization, industry leaders used advertisements to ask customers to delay their dreams until after the war was won. "Everything Electric for After-Victory Homes" proclaims this General Electric ad from *Life* magazine, February 7, 1944. While the text is filled with statements linking wartime sacrifices with the promised affluence of a postwar world, the image presented (happy baby, cheerful [white] mother, lushly landscaped garden, large house, even the picket fence) was a reality for only a minority of American families at war's end.
(Credit: By permission of General Electric Company)

CIVIL RIGHTS ACTIVISM IN AN ERA OF CONFORMITY

Rosa Parks represents the large role that black women played in the Civil
Rights revolution that rocked American society in the 1950s and beyond. Here
she is fingerprinted at the Montgomery, Alabama, police station in 1955 after
being arrested for failing to give up her seat on a city bus to a white person. "I
felt it was just something I had to do," Parks said simply. Black activist
Eldridge Cleaver captured the broader significance of her personal stand:
"Somewhere in the universe a gear in the machinery shifted."
(Credit: Wide World Photos, Inc.)

CHAPTER 8

Rosie the Riveter and Other Wartime Women

World War II had an unmistakable impact on American society. The task of fighting and winning a global war greatly accelerated the growth of the federal bureaucracy that had begun during the New Deal; federal budgets and functions never returned to their prewar levels. Nor did the United States return to its prewar stance of isolation from international relations. The war also encouraged dramatic social changes on the home front, especially an increase in mobility as people flocked to war jobs or entered the armed services. African-Americans were able to lay the groundwork for the postwar civil rights revolution by equating segregation with Nazi white supremacist ideology. Most importantly, defense mobilization brought a return to prosperity after a decade of depression.

The specific impact of the wartime experience on the nation's women is less clear-cut. Some historians have argued that the war represented a major turning point for women because of their dramatic roles in the war effort, especially in defense plants. Others have focused on the persistence of sexism and discrimination against women on the job, in families, and in society as a whole. The weight of the evidence in this historical debate tilts toward analyzing women's wartime experiences in light of long-term trends of employment, demographics, and family roles, rather than seeing the war as a dramatic period of social change.

One of the difficulties of coming to an assessment of the impact of World War II on women is that the impact varies depending on which women are examined. Despite all the media attention to the "Rosie the Riveters" who took on defense jobs, the majority of American women were homemakers during the war. The war permeated every aspect of their daily life. Popular culture and advertising were saturated with patriotic war themes, especially the movies. Household management was challenging during wartime, notably coping with the high inflation rate and the shortages and rationing of most durable consumer goods, food, and gasoline. Women also performed volunteer services for their communities.

Many women were more directly involved in the war effort. For example, 350,000 women joined the armed services, supplying approximately 2 percent of the total fighting forces. Equally dramatic were changes for the nation's female workers. The female work force grew by 50 percent between 1940 and 1945.

These war workers were drawn both from the ranks of women already working (they used the opportunity to leave such traditional female jobs as domestic and personal service for higher-paying industrial work) and new workers, including recent students and former full-time homemakers who joined the war effort for reasons both of patriotism and economics. The wartime economic and social climate was especially liberating for single women, who experienced increasing autonomy and independence in the conduct of their personal lives. Such opportunities were also an important breakthrough for black workers of both sexes, who until the war-induced labor shortage had been barred from most manufacturing and industrial jobs.

These women workers were welcomed into the work force, a stark contrast to the public disapproval that greeted women during the Depression. But much of the public support derived from the conviction that these women workers were only temporary, that they would happily trade their overalls and welding tools for aprons when the men came home from war. Women workers had other ideas. When surveyed, the vast majority wanted to keep their new jobs. In the reconversion process, women did in fact lose many of the gains made during wartime, but they did not return to the home—they just went back to the traditional kinds of female jobs they had always held. After a slight dip after the war, the percentage of women who worked began a steady climb upwards. By 1950, 28.6 percent of adult women were working (down from the wartime peak of 37 percent), comprising 30 percent of the work force. In the postwar period, women showed an increasing propensity to combine marriage and work, a trend first noticed during the Depression but vastly accelerated during wartime.

World War II left other legacies for the nation's women. Because women's work was seen as temporary, there was no underlying shift in public attitudes about women's traditional responsibilities for home and family. In fact, "the unshaken claim of family" was probably intensified by the war: after the years of home front dislocation, returning soldiers and their spouses welcomed a return to normalcy. The marriage and birth rates, which had been artificially suppressed during the Depression, had already begun to rise during the war and would shoot up soon afterwards. So did the divorce rate.

Concentrating on women's displacement from industrial jobs and the continuity of traditional attitudes about women's place leads to fairly negative assessments about the impact of the war on women's lives. Such a view, however, is too shortsighted, for it misses what the wartime experience meant to individual women. Historian Sherna Gluck, who collected oral histories from female war workers in California, found this common thread to many women's recollections: "I never realized what I could do." Gluck posits that this increase in self-esteem and belief in women's own capabilities spilled over into more egalitarian family and marital relations in the postwar years, but was not translated into a direct challenge of the status quo in the public realm: "Changes in consciousness are not *necessarily* or *immediately* reflected in dramatic alterations in the public world. They may be very quietly played out in the private world of women, yet expressed in a fashion that can both affect future generations and eventually be expressed more openly when the social climate is right." Taking this perspective on the impact of the war on individual women's lives, World War II may turn out to have been more of a watershed for women than historians have realized.

Rosie the Riveter

Fanny Christina Hill

No image captured the popular view of women's contributions to the war effort better than Norman Rockwell's *Saturday Evening Post* cover of "Rosie the Riveter": a patriotic housewife who dons overalls and goes to work in a defense plant "for the duration." Yet, there was no one Rosie the Riveter: She was a recent high school graduate taking her first job or a mother with a son in the service; she had been working before the war or was taking her first full-time job after years of homemaking; she was single or married, white or black or Latina, middle- or working-class. What unified the experiences of these women was that they proved to themselves (and the country) that they could do a "man's job" and could do it well.

The experiences of black women in the defense industry are especially instructive. World War II's labor shortage opened up skilled work in industry, providing better working conditions and dramatic increases in pay over black women's previous concentration in domestic service or farm labor. The jobs opened to blacks, however, were always less desirable and less numerous than those available to whites. But the process of whites working alongside blacks (and, to a lesser degree, Latinas) encouraged a breaking down of social barriers and a healthy recognition of diversity.

The oral history of Fanny Christina (Tina) Hill illuminates these broader trends. A black woman who was born in Texas but migrated to California, she had been trapped in domestic service until at age 24 she got a job at North American Aircraft. Her memoir balances excitement at the opportunity with an awareness of the discrimination blacks faced on the job. Her story also confirms the need to look beyond just the war years to understand the life cycles of the Rosie the Riveters. After quitting work near war's end to have a child, she returned to North American Aircraft in 1946 (one of the minority of wartime women who got their jobs back), remaining there until her retirement in 1980. As her final comment underscores, Tina Hill realizes that World War II had a positive impact on her life.

I don't remember what day of the week it was, but I guess I must have started out pretty early that morning. When I went there, the man didn't hire me. They had a school down here on Figueroa and he told me to go to the school. I went down and it was almost four o'clock and they told me they'd hire me. You had to fill out a form. They didn't bother too much about your experience because they knew you

Source: From *Rosie the Riveter Revisited,* by Sherna Berger Gluck. Copyright © 1987. Reprinted by permission of The Gale Group.

didn't have any experience in aircraft. Then they give you some kind of little test where you put the pegs in the right hole.

There were other people in there, kinda mixed. I assume it was more women than men. Most of the men was gone, and they weren't hiring too many men unless they had a good excuse. Most of the women was in my bracket, five or six years younger or older. I was twenty-four. There was a black girl that hired in with me. I went to work the next day, sixty cents an hour.

I think I stayed at the school for about four weeks. They only taught you shooting and bucking rivets and how to drill the holes and to file. You had to use a hammer for certain things. After a couple of whiles, you worked on the real thing. But you were supervised so you didn't make a mess.

When we went into the plant, it wasn't too much different than down at the school. It was the same amount of noise; it was the same routine. One difference was there was just so many more people, and when you went in the door you had a badge to show and they looked at your lunch. I had gotten accustomed to a lot of people and I knew if it was a lot of people, it always meant something was going on. I got carried away: "As long as there's a lot of people here, I'll be making money." That was all I could ever see.

I was a good student, if I do say so myself. But I have found out through life, sometimes even if you're good, you just don't get the breaks if the color's not right. I could see where they made a difference in placing you in certain jobs. They had fifteen or twenty departments, but all the Negroes went to Department 17 because there was nothing but shooting and bucking rivets. You stood on one side of the panel and your partner stood on this side, and he would shoot the rivets with a gun and you'd buck them with the bar. That was about the size of it. I just didn't like it. I didn't think I could stay there with all this shooting and a'bucking and a'jumping and a'bumping. I stayed in it about two or three weeks and then I just decided I did *not* like that. I went and told my foreman and he didn't do anything about it, so I decided I'd leave.

While I was standing out on the railroad track, I ran into somebody else out there fussing also. I went over to the union and they told me what to do. I went back inside and they sent me to another department where you did bench work and I liked that much better. You had a little small jig that you would work on and you just drilled out holes. Sometimes you would rout them or you would scribe them and then you'd cut them with a cutters.

I must have stayed there nearly a year, and then they put me over in another department, "Plastics." It was the tail section of the B-Bomber, the Billy Mitchell Bomber. I put a little part in the gun sight. You had a little ratchet set and you would screw it in there. Then I cleaned the top of the glass off and put a piece of paper over it to seal it off to go to the next section. I worked over there until the end of the war. Well, not quite the end, because I got pregnant, and while I was off having the baby the war was over . . .

You had a spot where you always stayed around, close to where you worked, because when the whistle blew, you wanted to be ready to get up and go to where you worked. The leadman always come by and give you a job to do or you already had one that was a hangover from the day before. So you had a general idea what you was going to do each day.

Then we'd work and come home. I was married when I started working in the war plant, so I wasn't looking for a boyfriend and that made me come home in the evening. Sometimes you'd stop on the way home and shop for groceries. Then you'd come home and clean house and get ready for bed so you can go back the next morning. Write letters or what have you. I really wasn't physically tired . . .

Some weeks I brought home twenty-six dollars, some weeks sixteen dollars. Then it gradually went up to thirty dollars, then it went up a little bit more and a little bit more. And I learned somewhere along the line that in order to make a good move you gotta make some money. You don't make the same amount everyday. You have some days good, sometimes bad. Whatever you make you're supposed to save some. I was also getting that fifty dollars a month from my husband and that was just saved right away. I was planning on buying a home and a car. And I was going to go back to school. My husband came back, but I never was laid off, so I just never found it necessary to look for another job or to go to school for another job.

I was still living over on Compton Avenue with my sister in this small little back house when my husband got home. Then, when Beverly was born, my sister moved in the front house and we stayed in the back house. When he came back, he looked for a job in the cleaning and pressing place, which was just plentiful. All the people had left these cleaning and pressing jobs and every other job; they was going to the defense plant to work because they was paying good. But in the meantime he was getting the same thing the people out there was getting, $1.25 an hour. That's why he didn't bother to go out to North American. But what we both weren't thinking about was that they did have better benefits because they did have an insurance plan and a union to back you up. Later he did come to work there, in 1951 or 1952.

I worked up until the end of March and then I took off. Beverly was born the twenty-first of June. I'd planned to come back somewhere in the last of August. I went to verify the fact that I did come back, so that did go on my record that I didn't just quit. But they laid off a lot of people, most of them, because the war was over.

It didn't bother me much—not thinking about it jobwise. I was just glad that the war was over. I didn't feel bad because my husband had a job and he also was eligible to go to school with his GI bill. So I really didn't have too many plans—which I wish I had had. I would have tore out page one and fixed it differently; put my version of page one in there.

I went and got me a job doing day work. That means you go to a person's house and clean up for one day out of the week and then you go to the next one and clean up. I did that a couple of times and I discovered I didn't like that so hot. Then I got me a job downtown working in a little factory where you do weaving—burned clothes and stuff like that. I learned to do that real good. It didn't pay too much but it paid enough to get me going, seventy-five cents or about like that.

When North American called me back, was I a happy soul! I dropped that job and went back. That was a dollar an hour. So, from sixty cents an hour, when I first hired in there, up to one dollar. That wasn't traveling fast, but it was better than anything else because you had hours to work by and you had benefits and you come home at night with your family. So it was a good deal.

It made me live better. I really did. We always say that Lincoln took the bale off of the Negroes. I think there is a statue up there in Washington, D.C., where he's lifting something off the Negro. Well, my sister always said—that's why you can't interview her because she's so radical—"Hitler was the one that got us out of the white folks' kitchen."

Women in the Armed Forces

Marion Stegeman

Of the more than 15 million Americans who entered the armed services during World War II, approximately 350,000 were women. Like the Rosie the Riveters, women who joined the armed forces experienced new challenges, greater geographical mobility, and increased responsibility. The largest number served in the Women's Army Corps (WACS)—140,000—followed by 100,000 volunteers for the WAVES (Women Appointed for Volunteer Emergency Service) in the Navy. There were women's branches of the Marines and Coast Guard, and 1,000 WASPs (Women's Airforce Service Pilots) did stateside and noncombat air duty.

Avenger Field in Sweetwater, Texas, was the place to be if you were a woman and a pilot in World War II. The letters that Marion Stegeman wrote home convey the excitement of being a WASP, a thrill that was part patriotism but mainly the sheer joy of flying. They also convey the disappointments, like a friend "washing out" (being asked to leave) or, worse, the death of classmates in training exercises. In all, 38 WASPs lost their lives during the war.

Marion Stegeman had learned to fly in a Civilian Pilot Training Program while a student at the University of Georgia, from which she graduated with a degree in journalism and art in 1941. She became a WASP because she "wanted to be part of the action." After her training at Sweetwater, she was stationed at Love Field in Dallas. But, as her last letter shows, she realized that there was no future for women as pilots in the armed services and in 1944 she resigned to marry her boyfriend Ned Hodgson, a Marine stationed in Texas. After the war, they settled in Fort Worth to raise a family, both their lives dramatically and irrevocably affected by their service during World War II.

Sweetwater, Texas
April 24, 1943

Dearest Mother,

The gods must envy me! This is just too, *too* to be true. (By now you realize I had a good day as regards flying. Nothing is such a gauge to the spirits as how well or how poorly one has flown.) Where was I? Oh, yes, I'm far too happy. The law of compensation must be waiting to catch up with me somewhere. Oh, God, how I love it! Honestly, Mother, you haven't *lived* until you get way *up* there—all alone—just you and that big, beautiful plane humming under your control. I just sit there and sing at the top of my lungs while I'm climbing up to 4,000 feet—or however high I want to go. Of course, I'm too busy to sing while in the middle of aerobatics—but you ought to hear me let loose when I'm "clearing my area" between maneuvers. (We always clear the area first to make sure there are no planes underneath or close by —safety foist!)

The only thing that I know that's going to happen that I won't like is that they are changing my instructors some day soon. Mine is going on to the B.T.'s (Basic trainers—one step ahead of primary trainers) but maybe I'll get him again when I get to the B.T.'s. Hope so! I have no idea who my new instructor will be—I hope I'll like him as much as I do this one. He'll have to be pretty good and mighty nice though, to beat Mr. Wade's time . . .

Smackers and much love to John, Janet, Joanna and you—M.

*   *   *

Sweetwater, Texas
[June 10, 1943]

Mother, Dear,

. . . I went on my fourth solo cross-country ("X-C") yesterday and at last something happened to break the monotony. Each trip is around 400 miles and takes about three hours, and they really get boring. But yesterday a strong wind blew me off course and made me temporarily uncertain. I decided to head out for home anyway, but things started looking *wrong,* and the check points didn't jibe with the map. I buzzed a couple of towns but couldn't find the names of them anywhere, so I turned around and went back to a town I had just passed over that had an airport. I knew it was either Ballinger or another town north of Ballinger, both of which had army airports. The roads leading out of each town made a similar pattern and the fields were located in the same place in relation to the towns. So I entered the traffic pattern with a bunch of P.T's and landed. I could've tried to get on home, but I didn't have a heck of a lot of gas and I was bored with it all anyway, and didn't want to waste time. The Army cadets and instructors nearly fell out of their planes when they saw a *girl* taxiing by in a *B.T.!* I beamed at them all and got out at a hangar where I telephoned our squadron commander, after I had found it was Ballinger, after all . . .

The Sqn. Cmdr. here (when I got him on the phone) told me I had done the right thing and to come on home if I could get clearance to take off from Ballinger. So I sacheted over to Major McConnell's office and got the most cordial greeting, I've ever had. He said, "Sure I'll clear you, but I refuse to do it for a couple of hours." So he took me to the PX for cokes and cigarettes and showed me around the post. He devoted his entire time to me, and then—and then!—flew formation home with me! I had a wonderful time and the girls were really impressed and refuse to believe it wasn't all planned. The major's parting words, before he took off for Ballinger after delivering me here safely, were: "Next time make it late in the afternoon!" . . .

Darling, I do miss you so! Please don't worry about me when you miss me, though, because, honestly, I'm so happy and having so much fun it's worth any chance in the world I could take. And, actually, I'm not doing anything dangerous at all. I fly well-kept-up planes in a country where no one will shoot me down, so I'm not really brave at all, though you may keep on thinking so if you like!

LOVE YA, M.

*   *   *

Sweetwater, Texas
[Summer 1943]

Mother dear,

. . . Mother, the most heart-breaking thing has happened. Jane . . . the older roommate—washed out yesterday. The check pilots said the B.T. was just too much for her to handle, that it was no reflection on her flying . . . Some people just aren't capable of handling the faster, heavier ships and still they make good pilots on lighter planes. Poor Jane, though! Next to Shirley and Sandy she was my favorite, and I'll sure miss her and her inimitable sense of humor. She was loads of fun and it just about broke my heart to watch what she was going through while waiting for what she knew was to be her last ride. Of course, this doesn't hit her as hard as it would someone like the other roommates because Jane has a husband and daughter—but, as she put it, that didn't keep her "from being heartsick." Poor gal cried for two days, and I cried right with her most of the time . . .

Love you *deely.* M.

*   *   *

[Sweetwater, Texas
Late summer, 1943]

Dear Mom,

. . . Mother, this was to be a short letter, but now something has happened that I must tell you about.

You may just as well get used to hearing about these things, Mom, because so long as I'm in the flying racket they are bound to happen. Two of my classmates and their instructor were killed yesterday afternoon near Big Spring . . .

This is no doubt another of those undetermined causes that brings about crashes, and no one will ever know what it was. Maybe it was one of those rare structural failure cases—no one knows. It seems likely, since the instructor was in the plane—Or it could have been that the girls were changing seats in mid air and one of them could've grabbed the wheel for support, thus stalling the plane. There are endless possibilities—Most of them things that *could* have been avoided, as most crashes seem to be . . .

Don't worry about it, though, Mom, because it's very unusual for anything so mysterious to happen (especially *here*) and they're inspecting all the airplanes before we go up in them again.

As I've told you before, we *do* take chances, but they are small compared to those that thousands take every day all over the world. And we could fall down in our bathtubs at home and be killed, or get in a car and meet death. It's just not up to us to say where or when. You believe that, don't you? We'll talk about it more when I get home . . .

I love you, Marion

*   *   *

Tallahassee, Florida
March 30, 1944

Mother, dear:

(1) General Arnold [Henry H. "Hap" Arnold, Chief of the Army Air Forces] says openly that the Army Air Forces has more than enough pilots.

(2) There are experienced instructors now being forced into the foot army— and others out of jobs.

(3) If I go into the Army, they could chain me to a typewriter for the duration plus six months, in spite of anything they might promise.

(4) I can't see myself running around saluting and kow-towing and obeying orders from [those who] . . . will really dish out the works to those of us who have been in only a year and will be mere Second Lieutenants. I can do what I'm told gracefully now only because—underneath it all—I know I don't *have* to.

Summary: All this adds up to a great deal of rationalization that has been taking place since I last saw my love. I want to marry him—now! Of course, though, I'd stay on the job indefinitely as a civilian, because I owe so much, but since the Army is forcing me to become a puppet or resign, I'm tempted to go my own way,—mine and Ned's.

I don't think the airplane will replace the man, do you?

It may be days, weeks, or months before it is necessary for me to decide. How's about a long letter of advice from you—and also please ask Aunt Helvig and Grannie what they think.

I love you, M.

Wartime Migration

Harriette Arnow

One of the most far-reaching changes on the home front during World War II was the dramatic increase in migration. Just the sheer fact of mobilizing 15 million men and women for military service encouraged a huge amount of internal migration, as people left their homes (often for the first time) to report to service camps and training centers. In addition, the Census Bureau estimated that another 15.3 million Americans moved during wartime, with more than half of those crossing state lines. The largest single influx was westward to the state of California, the site of much of the new defense mobilization and hence jobs. During the war alone, California gained 1.4 million newcomers.

Harriette Arnow's novel, *The Dollmaker* (1954), conveys the dislocation and confusion that often accompanied such wartime uprootings. Set in the closing years of World War II (although the war is barely mentioned), the book traces the story of the Nevels family as they leave rural Kentucky for war-induced industrial opportunities in Detroit. Clovis, the husband, excited about the prospects for higher wages and a better life in a big city, initiates the move, even though his wife Gertie's dream is to own a farm of her own. In this excerpt, Gertie and her children have just arrived in Detroit at the home Clovis has rented for them. We see Detroit, and by extension, modern urban industrial life, through the eyes of a rural migrant. We follow her fumbling attempts to acquaint herself with such unfamiliar consumer items as gas stoves, bottled milk, and city water. We also see the poverty and barrenness of the urban landscape: no yard, railroad near by, tiny house with flimsy walls and little furniture, never enough money, even with everything bought on credit.

This novel does not offer a happy ending. One of Gertie's children runs away back to Kentucky, and another is killed by a train. The family sinks deeper in debt, as Clovis finds himself working only sporadically while expenses rise due to wartime inflation. The novel ends with Gertie Nevels, a skilled woodcarver, turning a large Christ figure she has been creating into cheap trinkets and wooden dolls that she can sell to make ends meet, thus supplying the ironic title of *The Dollmaker.*

Gertie stood, her outspread hands pressed against the door, closed behind her. She realized she stood in the kitchen of her new home, but it seemed more like a large closet with rows of uncurtained shelves above a sink, and smotheringly crowded with curious contrivances. A few feet in front of her was a doorless doorway into a small hall-like living room. In this room, no more than a dozen feet past the doorway, was another outside door, exactly opposite and exactly like the one behind her. The place seemed all halls and walls and doors and windows.

"It's so little, Mom. We cain't never cook an eat an—" Clytie's voice wavered, then died as she stared at a large black heating stove in a corner by the doorway.

Gertie continued to stand a moment longer, staring, choking, swallowing hard to prove to herself that she was not choking. "I figger," she said in a moment, "that it's about twenty-five feet frum inside to outside. If it jist wasn't broke up so, but we can—" Clytie, she realized, had disappeared like the rest of the children. She heard their cries and comments of exploration behind the kitchen walls. She drew a deep breath, then took the few steps to the other outside door. She opened the inner door, and scraped a hole in the dirt and frost on the outer door. She saw across a narrow strip of soot-blackened snow another building exactly like her own, telephone wires and poles, smoke, steel-mill light, and steam. She suddenly bent close to the glass, smiling. Quickly, she scraped the hole larger, then looked again; dim it had been through the steam and the smoke, and far away on the other side of the railroad fence, but it was a hill. She turned away; when seen more clearly the hill had become a great pile of coal.

She struck her shin bone against a chair as she closed the door. She bent to rub the pain, sharp in her half numb leg, and in bending her hips struck a corner of the low head of a cot-like bed. There was between the door and wall room for the head of the narrow bed, and on the other side of the door almost room for a chair. Touching the chair was a sofa, holding three cushions of some slippery, rubbery material. The wood of the sofa, like that of the chair, was a pale but shiny oak.

She stood a moment, her hands clenched by her sides, then carefully walked through the narrow space between bed and sofa. Two halls, scarce wider than her shoulders, led to the bathroom and the three bedrooms. Two of these were big enough for a double bed and four chairs each. The other was smaller still, but into it two single beds were jammed so close together there was no room to walk between them.

Clytie bumped her as she turned away. "Mom, they ain't no dressers, an no looken glass, but I bet they's twenty chairs, all alike. An jist one table fer all our cooken an eaten."

Clytie's voice had grown closer and closer to sobs, and Gertie patted her shoulder. "I recken th gover'ment thinks people won't be a doen much in their houses but setten an sleepen. An anyhow it won't be fer long an—" she was comforting when Enoch's laughter and Amos's frightened scream came from the other side of the kitchen. She bumped into the stove as she whirled toward the sound. Amos, water dripping from his hair, came running, with Enoch behind him, explaining between giggles, "He clumb into a little box uv a thing, Mom, an turned a round thing an water squirted all over."

Cassie trailed behind them, whimpering, "Th water stinks, Mom."

"It's city water, silly," Clytie explained. "It's purified like in th health books, and that thing in th bathroom, it's a shower, like in th catalogue."

Gertie tried a glass of water, but after one taste emptied it into the sink with a suspicious frown. "They's somethen in it besides water. It's worse'n that on th train."

Enoch was holding a match he had found above the kitchen sink and begging: "Light th gas, Mom. It'll warm up Amos, an we're all freezen."

Gertie turned to consider the little cooking stove in a corner of the kitchen. The top was hardly a fourth as big as that of her range cookstove back home, and no warming oven at all. Enoch, climbed on the edge of the sink to watch, pointed out the knobs she must turn, while Clytie warned, "Watch out, Mom. Vadie Tucker—recollect she'd been in Cincinnati—said a body had to be mighty careful a gas."

Gertie struck a match, and held it waveringly, looking first at the row of small black handles, then at the blank wall behind. "It ain't got no pipe. Mebbe it ain't ready to light."

"I'll bet gas stoves don't need pipes. Go on, turn one," Enoch urged.

"I don't know which is which," Gertie said in a whimpering voice, new to her.

Enoch turned a knob just as her match went out. She reached for another, while Enoch cried: "Hurry up, Mom. I'm turnen em all on."

She struck the match and held it toward the burners, all hissing now. Flame leaped at her; the corner of the kitchen seemed a wall of flame. She, like the children, jumped away, but her head struck a corner of the row of open shelves across from the stove. She saw stars and whirling lights, smelled smoke, and heard the screams of the children. Then Reuben was slapping her forehead. Clytie was throwing a glass of water on her, and Enoch was laughing. "Mom, you look so funny. Your hair's all swinged." . . .

The dusk had deepened until the flickering steel-mill lights made a bloody brightness on the windows, when there came another banging on the door. Clovis. He looked peaked, she thought, but hardly had a chance to look at him before the children came swarming over him, so crowding the tiny kitchen that she backed against the icebox, watching. Clytie was almost crying, and even Amos, little as he was, remembered his daddy as if he'd never been away.

She felt a sharp thrust of guilt. It was in truth like her mother said: the children had a right to live with their father. Seemed like sometimes they loved him better than her, especially Enoch and Clytie. But then she'd always been the one to give them the work and the scoldings. Clovis had brought the fun—trips in the coal truck, the river in summer, grape hunting in the fall. She'd never had the time.

In a moment he looked across their heads and smiled. "Supper ready, Gert? I'm starved fer some a yer good cooken. I ain't had a bite a fried meat, seems like, since I got up here."

"I ain't got no fried meat," she said, "but I've got supper."

"I'm figgeren on some good eaten. You ought tu have a heap a ration points. You never used none at home."

They pulled the table out from the wall, and there was room for Clovis and the older children to squeeze into their chairs, with space enough left at the corners for Amos and Cassie to stand. Gertie never sat down, but, as she had often done at home, stood between table and stove waiting on them all. Clovis, she saw, was displeased with the food. He looked resigned and disgusted as he had used to be when she left eggs out of the cornbread in order to have a few more to sell. Some of Sophronie's beans were left, and they were good, better than her own scrambled eggs and cornbread. The eggs had stuck for lack of grease and the bread, badly baked to begin with, was dry and hard and lifeless, as the meal that had gone into it.

He chirked up when Clytie praised the new dishes, and Enoch started carrying on about the wonders of the radio, and Cassie admired his new work clothing. Gertie, sorry that after he had bought so many things for them she didn't have a better kind of supper, said, trying hard to act pleased, "You've done good, real good, Clovis, to buy so much stuff, an send us th truck money besides."

He looked at her with a great showing of surprise. "Law, woman, you shorely don't think I've paid fer all this. Up here everybody buys everything on time."

She had fixed herself a plate of cornbread and beans, set it on the rim of the sink, and started to eat, standing up. But now she turned away from the food, asking, "How much we owe, Clovis?"

"Gert, don't start a worryen. Jist git it into yer head that I'm a maken big money. I ain't no sweeper maken th lowest. I done what I aimed to do, got on as a machine repair man. An it shore took some tall talken, an a heap a white lies. But it was worth it. I git in a heap a overtime, too. Do you know what my pay checkull be this week?" he went on, laying down his knife and fork and twisting about in his chair to look at her, "Why, better'n a hundred dollars."

She heard the admiring gasp of Reuben, hurt and sullen as he still was from his attempts to borrow kindling. Big as he was, he'd worked many a day for seventy-five cents. Clytie, her voice all jerky with surprise and delight, was exclaiming, "Oh, Pop—why we're rich. That's way more'n a schoolteacher makes back home in a month."

"I don't make it ever week," Clovis explained, "an recollect that's afore hospitalization, an union dues, an OAB, an taxes. An right now, with everything tu buy, it ain't no fortune. It took saven to git a down payment on all this an on a car, too."

Gertie backed against the sink, heard her plate of beans and cornbread flop off the rim into the dishwater, but did not look around. "But Clovis," she began haltingly, not wanting to darken the family joy, "if'n you've already run intu debt 'fore me an th youngens comes, why how can you manage with us? An we cain't, jist cain't keep on a liven in this little hole. Cain't you git along without a car?"

He pushed his plate away. "Gert, we ain't hardly seen each other 'fore you start a quarrelen about money an th place I got fer ye. What was you expecten—a castle in Grosse Pointe where them rich dagoes lives? I was lucky, mighty lucky, tu git this. They ain't hardly standen room in Detroit—I'd meant tu surprise th youngens with a ride when the weather was fitten." He held out his cup for more coffee. "But I've already got me a car. It's in th parken place now. A body cain't git along in this town thout a car."

The delighted squeals of the children, all save Reuben, only subsided under his animated discussion of the car, especially the sweetness of the motor's running, now that he had worked on it. Gertie had heard little past the words "got me a car." She turned and looked down at the gray dishwater. If just for one minute she could walk outside, go to the barn, the spring, somewhere—walk, see her father, get away from the gas smell, the water smell, the steamy heat; the hard white light beating into her eyeballs. She turned toward the outside door. A corner of the pulled out table barred her way. She looked toward the passway. Clovis's chair was there. Her empty hands found the dishrag. Somehow she washed the dishes. Hemmed in, shut down, by all this—and debts.

The evening in the hot, overcrowded, noise-laden place seemed endless. She answered questions about back home, learned that Sophronie's man, Whit Meanwell, worked in the same Flint plant as Clovis, though on a different job and shift. She wanted to ask Clovis questions: how much did they owe, how much was the interest on the debts for the car and the house plunder, where was the school, and how far away? But the radio was on, and she talked but little.

As soon as the children were asleep, Clovis had no thought for answering questions. Amos had been put to bed on the cot in the middle room, so that Gertie and Clovis were alone in the room beside the kitchen. Still, she was conscious of the restless sleep of the children on the other side of the thin walls. They were all so close together it didn't seem decent. The whole place wasn't as big as either of the two main rooms at the Tipton Place.

She shut her eyes and tried to think that she was there when Clovis fell quickly into a deep, satisfied sleep. She drowsed and dreamed of pines talking. The talking rose, became the roar of a fast through train, its screeching whistle rising above the roar as it neared the through street. This was followed at once by the tumultuous sound of its passing, so close it seemed in the very house. Amos and Cassie screamed out in fright, then as the sounds subsided they sank gradually into a whimpering half-sleep. There remained only the quiverings—the windows, the steel springs of the bed, the dishes, a chair touching the wall.

There came at last a silence so complete she could hear the ticking of the clock under the bed, and the snoring of Sophronie's children behind the wall of the girls' bedroom. The feeling that had followed her at times since she had got on the train came back in the silence—she had forgotten something, something very important. But what? She was sorting out the things she'd left behind when she found herself lifted on one elbow, listening.

Someone was moving about on the other side of the wall. She heard running water, the soft thud of a pot going over the gas flame, the creak and slam of an icebox door—breakfast getting sounds. Soon she heard the opening and closing of the outside door, and whoever it was did not come back. He had not taken time to eat his breakfast. He was most likely the husband of that Sophronie in the sleazy nightgown. She was too lazy to get up and cook breakfast.

She drowsed, but sleep enough never came to drown the strangeness of the bed or the closeness of the air. It seemed only a little while before she found herself listening again. A singing it was in the alley now. Tipsy he was, and a tenor,

"They'll be pie in a sky—" A woman's voice cut him off, something like the girl Maggie's, but near crying, "Please, Joseph, please. Du neighbors—"

"Quitcha tucken," the man said, and a door on the other side of the alley slammed.

"Tucken." What was "tucken," she wondered. Then the door next her own was opened quietly, but slammed shut so loudly that Clovis turned in his sleep. She heard the opening of the oven door, the little whoosh of the lighting gas, then the opening and closing of the icebox door. A chair was pulled out followed by the hissing sound of the cap jerked off a bottle of something fizzy like pop. She heard a chair tip back against the wall, so close through the thinness seemed like she could feel it. She could see the man's chair leaning against the wall, his cold feet warming in the oven, as he drank from the bottle. She heard the soft clink of glass on steel as he put it down. But where had he been and why, at this time of night? She sat straight up in bed with wonder and surprise when the voice came, low, more like a sigh than a voice, "Oh, Lord, that moven line," for the voice was a woman's voice, Sophronie's.

The sounds of the other side of the wall or her own abrupt movement awakened Clovis enough that he mumbled sleepily: "Don't be afeared, Gert. Th doors locks good."

"Oh, I ain't afeared," she whispered. "It's that Sophronie. Why, she's jist got in home."

He clamped one ear against the pillow, put an arm over the other. "When else would a woman on th three-tu-twelve shift git home?"

Japanese Relocation

Monica Sone

at was Racial grounds.

The internment of 110,000 Japanese-Americans from 1942 to 1945 represented the largest denial of civil liberties during the war. After the Japanese attack on Pearl Harbor in December 1941, the federal government ordered all Japanese-Americans relocated from the West Coast war zone to internment camps in the interior. The Japanese community did not strenuously contest this policy, fearing further reprisals and charges of treason or spying; public opinion, federal officials, and (in 1944) the Supreme Court all upheld the detention as a necessary military decision during wartime. Only after the war, and among later generations, did the shame of this episode sink in.

Monica (Itoi) Sone's autobiography, *Nisei Daughter* (1953), tells the story of Japanese relocation from the perspective of a young woman in Seattle, Washington. (The Japanese character *sei* means generation; by adding a number as a prefix, such as *Issei, Nisei, Sansei,* and most recently, *Yonsei,* it enumerates the successive generations.) The Issei generation, Monica's

Source: From *Nisei Daughter* by Monica Sone. Copyright 1953 by Monica Sone; © renewed 1981 by Monica Sone. By permission of Little, Brown and Company (Inc.).

parents, were permanently barred from citizenship by the 1924 law that cut off immigration from Japan (and China) completely. But their American-born children, the Nisei, were citizens and much more part of American culture than their parents. This autobiography, like many stories of immigrant children and their parents, concerns the struggle to balance the dual heritages. As the war hysteria mounts, Monica can only describe herself as "a despised, pathetic two-headed freak," but at story's end she feels that her Japanese   and   American   parts   have   now   melded   into   one.

This section describes the Itoi family's forced evacuation to a temporary encampment called Camp Harmony; later they will be moved to a settlement in Idaho. They are now Family #10710, trying to make the best of a terrible situation. Monica Sone's memoir suggests the generational conflicts between elders and their children, and it conveys the strain that the prison-like barrack conditions imposed on family life and parental authority. It also displays the physical and mental resourcefulness necessary to survive this enforced internment. Although her parents spent the entire war in the camp, Monica Sone was allowed to leave in 1943 to attend college in Indiana.

When our bus turned a corner and we no longer had to smile and wave, we settled back gravely in our seats. Everyone was quiet except for a chattering group of university students who soon started singing college songs. A few people turned and glared at them, which only served to increase the volume of their singing. Then suddenly a baby's sharp cry rose indignantly above the hubbub. The singing stopped immediately, followed by a guilty silence. Three seats behind us, a young mother held a wailing red-faced infant in her arms, bouncing it up and down. Its angry little face emerged from multiple layers of kimonos, sweaters and blankets, and it, too, wore the white pasteboard tag pinned to its blanket. A young man stammered out an apology as the mother gave him a wrathful look. She hunted frantically for a bottle of milk in a shopping bag, and we all relaxed when she had found it.

We sped out of the city southward along beautiful stretches of farmland, with dark, newly turned soil. In the beginning we devoured every bit of scenery which flashed past our window and admired the massive-muscled work horses plodding along the edge of the highway, the rich burnished copper color of a browsing herd of cattle, the vivid spring green of the pastures, but eventually the sameness of the country landscape palled on us. We tried to sleep to escape from the restless anxiety which kept bobbing up to the surface of our minds. I awoke with a start when the bus filled with excited buzzing. A small group of straw-hatted Japanese farmers stood by the highway, waving at us. I felt a sudden warmth toward them, then a twinge of pity. They would be joining us soon.

About noon we crept into a small town. Someone said, "Looks like Puyallup, all right." Parents of small children babbled excitedly, "Stand up quickly and look over there. See all the chick-chicks and fat little piggies?" One little city boy stared hard at the hogs and said tersely, "They're *bachi*—dirty!"

Our bus idled a moment at the traffic signal and we noticed at the left of us an entire block filled with neat rows of low shacks, resembling chicken houses.

Someone commented on it with awe, "Just look at those chicken houses. They sure go in for poultry in a big way here." Slowly the bus made a left turn, drove through a wire-fenced gate, and to our dismay, we were inside the oversized chicken farm. The bus driver opened the door, the guard stepped out and stationed himself at the door again. Jim, the young man who had shepherded us into the busses, popped his head inside and sang out, "Okay, folks, all off at Yokohama, Puyallup."

We stumbled out, stunned, dragging our bundles after us. It must have rained hard the night before in Puyallup, for we sank ankle deep into gray, gluttinous mud. The receptionist, a white man, instructed us courteously, "Now, folks, please stay together as family units and line up. You'll be assigned your apartment."

We were standing in Area A, the mammoth parking lot of the state fairgrounds. There were three other separate areas, B, C and D, all built on the fair grounds proper, near the baseball field and the race tracks. This camp of army barracks was hopefully called Camp Harmony.

We were assigned to apartment 2-1-A, right across from the bachelor quarters. The apartments resembled elongated, low stables about two blocks long. Our home was one room, about 18 by 20 feet, the size of a living room. There was one small window in the wall opposite the one door. It was bare except for a small, tinny wood-burning stove crouching in the center. The flooring consisted of two by fours laid directly on the earth, and dandelions were already pushing their way up through the cracks. Mother was delighted when she saw their shaggy yellow heads. "Don't anyone pick them. I'm going to cultivate them."

Father snorted, "Cultivate them! If we don't watch out, those things will be growing out of our hair."

Just then Henry stomped inside, bringing the rest of our baggage. "What's all the excitement about?"

Sumi replied laconically, "Dandelions."

Henry tore off a fistful. Mother scolded, *"Arra! Arra!* Stop that. They're the only beautiful things around here. We could have a garden right in here."

"Are you joking, Mama?"

I chided Henry, "Of course, she's not. After all, she has to have some inspiration to write poems, you know, with all the *'nali keli's.'* I can think of a poem myself right now:

Oh, Dandelion, Dandelion,
Despised and uprooted by all,
Dance and bob your golden heads
For you've finally found your home
With your yellow fellows, *nali keli,* amen!"

Henry said, thrusting the dandelions in Mother's black hair, "I think you can do ten times better than that, Mama."

Sumi reclined on her seabag and fretted, "Where do we sleep? Not on the floor, I hope."

"Stop worrying," Henry replied disgustedly.

Mother and Father wandered out to see what the other folks were doing and they found people wandering in the mud, wondering what other folks were doing. Mother returned shortly, her face lit up in an ecstatic smile, "We're in luck. The latrine is right nearby. We won't have to walk blocks."

We laughed, marveling at Mother who could be so poetic and yet so practical. Father came back, bent double like a woodcutter in a fairy tale, with stacks of scrap lumber over his shoulder. His coat and trouser pockets bulged with nails. Father dumped his loot in a corner and explained, "There was a pile of wood left by the carpenters and hundreds of nails scattered loose. Everybody was picking them up, and I hustled right in with them. Now maybe we can live in style with tables and chairs."

The block leader knocked at our door and announced lunchtime. He instructed us to take our meal at the nearest mess hall. As I untied my seabag to get out my pie plate, tin cup, spoon and fork, I realized I was hungry. At the mess hall we found a long line of people. Children darted in and out of the line, skiing in the slithery mud. The young stood impatiently on one foot, then the other, and scowled, "The food had better be good after all this wait." But the Issei stood quietly, arms folded, saying very little. A light drizzle began to fall, coating bare black heads with tiny sparkling raindrops. The chow line inched forward.

Lunch consisted of two canned sausages, one lob of boiled potato, and a slab of bread. Our family had to split up, for the hall was too crowded for us to sit together. I wandered up and down the aisles, back and forth along the crowded tables and benches, looking for a few inches to squeeze into. A small Issei woman finished her meal, stood up and hoisted her legs modestly over the bench, leaving a space for one. Even as I thrust myself into the breach, the space had shrunk to two inches, but I worked myself into it. My dinner companion, hooked just inside my right elbow, was a bald headed, gruff-looking Issei man who seemed to resent nestling at mealtime. Under my left elbow was a tiny, mud-spattered girl. With busy runny nose, she was belaboring her sausages, tearing them into shreds and mixing them into the potato gruel which she had made with water. I choked my food down.

We cheered loudly when trucks rolled by, distributing canvas army cots for the young and hardy, and steel cots for the older folks. Henry directed the arrangement of the cots. Father and Mother were to occupy the corner nearest the wood stove. In the other corner, Henry arranged two cots in L shape and announced that this was the combination living room-bedroom area, to be occupied by Sumi and myself. He fixed a male den for himself in the corner nearest the door. If I had had my way, I would have arranged everyone's cots in one neat row as in Father's hotel dormitory.

We felt fortunate to be assigned to a room at the end of the barracks because we had just one neighbor to worry about. The partition wall separating the rooms was only seven feet high with an opening of four feet at the top, so at night, Mrs. Funai next door could tell when Sumi was still sitting up in bed in the dark, putting her hair up. *"Mah, Sumi-chan,"* Mrs. Funai would say through the plank wall, "are you curling your hair tonight again? Do you put it up every night?" Sumi would put her hands on her hips and glare defiantly at the wall.

The block monitor, an impressive Nisei who looked like a star tackle with his crouching walk, came around the first night to tell us that we must all be inside our room by nine o'clock every night. At ten o'clock, he rapped at the door again, yelling, "Lights out!" and Mother rushed to turn the light off not a second later.

Throughout the barracks, there were a medley of creaking cots, whimpering infants and explosive night coughs. Our attention was riveted on the intense little wood stove which glowed so violently I feared it would melt right down to the floor. We soon learned that this condition lasted for only a short time, after which it suddenly turned into a deep freeze. Henry and Father took turns at the stove to produce the harrowing blast which all but singed our army blankets, but did not penetrate through them. As it grew quieter in the barracks, I could hear the light patter of rain. Soon I felt the "splat! splat!" of raindrops digging holes into my face. The dampness on my pillow spread like a mortal bleeding, and I finally had to get out and haul my cot toward the center of the room. In a short while Henry was up. "I've got multiple leaks, too. Have to complain to the landlord first thing in the morning."

All through the night I heard people getting up, dragging cots around. I stared at our little window, unable to sleep. I was glad Mother had put up a makeshift curtain on the window for I noticed a powerful beam of light sweeping across it every few seconds. The lights came from high towers placed around the camp where guards with Tommy guns kept a twenty-four hour vigil. I remembered the wire fence encircling us, and a knot of anger tightened in my breast. What was I doing behind a fence like a criminal? If there were accusations to be made, why hadn't I been given a fair trial? Maybe I wasn't considered an American anymore. My citizenship wasn't real, after all. Then what was I? I was certainly not a citizen of Japan as my parents were. On second thought, even Father and Mother were more alien residents of the United States than Japanese nationals for they had little tie with their mother country. In their twenty-five years in America, they had worked and paid their taxes to their adopted government as any other citizen.

Of one thing I was sure. The wire fence was real. I no longer had the right to walk out of it. It was because I had Japanese ancestors. It was also because some people had little faith in the ideas and ideals of democracy. They said that after all these were but words and could not possibly insure loyalty. New laws and camps were surer devices. I finally buried my face in my pillow to wipe out burning thoughts and snatch what sleep I could.

Americans didn't trust them to be loyal.

Women of Wartime Los Alamos

Ruth Marshak

Among American women affected by wartime dislocations, one of the most unusual situations concerned the Manhattan Project, the secret government project that designed, assembled, and tested the first atomic weapons. In 1943 many of the country's top physicists and scientists were sent to a

Atomic Bomb [handwritten note in left margin]

remote area called Los Alamos 35 miles west of Santa Fe, New Mexico. This being the 1940s, all of these scientists were men, but the U.S. Army (which ran the project) allowed them to bring their families. As this selection from Ruth Marshak opens, she and her husband (who was deputy head of a theoretical physics group) had been sworn to secrecy about where they were going, and they had no idea what would await them when they arrived.

The men were quickly absorbed into their research, leaving the women to cope with problems of housekeeping and child care in this remote and somewhat primitive location. In many ways it was like living in a company town. Many of the women's memories concern such mundane details as how big their house (or more accurately, trailer or hut) was, the difficulty of doing laundry, and problems with their domestic workers, local Pueblo Indian women hired for $1.50 a half day. But complaints were balanced by the beautiful scenery and recreational opportunities, and Saturday evenings of square dancing and camaraderie with other Los Alamos residents thrown together in this unusual wartime situation.

The Manhattan Project grew rapidly, its population swelled by new recruits and by the burgeoning baby boom caused by the fertile young scientific couples, who arrived with young children or quickly had more on the way. The first baby was born in August 1943, and 80 more arrived the next year. Babies kept coming at the rate of about 10 a month, keeping the staff pediatrician quite busy and allowing project residents to joke about "rural free delivery." Many of the women were recruited to staff the child care center or teach in the school. Ruth Marshak, for example, taught third grade and also worked in the Housing Office. Her recollections, originally written in 1946, are typical of the mix of the travails of daily life and wartime patriotism of the women and men who were part of the Manhattan Project.

A physicist's wife in peacetime and a physicist's wife in wartime are, I have discovered, two very different things. In the years before our country was at war, this wife's interests were identical with those of any other academic lady. She went to faculty teas, fretted over her budget, and schemed for her husband's advancement. Although a physicist was inclined to work rather longer hours than his colleagues in other departments of the university, his wife's life was no different from that of the wife of a history professor. It was a good life, too.

Even before the Pearl Harbor attack, however, the physicist's routine had changed. Defense projects were started in college laboratories; armed guards began to pace the thresholds of physics buildings. One's husband grew more secretive about his work, and one knew that his job must be important, for he was immune from the draft. The physicist's wife realized that her husband, in wartime, was more than just a college professor—his was a key profession in the defense of his country.

Some physicists remained at home to teach the few students who were left in the universities. Others worked on subcontracts for the Army or the Navy in their

Source: From Ruth Marshak, "Secret City," in Jane S. Wilson and Charlotte Serber, eds., *Standing By and Making Do: Women of Wartime Los Alamos,* pp. 1–2, 3–5, 8–9, 10–11, 19. Copyright © 1988. Reprinted by permission of Los Alamos Historical Society.

own laboratories. But many were forced to leave home in order to do their part in developing and perfecting the weapons of war. They went to a giant installation at the Massachusetts Institute of Technology to work on radar. They went to Washington as Naval Ordnance men. They went to the Aberdeen Proving Grounds. Then, sometimes, the wives who accompanied them found that they were moving to a destination without a name.

I was one of the women thus bound for an unknown and secret place. "I can tell you nothing about it," my husband said. "We're going away, that's all." This made me feel a little like the heroine of a melodrama. It is never easy to say good-bye to beloved and familiar patterns of living. It is particularly difficult when you do not know what substitute for them will be offered you. Where was I going and why was I going there? I plied my husband with questions which he steadfastly refused to answer.

"Be very careful what you say," he warned me over and over again. As if I, confused and distraught, knew anything which might be of aid and comfort to the enemy! German agents could probably tell me a thing or two, I reflected bitterly. I went about my packing in a daze. Many questions quivered on my lips, but I would have to wait two years to find out most of their answers. "What's it all about?" I cried to my husband. "At least tell me why we are going away?"—That was in 1943, and only when an atomic bomb ripped Hiroshima in the fall of 1945 did I really understand.

When I left home, I had never even heard the name, "Los Alamos." I gradually became aware, however, that we were going to the Southwest. My husband had received a letter of instructions which said, in part, "Go to 109 East Palace Street, Santa Fe, New Mexico. There you will find out how to complete your trip." What should I expect? Rattlesnakes? Outdoor privies? My concern as a housewife over the mechanics of living seemed rather petty in the face of the secrecy surrounding our destination. I felt akin to the pioneer women accompanying their husbands across the uncharted plains westward, alert to danger, resigned to the fact that they journeyed, for weal or for woe, into the Unknown. The analogy is incomplete, for I rode, not in a covered wagon, but in a red coupe, comfortably, over silver highways. The hazards of the road were not Indians but the broken glass that menaced our thin, irreplaceable tires.

Just before reaching New Mexico, we stopped at a gasoline station in Colorado. The attendant looked over the loaded car, examined our license plates, and asked us where we were heading. We replied that we were bound for New Mexico. The man studied my husband and said, "Oh, you folks must be going to that secret project!" He needed no encouragement to launch into a detailed and accurate description of our new home. Thus for my husband's caution! We proceeded on our way, feeling considerably less important . . .

The first thing I learned about my new home was that it was not, as I had supposed, in the desert, but rather was on the top of a mesa thirty-five miles from Santa Fe. The most direct road to it was a treacherous washboard running through the Indian pueblo of San Ildefonso, over the muddy Rio Grande, and then up a series of narrow switchbacks. As we neared the top of the mesa, the view was breathtaking. Behind us lay the Sangre de Cristo Mountains, at sunset bathed in changing waves of color—scarlets and lavenders. Below was the desert with its flatness broken by majestic palisades that seemed like the ruined cathedrals and palaces of some old, great, vanished race. Ahead was Los Alamos, and beyond the flat plateau on which it sat was its backdrop, the Jemez Mountain Range. Whenever things went wrong at Los Alamos, and there was never a day when they didn't, we had this one consolation—we had a view.

A mile or two before reaching the settlement itself, we had to show our temporary passes to the MP on duty. He jotted our pass and car license numbers on the record for the day. Passes were to be a solemn business in our lives. A lost pass meant hours of delay in the guard's hutment, an elemental little structure, its stark walls decorated with starkly naked pinup girls. The expiration date of a pass was apt to creep up, finding one unaware on just the day one had planned an outing. Many a tearful woman or belligerent gent found themselves stopped at the guardhouse, while the rest of the party sailed gaily by. The fence penning Los Alamos was erected and guarded to keep out the treasonable, the malicious, and the curious. This fence had a real effect on the psychology of the people behind it. It was a tangible barrier, a symbol of our isolated lives. Within it lay the most secret part of the atomic bomb project. Los Alamos was a world unto itself, an island in the sky.

So we arrived at the place we would call home. My first impression was discouraging. The rickety houses looked like the tenements of a metropolitan slum area; washing hung everywhere, and the garbage cans were overflowing. Dust rose in great clouds around our car. Later, we learned that the homes were not as hideous as they had seemed at first. Often, they had large yards and attractive interiors. Always, the mountains were behind them, and there was no time of year when the mountains were not beautiful . . .

Los Alamos is about 7200 feet above sea level. Many people found the altitude a bit uncomfortable at first. Typical manifestations were a shortness of breath and insomnia. I happened to feel fine, but the altitude affected my cooking and baking. It took much longer for water to boil, so my first few meals were on the tardy side. Cakes rose beautifully in the oven, but fell magically the moment they were removed. I'd never enjoyed baking anyhow, so I now had an excuse not to bake at all. There were, however, no commercial bakeries on the Hill.

After one grew acclimated to the altitude, one began really to enjoy the Los Alamos climate. Los Alamos was a secret place, and the job of its large Security Division was to avoid publicity, not to court it. Had it had a Chamber of Commerce or a bigger booster club, however, wonderful advertisements might have been written about its weather. The sun shone almost every day. Although summer days might be warm, they were never unendurable, for the air was dry. Winters were without penetrating cold. The citizens of our community seemed to draw vigor from the air. They not only worked inhuman hours to perfect the bomb; they also had energy to dissipate on skiing and horseback riding, mountain climbing and folk dancing, and gay parties which lasted until dawn.

The social life of the Hill was surely one of its redeeming features. I found much friendliness and informality, but I discovered also that Los Alamos was not a casteless society. Lines were drawn principally, not on wealth, family, or even age, but on the position one's husband held in the Laboratory . . .

The Tech Area was a great pit which swallowed our scientist husbands out of sight, almost out of our lives. The men were drawn to their work not only by curiosity and zeal, but also by an inspiring patriotism. They worked as they had never worked before. They worked at night and often came home at three or four in the morning. Sometimes, they set up Army cots in the laboratories and did not come home at all. Other times, they did not sleep at all. Few women understood what the men were seeking there or comprehended the magnitude of the search. The loneliness and heartache of some scientists' wives during the years before the atomic bomb was born were very real . . .

In a broader sense, for most of us elders, the Los Alamos experience was one of the most educational of our lives. Sequestered, regimented, we had to make the most of the little we had. Perhaps it was a good thing, three years ago when I left home and started westward, that I knew so little of what awaited me. There was much amiss in the ugly town where the bomb was born. Yet I have only to think of the neighborliness and warmth and esprit de corps of Los Alamos to be heartily glad for the chance that took me there. Nor is it surprising that most people enjoyed their years on the mesa. Los Alamos was our town, our own creation. To no other community will we ever give so much of ourselves.

CHAPTER 9

The 50s: The Way We Were?

On the surface, the 1950s is full of seeming contradictions for American women. For example, a heightened emphasis on domesticity, which Betty Friedan tagged *the feminine mystique,* coexisted alongside a steady, indeed dramatic increase in the number of married women working outside the home. Another contradiction is the stark contrast between women's supposed political apathy and nonpartici-pation in the 1950s and the explosion of social turmoil in the 1960s and 1970s, es-pecially the revival of feminism. Historians are still trying to unravel the mysteries of the decade (which in terms of women's history more accurately refers to the period between 1946 and 1963, a generational cohort). Tentative find-ings suggest a far more complex picture than our nostalgic views of "Father Knows Best," hula hoops, and '57 Chevies provide.

After two decades of dislocation from depression and war, traditional family values looked fairly appealing to the younger generation coming of age in the 1940s. The average age of marriage for women dropped to 20, and a third of all women in 1951 were married by 19. The birthrate, after steadily declining since 1800, and falling below the replacement level briefly during the Depression, sud-denly shot up and stayed high well into the early 1960s. (Demographers call this phenomenon the *baby boom.*) American women on average were now having close to four children. The baby boom was accompanied by the growth of subur-bia, one of the most far-reaching trends of postwar America; by 1960, more peo-ple lived in suburbs than cities. And the baby boom took place in a period of general affluence—Americans experienced a 25 percent rise in real income be-tween 1946 and 1959. This affluence in turn heightened the cultural emphasis on consumption, which characterized postwar society. The way that such factors re-inforced the identification of women with the home was well captured by Betty Friedan in her best-selling *The Feminine Mystique* (1963), which more than any other source has shaped our views of women's lives in the 1950s.

One key to unraveling the experiences of women in the 1950s is to remember that the prescriptive literature that Betty Friedan drew on to write *The Feminine Mystique* does not necessarily reflect the reality of women's lives. For one thing, many families could not afford to live the child-centered suburban lifestyle glori-fied in the pages of *Good Housekeeping* or *McCall's.* What relevance did it have to black or Latina women trapped in urban ghettos, farm women still living in rural areas, or even working-class families, where such a lifestyle would have represented an almost unattainable standard of upward mobility? Looking at it another way, perhaps the popular culture so relentlessly and shrilly pushed this domestic ideal precisely because so many women were no longer willing or able to accept its basic tenet that women belonged at home. Nowhere is this more suggestive than in explaining the continuing increase in women who worked outside the home.

Women continued to enter the work force throughout the postwar period, especially married women who should have been the prime candidates for the "togetherness" glorified by the feminine mystique. Some women worked for personal reasons (they needed the stimulation of interaction on the job), but most women worked for economic ones: supporting the consumer lifestyle of postwar America often required two incomes, even in a time of rising affluence. And women worked for structural reasons related to the maturation of the American economy: The economy needed clerical and service workers, precisely the occupations women have traditionally filled. So despite the prescriptive ideology telling women to stay home, many women found sufficient reasons to make different choices. When the life choices of these women are included in the history of the decade, the experiences of women in the 1950s look far more diverse and heterogeneous than one would ever expect from only reading the popular literature.

Another area where we need to modify our simplistic views of the 1950s is as a period of political apathy. To be sure, there were few large-scale protest movements in this time of complacency and satisfaction with the rewards of the American way of life. But that does not mean the decade was devoid of political action. The most obvious example is the developing civil rights movement, which gained strength throughout the 1950s. Women, both black and white, played important roles in the early stages of this struggle. Also important were the efforts of the peace movement against nuclear testing and in favor of disarmament. Such activism makes the contrast between the apathetic 1950s and the turbulent 1960s harder to sustain.

The root problem, it seems, to our interpretation of women in the decade is that we see the 1950s only in terms of one group of women: young white mothers with small children. If historians looked at that age cohort in any decade, they would not likely see much activity beyond the home, because those are the years when women's child-rearing responsibilities are most extensive. But the 1950s were not just populated by young mothers in their 20s; a generational approach reminds us that there were older women whose life patterns were set in the 1920s, 1930s, and 1940s for whom the feminine mystique is hardly the most relevant analytical tool.

It is also important to let the archetypical women of the 1950s grow up and get on with their lives rather than being forever frozen in time. Because of their young age at marriage, these postwar wives and mothers finished their intensive child-rearing responsibilities (even if they have four children) by their late 30s. Given the demographic aging of the population, that left women approximately 35 years of their lives when domestic responsibilities would be less central. Many full-time suburban housewives of the 1950s later entered the work force, joining the significant minority who had already done so by the 1950s. When we take this broader view of women's lives in the postwar period, the picture does not look as vapid and devoid of progress. Once again, small, incremental change has the power to shape the lives of women in 20th century America.

 Balancing Work and Family

Betty Jeanne Boggs

Besides the heightened media emphasis on domesticity, the other major trend of the 1950s was the growing number of women who were working outside the home. Women made up 29 percent of the work force in 1950 and 35 percent in 1965; whereas one-fifth of wives worked in 1950, the figure approached one-third by 1960. Women's work was not necessarily a challenge to the values of home and family, however, since many women justified taking jobs in order to improve their family lifestyle. But it did point to the emerging centrality of paid work to women's lives, especially for married women whose children were in school.

Betty Jeanne Boggs is one of the women who alternated work with home responsibilities in the 1950s. Born in 1926, she had been a Rosie the Riveter in the aircraft industry in California during World War II. When the war ended, she returned to her native Seattle to resume her education, marry, and raise a family. She had always had nontraditional aspirations (she wanted to be a test pilot and major in aeronautical engineering) and began a career as a lab technician. But after her second child was born, she left the work force completely, although not without a great deal of ambivalence, as this selection shows. After her children were older, she went back to school to earn her masters in fine arts; as a sculptor, she works with heavy metals in ways that hark back to her experiences in World War II.

I worked in a war plant and it was one of the things you did when your country was at war, and it had been an enjoyable experience. Even today, I'm very proud of that job. I can always say "Hey, I was a riveter during World War II!". . .

I started to major in math, and you know how people'll ask, "Well, what are you going to do with it? Are you going to teach?" "Oh, is that all you can do, is teach?" "Well, there's not much else you can do with it because you're a woman." Always this—"because you're a woman." So I thought, "Teach? I can't imagine me being up in front of a class trying to teach kids." Still there was this shyness. So I think I finished calculus and also got through physics.

I was working part time at a scientific supply house. They brought in an auditor and his desk was next to mine. Naturally, you get to talking. He told me that

Source: From *Rosie the Riveter Revisited* by Sherna Berger Gluck. Copyright © 1987. Reprinted by permission of The Gale Group.

at Stanford University they had a test which you could write for. You answer all
these questions: "What are you best suited for?" So I wrote for the test. When the
results came back, the two top things—it was equal—was either an artist or a laboratory technician. I had never given either one of them any thought. In fact, a laboratory technician—I'd never even heard of it. Then it went down to a dentist, a
librarian. Oh, I think even an engineer was kind of high. Anyway, it introduced
new ideas.

So I thought, okay, look into a laboratory technician. That's when I changed
my major from math into biological science. That made a big difference because
before, in math, I just couldn't figure out—what am I going to do with it? Also my
social life sort of got in the way. I knew a fellow at that time, and he kept telling
me he couldn't figure out why I was taking calculus. He was in one of my calculus classes and his presence bothered me. I just didn't quite get a hold of the idea
of calculus as well as if I'd been in there by myself. In the engineering classes, I
may have been the only girl but I wasn't going on dates with them, and I seemed
to get those subjects a lot better. Anyway, in chemistry I felt, "This is my place."
It has that nice feeling to it . . .

My girlfriend, Shirley, was in a couple of my classes and we would do things
together. Pretty soon she started talking about this character she met in one of her
classes, and his name was Josh. Being a lab technician, there was a club that you
joined, and she and I would go to these meetings. Josh was there because he was
going to be premed. He would take us both home from these meetings, and I gradually got acquainted with him. There was nothing going on at first, except that he
had such a terrific sense of humor that I just really was quite fascinated by him.

I didn't go out with him until February. It was one of these dances where the
girls ask the boys. He will deny it to this day—I'm glad he's not here because he
can't argue with me—but I stopped to talk to him in the hall and he said something
about going to that dance, and I said, "Well, I just hadn't thought of who I'm going
to take." And he said something like "I think it would be nice if you took me." So
that was the first date with him, and from then on there wasn't anybody else. We
got married September the first, and so here we are a hundred years later . . .

Josh said, "I want you to finish school, and then I'll go back and won't have
to work because you'll work full time. We can live better off of your salary than
we can this other way and I can get through faster." . . .

I started out at two hundred dollars and something. I remember I got a raise
to three hundred dollars, and there was some other engineer that was provoked because he didn't get as big a raise as I did. About a year after that, they transferred
my boss to another part of that lab. I was then supervisor. Because I had a degree
and was a white-collar worker and working out in the plant, they gave me the title of engineer. There was a couple of girls under me, maybe one or two. The most
I had reporting to me at one time were ten girls. They had lead-girls, but as far as
being a supervisor, I think I was the only woman. From what I've been told, I was
supposed to be the first woman engineer, which naturally was very thrilling to me.

When they talk about women's lib, boy, oh boy, this is where the whole darn
thing came in. If I'd known then, I really would have told the son of a gun off and

I really would have run him right into the president's office. He was the production manager, and I think he was one of these people that came out of the plant back in West Virginia. He didn't have a college education but was one that came up through the ranks. Not that there's anything wrong with it, but when it affects the male ego, then there's a lot wrong with it. He could not stand to think that there was a woman white-collar worker, and he didn't like it one bit. He thought that I should be at home, and he hassled me every way he possibly could. He hassled me right up until practically the day I quit.

When we married, Josh's health wasn't that great and we got a sperm count. He was just so sterile at that time, we just sort of figured, okay, kids are for everybody else. We didn't do anything for or against. I don't think we even gave it any thought like "Well, are we going to adopt later on?" It was like "Oh, I guess kids are for everybody else, and maybe one of these days we'll sit down and think about it seriously."

Then when I did get pregnant: "Wow, I'm pregnant!" It was bewildering, in a way. Like "Oh, for heaven sakes!" So I will jokingly say to this day, "Well, shrugging the shoulders did it."

Then I was really torn up. For one thing, I wanted to stay home with the baby; two, I wanted to help Josh get through; three, I really enjoyed that job. I just didn't know what to do about it, because I enjoyed working and yet I thought I should really be home with that baby. My mind was sort of made up for me because Josh kept saying, "I've got to get through school. It's better that you work. I can spend all my time studying and get through engineering. When I get through, then we'll take it from there."

We kept trying to find baby-sitters and I think I went through five of them. That was a chore because you just didn't want any old body. At that time there weren't any of those places where they have preschool—which would really have worked out nice. So I'd find somebody that could take him for a while. I was paying ten dollars a week at that time for child care. Then the last one, oh gad, she was taking care of some other little baby about the same age as my son. She caused more trouble than any of the others put together: "Don't do this, don't do that. No, no, no."

When I stayed home with Tad when he was a little over two years old, his attitude was rather antagonistic. I'd go to be affectionate with him and he'd just kind of close up. I thought, "Okay, doggone child, you're going to love me and you're going to be affectionate. I'm just going to keep working away at you."

Josh had a good relationship built up, because he'd have Tad to himself. Sometimes he'd be home earlier and then he would pick up Tad, or he'd have a day off and he'd keep Tad with him, or if he was out working in the yard, he'd have Tad with him. And he took care of him. He never once hesitated to change diapers or to feed the baby. Absolutely no holding back as far as caring for him. The only thing I think that held him back was if he had a lot of homework.

I felt terrible—terrible, because I really enjoyed my job; good, because I could be at home. It was really a mixed emotion. You wanted to be in two places at one time and how can you resolve that? So in one way it was resolved for me, because then I didn't go back to work. I was at home with the kids all the time.

We took them everywhere. We never went on a trip that we left them at home. We didn't do any camping at that time, but we'd go to parks, we'd take them to the city—San Francisco—we'd picnic. Of course, Josh and I always did a lot together right from the time we got married. In fact, people are going to think I'm archaic when I mention this, but I would never go anywhere unless he could go. We always had the philosophy, "Well, why should I go enjoy myself when you're not here to enjoy it with me?" I think we've carried that out even today.

I gave it some thought that someday I would go back to work, but I didn't really think about it too much, 'cause my time was taken up pretty much by the kids. I don't regret one moment of ever staying home with them, because to me, it's very important that I was there. I think it has paid off. My daughter has told me, she's glad I didn't work. I think it's important for a woman to do something, 'cause I think she's got a brain, the same as a man. But I can't quite come to grips with women working full time and having children. It's either one way or the other, 'cause I feel that there's a lot of problems nowadays that are caused by women working and you've got everybody else raising your kids. I think a mother should be there the first couple of years of a child's life, and like high school, I definitely think that she should be there. I know they're old enough to take care of themselves, but it seems to make a difference. You just sense it: a parent cares, they're there.

Indian Relocation

Wilma Mankiller

While magazines in the 1950s celebrated suburbia and traditional gender roles, Native Americans confronted a far different reality: In 1953 Congress approved legislation suggested by the Bureau of Indian Affairs (BIA) designed to break up Indiana reservations and relocate Indians to urban areas, where they supposedly would find better living and employment opportunities. The idea was to "mainstream" Native Americans into the general population, but at the cost of tribal autonomy and community survival. Before the program was halted in 1958, some 60,000 Indians had been relocated to urban and industrial areas, where conditions were rarely better than the poverty they had left behind on their tribal reservations.

Wilma Mankiller's family was part of this termination policy. In 1956, just one month before her 11th birthday, her family left Mankiller Flats, Oklahoma, for San Francisco. Mankiller later called it their own Trail of Tears, a reference to the brutal forced relocation in 1838–1839 of Cherokees from Tennessee to what was then Indian Territory (now Oklahoma) in which her great-grandfather had participated. "It was then that I came to know in some small way what it was like for our ancestors when the government troops made them give up their houses and property. It was a time for me to be sad."

Source: From Wilma Mankiller and Michael Wallis, *Mankiller: A Chief and Her People*, pp. 62, 69–71, 72–74. Copyright © 1993. Reprinted by permission.

The promised aid from the BIA never materialized, and the entire Mankiller family struggled to adjust to its new urban existence.

Wilma Mankiller is a survivor, and she has dedicated her life to serving her people. She eventually returned to Oklahoma, where she became the first woman deputy chief and then, in 1985, the first woman principal chief of the Cherokee Nation of Oklahoma. In 1998 she was awarded the Presidential Medal of Freedom.

I experienced my own Trail of Tears when I was a young girl. No one pointed a gun at me or at members of my family. No show of force was used. It was not necessary. Nevertheless, the United States government, through the Bureau of Indiana Affairs, was again trying to settle the "Indian problem" by removal. I learned through this ordeal about the fear and anguish that occur when you give up your home, your community, and everything you have ever known to move far away to a strange place. I cried for days, not unlike the children who had stumbled down the Trail of Tears so many years before. I wept tears that came from deep within the Cherokee part of me. They were tears from my history, from my tribe's past. They were Cherokee tears . . .

Our poverty had prompted the move. In 1955, my father first started talking to Bureau of Indian Affairs officials about the various forms of assistance for Cherokees. Relocation was a possibility. I recall hearing at that time that the relocation program was being offered as a wonderful opportunity for Indian families to get great jobs, obtain good educations for their kids and, once and for all, leave poverty behind. In truth, the program gave the government the perfect chance to take Indian people away from their culture and their land. The government methods had softened since the nineteenth century, but the end result was the same for native people. Instead of guns and bayonets, the BIA used promotional brochures showing staged photographs of smiling Indians in "happy homes" in the big cities.

Some of the BIA people came to our house. They talked to my father, explaining the particulars of the program. They said the government wanted to "get out of the Indian business," and one of the ways to do that was by helping individuals and families relocate in larger cities. Dad listened to their pitch. The BIA people came out to our place a couple of times. I think Dad initially was opposed to our leaving Oklahoma and our land. As a boy, he had been taken from his home against his will to attend Sequoyah Boarding School. He did not want to leave his community and people again. But he talked it over with some Cherokee friends, and eventually he decided it would be a good idea to move. He must have honestly believed that in a distant city he could provide a better life for his children, with all the modern amenities.

I never liked the idea of our moving away. I can still remember hiding in a bedroom in our house of rough-hewn lumber, listening while my father, mother, and oldest brother talked in the adjoining room about the benefits and drawbacks of relocating our family. We younger children tried to listen through the door. We were terrified. They were talking about possible destinations. They spoke of places we had barely heard of—Chicago, New York, Detroit, Oakland, and San Francisco. California seemed to be their favorite. Finally my parents chose San Francisco because Grandma Sitton, my mother's mom, had moved to California in 1943. A widow when she left Oklahoma, she had remarried and settled in Riverbank, a community in the farm belt about ninety miles east of San Francisco.

None of us little kids could visualize California. We had been as far as Muskogee to go to the fair on a school field trip. We had been to Stilwell and Tahlequah, but that was about it. My world lay within a ten-mile radius of our family house at Mankiller Flats. Dad and my oldest brother had traveled to Colorado to cut broomcorn. My mother had been to Arkansas to see her sister, but no farther than that. My mother was scared about leaving, and hated the idea of moving to California. She really opposed it at first, more than anyone else. But finally, knowing she would be living close to her mother, she was convinced to go along with my father, believing that life might be better for us all.

Despite my mother's decision, I still was not ready to leave. Neither was my sister Frances. We asked about the possibility of staying behind with friends, but my folks said we had to go with the others. So then we talked about running away to avoid the move, but we never did that. We kept hoping right up until the day our family left that something would happen—some kind of miracle—and we would stay put and not have to go to San Francisco. We did not have very much materially, but we really did not need much either. We had always managed to get by. From my point of view as a child, I could see no value in leaving our home. If life was not idyllic, at least it was familiar.

Finally, the day arrived in October of 1956 for us to depart for California. That day is branded into my memory. There were nine of us kids then. It was before the last two were born. My oldest sister, Frieda, was attending Sequoyah High School and did not move with us. My folks had sold off everything, including the old car. We all piled in a neighbor's car, and he drove us to Stilwell so we could catch the train headed west to California. As we drove away, I looked at our house, the store, my school. I took last looks. I wanted to remember it all. I tried to memorize the shapes of the trees, the calls of animals and birds from the forest. All of us looked out the windows. We did not want to forget anything.

When we got to Stilwell, Dad took us to a restaurant, and we had bowls of chili. We were not a very happy crew—two adults and eight children leaving everything behind for an unknown place. Just getting aboard the train was terrifying for the smaller children. It was a new experience. We settled in all over the place. Some of the children were more comfortable sleeping on the floor, others stayed on the seats or beneath them. My youngest baby sister was marking the back of a seat with a crayon. We were a wild bunch. We must have looked like a darker version of the Joad family from John Steinbeck's novel, *The Grapes of Wrath.*

My mother was still scared about the move. Dad was also worried, but he was excited about the chance for a better life for all of us. As we got settled on the train, he turned to my mother and said, "I don't think I will ever be back until I come home in a coffin." As it turned out, Dad was right. The next time he came home was more than fourteen years later when he was buried in his native land.

As soon as we were all on the train, my sister Frances started to cry. It seemed as if she cried without stopping all the way from Oklahoma to California, although I am sure she did not. The conductor came along and asked her why she was crying. She could not answer him. I cried, too. All of us did. The train headed north. Then we had to change to another train in Kansas City. The trip took two days and two nights. We finally reached California, passing through Riverbank, where my grandmother lived. We kept on going until we stopped in San Francisco . . .

After a couple of weeks, the BIA was finally able to find us a permanent place to live in San Francisco. We left the hotel and moved into a flat in a working-class neighborhood in the old Potrero Hill District. The apartment was quite small and crowded, but it seemed to be the best location for us. The rope factory where my father was able to get a job was not too far away. He was paid the grand sum of forty-eight dollars a week. There was no way, even then, that a man could support a big family in San Francisco on that salary. That is why my big brother Don also worked in the factory making ropes. He and my father walked to the factory every day and worked long hard hours. Even with both of them bringing home paychecks, we had a tough time, and our family was growing. My brother James Ray was born while we lived in the Potrero Hill District.

Many Hispanics lived in our neighborhood, and we became good friends with a Mexican family next door named Roybal. They took us under their wing, and made our adjustment a pet project. For example, we had never had a telephone before, so the Roybals showed us how one worked. None of us had ever ridden bicycles, so they taught us how to bike and roller-skate.

Still, I did not like living in the city. I especially hated school. The other kids seemed to be way ahead of us in academic and social abilities. We could hold our own in reading because of what our folks had taught us, but the other students were much more advanced at mathematics and language skills. I spent most of the time trying my best to make myself as inconspicuous as possible.

I was placed in the fifth grade, and I immediately noticed that everyone in my class considered me different. When the teacher came to my name during roll call each morning, every single person laughed. Mankiller had not been a strange name back in Adair County, Oklahoma, but it was a very odd name in San Francisco. The other kids also teased me about the way I talked and dressed. It was not that I was so much poorer than the others, but I was definitely from another culture.

My sister Linda and I sat up late every night reading aloud to each other to get rid of our accents. We tried to talk like the other kids at school. We also thought about our old home in Oklahoma. My big sister Frances and I talked about our life back at Mankiller Flats. We tried to remember where a specific tree was located and how everything looked. That helped a little, but I still had many problems trying to make such a major adjustment. We simply were not prepared for the move. As a result, I was never truly comfortable in the schools of California. I had to find comfort and solace elsewhere.

I was not alone in my feelings. I have met many native people from different tribes who were relocated from remote tribal communities. They discovered, as we did, that the "better life" the BIA had promised all of us was, in reality, life in a tough, urban ghetto. Many people were unable to find jobs, and those who did were often offered only marginal employment. I later learned that many native people endured a great deal of poverty, emotional suffering, substance abuse, and poor health because of leaving their homelands, families, and communities. Children seemed to be especially vulnerable without the traditional support of the extended family at home. Urban Indian families banded together, built Indian centers, held picnics and powwows, and tried to form communities in the midst of large urban populations. Yet there was always and forever a persistent longing to go home. "I was as distant from myself as the moon from the earth," is how James Welch, a native writer, described the sense of alienation he experienced in an urban setting.

The termination and relocation policies of the 1950s clearly failed to solve the "Indian problem." Most of the relocatees eventually returned to their communities to live and work, some of them trying even harder to strengthen tribal communities and governments. In the end, we survived.

An Unplanned Pregnancy

Joanna Rubin

When countless mothers told countless daughters that they could get pregnant the first time they had sexual intercourse, the daughters often looked the other way and laughed it off. And yet for women who were sexually active in the 1950s and early 1960s, a time when abortion was illegal and birth control not always effective (the birth control pill was introduced in 1960), one mistake literally could change your life. What was a young unmarried woman to do if she found herself pregnant? Often she hastily married the man who had impregnated her and had the baby, not the ideal circumstances under which to start married life. Or she could confess her plight to her parents, who if they were white, might arrange for her to go away once she began to "show" to a home for unwed mothers and then put the baby up for adoption. (If a black teenager got pregnant in the 1950s, historian Rickie Solinger has shown, she usually went through with pregnancy and kept her baby.) Or she could seek an illegal abortion to terminate the pregnancy.

The decision to have an abortion is rarely lightly taken, but the stakes were much higher when the procedure was illegal. Would it be performed in sterile conditions? What about the risk of infection? How painful would it be? Would there be decent care afterward? If a woman was desperate, she often had to take what was available, and what she could pay for. (Most abortionists accepted cash only, and since their services were in such demand, they could charge exorbitant prices without fear of losing clients.) In the case of Joanna Rubin, she and her boyfriend learned through the grapevine of a

Source: From *Generations: A Century of Women Speak about Their Lives* by Myriam Miedzian and Alisa Malinovich. Used by permission of Grove/Atlantic, Inc.

clinic in Puerto Rico where she had the 1962 abortion that she describes in this piece.

Starting in the 1960s a movement grew to challenge the laws that restricted women's access to abortion. In 1970 New York became the first state to reform its abortion laws, an act followed by 15 other states and the District of Columbia by 1972. In 1973, in one of the most controversial Supreme Court decisions ever handed down, a 7–2 majority ruled in *Roe v. Wade* that the constitutional right of privacy "is broad enough to encompass a woman's decision whether or not to terminate her pregnancy," in effect legalizing abortion. In the decades since *Roe v. Wade,* the issue has become so polarized, among the public at large, in politics, and in legal and medical circles, that the future of abortion in the United States remains in doubt.

It was 1962, and I was twenty-two. It was my first year of graduate school. Michael and I studied together. One night we stayed up all night talking, and it was very intense, intellectual. Maybe it was that night, maybe it was some other night, but we became sexually involved. The first or second time I had sex with him, I got pregnant. He didn't ejaculate inside of me—he came out—but I got pregnant. I certainly got birth control right after that, a diaphragm. Before that I hadn't really been seeing anyone. I wasn't particularly promiscuous. I liked Michael as a person, but I was ready to stop seeing him except that I got pregnant.

He knew through the grapevine about this place in Puerto Rico—Dr. Pardo's Clinic—that did abortions. I'm not sure if abortions were illegal at that point in Puerto Rico. They certainly were illegal in this country. Having a safe place alleviated a tremendous amount of anxiety and fear. I was scared until he found that clinic. I was afraid that I might end up having to go to some dirty back room.

I remember having lunch with my father. I wanted to tell him. I remember the intensity of the feelings; I felt alone. I didn't have any support from my parents in general. I had the sense that he knew something was wrong, but he didn't ask, and so I didn't tell him.

I must have borrowed the money to go down there, or Michael may have paid for the plane fare. He didn't have any money, and I didn't have any money. Anyway, I flew to Puerto Rico with him. I was about four to six weeks pregnant. We stayed two or three days. I was fairly confident that this place was okay. Michael knew people who had been there. We stayed in some hotel and took a bus out to the clinic: it was in a free-standing building outside of San Juan. There were other women in the waiting room, but I don't remember seeing any other American women. I remember them putting a mask over my face—they gave me some kind of anesthesia—and telling me to count and then waking up in bed bleeding. There were nurses. It was a real clinic; it wasn't a back room. The place was very clean. I don't know whether it's normal to bleed as much as I bled, but they reassured me and gave me sanitary napkins. I felt very vulnerable and physically weak. I had never felt that way before. I walked out of the clinic not too long after the abortion, and we took the bus back to San Juan. I remember needing to lean on Michael, and I didn't like being dependent. I can picture what I was wearing—a brown and white checked dress, short sleeves, straight skirt, organza, sheer cotton material. It was quite warm there. We went back to the hotel, and I rested.

When I found out I was pregnant, I went to see a doctor, and he had told me to come and see him afterwards. I had a low-grade infection. He was very sweet, supportive, gave me antibiotics. I remember I had an extremely intense dream. I think it was on the way down to Puerto Rico. I remembered it for years. It had something to do with being in a bathtub and bleeding, having a bloody leg. It had to do with wishing that I was pregnant with somebody else's baby. I think if I had had the baby with someone I was in love with, I might have kept it. The dream was real regret, a sadness. I never at all considered having that baby, and I never regretted having had the abortion. It would have been a total disaster in terms of my education, my relationship with Michael—I was already involved with him longer than I would have been because of the abortion. Although I didn't for a minute think I didn't want the abortion, it was still a very, very heavy experience. It isn't "Oh, this is a cool, easy decision to make, and there are no consequences."

Women Strike for Peace

Ethel Barol Taylor

Although the 1950s are often labeled a period of apathy and conservatism, the decade was hardly the political wasteland usually portrayed. Ethel Barol Taylor's lifelong activism began in reaction to the dropping of the atomic bombs on Hiroshima and Nagasaki in 1945, the very bombs that the husbands of the women at Los Alamos had worked so hard to produce. As a mother, Taylor was profoundly concerned about the effect of atomic weapons on the human race, especially the harmful effects of fallout released into the atmosphere. Soon she found other women who shared her concerns.

In 1961 more than 50,000 women came together in a nationwide Women Strike for Peace (WSP) to build support for a treaty to ban nuclear testing. Like Ethel Barol Taylor, who quickly found her home in this movement, participants were mainly white, middle-class, college-educated women from left to liberal political backgrounds; most were married with small children. Their appeal was unabashedly maternalist; that is, they used their status as wives and mothers, especially their concern for children, as the reason why they should have a political say about such vital issues as peace and nuclear testing. As Taylor attests, they dressed the part, always going to sit-ins and protests in hats and white gloves, symbols of middle-class ladies. This was a very effective appeal, and WSP's mobilization was a major factor in the passage of the 1963 treaty banning nuclear testing.

But along the way, Women's Strike for Peace drew the attention of the House Un-American Activities Committee (HUAC), the major congressional body charged with investigating concerns about internal communist subversion. Historians refer to the domestic witch-hunting of the postwar period as McCarthyism for one of the most vocal anti-communists, Senator Joseph McCarthy of Wisconsin, but the phenomenon was broader than one man. In the Cold War climate, any peace activism was seen as suspicious and potentially helpful to the Soviet Union.

Here Ethel Barol Taylor retells the story of what happened when HUAC subpoenaed 14 WSP women to quiz them on the supposedly communist leanings of their organization. HUAC was no match for the women, as newspaper headlines such as "It's Ladies Day at Capitol" and "Peace Gals Make Red Hunters Look Silly" affirmed. The full caption of the Herblock cartoon mentioned in the text says it even better: "I came in late, which was it that was un-American—women or peace?"

I was catapulted into the peace movement with the dropping of the bomb on Hiroshima. I was pretty apolitical up to that point. I used to get up in the morning and start polishing the furniture until I was polishing the polish. I thought, "There must be more to life than this."

I had a daughter, who was a small child at the time of the bombing of Hiroshima. When I read that the blast was so hot that in some circumstances it incinerated people and left just a shadow against a stone wall, creating instant fossils, I was numbed. I realized there were wars and there were wars, but this kind of war must never happen again.

There were others who felt as I did, and a few of us got together and talked. We formed a little group of women to study issues. I think even then, even though I was not political, I had this feeling that because women are not in positions of power and they have no role in policy-making, that maybe what we had to do was to make policy outside of government and demand of government that it listen to us.

A columnist once wrote a piece about me, and she called it "Rebel in White Gloves" because in the early days of Women Strike for Peace, women in the demonstrations, who were generally middle-class women, wore white gloves and hats. We used to do things like sit down and not move in the middle of the street, or whatever, but we would have our hats and white gloves on. I always thought that was a real protection until once we had an action, and hundreds of people went to Washington as a symbolic takeover of Congress. We walked and we came to a narrow street. The police said, "Cross this street and you get arrested." Well, I realized then that, what could they do? They're not going to electrocute me. They're not going to shoot me. It was much easier to cross that street than not to cross that street, so I crossed that street. Then we sat on the ground and waited to be arrested. We sat down, but we decided we weren't going to be yanked by our armpits, we were going to walk like ladies to the police van. We did. We got to the jail, and they opened the back door of the van. I looked out, and there was a five-foot drop to the ground. I waited for the policeman to help me down. The policeman came around and said, "Jump, sister." So I jumped into an entirely new world.

I didn't realize when I first got involved, when our government dropped the bomb on Hiroshima and Nagasaki, that this was going to be a lifetime commitment. I think if I had realized it I might have thought twice, because it's a terrible business to be in.

I think most of the pressures were because of the issues, not just because I was a woman—although there were those pressures too. You can really go nuts working for something and never have a success, never see enough change. Camus said, and I'm paraphrasing, that just because a thing is hopeless doesn't mean you don't get involved. That sounds gloomy. We have had some successes, but when I first got in, there were two bombs and they were both ours. Now there are 50,000 in the world. Someone once said, "Ethel, that's going to look lousy on your resumé." I think I developed an early anger that leaders had such contempt for the people they were supposed to be leading. That anger really has sustained me.

My anger is directed towards leaders who threaten the lives of children now and those yet unborn with their inhumane policy of nuclear weapons. We started because of children, because the scientists and doctors said that the strontium 90 and iodine 131 from the atomic tests would poison our children's milk and cause cancer. When we first organized we sent out a call throughout the streets with leaflets saying, "Take your children off milk." We sent our children's baby teeth to a lab in St. Louis to determine if strontium 90 was present. We were concerned about an epidemic, like polio before vaccines, except that polio is viral and these were man-made epidemics. Those who were then children now have children themselves.

My work in Women Strike for Peace sustains me. Outside of my family and my friends, WSP to me is the most important entity. It started out as a one-day action. We would meet every week around my dining room table to plan our "strike." There was a sugar bowl in the middle of the table for contributions toward the action. Some women stopped going to the hairdresser and did their own hair and put the money in the bowl. Some put birthday checks in. In one remarkable case, a woman who had very little money would occasionally give blood to the Red Cross and put the five dollars in the bowl. There was a wonderful outpouring of feeling and sisterhood. We were the harbingers of the women's movement—our weekly round table discussions were certainly consciousness raising. It was really an amazing experience. We never pledged solidarity, but we really were solid.

It was like an electric current running through the country with these women who decided that this couldn't just be a one-day action; it would have to go on. That has been our strength and weakness, to try to make a permanent organization out of a one-day action. WSP is more than an organization; it's a state of mind. I've never been part of a group—and I've been in a lot of them—where there was such a feeling of sisterhood. That is not to say that we don't sometimes get furious at each other.

In 1962 some WSP members were brought before the House Un-American Activities Committee [HUAC]. In order to show solidarity, many of us wrote to the chair of the committee asking for an opportunity to testify. The hearing was in 1962. It was pure theater. There is a wonderful cartoon about the HUAC hearings and WSP. There are these two guys sitting up at the HUAC table, and one of them says, "What are we against, women or peace?" They were against both. When some of us walked in, the guards were standing out in the hall outside the hearing room minding baby carriages and babies. We all carried red roses, and each time a woman would step down from testifying, we would present her with a bouquet, and we would applaud. The committee kept threatening to clear the room. They were in real trouble! They couldn't get out of the sessions, and they became more and more permissive because we were all so good-natured. The committee was just ridiculed away. It was a tremendous victory against the hearings.

When Dagmar Wilson was asked if there were Communists in WSP, she responded very pleasantly by saying something like, "We welcome everyone as long as they are for disarmament." That was quite a statement to make. I can't really speak for the women who faced the committee, and what the effect was on their lives, but it wasn't like the early McCarthy days, when people informed on others because they feared for their jobs—or the brave ones who refused to buckle under were ruined professionally. Then there was the real unadulterated fear and panic, because once you were blacklisted, that was it. But these were middle-class women whose jobs did not depend on whether or not they were cleared by this committee. I'm sure the HUAC experience for the women questioned was pretty scary, but the great difference was the tremendous, enthusiastic support they received publicly. We had a clipping service of all of the newspapers that covered the hearings. It was all "hats off to the ladies," as I remember . . .

I think one of the amazing things about my own personal life is that on the day of that first protest, where we were challenged to cross the street, it was easier to do it than not to do it. The next time it was a natural thing to do. So many women in the movement did things that they never thought would be possible to do because of the deep feelings they had against war . . .

I've survived by maintaining a sense of humor. It's better to laugh than to cry. I always got a tremendous amount of satisfaction and strength from the women with whom I worked. We can't always see immediate results from our work, but we have had an effect; we women have been dedicated and have made these issues ones that the government has to reckon with.

Civil Rights Activists

Rosa Parks and Virginia Foster Durr

Civil rights was the major social movement to rock the complacency of the 1950s. Although seeds of change for black Americans had been planted during World War II, it was the 1954 Supreme Court decision on school desegregation in *Brown v. Board of Education of Topeka* that marked the beginning of civil rights as a national issue.

On December 1, 1955, Montgomery, Alabama, seamstress Rosa Parks was arrested on a city bus for failing to give up her seat to a white person. The local National Association for the Advancement of Colored People (NAACP), headed by E. D. Nixon and to which Parks belonged, decided to challenge the constitutionality of the segregation ordinance. To further build support in the black community, Nixon and others called for a one-day boycott of the buses on December 5, the day of Parks's trial. More than 90 percent of Montgomery's black community stayed off the buses that day, and for the following 381 days, in a show of solidarity. A new leader emerged in the process: the 26-year-old Rev. Martin Luther King, Jr., who had recently become pastor of Montgomery's Dexter Avenue Baptist Church. The Supreme Court eventually ruled that Alabama laws requiring segregation on buses were unconstitutional, and on December 21, 1956, the city of Montgomery begrudgingly complied.

The quiet determination of Rosa Parks not to give up her seat comes through in her description here of the events that fateful day. The story is then picked up by Virginia Foster Durr, a liberal white Alabaman and early crusader against the poll tax, who with her lawyer husband Clifford Durr was deeply committed to the cause of civil rights. Durr's story (she was personally acquainted with Parks through the NAACP) shows the roles that whites played in the developing civil rights movement, as well as demonstrating how the bus boycott affected the relations between white women and their black servants.

I had left my work at the men's alteration shop, a tailor shop in the Montgomery Fair department store, and as I left work, I crossed the street to a drugstore to pick up a few items instead of trying to go directly to the bus stop. And when I had finished this, I came across the street and looked for a Cleveland Avenue bus that apparently had some seats on it. At that time it was a little hard to get a seat on the bus. But when I did get to the entrance to the bus, I got in line with a number of other people who were getting on the same bus.

As I got up on the bus and walked to the seat I saw there was only one vacancy that was just back of where it was considered the white section. So this was the seat that I took, next to the aisle, and a man was sitting next to me. Across the aisle there were two women, and there were a few seats at this point in the very front of the bus that was called the white section. I went on to one stop and I didn't particularly notice who was getting on the bus, didn't particularly notice the other people getting on. And on the third stop there were some people getting on, and at this point all of the front seats were taken. Now in the beginning, at the very first stop I had got on the bus, the back of the bus was filled up with people standing in the aisle and I don't know why this one vacancy that I took was left, because there were quite a few people already standing toward the back of the bus. The third stop is when all the front seats were taken, and this one man was

Sources: The interview with Rosa Parks is from *My Soul is Rested* by Howell Raines. Used by permission of Putnam Berkeley, a division of Penguin Putnam Inc. Reprinted from *Outside the Magic Circle: The Autobiography of Virginia Foster Durr,* edited by Hollinger F. Barnard. Copyright © 1985 The University of Alabama Press. Reprinted by permission of the publisher.

standing and when the driver looked around and saw he was standing, he asked the four of us, the man in the seat with me and the two women across the aisle, to let him have those front seats.

At his first request, didn't any of us move. Then he spoke again and said, "You'd better make it light on yourselves and let me have those seats." At this point, of course, the passenger who would have taken the seat hadn't said anything. In fact, he never did speak to my knowledge. When the three people, the man who was in the seat with me and the two women, stood up and moved into the aisle, I remained where I was. When the driver saw that I was still sitting there, he asked if I was going to stand up. I told him, no, I wasn't. He said, "Well, if you don't stand up, I'm going to have you arrested." I told him to go on and have me arrested.

He got off the bus and came back shortly. A few minutes later, two policemen got on the bus, and they approached me and asked if the driver had asked me to stand up, and I said yes, and they wanted to know why I didn't. I told them I didn't think I should have to stand up. After I had paid my fare and occupied a seat, I didn't think I should have to give it up. They placed me under arrest then and had me get in the police car, and I was taken to jail and booked on suspicion, I believe. The questions were asked, the usual questions they ask a prisoner or somebody that's under arrest. They had to determine whether or not the driver wanted to press charges or swear out a warrant, which he did. Then they took me to jail and I was placed in a cell. In a little while I was taken from the cell, and my picture was made and fingerprints taken. I went back to the cell then, and a few minutes later I was called back again, and when this happened I found out that Mr. E. D. Nixon and Attorney and Mrs. Clifford Durr had come to make bond for me.

* * * * *

This particular afternoon, Mrs. Parks later told me, she was exhausted. The bus she took went out to the housing project and was full of blacks, but some white men got on. The bus driver turned around and said, the way they always said, "Niggers, move back." And she just sat. The driver stopped the bus and came up to her. He said, "Did you hear me say to move back?" She said yes. He said, "Are you going to move back?" She said no. He called the police, and they came and arrested her and took her to jail. She was booked and put behind bars.

We got home about five o'clock from the office. Only Lulah was at home then, and she always had coffee ready for us. Lucy had graduated from high school and had gone to college, and we had sent Tilla north to school. Lulah was pretty lonesome because she didn't have any friends in the neighborhood, so we always tried to get home on time. We had just walked in and poured some coffee when the telephone rang. It was Mr. Nixon. He said, "Mr. Durr, will you call the jail and see why Mrs. Parks has been arrested?" The police recognized his voice as being that of a black man, and they wouldn't tell him anything. They treated him with the utmost disdain. Cliff called the jail and said he was Clifford J. Durr and he was a lawyer. They knew who he was, I think. He asked why Mrs. Parks was in jail. They told him she'd been booked on the city segregation ordinance.

So Cliff called Mr. Nixon back. Mr. Nixon asked if Cliff would go down with him to make bail. Cliff said, "Mr. Nixon, I don't have anything to make bail with." We didn't own any property at that time, and we only had three or four hundred dollars a month to live on. Mr. Nixon said, "That's all right. I can make bail, if you'll just go with me." He was afraid they wouldn't let him make bail. I was determined to go, too, so I put on my coat and came running out.

I waited for them while they made bail. Everything went very smoothly. They brought Mrs. Parks out from behind the bars. That was a terrible sight to me to see this gentle, lovely, sweet woman, whom I knew and was so fond of, being brought down by a matron. She wasn't in handcuffs, but they had to unlock two or three doors that grated loudly. She was very calm. I asked her how they had treated her and she said, "Very nicely." Just at that moment her husband arrived. He was very excited and upset. She went home with him in the car that some friend had brought. We told her we would follow her home in Mr. Nixon's car and would discuss the case in her apartment.

We all went to her apartment, and after she had freshened up and had a little supper, Cliff and Mr. Nixon and Mrs. Parks and her husband and her mother and I discussed the case. Of course, Mr. Nixon wanted her to make a test case of it. Mr. Nixon remembers her as being extremely reluctant to do so, but I remember that it was her husband who was so reluctant. He kept saying over and over again, "Rosa, the white folks will kill you. Rosa, the white folks will kill you." It was like a background chorus, to hear the poor man, who was as white as he could be himself, for a black man, saying, "Rosa, the white folks will kill you." I don't remember her being reluctant.

Part of the city bus ordinance said that the white people got on in the front and sat from the front back; the black people got on in the back and sat from the back toward the front. No signs were posted and the center was always a no-man's land. When more whites got on, the bus driver would make the blacks get up and go stand up in the back. But the city ordinance included a phrase that said the bus driver couldn't order a black to give up a seat unless there was another seat available farther back in the black section. In other words, he couldn't just say, "Nigger, get back." Cliff asked Mrs. Parks if she wanted to test the constitutionality of the law itself or if she wanted him to try to get her off on the fact that the bus driver hadn't been following the law. She said she wanted to test the constitutionality of the law.

Cliff told Mrs. Parks he thought he could get the charges dropped, if that's what she wanted, to prevent her going through a long court session. Cliff told her, "Now if you're going to fight this on a constitutional basis, you will have to get the NAACP to finance it because it's going to cost you a fortune. It'll have to go all the way up to the Supreme Court of the United States and it's going to cost a lot of money. You don't have it and of course we don't have it." Certainly the Montgomery NAACP or even the Alabama NAACP didn't have it, but Fred Gray, a lawyer for the NAACP in Montgomery, had connections with the NAACP Legal Defense Fund in New York. So that night it was decided that Mrs. Parks would challenge the bus ordinance on constitutional grounds, and Fred Gray would represent her. It would be an NAACP case and Cliff would do all he could to help Fred, but Cliff would not be the lawyer of record.

Mrs. Parks was brought up to trial on the Monday after her arrest. In the meantime, Mr. Nixon had organized a boycott of the buses on the day of her trial. It was supposed to be just a one-day boycott. I can very well remember going to a meeting Mr. Nixon had that Sunday afternoon at a black church. It was an NAACP meeting and Mr. Nixon asked me to come. I remember that he was very emotional. He said to the people, "I'm a Pullman porter and every time I go on my job, I put on an apron or a jacket." He said, "You know, we've been wearing aprons for three hundred years. It's time we took off our aprons." I always thought that was a vivid phrase. He asked them not to get on the bus the next day. He had spread the word to all the preachers and they all told their congregations to stay off the buses on that Monday, the day of Mrs. Parks's trial. They announced they would have a meeting at the Holt Street Baptist Church on Monday night.

Fred Gray represented Mrs. Parks in the courtroom. She was found guilty and fined. Then he announced they were going to appeal the case.

That night I left the house to go to the mass meeting. Mr. Nixon had had to go off on his run as a Pullman car porter, and Martin Luther King was selected to be the speaker. There must have been ten or fifteen thousand black people crowding in and around that church. At that time I felt on very friendly terms with all the black community. I hadn't the slightest feeling of fear being the only white person, but I couldn't get into the church because of the crowd. King made a magnificent speech that electrified the black people. He became their undoubted leader that night.

The Parks case went on and on, and so did the boycott. The black people formed car pools, and the city tried cracking down on them by arresting the drivers for going two miles an hour over the speed limit. The police were harassing them. So Cliff got in touch with Fred Gray, and they decided to transfer the case to federal court. It came before a three-judge panel: Judge Rives and Judge Johnson declared the ordinance unconstitutional; Judge Lynne dissented, saying the panel shouldn't declare the ordinance unconstitutional until a higher court had ruled in that area of the law. Then the case went to the Fifth Circuit Court of Appeals and then to the Supreme Court. Finally the Supreme Court declared the ordinance unconstitutional, and the Negroes began to ride the buses again.

The boycott lasted the entire year, December 1955 until December 1956. I would see the black women walking to work every morning and walking back at night. It was like the black tides would come up out of the black section of town and go to work and then sweep back again. We would offer the women rides when we saw them walking, particularly out in the country club area where the distances were rather great. I would say to a complete stranger, "Would you like a ride?" They'd say, "Yes, thank you very much." They'd get in the car, and I'd ask them where they lived. They always lived on the west part of town. I'd say, "I'm glad to see that you're supporting the boycott." "No, ma'am. I hadn't nothing to do with that boycott. The lady I work for, she wasn't feelin' so good this afternoon, so that's why I was walkin' home." "No, ma'am, I don't have nothin' to do with that boycott. It's just that her little girl's sick." One reason after another, but they wouldn't admit they were supporting the boycott.

Then the policemen began giving tickets to the white women who were taking black women home. I had a washwoman who came once a week, an older lady who belonged to the Church of Christ. She admired Dr. King greatly. She said she had seen the angels come down and stand on his shoulders every Monday night. In everything he said he was speaking with the voice of God. Now, everything she did was also dictated by the voice of God. She got so she talked to God so much that she didn't do much ironing. She was really a sweet old lady, but she was a religious fanatic. I was taking her home one afternoon and we were stopped. I knew positively I had stopped at the stop sign, but a policeman came roaring up to me. He said that I had stopped too late. I'd gone two or three feet over the line. I knew there was no use in arguing, so I told him I was sorry and got my ticket and took this old lady home. I had to pay five dollars. This incident was typical of what happened over and over again all over town.

The mayor of the city, Tacky Gayle, issued a plea for the white women of Montgomery to stop taking their black maids home. He said they could break the boycott if the white women would stop taking their black maids home, or even stop hiring them. Well, you have never heard a roar of indignation in your life as came from the white women of Montgomery. They were just furious at Tacky Gayle. They said, okay, if Tacky Gayle wants to come out here and do my washing and ironing and cleaning and cooking and look after my children, he can do it, but unless he does, I'm going to get Mary or Sally or Suzy. And they said, "Sally has never had a thing to do with that boycott in the first place. She told me she only stays off the buses because she's scared of those hoodlums that might hurt her."

A vast deceit went on. Everybody knew everybody else was lying, but to save face, they had to lie. The black women had to say they weren't taking any part in the boycott. The white women had to say that their maids didn't take any part in the boycott. We had a good example of that in Mary, Mrs. Durr's old cook who came from Hardaway, in Macon County. She'd been with the Durrs for years and now was Mrs. Durr's nurse. Mrs. Durr by that time was quite old and feeble and had to stay in bed, but a lot of people would drop by in the afternoons. Mary would sit in the room.

Mrs. Durr was a beautiful old woman, all propped up in bed, with a pink bed jacket and a pink ribbon in her hair and looking so pretty. Her mind was failing her, but she was still able to carry on a conversation. One afternoon when I was in the room somebody said to Mary, "Mary, I hope you don't have anything to do with that boycott." Mary said, "No, ma'am, I hadn't had nothing to do with that boycott. There's my sister Olla. She don't live very far from her job so she just walks to work. And my brother, he's got a job at the cotton mill and he just goes to work with some other men who are driving a car. And my other sister she just walks to work cause it's so close. No, ma'am, none of us has a thing to do with that boycott. We just stays off the buses." The white people really believed that. They didn't see through it at all.

In truth, Mary was a passionate advocate of the boycott. She'd meet us as we came in the driveway to ask how the bus boycott was getting on, how Dr. King was. She couldn't read and write, but she listened to the radio. That afternoon after the guests had left and Mary was fixing supper, Cliff and I said to her, "Mary, you are the biggest storyteller in the world. You know very well you're supporting the boycott and all of your family are. Why in the world did you make up that tale about how none of you were, and you were all walking just because you wanted to?" She laughed and she said, "Well, I tell you, Mr. Cliff, I tell you, I learned one thing in my life and that is, when your hand's in the lion's mouth, it's just better to pat it on the head." That expressed the feeling in the black community. The black women needed those jobs. They weren't paid very much, but that's all the income many of them had. They couldn't afford to say, "I'm supporting the boycott." So the white women lied and the black women lied. And the maids kept coming and the white women kept driving them back and forth to work.

Rachel Carson Answers Her Critics

Like civil rights and feminism, the environmental movement also traces its roots to this supposedly quiescent period of American political activism. Any movement for change will have multiple causes, of course, but many date the beginnings of modern environmentalism to the 1962 publication of one book—Rachel Carson's *Silent Spring*. Both a condemnation of the effects of pesticides, especially DDT, on the environment and a plea for a better balance between nature and human endeavor, the best-selling book permanently affected the way that Americans, scientists and general readers, thought about chemicals and their use in modern life.

Rachel Carson was that rare creature: both a scientist and a writer. For most of her career she was employed as a biologist and editor with the United States Bureau of Fisheries, later the Fish and Wildlife Service, in Washington, D.C. She never married, living with her widowed mother and taking on financial responsibility for various family members, including the child of a beloved niece whom she adopted as her own. The success of her 1951 book *The Sea Around Us* allowed her to quit her government job and devote herself to writing. The philosophy she wanted to share with readers was deceptively simple: "Instead of always trying to impose our will on Nature we should sometimes be quiet and listen to what she has to tell us."

Rachel Carson never saw herself as a muckraker, but she became imbued with a sense of moral crisis and the need to bear witness against the effects of pesticides on the natural environment. *Silent Spring* took its title from one of the main side effects of extensive aerial spraying of DDT: the inadvertent killing of songbirds along with the insects the chemicals were meant to destroy. Without songbirds, there would of course be a silent spring.

Source: Rachel Carson, "Rachel Carson Answers Her Critics," *Audubon Magazine* 65 (September/October 1963), pp. 262–64. Copyright © 1963. Reprinted by permission.

When the book was published, Carson immediately found herself the center of vicious attacks from the agricultural pesticide and chemical industries, who feared (rightly, it turned out) that her research would lead to federal legislation limiting or banning the use of certain chemicals. Here she answers her critics in a 1963 article in *Audubon Magazine.* Even though she would be dead within the year of breast cancer at age 56, her prediction that the controversy over pesticides would not meekly go away was absolutely on target.

criticized b/t her radical beliefs

Not often is it given to a generation to be able to change the course of events in ways that may significantly affect the future. Yet this is at once the privilege and the responsibility of us who live today.

We live in a time of challenge, which is also a time of opportunity. We live in a time when it is easy to despair, but which is also a time of great hope. We live in a time when it is necessary to know for what we stand, and to take that stand with courage.

It is, then, a time when we must have a realistic sense of values. We must decide what is worth while. We must be able to separate the trivia of today from the enduring realities of the long tomorrow.

"A thing of beauty is a joy forever," said the poet Keats. In modern times that humane and perceptive jurist, Justice William O. Douglas, has said that the right to search out a rare wildflower is just as inalienable as the right of a stock man to search out grass or of a lumberman to claim a tree.

There are scientific reasons as well as those which are esthetic. The world is inhabited by living species that are not only beautiful but full of meaning and significance. The evolution of the plants of today took millions upon millions of years. Who are we to assume the right, in this 20th century—a mere instant in time—who are we to say that those who come after us may never see some of today's rare and endangered species?

What right do we have to destroy the scientific record contained in a living species? How do we know that we may not have great need of what it has to tell us—or of the function it performs?

People who consider themselves practical may sometimes make judgments that are extremely impractical. A Canadian forester recently wrote me of a meeting attended by industrial and research foresters. Everyone present was agreed on a campaign to get rid of a species of alder that invades cutover black spruce lands. Yet, no one knew anything about the life history of the alder, or its ecological relationships.

Apparently it had never occurred to anyone that they should find out. Later it was discovered that this shrub performs a necessary function—a nitrogen-fixing process in the soil—and so is definitely beneficial to the spruce and to the other trees.

In this rather tough and materialistic world, then, how much room is there for concern about our wildflowers? About all of nature? Are we being impractical when we protest the substitution of the "brownout" for the color and beauty of flowers along our roads? Are we being sentimental when we care whether the robin returns to our dooryard and the veery sings in the twilight woods?

I am confident that the verdict of history will show that we—far from being the heedless sentimentalists—were indeed the tough-minded realists.

A world that is no longer fit for wild plants, that is no longer graced by the flight of birds, a world whose streams and forests are empty and lifeless is not likely to be fit habitat for man himself, for these things are symptoms of an ailing world.

In a recent speech in behalf of the World Wildlife Fund, Britain's Prince Philip put the matter very simply: "Miners," he reminded his hearers, "used canaries to warn them of deadly gases. It mightn't be a bad idea if we took the same warning from the dead birds in our countryside."

So today, as thousands of hapless wild creatures serve as canaries in the mines of our heedless technology, we have graphic reminders that all is not well in the environment of man.

In *Silent Spring* I gave many examples of the destruction of wildlife following the use of insecticides. I am sure I do not need to tell you that a determined effort is now being made to discredit these reports. People are told that the incidents I reported happened years ago, that better methods, better controls now make this sort of thing impossible. We are told that destruction of wildlife occurs only when insecticides are improperly used—"follow the directions and no harm will result."

Even as these reassurances are anxiously being given out, the newspapers carry other reports. These make it clear that incidents linking wildlife and pesticides did not stop with the publication of *Silent Spring*.

Let me give you a few examples:

- A few weeks ago, Canadian newspapers carried a warning that woodcock being shot during the hunting season in New Brunswick were carrying residues of the insecticide heptachlor and might be dangerous if used as food. These birds had wintered in the Southern United States, where heptachlor was used in the fire ant program. This was a program sponsored and carried out by the state and federal governments. It was no unplanned or accidental application.

- For a number of years the eagle populations have shown an alarming decline. The Fish and Wildlife Service recently made news by announcing its discovery of lethal quantities of DDT in eagles found dead in the wild. It also discovered DDT in eagle eggs that failed to hatch.

- In Southern Michigan, state agricultural officials are again using the very poisonous insecticide dieldrin in their campaign against the Japanese beetle. According to a report sent me by a biologist on the scene the destruction of rabbits, squirrels, pheasants, and many songbirds is again great. This time the farmers themselves are protesting against the program presumably intended for their benefit.

- Strong protests are also being heard in Southern Illinois where a similar program has destroyed several hundred quail and rabbits in two small areas.

- And in the Boston area, as a legacy from years of insecticide spraying, fish in the Framingham, Mass. reservoir are carrying DDT in amounts 10 times the legally permissible level. This was discovered by the excellent researches of biologists of the Massachusetts Fish and Game Department.

No, the problem of pesticides is not merely the dream of an avaricious author, out to pile up royalties by frightening the public—it is very much with us, here and now.

I was amused recently to read a bit of wishful thinking in one of the trade magazines. Industry "can take heart," it said, "from the fact that the main impact of the book (i.e., *Silent Spring*) will occur in the late fall and winter—seasons when consumers are not normally active buyers of insecticides . . . it is fairly safe to hope that by March or April *Silent Spring* no longer will be an interesting conversational subject."

If the tone of my mail from readers is any guide, and if the movements that have already been launched gain the expected momentum, this is one prediction that will not come true.

SUGGESTIONS FOR FURTHER READING

Anderson, Karen. *Wartime Women: Sex Roles, Family Relations, and the Status of Women during World War II.* Westport, 1981.

Bailey, Beth. *From Front Porch to Back Seat: Courtship in 20th Century America.* Baltimore, 1988.

Berube, Alan. *Coming Out Under Fire: Gay Men and Women in World War II.* New York, 1990.

Blackwelder, Julia Kirk. *Women of the Depression: Caste and Culture in San Antonio, 1929–1939.* College Station, TX, 1984.

Blee, Kathleen. *Women of the Klan: Racism and Gender in the 1920s.* Berkeley, 1991.

Breines, Wini. *Young, White, and Miserable: Growing Up Female in the Fifties.* Boston, 1992.

Brown, Dorothy M. *Setting a Course: American Women in the 1920s.* Boston, 1987.

Cook, Blanche Wiesen. *Eleanor Roosevelt: Volume I, 1884–1933.* New York, 1992.

Cook, Blanche Wiesen. *Eleanor Roosevelt: Volume II, 1933–1938.* New York, 1999.

Cott, Nancy F. *The Grounding of Modern Feminism.* New Haven, 1987.

Crawford, Vicki, Jacqueline Ann Rouse, and Barbara Woods, eds. *Women in the Civil Rights Movement: Trailblazers and Torchbearers, 1941–1965.* New York, 1990.

D'Emilio, John, and Estelle Freedman. *Intimate Matters: A History of Sexuality in America.* New York, 1988.

Farnham, Christine Anne. *Women of the American South: A Multicultural Reader.* New York, 1997.

Fass, Paula. *The Damned and the Beautiful: American Youth in the 1920s.* New York, 1977.

Faue, Elizabeth. *Community of Suffering and Struggle: Women, Men, and the Labor Movement in Minneapolis, 1915–1945.* Chapel Hill, 1991.

Gluck, Sherna B. *Rosie the Riveter Revisited: Women, the War, and Social Change.* Boston, 1987.

Gordon, Felice D. *After Winning: The Legacy of the New Jersey Suffragists, 1920–1947.* New Brunswick, 1986.

Gordon, Linda, ed. *Women, the State, and Welfare.* Madison, 1990.

Hall, Jacqueline Dowd. *Revolt against Chivalry: Jessie Daniel Ames and the Women's Campaign against Lynching.* New York, 1979.

Hartmann, Susan M. *The Home Front and Beyond: American Women in the 1940s.* Boston, 1982.

Hoff-Wilson, Joan, and Marjorie Lightman. *Without Precedent: The Life and Career of Eleanor Roosevelt.* Bloomington, 1984.

Honey, Maureen. *Creating Rosie the Riveter: Class, Gender, and Propaganda during World War II.* Amherst, 1984.

Janiewski, Dolores E. *Sisterhood Denied: Race, Gender, and Class in a New South Community.* Philadelphia, 1985.

Jones, Jacqueline. *Labor of Love, Labor of Sorrow: Black Women, Work, and the Family from Slavery to the Present.* New York, 1985.

Kaledin, Eugenia. *Mothers and More: American Women in the 1950s.* Boston, 1984.

Kessler-Harris, Alice. *Out to Work: A History of Wage-Earning Women in America.* New York, 1982.

Lear, Linda. *Rachel Carson: Witness for Naure.* New York, 1997.

Litoff, Judy Barrett, and David C. Smith. *We're in This War, Too: World War II Letters from Women in Uniform.* New York, 1994.

Lynn, Susan. *Progressive Women in Conservative Times: Racial Justice, Peace, and Feminism, 1945 to the 1960s.* New Brunswick, 1992.

Martin, Patricia Preciado, ed. *Songs My Mother Sang to Me: An Oral History of Mexican-American Women.* Tucson, 1992.

May, Elaine Tyler. *Homeward Bound: American Families in the Cold War Era.* New York, 1988.

Meyer, Leisa D. *Creating G.I. Jane: Sexuality and Power in the Women's Army Corps during World War II.* New York, 1996.

Meyerowitz, Joanne, ed. *Not June Cleaver: Women and Gender in Postwar America, 1945–1960.* Philadelphia, 1994.

Milkman, Ruth. *Gender at Work: The Dynamics of Job Segregation by Sex during World War II.* Urbana, 1987.

Muncy, Robyn. *Creating a Female Dominion in American Reform, 1890–1930.* New York, 1991.

Neff, Mary. *Preserving the Family Farm: Women, Community, and the Foundations of Agribusiness in the Midwest, 1900–1940.* Baltimore, 1995.

Palmer, Phyllis. *Domesticity and Dirt: Housewives and Domestic Servants in the United States, 1920–1945.* Philadelphia, 1989.

Reagan, Leslie J. *When Abortion Was a Crime: Women, Medicine, and the Law 1867–1973.* Berkeley, 1997.

Rossiter, Margaret. *Women Scientists in America: Struggles and Strategies to 1940.* Baltimore, 1982.

Ruiz, Vicki L. *Cannery Women, Cannery Lives: Mexican Women, Unionization, and the California Food Processing Industry, 1930–1950.* Albuquerque, 1987.

Ruiz, Vicki L. *From Out of the Shadows: Mexican Women in Twentieth-Century America.* New York, 1998.

Rupp, Leila J. *Worlds of Women: The Making of an International Women's Movement.* Princeton, 1998.

Rupp, Leila J., and Verta Taylor. *Survival in the Doldrums: The American Women's Rights Movement, 1945 to the 1960s.* New York, 1987.

Scharf, Lois. *To Work and To Wed: Female Employment, Feminism, and the Great Depression.* Westport, 1980.

Showalter, Elaine, ed. *These Modern Women: Autobiographical Essays from the 1920s.* Old Westbury, NY, 1978.

Storrs, Landon R. Y. *Civilizing Capitalism: The National Consumers' League, Women's Activism, and Labor Standards in the New Deal Era.* Chapel Hill, 2000.

Swerdlow, Amy. *Women Strike for Peace: Traditional Motherhood and Radical Politics in the 1960s.* Chicago, 1993.

Wandersee, Winifred. *Women's Work and Family Values, 1920–1940.* Cambridge, 1981.

Ware, Susan. *Beyond Suffrage: Women in the New Deal.* Cambridge, 1981.

———. *Holding Their Own: American Women in the 1930s.* Boston, 1982.

———. *Still Missing: Amelia Earhart and the Search for Modern Feminism.* New York, 1993.

Westin, Jeane. *Making Do: How Women Survived the 30s.* Chicago, 1976.

The Personal Becomes Political

1963 to the Present

*I*n the last four decades of the 20th century, the United States faced major challenges at home and abroad: Vietnam, the end of the Cold War, globalization, an increasingly multicultural and pluralistic society, debates over the role of the federal government, and struggles over the core values to shape American public life. The period of activism and social change associated with the 1960s and 1970s gradually gave way to a more conservative tenor to public life after 1980. Despite heated cultural debates about many of the challenges reshaping American society, the country showed no signs of returning to its old ways. Changes had become so deeply imbedded in modern life, and so quickly, that it would have been impossible to go back.

Nowhere is the cumulative effect of social change more apparent than in women's lives. Of all the transformations that reshaped American life in the second half of the 20th century, the revolution in women's lives was one of the most profound and far-reaching. Some of those changes were economic and structural, but many were propelled by the revival of feminism in the 1960s and 1970s. Historian Ruth Rosen used the image of "the world split open" to capture how the modern women's movement changed America. While the fortunes of feminism have ebbed and flowed, the movement continues to redefine itself in response to new issues and new converts. In the words of two young feminists (born in 1970), "After thirty years of feminism, the world we inhabit barely resembles the world we were born into. And there's still a lot left to do."

This final section aims to capture the revolutionary changes that have occurred in women's lives since 1963 (the publication date of Betty Friedan's *The Feminine Mystique),* as well as the controversies that these changes have engendered. Feminists share the stage with conservative critics such as Phyllis Schlafly and Christina Hoff Sommers. Different generations are represented: 1960s feminists and "third wave" feminists from the 1990s who are their symbolic (and sometimes actual) daughters. We see women at work, struggling to make a living for themselves and their families. Issues that shape contemporary women's lives, such as sexuality, body image, women and disabilities, and abortion, are presented and debated. Finally, this section ends with a glance forward into the 21st century, symbolized by the dramatic upsurge of global feminism.

CHAPTER 10

The Revival of Feminism

The *60s,* as the term is commonly used to describe a period of political upheaval and dissent, did not really start in 1960 nor did it end in 1970. The women's movement helps to correct this chronology. Just as the civil rights movement pushes the period of activism back to its beginnings in the 1950s, so does the women's movement extend the activism well past the end of the decade.

In 1960, feminism was a topic of interest only to a small minority of American women. Over the next 15 years feminism became a major item on the national agenda. The revival of feminism initially followed two different paths—through "women's rights" and "women's liberation." By the 1970s, however, those distinctions had blurred and supporters began to talk about "the women's movement" or "feminism" without dividing it into two branches. The widening public discussion of women's issues continues today, although the terms of the debate have changed over the intervening decades.

Several events set the stage for the revival of feminism as a national issue in the early 1960s. The establishment of the Presidential Commission on the Status of Women by President John F. Kennedy in 1961 brought together women and men concerned about women's issues; although its final recommendations were rather limited, just the fact of its existence raised expectations that women's issues were going to be addressed. The publication of Betty Friedan's *The Feminine Mystique* in 1963 suggested a groundswell of popular dissatisfaction with women's lives that could be tapped for an emerging political movement.

An especially important event was the passage of the 1964 Civil Rights Act, which had as great an impact on women as it did on blacks. The key provision was Title VII, which in its original formulation outlawed discrimination in public accommodations or employment on the basis of race, color, religion, or national origin. At the last moment, *sex* was added as a category, and women had an important legal tool to challenge discrimination on the job.

The Civil Rights Act set up the Equal Employment Opportunity Commission to deal with complaints, but dissatisfaction with how the EEOC was implementing its mandate against sex discrimination led to the founding of the National Organization for Women in 1966. NOW best represents the women's rights branch of feminism. Composed mainly of professional women who had long been active in politics and public life, its members considered themselves a civil rights organization for women. Their main goal was, in the words of their statement of purpose, "to take action to bring women into full participation in the mainstream of American society now, exercising all the privileges and responsibilities thereof in truly equal partnership with men." By the 1970s, NOW had grown to the largest feminist organization in the country, a position it still holds today.

Women's liberationists came to feminism by a different path. Radical women, who tended to be much younger than the politicos of NOW, had been active in the civil rights movement in the early 1960s. Their experiences on the front line of voter registration drives and protest marches increased their self-confidence, but also fed their frustration about the way that women were treated within the movement. For example, women were automatically expected to take notes at meetings, make coffee, do all the housework, and often be available as sexual partners for male co-workers. But women found it difficult in the mid-1960s to pinpoint their generalized dissatisfactions because they lacked the ideological context of feminism to frame the questions. Civil rights activists began tentatively by comparing women's position to that of blacks, but when they tried to raise such issues with their male colleagues, both black and white, they were rebuffed.

By the mid-1960s, whites had been kicked out of the civil rights movement, which was entering its black power phase. Radical women did not find the male-dominated New Left much more congenial. As the men debated ending the war in Vietnam and taking over the universities, women continued to be expected to make coffee and take notes. By 1967 and 1968, groups of radical women in several cities across the country had begun to come together to share common concerns. At first, none of them thought they were founding a separate women's movement, but when the New Left refused to include a commitment to fighting sexism as part of its agenda, the women walked out.

Around 1969 and 1970, the media discovered feminism. With wide coverage of such events as the August 26, 1970, marches and demonstrations to honor the 50th anniversary of the suffrage amendment, the media brought the stimulating ideas of feminism to a far wider audience than had been reached by the members of NOW or the small constituencies of the New Left. Women started to join the movement or call themselves feminists who had not been part of either women's rights or women's liberation, and the distinctions between the two branches began to blur.

There was also a certain breaking down of barriers because each side was learning from the other. Radical women, who had devoted much of their energy to critiquing patriarchal institutions such as marriage and the family, saw the relevance of such legislative changes as increased child care services or protection of battered women. The women of NOW, on the other hand, while still wedded to working within the system, began to embrace a broader critique of women's place in American society than could be cured simply by legal reform. By 1970, feminism was on the way to becoming a mass movement.

The symbol of the new women's movement was the Equal Rights Amendment. No longer a divisive issue between feminists as it had been in the 1920s, the

ERA seemed a perfect vehicle for mobilizing the nation around a commitment to equality and a strong tool to correct the legal disabilities under which women still labored. In large part in response to the new political muscle of organized feminism, the ERA passed the Congress in 1972 and was sent to the states for what was predicted as a speedy ratification. At that point, the women's movement was at high tide, taking as its mind-set the title of Robin Morgan's best-selling 1970 book, *Sisterhood Is Powerful.*

Founding the National Organization for Women, 1966

At a 1966 convention in Washington, D.C., of state commissions mandated in the aftermath of the Presidential Commission on the Status of Women, Betty Friedan, lawyer Pauli Murray, ERA supporter Marguerite Rawalt, Women's Bureau staffer Catherine East, Wisconsin activist Kay Clarenbach, and others met in Friedan's hotel room to draw up plans for what they saw as a civil rights organization for women. The immediate backdrop was frustration over the failure of the Equal Employment Opportunity Commission (EEOC) to take action against sex discrimination as required under Title VII. More generally, these women had become increasingly aware of the discrimination that women faced in American life and they wanted to organize a pressure group to seek change. As Friedan later put it dramatically, "The absolute necessity for a civil rights movement for women had reached such a point of subterranean explosive urgency by 1966, that it only took a few of us to get together to ignite the spark—and it spread like a nuclear chain-reaction."

The National Organization for Women was officially launched in October 1966, with Betty Friedan as its first president; it counted 300 charter members, of whom perhaps one-quarter were men. NOW's statement of purpose reprinted here is a classic document of liberal feminism: rather than challenging the system, it asks for women's full inclusion into the mainstream of American society; rather than being antagonistic to men, it strives toward a "truly equal partnership." But its recommendations are more wide ranging than the Presidential Commission's just three years before, and its tone conveys an urgency about action now.

It is interesting to note what issues are not mentioned in the NOW document, notably the Equal Rights Amendment and support for reproductive rights. By its second national convention in November of 1967, NOW had added those demands to its "Bill of Rights for Women," but only after heated debate. Showing the ability of the women's movement to mobilize a constituency, NOW grew from 1,000 members in 1967 to over 40,000 just seven years later.

Source: Reprinted by permission of the National Organization for Women. This is a historical document (1966) and does not reflect the current language or priorities of the organization.

We, men and women who hereby constitute ourselves as the National Organization for Women, believe that the time has come for a new movement toward true equality for all women in America, and toward a fully equal partnership of the sexes, as part of the world-wide revolution of human rights now taking place within and beyond our national borders.

The purpose of NOW is to take action to bring women into full participation in the mainstream of American society now, exercising all the privileges and responsibilities thereof in truly equal partnership with men.

We believe the time has come to move beyond the abstract argument, discussion and symposia over the status and special nature of women which has raged in America in recent years; the time has come to confront, with concrete action, the conditions that now prevent women from enjoying the equality of opportunity and freedom of choice which is their right as individual Americans, and as human beings.

NOW is dedicated to the proposition that women first and foremost are human beings, who, like all other people in our society, must have the chance to develop their fullest human potential. We believe that women can achieve such equality only by accepting to the full the challenges and responsibilities they share with all other people in our society, as part of the decision-making mainstream of American political, economic and social life.

We organize to initiate or support action, nationally or in any part of this nation, by individuals or organizations, to break through the silken curtain of prejudice and discrimination against women in government, industry, the professions, the churches, the political parties, the judiciary, the labor unions, in education, science, medicine, law, religion and every other field of importance in American society . . .

There is no civil rights movement to speak for women, as there has been for Negroes and other victims of discrimination. The National Organization for Women must therefore begin to speak.

WE BELIEVE that the power of American law, and the protection guaranteed by the U.S. Constitution to the civil rights of all individuals, must be effectively applied and enforced to isolate and remove patterns of sex discrimination, to ensure equality of opportunity in employment and education, and equality of civil and political rights and responsibilities on behalf of women, as well as for Negroes and other deprived groups.

We realize that women's problems are linked to many broader questions of social justice; their solution will require concerted action by many groups. Therefore, convinced that human rights for all are indivisible, we expect to give active support to the common cause of equal rights for all those who suffer discrimination and deprivation, and we call upon other organizations committed to such goals to support our efforts toward equality for women.

WE DO NOT ACCEPT the token appointment of a few women to high-level positions in government and industry as a substitute for a serious continuing effort to recruit and advance women according to their individual abilities. To this end, we urge American government and industry to mobilize the same resources of ingenuity and command with which they have solved problems of far greater difficulty than those now impeding the progress of women.

WE BELIEVE that this nation has a capacity at least as great as other nations, to innovate new social institutions which will enable women to enjoy true equality of opportunity and responsibility in society, without conflict with their responsibilities as mothers and homemakers. In such innovations, America does not lead the Western world, but lags by decades behind many European countries. We do not accept the traditional assumption that a woman has to choose between marriage and motherhood, on the one hand, and serious participation in industry or the professions on the other. We question the present expectation that all normal women will retire from job or profession for ten or fifteen years, to devote their full time to raising children, only to reenter the job market at a relatively minor level. This in itself is a deterrent to the aspirations of women, to their acceptance into management or professional training courses, and to the very possibility of equality of opportunity or real choice, for all but a few women. Above all, we reject the assumption that these problems are the unique responsibility of each individual woman, rather than a basic social dilemma which society must solve. True equality of opportunity and freedom of choice for women requires such practical and possible innovations as a nationwide network of child-care centers, which will make it unnecessary for women to retire completely from society until their children are grown, and national programs to provide retraining for women who have chosen to care for their own children full time.

WE BELIEVE that it is as essential for every girl to be educated to her full potential of human ability as it is for every boy—with the knowledge that such education is the key to effective participation in today's economy and that, for a girl as for a boy, education can only be serious where there is expectation that it will be used in society. We believe that American educators are capable of devising means of imparting such expectations to girl students. Moreover, we consider the decline in the proportion of women receiving higher and professional education to be evidence of discrimination. This discrimination may take the form of quotas against the admission of women to colleges and professional schools; lack of encouragement by parents, counselors and educators; denial of loans or fellowships; or the traditional or arbitrary procedures in graduate and professional training geared in terms of men, which inadvertently discriminate against women. We believe that the same serious attention must be given to high school dropouts who are girls as to boys.

WE REJECT the current assumptions that a man must carry the sole burden of supporting himself, his wife, and family, and that a woman is automatically entitled to life-long support by a man upon her marriage, or that marriage, home and family are primarily woman's world and responsibility—hers, to dominate, his to support. We believe that a true partnership between the sexes demands a different concept of marriage, an equitable sharing of the responsibilities of home and children and of the economic burdens of their support. We believe that proper recognition should be given to the economic and social value of homemaking and child care. To these ends, we will seek to open a reexamination of laws and mores governing marriage and divorce, for we believe that the current state of "half-equality" between the sexes discriminates against both men and women, and is the cause of much unnecessary hostility between the sexes.

WE BELIEVE that women must now exercise their political rights and responsibilities as American citizens. They must refuse to be segregated on the basis of sex into separate-and-not-equal ladies' auxiliaries in the political parties, and they must demand representation according to their numbers in the regularly constituted party committees—at local, state, and national levels—and in the informal power structure, participating fully in the selection of candidates and political decision-making, and running for office themselves.

IN THE INTERESTS OF THE HUMAN DIGNITY OF WOMEN, we will protest and endeavor to change the false image of women now prevalent in the mass media, and in the texts, ceremonies, laws, and practices of our major social institutions. Such images perpetuate contempt for women by society and by women for themselves. We are similarly opposed to all policies and practices—in church, state, college, factory, or office—which, in the guise of protectiveness, not only deny opportunities but also foster in women self-denigration, dependence, and evasion of responsibility, undermine their confidence in their own abilities and foster contempt for women.

NOW WILL HOLD ITSELF INDEPENDENT OF ANY POLITICAL PARTY in order to mobilize the political power of all women and men intent on our goals. We will strive to ensure that no party, candidate, President, senator, governor, congressman, or any public official who betrays or ignores the principle of full equality between the sexes is elected or appointed to office. If it is necessary to mobilize the votes of men and women who believe in our cause, in order to win for women the final right to be fully free and equal human beings, we so commit ourselves.

WE BELIEVE THAT women will do most to create a new image of women by *acting* now, and by speaking out in behalf of their own equality, freedom, and human dignity—not in pleas for special privilege, nor in enmity toward men, who are also victims of the current half-equality between the sexes—but in an active, self-respecting partnership with men. By so doing, women will develop confidence in their own ability to determine actively, in partnership with men, the conditions of their life, their choices, their future and their society.

Feminist Guerrilla Theater, 1968

Robin Morgan

Radical women presented a stark contrast to the National Organization for Women, the difference between dresses, makeup, and stockings versus jeans, T-shirts, and long hair. Women's liberation was all mass and no organization; groups formed and disbanded spontaneously, often not knowing of each other's existence; there were no leaders. Members tended to be young women in their 20s (only later did the women's movement reach the college campuses) who were far more hostile to men than the women's rights branch of the movement. They believed in revolution, not reform, of the dominant system.

Women's liberation first gained media attention with this protest organized by the Radical Women of New York at the Miss America Pageant in September 1968. In the spirit of counterculture street theater (such as had occurred at that summer's Democratic convention in Chicago, but without the violence), the protesters planned such antics as crowning a live sheep as Miss America and throwing items of women's oppression into a freedom trash can. The language in the following reprint of the broadside the feminists distributed is characteristic of the 1960s, with such words as *groovy, busted, dig that,* and *male chauvinism.* Its reasoning also closely links beauty pageants to other key issues of the 1960s, such as racism, a critique of affluence, and the war in Vietnam.

The protest was staged as a media event. When organizers announced they would speak only to women reporters, who were greatly underrepresented in journalism at the time, the demand helped to raise media interest in the event, and it became front page news. Such media coverage had a twofold effect. It spread the notion that women's liberation was growing (although *movement* is too strong a word for the loose structures of 1968), which in turn brought more women into the cause. At the same time, the media portrayed the protestors in fairly negative terms, such as coining the term *bra-burners* to denote all radical feminists, even though no bras were burned. Media coverage was thus a double-edged sword.

On September 7th in Atlantic City, the Annual Miss America Pageant will again crown "your ideal." But this year, reality will liberate the contest auction-block in the guise of "genyooine" de-plasticized, breathing women. Women's Liberation Groups, black women, high-school and college women, women's peace groups, women's welfare and social-work groups, women's job-equality groups, pro-birth control and pro-abortion groups—women of every political persuasion—all are invited to join us in a day-long boardwalk-theater event, starting at 1:00 P.M. on the Boardwalk in front of Atlantic City's Convention Hall. We will protest the image of Miss America, an image that oppresses women in every area in which it purports to represent us. There will be: Picket Lines; Guerrilla Theater; Leafleting; Lobbying Visits to the contestants urging our sisters to reject the Pageant Farce and join us; a huge Freedom Trash Can (into which we will throw bras,* girdles, curlers, false eyelashes, wigs, and representative issues of *Cosmopolitan, Ladies' Home Journal, Family Circle,* etc.—bring any such woman-garbage you have around the house); we will also announce a Boycott of all those commercial products related to the Pageant, and the day will end with a Women's Liberation rally at midnight when Miss America is crowned on live television. Lots of other

Source: Robin Morgan, "No More Miss America!" From *Sisterhood Is Powerful: An Anthology of Writings from the Women's Liberation Movement,* edited by Robin Morgan, pp. 584–88. Copyright © 1970. Reprinted by permission.
*Bras were never burned. Bra-burning was a whole-cloth invention of the media.—Ed. [Morgan]

surprises are being planned (come and add your own!) but we do not plan heavy disruptive tactics and so do not expect a bad police scene. It should be a groovy day on the Boardwalk in the sun with our sisters. In case of arrests, however, we plan to reject all male authority and demand to be busted by policewomen only. (In Atlantic City, women cops are not permitted to make arrests—dig that!)

Male chauvinist-reactionaries on this issue had best stay away, nor are male liberals welcome in the demonstrations. But sympathetic men can donate money as well as cars and drivers.

Male reporters will be refused interviews. We reject patronizing reportage. *Only newswomen will be recognized.*

THE TEN POINTS

We Protest:

1. *The Degrading Mindless-Boob-Girlie Symbol.* The Pageant contestants epitomize the roles we are all forced to play as women. The parade down the runway blares the metaphor of the 4-H Club county fair, where the nervous animals are judged for teeth, fleece, etc., and where the best "specimen" gets the blue ribbon. So are women in our society forced daily to compete for male approval, enslaved by ludicrous "beauty" standards we ourselves are conditioned to take seriously.
2. *Racism with Roses.* Since its inception in 1921, the Pageant has not had one Black finalist, and this has not been for a lack of test-case contestants. There has never been a Puerto Rican, Alaskan, Hawaiian, or Mexican-American winner. Nor has there ever been a *true* Miss America—an American Indian.
3. *Miss America as Military Death Mascot.* The highlight of her reign each year is a cheerleader-tour of American troops abroad—last year she went to Vietnam to pep-talk our husbands, fathers, sons and boyfriends into dying and killing with a better spirit. She personifies the "unstained patriotic American womanhood our boys are fighting for." The Living Bra and the Dead Soldier. We refuse to be used as Mascots for Murder.
4. *The Consumer Con-Game.* Miss America is a walking commercial for the Pageant's sponsors. Wind her up and she plugs your product on promotion tours and TV—all in an "honest, objective" endorsement. What a shill.
5. *Competition Rigged and Unrigged.* We deplore the encouragement of an American myth that oppresses men as well as women: the win-or-you're worthless competitive disease. The "beauty contest" creates only one winner to be "used" and forty-nine losers who are "useless."
6. *The Woman as Pop Culture Obsolescent Theme.* Spindle, mutilate, and then discard tomorrow. What is so ignored as last year's Miss America? This only reflects the gospel of our society, according to Saint Male: women must be young, juicy, malleable—hence age discrimination and the cult of youth. And we women are brainwashed into believing this ourselves!

7. *The Unbeatable Madonna-Whore Combination.* Miss America and Playboy's centerfold are sisters over the skin. To win approval, we must be both sexy and wholesome, delicate but able to cope, demure yet titillatingly bitchy. Deviation of any sort brings, we are told, disaster: "You won't get a man!!"

8. *The Irrelevant Crown on the Throne of Mediocrity.* Miss America represents what women are supposed to be: unoffensive, bland, apolitical. If you are tall, short, over or under what weight The Man prescribes you should be, forget it. Personality, articulateness, intelligence, commitment—unwise. Conformity is the key to the crown—and, by extension, to success in our society.

9. *Miss America as Dream Equivalent To—?* In this reputedly democratic society, where every little boy supposedly can grow up to be President, what can every little girl hope to grow to be? Miss America. That's where it's at. Real power to control our own lives is restricted to men, while women get patronizing pseudo-power, an ermine cloak and a bunch of flowers; men are judged by their actions, women by their appearance.

10. *Miss America as Big Sister Watching You.* The Pageant exercises Thought Control, attempts to sear the Image onto our minds, to further make women oppressed and men oppressors; to enslave us all the more in high-heeled, low-status roles; to inculcate false values in young girls; to use women as beasts of buying; to seduce us to prostitute ourselves before our own oppression.

NO MORE MISS AMERICA

The Politics of Housework

Pat Mainardi

One of the major contributions of the women's liberation movement was the idea of consciousness-raising, that is, using group discussions of women's personal experiences to understand how sexism (a word just coming into use in 1968) shaped their lives. Credit for the consciousness-raising tactic belongs to a group of radical women in New York who called themselves the Redstockings. In their 1969 Manifesto, they asserted: "We regard our personal experience, and our feelings about that experience, as the basis for an analysis of our common situation . . . Consciousness-raising is not 'therapy,' which implies the existence of individual solutions and falsely assumes that the male-female relationship is purely personal, but the only method by which we can ensure that our program for liberation is based on the concrete realities of our lives."

Source: Pat Mainardi, "The Politics of Housework." From *Sisterhood Is Powerful: An Anthology of Writings from the Women's Liberation Movement,* edited by Robin Morgan, pp. 502–6. Copyright © 1970. Reprinted by permission.

Painter Pat Mainardi was a member of Redstockings, and this piece on "The Politics of Housework" grew out of her experience. One of the slogans of the women's movement was that "the personal is political," and nowhere was that more clear than in who did the housework. In such sessions, many women who considered themselves liberated realized that the men with whom they were sharing their lives, as husbands or lovers, were often resistant to changing old patterns if they (the men) had something to lose. Her humorous, yet pointed, recounting of such dialogues in her own household shows the uneasiness and tension that could occur when women took the revolution home.

Dismissed by men as a trivial issue, housework in fact goes to the heart of a patriarchal family structure that deposits all responsibility for household management and child care on women. Furthermore, the discussion pinpoints the parallels between housework and women's work in general: its low status, its repetitiveness, its dull and boring nature. Women's liberation argued that not just women should change, but men must as well. And the change should occur not just in the public realm of law and politics, but in the private realm of family life and sexuality.

Liberated women—very different from women's liberation! The first signals all kinds of goodies, to warm the hearts (not to mention other parts) of the most radical men. The other signals—*housework.* The first brings sex without marriage, sex before marriage, cozy housekeeping arrangements ("You see, I'm living with this chick") and the self-content of knowing that you're not the kind of man who wants a doormat instead of a woman. That will come later. After all, who wants that old commodity anymore, the Standard American Housewife, all husband, home and kids. The New Commodity, the Liberated Woman, has sex a lot and has a Career, preferably something that can be fitted in with the household chores— like dancing, pottery, or painting.

On the other hand is women's liberation—and housework. What? You say this is all trivial? Wonderful! That's what I thought. It seemed perfectly reasonable. We both had careers, both had to work a couple of days a week to earn enough to live on, so why shouldn't we share the housework? So I suggested it to my mate and he agreed—most men are too hip to turn you down flat. "You're right," he said, "It's only fair."

Then an interesting thing happened. I can only explain it by stating that we women have been brainwashed more than even we can imagine. Probably too many years of seeing television women in ecstasy over their shiny waxed floors or breaking down over their dirty shirt collars. Men have no such conditioning. They recognize the essential fact of housework right from the very beginning. Which is that it stinks. Here's my list of dirty chores: buying groceries, carting them home and putting them away; cooking meals and washing dishes and pots; doing the laundry, digging out the place when things get out of control; washing floors. The list could go on but the sheer necessities are bad enough. All of us have to do these things, or get some one else to do them for us. The longer my husband contemplated these chores the more repulsed he became, and so proceeded the change from the normally sweet considerate Dr. Jekyll into the crafty Mr. Hyde who would stop at nothing to avoid the horrors of—*housework.* As he felt himself backed into a corner laden with dirty dishes, brooms, mops, and reeking garbage, his front teeth grew longer and pointier, his fingernails haggled and his eyes grew wild. Housework trivial? Not on your life! Just try to share the burden.

So ensued a dialogue that's been going on for several years. Here are some of the high points:

"I don't mind sharing the housework, but I don't do it very well. We should each do the things we're best at."

Meaning: Unfortunately I'm no good at things like washing dishes or cooking. What I do best is a little light carpentry, changing light bulbs, moving furniture *(how often do you move furniture?).*

Also Meaning: Historically the lower classes (black men and us) have had hundreds of years experience doing menial jobs. It would be a waste of manpower to train someone else to do them now.

Also Meaning: I don't like the dull stupid boring jobs, so you should do them.

"I don't mind sharing the work, but you'll have to show me how to do it."

Meaning: I ask a lot of questions and you'll have to show me everything everytime I do it because I don't remember so good. Also don't try to sit down and read while I'm doing my jobs because I'm going to annoy hell out of you until it's easier to do them yourself.

"We used to be so happy!" (Said whenever it was his turn to do something.)

Meaning: I used to be so happy.

Meaning: Life without housework is bliss. *(No quarrel here. Perfect agreement.)*

"We have different standards, and why should I have to work to your standards. That's unfair."

Meaning: If I begin to get bugged by the dirt and crap I will say "This place sure is a sty" or "How can anyone live like this?" and wait for your reaction. I know that all women have a sore called "Guilt over a messy house" or "Household work is ultimately my responsibility." I know that men have caused that sore—if anyone visits and the place *is* a sty, they're not going to leave and say, "He sure is a lousy housekeeper." You'll take the rap in any case. I can outwait you.

Also Meaning: I can provoke innumerable scenes over the housework issue. Eventually doing all the housework yourself will be less painful to you than trying to get me to do half. Or I'll suggest we get a maid. She will do my share of the work. You will do yours. It's women's work.

"I've got nothing against sharing the housework, but you can't make me do it on your schedule."

Meaning: Passive resistance. I'll do it when I damned well please, if at all. If my job is doing dishes, it's easier to do them once a week. If taking out laundry, once a month. If washing the floors, once a year. If you don't like it, do it yourself oftener, and then I won't do it at all.

"I *hate* it more than you. You don't mind it so much."

Meaning: Housework is garbage work. It's the worst crap I've ever done. It's degrading and humiliating for someone of *my* intelligence to do it. But for someone of *your* intelligence . . .

"Housework is too trivial to even talk about."

Meaning: It's even more trivial to do. Housework is beneath my status. My purpose in life is to deal with matters of significance. Yours is to deal with matters of insignificance. You should do the housework.

"This problem of housework is not a man-woman problem! In any relationship between two people one is going to have a stronger personality and dominate."

Meaning: That stronger personality had better be *me*.

"In animal societies, wolves, for example, the top animal is usually a male even where he is not chosen for brute strength but on the basis of cunning and intelligence. Isn't that interesting?"

Meaning: I have historical, psychological, anthropological, and biological justification for keeping you down. How can you ask the top wolf to be equal?

"Women's liberation isn't really a political movement."

Meaning: The Revolution is coming too close to home.

Also Meaning: I am only interested in how *I* am oppressed, not how I oppress others. Therefore the war, the draft, and the university are political. Women's liberation is not.

"Man's accomplishments have always depended on getting help from other people, mostly women. What great man would have accomplished what he did if he had to do his own housework?"

Meaning: Oppression is built into the System and I, as the white American male receive the benefits of this System. I don't want to give them up.

Postscript

Participatory democracy begins at home.

Thoughts on Indian Feminism

Kate Shanley

As a result of the consciousness raising from the civil rights and feminist movements, nonwhite women in the United States have had greater reasons to reach out to each other as women. Within each minority group, women have faced the simultaneous oppressions of race and gender (and since many minority women are also poor, of class) and consistently refused to rank one oppression above another. And yet when it has come to making links with the predominantly white feminist movement, suspicion and misunderstanding have reigned.

Source: From Kate Shanley, "Thoughts on Indian Feminism," in *A Gathering of Spirit,* ed. Beth Brant, pp. 213–15. Copyright © 1984 by Kate Shanley. Reprinted by permission of Firebrand Books, Ithaca, New York.

Kate Shanley's piece, "Thoughts on Indian Feminism," suggests reasons why such alliances have often been fraught with problems at the same time it argues that such coalitions are beneficial, indeed necessary, for feminism. Native-American women fear being made into tokens or mascots for a white woman's movement, and all too often have had the experience of seeing their concerns marginalized or ignored by white feminists. Shanley points to the different agenda that Indian women bring to feminism, notably their commitment to tribal sovereignty as the highest priority for the survival of the Indian peoples. The historical patterns governing Native-American life traditionally have given large roles to women to decide matters of family inheritance and control, and Indian women play a central role in the imagery of spirituality and identification with the land; as Shanley points out, concerns such as challenging the oppression of gender roles in the nuclear family have little relevance in such a context. But rather than suggesting that Indian women should only work in isolation, Shanley argues that the women's movement as a whole will profit from a recognition of diversity as its basis.

Kate Shanley refers to herself as an *academic squaw* because at the time this article was published in 1984 she was working toward a Ph.D. in literature at the University of Michigan. She is part Assiniboine Indian, part Irish, and was born and raised on the Fort Peck reservation in Montana.

Toward the end of the 1983 Ohoyo Indian Women's Conference on Leadership, I began to notice that the participants were not referring to themselves as feminists, although the group of women present are as strong and committed as any group of women in America today who are working for change. Why, then, do Indian women avoid the designation "feminist?" The more I thought about it, the more that question began proliferating into many questions: how many other women (of all colors and creeds) have I encountered in my travels (plenty!) who do not choose to identify as feminists? What do they have in common with Indian women? What is a feminist, anyway?

My thoughts on the questions raised thus far by no means represent a consensus among Indian women; in fact, before I could begin to deal objectively with the subject of Indian feminism, I had to come to terms with my own defensiveness about representing other women, particularly other Indian women. On the one hand, I am a woman who refers to herself as a feminist. If most Indian women do not refer to themselves as feminists, does that fact make me somehow *less* representative, *less* Indian? On the other hand, does the theoretical feminism of the university constitute something different from (though, perhaps giving it the benefit of the doubt, correlated to) the "grass-roots" feminism Ohoyo represents? To some extent I know that I suffer the conflicts of an "academic squaw" (to borrow a term from poet and educator Wendy Rose), a certain distance from the "real world."

Attending the Ohoyo conference in Grand Forks, North Dakota was a returning home for me in a spiritual sense—taking my place beside other Indian women, and an actual sense—being with my relatives and loved ones after finally finishing my pre-doctoral requirements at the university. Although I have been a full-time student for the past six years, I brought to the academic experience many years in the workaday world as a mother, registered nurse, volunteer tutor, social worker aide, and high school outreach worker. What I am offering in this article are my thoughts as an Indian woman on feminism. Mine is a political perspective that seeks to re-view the real-life positions of women in relation to the theories that attempt to address the needs of those women.

Issues such as equal pay for equal work, child health and welfare, and a woman's right to make her own choices regarding contraceptive use, sterilization and abortion—key issues to the majority women's movement—affect Indian women as well; however, equality *per se,* may have a different meaning for Indian women and Indian people. That difference begins with personal and tribal sovereignty—the right to be legally recognized as peoples empowered to determine our own destinies. Thus, the Indian women's movement seeks equality in two ways that do not concern mainstream women: (1) on the individual level, the Indian woman struggles to promote the survival of a social structure whose organizational principles represent notions of family different from those of the mainstream; and (2) on the societal level, the People seek sovereignty as a people in order to maintain a vital legal and spiritual connection to the land, in order to *survive* as a people.

The nuclear family has little relevance to Indian women; in fact, in many ways mainstream feminists now are striving to redefine family and community in a way that Indian women have long known. The American lifestyle from which white middle-class women are fighting to free themselves, has not taken hold in Indian communities. Tribal and communal values have survived after four hundred years of colonial oppression.

It may be that the desire on the part of mainstream feminists to include Indian women, however sincere, represents tokenism just now, because too often Indian people, by being thought of as spiritual "mascots" to the American endeavor, are seen more as artifacts than as real people able to speak for ourselves. Given the public's general ignorance about Indian people, in other words, it is possible that Indian people's real-life concerns are not relevant to the mainstream feminist movement in a way that constitutes anything more than a "representative" facade. Charges against the women's movement of heterosexism and racism abound these days; it is not my intention to add to them except to stress that we must all be vigilant in examining the underlying assumptions that motivate us. Internalization of negative (that is, sexist and racist) attitudes towards ourselves and others can and quite often does result from colonialist (white patriarchal) oppression. It is more useful to attack the systems that keep us ignorant of each other's histories.

The other way in which the Indian women's movement differs in emphasis from the majority women's movement, lies in the importance Indian people place on tribal sovereignty—it is the single most pressing political issue in Indian country today. For Indian people to survive culturally as well as materially, many battles must be fought and won in the courts of law, precisely because it is the legal recognition that enables Indian people to govern ourselves according to our own world view—a world view that is antithetical to the *wasicu* (the Lakota term for "takers of the fat") definition of progress. Equality for Indian women within tribal communities, therefore, holds more significance than equality in terms of the general rubric "American."

Up to now I have been referring to the women's movement as though it were a single, well-defined organization. It is not. Perhaps in many ways socialist feminists hold views similar to the views of many Indian people regarding private property and the nuclear family. Certainly, there are some Indian people who are capitalistic. The point I would like to stress, however, is that rather than seeing differences according to a hierarchy of oppressions (white over Indian, male over female), we must practice a politics that allows for diversity in cultural identity as well as in sexual identity.

The word "feminism" has special meanings to Indian women, including the idea of promoting the continuity of tradition, and consequently, pursuing the recognition of tribal sovereignty. Even so, Indian feminists are united with mainstream feminists in outrage against woman and child battering, sexist employment and educational practices, and in many other social concerns. Just as sovereignty cannot be granted but *must be recognized* as an inherent right to self-determination, so Indian feminism must also be recognized as powerful in its own terms, in its own right.

Feminism becomes an incredibly powerful term when it incorporates diversity—not as a superficial political position, but as a practice. The women's movement and the Indian movement for sovereignty suffer similar trivialization, because narrow factions turn ignorance to their own benefit so that they can exploit human beings and the lands they live on for corporate profit. The time has come for Indian women and Indian people to be known on our own terms. This nuclear age demands new terms of communication for all people. Our survival depends on it. Peace.

Black Feminism

Combahee River Collective

"The concept of the simultaneity of oppression is still the crux of a Black Feminist understanding of political reality and, I believe, one of the most significant ideological contributions of Black Feminist thought." So wrote Barbara Smith, one of the members of Combahee River Collective, a group of black feminists in Boston in the 1970s who drew their name from Harriet Tubman's 1863 guerrilla action in the Port Royal region of South Carolina that freed more than 750 slaves. This document, which is dated April 1977,

Source: Combahee River Collective, "A Black Feminist Statement," in *Capitalist Patriarchy and the Case for Socialist Feminism,* ed. Zillah Eisenstein (New York and London: Monthly Review Press, 1979), pp. 362–72. Copyright © 1979 by Zillah Eisenstein. Reprinted by permission of Monthly Review Foundation.

summarizes the major themes of black feminism as it developed in the 1970s. It functions not only as an ideological statement, but also as an attempt to describe "what oppression is comprised of on a day-to-day basis," thus reminding us that oppression is not just some abstraction but a concrete daily experience.

The Combahee River Collective statement refuses to separate the multiple oppressions that shape black women's lives. As it says, "We struggle together with Black men against racism, while we also struggle with Black men about sexism." An overriding commitment to combat racism need not negate the very personal (and political) need to work for women's own liberation within the black community. They name the reason: "because of our need as human persons for autonomy." Like the white women in the women's liberation movement of the late 1960s, for them, the personal is political. The identification of the members as lesbians also reinforces this awareness. But once again, it takes women of color to forcefully point out the unconscious racism that often afflicts the women's movement as a whole.

We are a collective of Black feminists who have been meeting together since 1974. During that time we have been involved in the process of defining and clarifying our politics, while at the same time doing political work within our own group and in coalition with other progressive organizations and movements. The most general statement of our politics at the present time would be that we are actively committed to struggling against racial, sexual, heterosexual, and class oppression and see as our particular task the development of integrated analysis and practice based upon the fact that the major systems of oppression are interlocking. The synthesis of these oppressions creates the conditions of our lives. As Black women we see Black feminism as the logical political movement to combat the manifold and simultaneous oppressions that all women of color face.

We will discuss four major topics in the paper that follows: (1) the genesis of contemporary black feminism; (2) what we believe, i.e., the specific province of our politics; (3) the problems in organizing Black feminists, including a brief herstory of our collective; and (4) Black feminist issues and practice.

1. THE GENESIS OF CONTEMPORARY BLACK FEMINISM

Before looking at the recent development of Black feminism we would like to affirm that we find our origins in the historical reality of Afro-American women's continuous life-and-death struggle for survival and liberation. Black women's extremely negative relationship to the American political system (a system of white male rule) has always been determined by our membership in two oppressed racial and sexual castes. As Angela Davis points out in "Reflections on the Black Woman's Role in the Community of Slaves," Black women have always embodied, if only in their physical manifestation, an adversary stance to white male rule and have actively resisted its inroads upon them and their communities in both dramatic and subtle ways. There have always been Black women activists—some known, like Sojourner Truth, Harriet Tubman, Frances E. W. Harper, Ida B. Wells Barnett, and Mary Church Terrell, and thousands upon thousands unknown—who had a shared awareness of how their sexual identity combined with their racial identity to make their whole life situation and the focus of their political struggles unique. Contemporary Black feminism is the outgrowth of countless generations of personal sacrifice, militancy, and work by our mothers and sisters.

A Black feminist presence has evolved most obviously in connection with the second wave of the American women's movement beginning in the late 1960s. Black, other Third World, and working women have been involved in the feminist movement from its start, but both outside reactionary forces and racism and elitism within the movement itself have served to obscure our participation. In 1973 Black feminists, primarily located in New York, felt the necessity of forming a separate Black feminist group. This became the National Black Feminist Organization (NBFO).

Black feminist politics also have an obvious connection to movements for Black liberation, particularly those of the 1960s and 1970s. Many of us were active in those movements (civil rights, Black nationalism, the Black Panthers), and all of our lives were greatly affected and changed by their ideology, their goals, and the tactics used to achieve their goals. It was our experience and disillusionment within these liberation movements, as well as experience on the periphery of the white male left, that led to the need to develop a politics that was antiracist, unlike those of white women, and antisexist, unlike those of Black and white men.

There is also undeniably a personal genesis for Black feminism, that is, the political realization that comes from the seemingly personal experiences of individual Black women's lives. Black feminists and many more Black women who do not define themselves as feminists have all experienced sexual oppression as a constant factor in our day-to-day existence. As children we realized that we were different from boys and that we were treated differently. For example, we were told in the same breath to be quiet both for the sake of being "ladylike" and to make us less objectionable in the eyes of white people. As we grew older we became aware of the threat of physical and sexual abuse by men. However, we had no way of conceptualizing what was so apparent to us, what we *knew* was really happening.

Black feminists often talk about their feelings of craziness before becoming conscious of the concepts of sexual politics, patriarchal rule, and most importantly, feminism, the political analysis and practice that we women use to struggle against our oppression. The fact that racial politics and indeed racism are pervasive factors in our lives did not allow us, and still does not allow most Black women, to look more deeply into our own experiences and, from that sharing and growing consciousness, to build a politics that will change our lives and inevitably end our oppression. Our development must also be tied to the contemporary economic and political position of Black people. The post World War II generation of Black youth was the first to be able to minimally partake of certain educational and employment options, previously closed completely to Black people. Although our economic position is still at the very bottom of the American capitalistic economy, a handful of us have been able to gain certain tools as a result of tokenism in education and employment which potentially enable us to more effectively fight our oppression.

A combined antiracist and antisexist position drew us together initially, and as we developed politically we addressed ourselves to hetero-sexism and economic oppression under capitalism.

2. WHAT WE BELIEVE

Above all else, our politics initially sprang from the shared belief that Black women are inherently valuable, that our liberation is a necessity not as an adjunct to somebody else's but because of our need as human persons for autonomy. This may seem so obvious as to sound simplistic, but it is apparent that no other ostensibly progressive movement has ever considered our specific oppression as a priority or worked seriously for the ending of that oppression. Merely naming the pejorative stereotypes attributed to Black women (e.g., mammy, matriarch, Sapphire, whore, bulldagger), let alone cataloguing the cruel, often murderous, treatment we receive, indicates how little value has been placed upon our lives during four centuries of bondage in the Western hemisphere. We realize that the only people who care enough about us to work consistently for our liberation is us. Our politics evolve from a healthy love for ourselves, our sisters and our community which allows us to continue our struggle and work.

This focusing upon our own oppression is embodied in the concept of identity politics. We believe that the most profound and potentially the most radical politics come directly out of our own identity, as opposed to working to end somebody else's oppression. In the case of Black women this is a particularly repugnant, dangerous, threatening, and therefore revolutionary concept because it is obvious from looking at all the political movements that have preceded us that anyone is more worthy of liberation than ourselves. We reject pedestals, queenhood, and walking ten paces behind. To be recognized as human, levelly human, is enough.

We believe that sexual politics under patriarchy is as pervasive in Black women's lives as are the politics of class and race. We also often find it difficult to separate race from class from sex oppression because in our lives they are most often experienced simultaneously. We know that there is such a thing as racial-sexual oppression which is neither solely racial nor solely sexual, e.g., the history of rape of Black women by white men as a weapon of political repression.

Although we are feminists and lesbians, we feel solidarity with progressive Black men and do not advocate the fractionalization that white women who are separatists demand. Our situation as Black people necessitates that we have solidarity around the fact of race, which white women of course do not need to have with white men, unless it is their negative solidarity as racial oppressors. We struggle together with Black men against racism, while we also struggle with Black men about sexism.

We realize that the liberation of all oppressed peoples necessitates the destruction of the political-economic systems of capitalism and imperialism as well as patriarchy. We are socialists because we believe the work must be organized for the collective benefit of those who do the work and create the products, and not for the profit of the bosses. Material resources must be equally distributed among those who create these resources. We are not convinced, however, that a socialist revolution that is not also a feminist and antiracist revolution will guarantee our liberation. We have arrived at the necessity for developing an understanding of class relationships that takes into account the specific class position of Black women who are generally marginal in the labor force, while at this particular time some of us are temporarily viewed as doubly desirable tokens at white-collar and professional levels. We need to articulate the real class situation of persons who are not merely raceless, sexless workers, but for whom racial and sexual oppression are significant determinants in their working/economic lives. Although we are in essential agreement with Marx's theory as it applied to the very specific economic relationships he analyzed, we know that his analysis must be extended further in order for us to understand our specific economic situation as Black women.

A political contribution which we feel we have already made is the expansion of the feminist principle that the personal is political. In our consciousness-raising sessions, for example, we have in many ways gone beyond white women's revelations because we are dealing with the implications of race and class as well as sex. Even our Black women's style of talking/testifying in Black language about what we have experienced has a resonance that is both cultural and political. We have spent a great deal of energy delving into the cultural and experiential nature of our oppression out of necessity because none of these matters has ever been looked at before. No one before has ever examined the multilayered texture of Black women's lives. An example of this kind of revelation/conceptualization occurred at a meeting as we discussed the ways in which our early intellectual interests had been attacked by our peers, particularly Black males. We discovered that all of us, because we were "smart" had also been considered "ugly", i.e., "smart-ugly." "Smart-ugly" crystallized the way in which most of us had been forced to develop our intellects at great cost to our "social" lives. The sanctions in the Black and white communities against Black women thinkers is comparatively much higher than for white women, particularly ones from the educated middle and upper classes.

As we have already stated, we reject the stance of lesbian separatism because it is not a viable political analysis or strategy for us. It leaves out far too much and far too many people, particularly Black men, women, and children. We have a great deal of criticism and loathing for what men have been socialized to be in this society: what they support, how they act, and how they oppress. But we do not have the misguided notion that it is their maleness, per se—i.e., their biological maleness—that makes them what they are. As Black women we find any type of biological determinism a particularly dangerous and reactionary basis upon which to build a politic. We must also question whether lesbian separatism is an adequate and progressive political analysis and strategy, even for those who practice it, since it so completely denies any but the sexual sources of women's oppression, negating the facts of class and race.

3. PROBLEMS IN ORGANIZING BLACK FEMINISTS

During our years together as a Black feminist collective we have experienced success and defeat, joy and pain, victory and failure. We have found that it is very difficult to organize around Black feminist issues, difficult even to announce in certain contexts that we *are* Black feminists. We have tried to think about the reasons for our difficulties, particularly since the white women's movement continues to be strong and to grow in many directions. In this section we will discuss some of the general reasons for the organizing problems we face and also talk specifically about the stages in organizing our own collective.

The major source of difficulty in our political work is that we are not just trying to fight oppression on one front or even two, but instead to address a whole range of oppressions. We do not have racial, sexual, heterosexual, or class privilege to rely upon, nor do we have even the minimal access to resources and power that groups who possess any one of these types of privilege have.

The psychological toll of being a Black woman and the difficulties this presents in reaching political consciousness and doing political work can never be underestimated. There is a very low value placed upon Black women's psyches in this society, which is both racist and sexist. As an early group member once said, "We are all damaged people merely by virtue of being Black women." We are dispossessed psychologically and on every other level, and yet we feel the necessity to struggle to change the condition of all Black women. In "A Black Feminist's Search for Sisterhood," Michele Wallace arrives at this conclusion:

> We exist as women who are Black who are feminists, each stranded for the moment, working independently because there is not yet an environment in this society remotely congenial to our struggle—because, being on the bottom, we would have to do what no one else has done: we would have to fight the world.

Wallace is pessimistic but realistic in her assessment of Black feminists' position, particularly in her allusion to the nearly classic isolation most of us face. We might use our position at the bottom, however, to make a clear leap into revolutionary action. If Black women were free, it would mean that everyone else would have to be free since our freedom would necessitate the destruction of all the systems of oppression.

Feminism is, nevertheless, very threatening to the majority of Black people because it calls into question some of the most basic assumptions about our existence, i.e., that sex should be a determinant of power relationships. Here is the way male and female voices were defined in a Black nationalist pamphlet from the early 1970's.

> We understand that it is and has been traditional that the man is the head of the house. He is the leader of the house/nation because his knowledge of the world is broader, his awareness is greater, his understanding is fuller and his application of this information is wiser . . . After all, it is only reasonable that the man be the head of the house because he is able to defend and protect the development of his home . . . Women cannot do the same things as men— they are made by nature to function differently. Equality of men and women is something that cannot happen even in the abstract world. Men are not equal to other men, i.e., ability, experience or even understanding. The value of men and women can be seen as in the value of gold and silver—they are not equal but both have great value. We must realize that men and women are a complement to each other because there is no house/family without a man and his wife. Both are essential to the development of any life.

The material conditions of most Black women would hardly lead them to upset both economic and sexual arrangements that seem to represent some stability in their lives. Many Black women have a good understanding of both sexism and racism, but because of the everyday constrictions of their lives cannot risk struggling against them both.

The reaction of Black men to feminism has been notoriously negative. They are, of course, even more threatened than Black women by the possibility that Black feminists might organize around our own needs. They realize that they might not only lose valuable and hardworking allies in their struggles but that they might also be forced to change their habitually sexist ways of interacting with and oppressing Black women. Accusations that Black feminism divides the Black struggle are powerful deterrents to the growth of an autonomous Black women's movement.

Still, hundreds of women have been active at different times during the three-year existence of our group. And every Black woman who came, came out of a strongly-felt need for some level of possibility that did not previously exist in her life.

When we first started meeting early in 1974 after the NBFO first eastern regional conference, we did not have a strategy for organizing, or even a focus. We just wanted to see what we had. After a period of months of not meeting, we began to meet again late in the year and started doing an intense variety of consciousness-raising. The overwhelming feeling that we had is that after years and years we had finally found each other. Although we were not doing political work as a group, individuals continued their involvement in Lesbian politics, sterilization abuse and abortion rights work, Third World Women's International Women's Day activities, and support activity for the trials of Dr. Kenneth Edelin, Joan Little, and Inéz García. During our first summer, when membership had dropped off considerably, those of us remaining devoted serious discussion to the possibility of opening a refuge for battered women in a Black community. (There was no refuge in Boston at that time.) We also decided around that time to become an independent collective since we had serious disagreements with NBFO's bourgeois-feminist stance and their lack of a clear political focus.

We also were contacted at that time by socialist feminists, with whom we had worked on abortion rights activities, who wanted to encourage us to attend the National Socialist Feminist Conference in Yellow Springs. One of our members did attend and despite the narrowness of the ideology that was promoted at that particular conference, we became more aware of the need for us to understand our own economic situation and to make our own economic analysis.

In the fall, when some members returned, we experienced several months of comparative inactivity and internal disagreements which were first conceptualized as a Lesbian-straight split but which were also the result of class and political differences. During the summer those of us who were still meeting had determined the need to do political work and to move beyond consciousness-raising and serving exclusively as an emotional support group. At the beginning of 1976, when some of the women who had not wanted to do political work and who also had voiced disagreements stopped attending of their own accord, we again looked for a focus. We decided at that time, with the addition of new members, to become a study group. We had always shared our reading with each other, and some of us had written papers on Black feminism for group discussion a few months before this decision was made. We began functioning as a study group and also began discussing the possibility of starting a Black feminist publication. We had a retreat in the late spring which provided a time for both political discussion and working out interpersonal issues. Currently we are planning to gather together a collection of Black feminist writing. We feel that it is absolutely essential to demonstrate the reality of our politics to other Black women and believe that we can do this through writing and distributing our work. The fact that individual Black feminists are living in isolation all over the country, that our own numbers are small, and that we have some skills in writing, printing, and publishing makes us want to carry out these kinds of projects as a means of organizing Black feminists as we continue to do political work in coalition with other groups.

4. BLACK FEMINIST ISSUES AND PROJECTS

During our time together we have identified and worked on many issues of particular relevance to Black women. The inclusiveness of our politics makes us concerned with any situation that impinges upon the lives of women, Third World and working people. We are of course particularly committed to working on those struggles in which race, sex and class are simultaneous factors in oppression. We might for example, become involved in workplace organizing at a factory that employs Third World women or picket a hospital that is cutting back on already inadequate health care to a Third World community, or set up a rape crisis center in a Black neighborhood. Organizing around welfare and daycare concerns might also be a focus. The work to be done and the countless issues that this work represents merely reflect the pervasiveness of our oppression.

Issues and projects that collective members have actually worked on are sterilization abuse, abortion rights, battered women, rape and health care. We have also done many workshops and educationals on Black feminism on college campuses, at women's conferences, and most recently for high school women.

One issue that is of major concern to us and that we have begun to publicly address is racism in the white women's movement. As Black feminists we are made constantly and painfully aware of how little effort white women have made to understand and combat their racism, which requires among other things that they have a more than superficial comprehension of race, color, and black history and culture. Eliminating racism in the white women's movement is by definition work for white women to do, but we will continue to speak to and demand accountability on this issue.

In the practice of our politics we do not believe that the end always justifies the means. Many reactionary and destructive acts have been done in the name of achieving "correct" political goals. As feminists we do not want to mess over people in the name of politics. We believe in collective process and a nonhierarchical distribution of power within our own group and in our vision of a revolutionary society. We are committed to a continual examination of our politics as they develop through criticism and self-criticism as an essential aspect of our practice. In her introduction to *Sisterhood Is Powerful* Robin Morgan writes:

> I haven't the faintest notion what possible revolutionary role white heterosexual men could fulfill, since they are the very embodiment of reactionary-vested-interest-power.

As Black feminists and Lesbians we know that we have a very definite revolutionary task to perform and we are ready for the lifetime of work and struggle before us.

A More Personal View of Black Feminism

Michele Wallace

Writer Michele Wallace's story of her personal route to black feminism contrasts with the primarily intellectual thrust of the Combahee River Collective statement, where it is mentioned in passing. Black women who identify themselves as feminists have been especially insightful about the dangers of claiming that all oppression comes from race, knowing from their own experiences that the element of sexism operates independently of the oppression of racism. Wallace's willingness to criticize black men for their treatment of black women, which she developed in her 1979 book *Black Macho and the Myth of the Superwoman,* was controversial in both the black

Source: From Michele Wallace, "A Black Feminist's Search for Sisterhood," *The Village Voice,* July 28, 1975. Reprinted in Gloria Hull, Patricia Bell Scott, and Barbara Smith, *But Some of Us Are Brave* (New York: The Feminist Press, 1982), pp. 5–12. Reprinted by permission of the author.

and white communities. Wallace's identification of this theme was foreshadowed in this 1975 article for *The Village Voice.*

Besides Wallace's perspective on black feminism, her autobiographical piece has resonance for many of the themes of this anthology. She describes the process of growing up female and growing up black, which at first meant accepting that her dreams were unrealistic, and then after the civil rights and women's movements raised expectations, learning that her early dreams did not have to be abandoned after all. As she grows toward womanhood, she is caught in many of the dilemmas of female adolescence: a weight problem, concern about hair and makeup, worrying if the rain would dampen her Afro haircut, and attempts to meet men. College is a time to test her ideas and link up with the movements for social change then reshaping American society. Her conclusion, that black feminists exist as individuals, not as part of a black women's movement, may be as true today as when she published this article in 1975.

When I was in the third grade I wanted to be president. I can still remember the stricken look on my teacher's face when I announced it in class. By the time I was in the fourth grade I had decided to be the president's wife instead. It never occurred to me that I could be neither because I was Black. Growing up in a dreamy state of mind not uncommon to the offspring of the Black middle class, I was convinced that hatred was an insubstantial emotion and would certainly vanish before it could affect me. I had the world to choose from in planning a life.

On rainy days my sister and I used to tie the short end of a scarf around our scrawny braids and let the rest of its silken mass trail to our waists. We'd pretend it was hair and that we were some lovely heroine we'd seen in the movies. There was a time when I would have called that wanting to be white, yet the real point of the game was being feminine. Being feminine *meant* being white to us.

One day when I was thirteen on my bus ride home from school I caught a brief but enchanting glimpse of a beautiful creature—slender, honey brown, and she wore her hair natural. Very few people did then, which made her that much more striking. *This* was a look I could imitate with some success. The next day I went to school with my hair in an Afro.

On my way out of my building people stared and some complimented me, but others, the older permanent fixtures in the lobby, gaped at me in horror. Walking the streets of Harlem was even more difficult. The men on the corners who had been only moderately attentive before, now began to whoop and holler as I came into view. Becoming exasperated after a while, I asked someone why. "They think you're a whore, sugar." I fixed my hair and was back to normal by the next morning. Letting the world in on the secret of my native naps appealed to my proclivity for rebellion but having people think I was not a "nice girl" was The War already and I was not prepared for it. I pictured myself in a police station trying to explain how I'd been raped. "Come on, baby, you look like you know your way around," sneered an imaginary policeman.

In 1968 when I was sixteen and the term Black consciousness was becoming popular, I started wearing my hair natural again. This time I ignored my "elders."

I was too busy reshaping my life. Blackness, I reasoned, meant that I could finally be myself. Besides recognizing my history of slavery and my African roots, I began a general housecleaning. All my old values, gathered from "playing house" in nursery school to *Glamour* Magazine's beauty tips, were discarded.

No more makeup, high heels, stockings, garter belts, girdles. I wore T-shirts and dungarees, or loose African print dresses, sandals on my feet. My dust-covered motto, "Be a nice well-rounded colored girl so that you can get yourself a nice colored doctor husband," I threw out on the grounds that it was another remnant of my once "whitified" self. My mind clear now, I was starting to think about being someone again, not some*thing*—the presidency was still a dark horse but maybe I could be a writer. I dared not even say it aloud: my life was my own again. I thanked Malcolm and LeRoi—wasn't it their prescription that I was following?

It took me three years to fully understand that Stokely was serious when he'd said my position in the movement was "prone," three years to understand that the countless speeches that all began "the Black man . . ." did not include me. I learned. I mingled more and more with a Black crowd, attended the conferences and rallies and parties and talked with some of the most loquacious of my brothers in Blackness, and as I pieced together the ideal that was being presented for me to emulate, I discovered my newfound freedoms being stripped from me, one after another. No I wasn't to wear makeup but yes I had to wear long skirts that I could barely walk in. No I wasn't to go to the beauty parlor but yes I was to spend hours cornrolling my hair. No I wasn't to flirt with or take shit off white men but yes I was to sleep with and take unending shit off Black men. No I wasn't to watch television or read *Vogue* or *Ladies' Home Journal* but yes I should keep my mouth shut. I would still have to iron, sew, cook, and have babies . . .

When I chose to go to Howard University in 1969, it was because it was all Black. I envisioned a super-Black utopia where for the first time in life I would be completely surrounded by people who totally understood me. The problem in New York had been that there were too many white people.

Thirty pounds overweight, my hair in the ultimate Afro—washed and left to dry without combing—my skin blue-black from a summer in the sun, Howard's students, the future polite society of NAACP cocktail parties, did not exactly greet me with open arms. I sought out a new clique each day and found a home in none. Finally I found a place of revelation, if not of happiness, with other misfits in the girls' dorm on Friday and Saturday nights.

These misfits, all dark without exception, all with Afros that were too nappy, chose to stay in and watch television or listen to records rather than take advantage of the score of one-night stands they could probably achieve before being taunted into running home to their parents as "fallen women." They came to Howard to get husbands; if you slept around, or if it got out that you had slept with someone you weren't practically engaged to, then there would be very little possibility of a husband for you at Howard.

Such restrictions are not unique in this world, but at Howard, the scene of student takeovers just the previous year, of riots and much revolutionary talk about casting aside Western values, archaic, Victorian morals seemed curiously "unblack." Baffled by my new environment, I did something I've never done before—I spent most of my time with women, often turning down the inevitable humiliation or, worse, boredom of a date (a growing possibility as I shed the extra pounds) even when it was offered to me. Most of the women were from small southern and midwestern communities. They thought me definitely straitjacket material with my well-polished set of "sophisticated" New York views on premarital sex and atheism. I learned to listen more than I spoke.

But no one talked about why we stayed in on Friday and Saturday nights on a campus that was well known for its parties and nightlife. No one talked about why we drank so much or why our hunger for Big Macs was insatiable. We talked about men—all kinds. Black and white, Joe Namath, Richard Roundtree, the class president who earned quite a reputation for driving coeds out on the highway and offering them a quick screw or a long walk home. "But girl, ain't he fine?" We talked about movie stars and singing groups into the wee hours of the morning. Guzzling gin, cheating at poker, choking on cigarettes that dangled precariously from the corners of our mouths, we'd signify. "If we could only be woman (white) enough" was the general feeling of most of us as we trotted off to bed.

Meanwhile the males on the campus had successfully buried the old standards of light, curly haired young men with straight noses. They sported large, unruly Afros, dashikis, and flaring nostrils. Their coal-black eyes seemed to say, "The nights *and* the days belong to me," as we'd pass one another on the campus green, a fashionable, thin, colorless little creature always on their arm.

Enough was enough. I left Howard for City College after one term, and the significance of all I'd seen there had not entirely escaped me, because I remember becoming a feminist about then. No one had been doing very well when I had left New York but now it seemed even worse—the "new Blackness" was fast becoming the new slavery for sisters.

I discovered my voice and when brothers talked to me, I talked back. This had its hazards. Almost got my eye blackened several times. My social life was like guerilla warfare. Here was the logic behind our grandmothers' old saying, "A nigga man ain't shit." It was shorthand for "The Black man has learned to hate himself and to hate you even more. Be careful. He will hurt you."

I am reminded of a conversation I had with a brother up at City College one mild spring day. We were standing on a corner in front of the South Campus gates and he was telling me what the role of the Black woman was. When a pause came in his monologue, I asked him what the role of the Black man was. He mumbled something about, "Simply to be a man." When I suggested that might not be enough, he went completely ape. He turned purple. He started screaming. "The Black man doesn't have to do anything. He's a man he's a man he's a man!" . . .

When I first became a feminist, my Black friends used to cast pitying eyes upon me and say, "That's whitey's thing." I used to laugh it off, thinking, yes there are some slight problems, a few things white women don't completely understand, but we can work them out. In *Ebony, Jet,* and *Encore,* and even in *The New York Times,* various Black writers cautioned Black women to be wary of smiling white feminists. The women's movement enlists the support of Black women only to lend credibility to an essentially middle-class, irrelevant movement, they asserted. Time has shown that there was more truth to these claims than their shrillness indicated. Today when many white feminists think of Black women, they too often think of faceless masses of welfare mothers and rape victims to flesh out their statistical studies of woman's plight . . .

In the spring of 1973, Doris Wright, a Black feminist writer, called a meeting to discuss "Black Women and Their Relationship to the Women's Movement." The result was the National Black Feminist Organization, and I was fully delighted until, true to Women's Movement form, we got bogged down in an array of ideological disputes, the primary one being lesbianism versus heterosexuality. Dominated by the myths and facts of what white feminists had done and not done before us, it was nearly impossible to come to any agreement about our position on anything; and action was unthinkable.

Many of the prime movers in the organization seemed to be representing other interest groups and whatever commitment they might have had to Black women's issues appeared to take a back seat to that. Women who had initiative and spirit usually attended one meeting, were turned off by the hopelessness of ever getting anything accomplished, and never returned again. Each meeting brought almost all new faces. Overhearing an aspiring political candidate say only half-jokingly at NBFO's first conference, "I'm gonna get me some votes out of these niggas," convinced me that Black feminists were not ready to form a movement in which I could, with clear conscience, participate.

It is very possible that NBFO was not meant to happen when it did, that the time was not yet ripe for such an organization.

I started a Black women's consciousness-raising group around the same time. When I heard one of my friends, whom I considered the closest thing to a feminist in the room, saying at one of our sessions, "I feel sorry for any woman who tries to take my husband away from me because she's just going to have a man who has to pay alimony and child support," even though she was not married to the man in question, I felt a great sinking somewhere in the chest area. Here was a woman, who had insisted (at least to me) upon her right to bear a child outside of marriage, trying to convince a few Black women, who were mostly single and very worried about it, that she was really married—unlike them. In fact, one of the first women to leave the group was a recent graduate of Sarah Lawrence, her excuse being, "I want to place myself in situations where I will meet more men." The group eventually disintegrated. We had no strength to give to one another. Is that possible? At any rate, that's the way it seemed, and perhaps it was the same on a larger scale with NBFO.

Despite a sizable number of Black feminists who have contributed much to the leadership of the women's movement, there is still no Black women's movement, and it appears there won't be for some time to come. It is conceivable that the level of consciousness feminism would demand in Black women wouldn't lead to any sort of separatist movement, anyway—despite our very separate problems. Perhaps a multicultural women's movement is somewhere in the future.

But for now, Black feminists, of necessity it seems, exist as individuals—some well known, like Eleanor Holmes Norton, Florynce Kennedy, Faith Ringgold, Shirley Chisholm, Alice Walker, and some unknown, like me. We exist as women who are Black who are feminists, each stranded for the moment, working independently because there is not yet an environment in this society remotely congenial to our struggle—because, being on the bottom, we would have to do what no one else has done: we would have to fight the world.

Houston, 1977

After a successful conference in Mexico City in 1975 to mark the International Year of the Woman, the United Nations designated the next 10 years as the International Decade for Women. In the United States, Congresswomen Bella Abzug and Patsy Mink won a $5 million appropriation from the U.S. Congress for a National Women's Conference to be held in Houston, Texas, in November 1977. (Feminists were pleased, but also pointed out that the appropriation amounted to less than seven cents for every adult woman in the country, not enough even to send them all a postcard.) The 2,000 official delegates were chosen at 56 state territorial meetings attended by 130,000 people, making this conference one of the most democratically selected gatherings in American history.

The conference opened with the symbolic lighting of a torch that had been relayed from Seneca Falls, New York, to Houston by volunteer runners. Then the delegates, alongside as many as 20,000 observers, spent four days of intense discussion and politicking to reach a consensus on the National Plan of Action, of which the preamble is reprinted here. Celebrating the diversity of American womanhood and the changes that are shaping women's lives, the *we* of the preamble call for the equality that is still withheld from women, asking policymakers to join them in forming "a more perfect union."

The rest of the National Plan of Action consisted of 26 resolutions adopted by the conference. The various planks addressed the topics that have formed the feminist agenda since the 1960s: violence against women (battered women, child abuse, rape, pornography); issues of credit employment and insurance; the rights of homemakers; the special problems of minority women, rural women, older women, and the disabled; education; health; political participation; and welfare and the feminization of poverty. The most controversial plank concerned reproductive freedom, especially support for women's right to abortion. Although not all delegates personally supported abortion, many endorsed the plank in order to present a unified front. While there has been some progress in the decades since Houston, the National Plan of Action will probably continue to serve more as a broad statement of goals rather than concrete achievements.

DECLARATION OF AMERICAN WOMEN

We are here to move history forward.
We are women from every State and Territory in the Nation.
We are women of different ages, beliefs, and life-styles.
We are women of many economic, social, political, racial, ethnic, cultural,
educational, and religious backgrounds.
We are married, single, widowed, and divorced.
We are mothers and daughters.
We are sisters.

We speak in varied accents and languages but we share the common language
and experience of American women who throughout our Nation's life have been
denied the opportunities, rights, privileges, and responsibilities accorded to men.

For the first time in the more than 200 years of our democracy, we are gathered in a National Women's Conference, charged under Federal law to assess the
status of women in our country, to measure the progress we have made, to identify the barriers that prevent us from participating fully and equally in all aspects
of national life, and to make recommendations to the President and to the Congress for means by which such barriers can be removed.

We recognize the positive changes that have occurred in the lives of women
since the founding of our nation. In more than a century of struggle from Seneca
Falls 1848 to Houston 1977, we have progressed from being non-persons and
slaves whose work and achievements were unrecognized, whose needs were ignored, and whose rights were suppressed to being citizens with freedoms and aspirations of which our ancestors could only dream.

We can vote and own property. We work in the home, in our communities and
in every occupation. We are 40 percent of the labor force. We are in the arts, sciences, professions, and politics. We raise children, govern States, head businesses
and institutions, climb mountains, explore the ocean depths, and reach toward the
moon.

Our lives no longer end with the childbearing years. Our Lifespan has increased to more than 75 years. We have become a majority of the population, 51.3
percent, and by the 21st Century, we shall be an even larger majority.

But despite some gains made in the past 200 years, our dream of equality is
still withheld from us and millions of women still face a daily reality of discrimination, limited opportunities, and economic hardship.

Man-made barriers, laws, social customs, and prejudices continue to keep a
majority of women in an inferior position without full control of our lives and
bodies.

From infancy throughout life, in personal and public relationships, in the
family, and the schools, in every occupation and profession, too often we find our

Source: "Declaration of American Women," official report to the President, National Women's Conference, Houston, 1977, reprinted in *What Women Want,* Caroline Bird, ed. (New York: Simon &
Schuster, 1979), pp. 85–86.

individuality, our capabilities, our earning powers diminished by the discriminatory practices and outmoded ideas of what a woman is, what a woman can do, and what a woman must be.

Increasingly, we are victims of crimes of violence in a culture that degrades us as sex objects and promotes pornography for profit.

We are poorer than men. And those of us who are minority women—blacks, Hispanic Americans, Native Americans, and Asian Americans—must overcome the double burden of discrimination based on race and sex.

We lack effective political and economic power. We have only minor and insignificant roles in making, interpreting, and enforcing our laws, in running our political parties, businesses, unions, schools, and institutions, in directing the media, in governing our country, in deciding issues of war or peace.

We do not seek special privileges, but we demand as a human right a full voice and role for women in determining the destiny of our world, our nation, our families, and our individual lives.

We seek these rights for all women, whether or not they choose as individuals to use them.

We are part of a worldwide movement of women who believe that only by brining women into full partnership with men and respecting our rights as half the human race can we hope to achieve a world in which the whole human race—men, women, and children—can live in peace and security.

Based on the views of women who have met in every State and Territory in the past year, the National Plan of Action is presented to the President and the Congress as our recommendations for implementing Public Law 97-167.

We are entitled to and expect serious attention to our proposals.

We demand immediate continuing action on our National Plan by Federal State, public, and private institutions so that by 1985, the end of the International Decade for Women proclaimed by the United Nations, everything possible under the law will have been done to provide American women with full equality.

The rest will be up to the hearts, minds, and moral consciences of men and women and what they do to make our society truly democratic and open to all.

We pledge ourselves with all the strength of our dedication to this struggle "to form a more perfect Union."

A Different View of Women's Nature

Phyllis Schlafly

The year 1977 marked not only the Houston conference, but also the publication of Phyllis Schlafly's *The Power of the Positive Women.* The incongruity of these two events shows the conflicting visions of women's lives by the 1970s. Phyllis Schlafly's rise to power was intimately connected with conservative Republican politics in the 1950s and 1960s and the rise of the New Right and the Moral Majority in the 1970s. Schlafly first made a splash in right-wing circles in 1963 when she published a best-selling campaign biography of Republican presidential candidate Barry Goldwater. Schlafly's years of political experience made her a superb organizer, and she was able to tap a grassroots movement mainly located in evangelical (or "born-again") protestant churches in support of her conservative views about the centrality of a traditional family life to the future of the United States. In her ability to weave together homilies about women's traditional feminine roles with a concrete political agenda (stop ERA, overturn the constitutional right of abortion, allow prayer in the schools), Schlafly went beyond other conservative writers such as Marabel Morgan, whose *The Total Woman* (1973) offered advice about how women should downplay their own needs to make men happy but failed to connect such traditional gender roles with a wider conservative world vision.

In this selection from *The Power of the Positive Woman,* Schlafly lays out her complaints against the feminist movement. At the core, they come down to Schlafly's acceptance, indeed glorification, of the differences between men and women; she accuses feminists of trying to remove all vestiges of difference in their rush to equality. For her, biological roles are important for a stable and profitable society; the Positive Woman knows that her loyalties should lie in the domestic sphere of home, marriage, and family. Schlafly's message that women had something to lose, instead of something to gain, from women's liberation proved very appealing in the increasingly conservative political climate of the 1970s and 1980s.

The first requirement for the acquisition of power by the Positive Woman is to understand the differences between men and women. Your outlook on life, your faith, your behavior, your potential for fulfillment, all are determined by the parameters of your original premise. The Positive Woman starts with the assumption that the world is her oyster. She rejoices in the creative capability within her body and the power potential of her mind and spirit. She understands that men and women are different, and that those very differences provide the key to her success as a person and fulfillment as a woman.

The women's liberationist, on the other hand, is imprisoned by her own negative view of herself and of her place in the world around her. This view of women was most succinctly expressed in an advertisement designed by the principal women's liberationist organization, the National Organization for Women (NOW), and run in many magazines and newspapers and as spot announcements on many television stations. The advertisement showed a darling curlyheaded girl with the caption: "This healthy, normal baby has a handicap. She was born female."

This is the self-articulated dog-in-the-manger, chip-on-the-shoulder, fundamental dogma of the women's liberation movement. Someone—it is not clear who, perhaps God, perhaps the "Establishment," perhaps a conspiracy of male chauvinist pigs—dealt women a foul blow by making them female. It becomes necessary, therefore, for women to agitate and demonstrate and hurl demands on society in order to wrest from an oppressive male-dominated social structure the status that has been wrongfully denied to women through the centuries.

By its very nature, therefore, the women's liberation movement precipitates a series of conflict situations—in the legislatures, in the courts, in the schools, in industry—with man targeted as the enemy. Confrontation replaces cooperation as the watchword of all relationships. Women and men become adversaries instead of partners.

The second dogma of the women's liberationists is that, of all the injustices perpetrated upon women through the centuries, the most oppressive is the cruel fact that women have babies and men do not. Within the confines of the women's liberationist ideology, therefore, the abolition of this overriding inequality of women becomes the primary goal. This goal must be achieved at any and all costs—to the woman herself, to the baby, to the family, and to society. Women must be made equal to men in their ability *not* to become pregnant and *not* to be expected to care for babies they may bring into the world.

This is why women's liberationists are compulsively involved in the drive to make abortion and child-care centers for all women, regardless of religion or income, both socially acceptable and government-financed. Former Congresswoman Bella Abzug has defined the goal: "to enforce the constitutional right of females to terminate pregnancies that they do not wish to continue."

If man is targeted as the enemy, and the ultimate goal of women's liberation is independence from men and the avoidance of pregnancy and its consequences, then lesbianism is logically the highest form in the ritual of women's liberation. Many, such as Kate Millett, come to this conclusion, although many others do not.

The Positive Woman will never travel that dead-end road. It is self-evident to the Positive Woman that the female body with its baby-producing organs was not designed by a conspiracy of men but by the Divine Architect of the human race. Those who think it is unfair that women have babies, whereas men cannot, will have to take up their complaint with God because no other power is capable of changing that fundamental fact. On some college campuses, I have been assured that other methods of reproduction will be developed. But most of us must deal with the real world rather than with the imagination of dreamers.

Another feature of the woman's natural role is the obvious fact that women can breast-feed babies and men cannot. This functional role was not imposed by conspiratorial males seeking to burden women with confining chores, but must be recognized as part of the plan of the Divine Architect for the survival of the human race through the centuries and in the countries that know no pasteurization of milk or sterilization of bottles.

The Positive Woman looks upon her femaleness and her fertility as part of her purpose, her potential, and her power. She rejoices that she has a capability for creativity that men can never have.

The third basic dogma of the women's liberation movement is that there is no difference between male and female except the sex organs, and that all those physical, cognitive, and emotional differences you *think* are there, are merely the result of centuries of restraints imposed by a male-dominated society and sex-stereotyped schooling. The role imposed on women is, by definition, inferior, according to the women's liberationists.

The Positive Woman knows that, while there are some physical competitions in which women are better (and can command more money) than men, including those that put a premium on grace and beauty, such as figure skating, the superior physical strength of males over females in competitions of strength, speed, and short-term endurance is beyond rational dispute . . .

The Positive Woman recognizes the fact that, when it comes to sex, women are simply not the equal of men. The sexual drive of men is much stronger than that of women. That is how the human race was designed in order that it might perpetuate itself. The other side of the coin is that it is easier for women to control their sexual appetites. A Positive Woman cannot defeat a man in a wrestling or boxing match, but she can motivate him, inspire him, encourage him, teach him, restrain him, reward him, and have power over him that he can never achieve over her with all his muscle. How or whether a Positive Woman uses her power is determined solely by the way she alone defines her goals and develops her skills.

The differences between men and women are also emotional and psychological. Without woman's innate maternal instinct, the human race would have died out centuries ago. There is nothing so helpless in all earthly life as the newborn infant. It will die within hours if not cared for. Even in the most primitive, uneducated societies, women have always cared for their newborn babies. They didn't need any schooling to teach them how. They didn't need any welfare workers to tell them it is their social obligation. Even in societies to whom such concepts as "ought," "social responsibility," and "compassions for the helpless" were unknown, mothers cared for their new babies.

Why? Because caring for a baby serves the natural maternal need of a woman. Although not nearly so total as the baby's need, the woman's need is nonetheless real.

The overriding psychological need of a woman is to love something alive. A baby fulfills this need in the lives of most women. If a baby is not available to fill that need, women search for a baby-substitute. This is the reason why women have traditionally gone into teaching and nursing careers. They are doing what comes naturally to the female psyche. The schoolchild or the patient of any age provides an outlet for a woman to express her natural maternal need.

This maternal need in women is the reason why mothers whose children have grown up and flown from the nest are sometimes cut loose from their psychological moorings. The maternal need in women can show itself in love for grandchildren, nieces, nephews, or even neighbors' children. The maternal need in some women has even manifested itself in an extraordinary affection lavished on a dog, a cat, or a parakeet.

This is not to say that every woman must have a baby in order to be fulfilled. But it is to say that fulfillment for most women involves expressing their natural maternal urge by loving and caring for someone.

CHAPTER 11

Women, Work, and Social Change

Demographic changes affecting women's lives had been gathering force over the course of the 20th century, and these changing social realities were an important precondition for the revival of feminism. Women were living longer, bearing fewer children, and enjoying increased access to education. They were working in far greater numbers outside the home. Marital instability, notably the dramatic rise in divorce, meant that women could no longer assume that the roles of wife and mother would provide the primary identification for their entire lives. All these changes reinforced each other to produce very different life patterns for postwar women than those of their mothers and grandmothers.

There is no dearth of statistics to convey the postwar revolution in women's work. The growth in women's share of the work force between 1950 and 1975 (from 29 percent in 1950 to 40 percent in 1975) surpassed the increase for the entire 60-year period that preceded it. And the trend continues to accelerate into the 21st century. In 1950, 56 percent of the nation's households conformed to the traditional image of male breadwinner and female housewife, but by 1980, the figure had dropped to 27 percent, and by 1992 it was down to only 15 percent. Two-income families or female-headed households are replacing the older pattern of a man serving as the sole means of support for his dependent wife and children.

In the postwar period, paid employment has emerged as a central definition of women's lives. No longer a temporary stint before marriage, more women are becoming, like men, lifelong paid workers. The kind of women who work has also undergone permanent changes from the turn-of-the-century poor, single, immigrant girl. Between 1940 and 1970, the number of married women in the work force (usually old enough for their children to be in school and increasingly middle-class) surpassed the number of single women. Since the 1970s, the fastest growing group of new female workers has been working mothers with preschool children. In 1982, nearly half of women with preschoolers were working, straining the country's inadequate child care system and causing concern in the media about who was raising the nation's children. Note how working mothers with small children emerged as the focal point of public debate in the 1980s. Just as single women workers had become accepted by 1920, few thought twice by the postwar period about older women entering the work force once their children were in school. But mothers with small children were another matter.

Because of the women's movement and the passage of such legislation as Title VII of the 1964 Civil Rights Act, the media played up women who moved into nontraditional jobs. We heard stories about women bus drivers, construction workers, and electricians; we also read about the elite women who were moving into corporate hierarchies. While a small minority of women have been able to assault traditionally male jobs, the most striking thing about women's occupational structure is how little it has changed since the 1960s. Despite small breakthroughs, women continue to work predominantly in stereotyped female jobs, especially in expanding areas such as clerical and sales work and service jobs. Continuity, rather than revolutionary change, is the story here.

Along with women's jobs continue to go women's wages. In 1984, the median earnings of full-time women workers were $14,479 versus $23,218 for men. A female college graduate still earns less than a male high school dropout, basically 64 cents for every man's dollar. One area where there has been a significant narrowing of the wage gap is between black and white women. As late as 1940, black women earned only 38 percent of white women's median wage, largely because blacks were excluded from fields other than agricultural work or domestic service. By 1977, black women earned 88 percent of what white women did, in large part because the civil rights revolution and Title VII opened higher-paying manufacturing, clerical, and retail work to black women for the first time.

The old pattern of indifference to women has continued in the labor movement in the postwar period, although women have made strides in certain areas of union organizing. In 1980, 15.9 percent of working women belonged to unions (the comparable figure for men was 28.4 percent). In large part, women's low rates of unionization were linked to the general decline in the labor movement since the 1950s, a trend with far-reaching consequences. And yet the situation is not totally bleak. As the manufacturing sector of the economy declines (traditionally the stronghold of the American labor movement), unions have turned to organizing employees in the public sector. Since women hold many of the clerical and service jobs in this area, they have benefited from this upsurge. For example, over 40 percent of the 7.7 million women in public sector jobs in the early 1980s were unionized, more than twice the general level. But these labor breakthroughs came less from attention to organizing women per se, than from targeting certain occupational groups where women happened to predominate.

One of the most disturbing trends related to women's work has been the feminization of poverty. The Census Bureau reported in 1985 that almost half (48 percent) of families living below the poverty level were headed by women, an increase from 30 percent in 1966. Because of the low wages commanded by women (in 1984, at least one-quarter of the nation's full-time women workers earned less than $10,000 a year), women can easily slip below the poverty line when they choose or are forced to set up households of their own. The line between welfare and women's wages is often very thin: By 1980, some two-thirds of female-headed households received child welfare payments such as AFDC. But because women are denied access to higher paying work, because women continue to come out of divorce in far worse economic shape than men, and because the numbers of births to unwed mothers continues to rise, the feminization of poverty will continue to worsen.

The revolution in women's work outside the home, which built throughout the 20th century, has thus had an ambiguous effect. One historian referred to it as "the radical consequences of incremental change." Waged work is now accepted as something that most women will do for most of their adult lives. But society has been slower in changing attitudes. While it is no longer a public scandal for women to work, there has been very little concrete attention paid to the problems raised by women working, such as the lack of good day care, inadequate maternity-leave policies, and inflexibility in the workplace. The labor movement has proven an imperfect vehicle for addressing these issues. Most married working women are still stuck with (in the words of one harried worker) "two full-time jobs instead of just one." When, if ever, attitudes and public policy will catch up with changing realities remains uncertain.

Clerical Workers Unite

Cathy Tuley

Many women who work hold jobs like the one Cathy Tuley describes here as a billing clerk in an Alameda County, California, hospital. But not all working women do what Cathy Tuley did: get so involved in starting and running a union of clerks that it dramatically changed her life.

Cathy Tuley was born in 1950 in Kansas City. She dropped out of a local college and got what she described as a "deadening" job as a clerk. She got married and moved to California. She has worked throughout most of her marriage, except for short stretches after the birth of her two children; her husband's periodic unemployment and the need for two incomes to keep the family afloat have kept her in the workplace. The job at the Highland General Hospital billing office she describes in this piece was the longest she ever stayed in one place: two and a half years. Her commitment to the union, and her responsibilities as a shop steward, kept her there until the birth of her second child. When she returned to work, she landed a better job as a ward clerk in a county hospital.

Cathy Tuley did not organize her hospital's clerks single-handedly: coworker Kay Eisenhower figures prominently in the story. Eisenhower had been active in civil rights in the South in the 1960s, as well as in community organizing in Berkeley and the Bay Area. Her involvement in the emerging women's movement and health issues got her interested in organizing hospital workers. Realizing that "the only way any real changes were going to be made was through the activities of working people," she joined Tuley in the

Source: From Nancy Seifer *Nobody Speaks for Me!* pp. 229–231, 232–233, 235–236. Copyright © 1976 by Nancy Seifer.

Alameda County Employees local and with the Coalition of Labor Union Women. Union activities allowed women to challenge the depersonalized conditions under which they worked as well as work for broader social change. For a mother of two like Cathy Tuley, her union work also gave her the self-confidence to share her story with writer Nancy Seifer for the book *Nobody Speaks for Me! Self-Portraits of American Working Class Women* (1976).

I met Kay Eisenhower the first day on my job. We were in the same section. She came about a month before I did, and she was kind of like the lead clerk. We have a pretty high turnover! So we just started having lunch together and talking, and she was interested in organizing a union.

I don't know if she has her master's or what in political science, but she was really active in student movements and in and out of the women's liberation movement, that type of thing. I think she thought that, rather than teach, which is what she would have been doing, she wanted to meet people and work with them and get to know their politics.

Kay was probably the biggest influence on me. She had been involved in politics for a long time, and at the same time she always worked alongside me, in the same area and everything. I don't think I would have become as openly involved in organizing if I didn't have somebody there to push me. I might have, but I think it would've taken a lot longer and I might have been more afraid. I just wasn't the type to start doing it on my own, and she made me feel I could contribute something. Before that, I never really felt I could.

We started off talking about problems in the immediate workplace. Our supervisor let us organize the work pretty much the way we wanted to. Kay is very good at that, and I was interested in it, too. So we talked about trying to get things running smoothly, problems with various other workers, supervisors, that type of thing. We really just spent a lot of time sitting around analyzing things.

Then we just felt that we could do more if we were all in one organization— things like getting a contract and having shop stewards, that we never had before. In general, just getting better working conditions. The employees' association they had at Highland then was not representing the right people. It was really representing management more and it was more like a social group than a union. They had picnics and this type of thing. And when a clerk would call in to the association for help, they would notify her supervisor that she was calling and she would get jumped on for calling in without going through the channels.

Well, then SEIU—the Service Employees International Union—was organizing hospital workers in the area—maintenance people, LVN's, social workers. Kay knew quite a few other clerks, and SEIU started having organizing dinners, trying to get us to join and help organize the clerks. So Kay invited me and we started going to these dinners and talking about our problems at work, and I started finding out more about unions.

I'd never been a union member before and I felt I had a lot to learn. This was my first association with it all. Before, the word "union" always made me think about blue-collar workers and men. My father was in one. He never talked about it that much. I guess he didn't participate much. But his being a man and a blue-collar worker, I guess that's why I made that association.

In my previous experiences being a clerk, I was never aware of things. I just went and did my job and went home. All of a sudden I was aware of problems between supervisors and workers and the kind of power games people play. In fact, that was the kind of thing that really started us organizing . . .

In our shop Kay and I have gotten almost everybody to join the union. There's about 2,500 clerks in the county and about 40 percent are members of the union now. But in terms of negotiations, that's not enough if you want to show your power. And that's what management relates to, your power. I have people telling me, "Look, I'll join if you get this and that at negotiations. I'm behind you all the way." But I say, "It doesn't help to be behind me, you have to join the union and participate."

It's hard for people to realize that management relates to us in terms of numbers, and they keep very close track of how many members we have. Also, I would just like more people to join so that they can know their rights. And I think the union is the best way to learn them.

I think maybe it's harder to organize clerks than some other kinds of workers, because sometimes they feel that they're halfway into professionalism, like maybe they have one foot in the door. The way it works within the county, you can get a promotion and all of a sudden be management if you know the right people, and that type of thing.

Also, maybe because they're women, they're not as aggressive. They have been taking things the way they are for so long without saying anything, whereas the men . . . Well, like if Tom blew his stack and cussed somebody out at work I think they would accept it more. Sometimes I'd really like to say exactly what I feel when something happens, but I have to kind of control myself more. I feel that if I said what came to my mind, it would probably go on my record. It's more structured, the things that you're allowed to do as a clerk, the things you're allowed to wear. There's the public out there, you know, and all this junk.

I've been a shop steward for a year and a half now. We were the first class, several of our Clerks' County caucus. We all took it together. It wasn't really much training, just four sessions. But we learned union language, and we talked about how to process grievances, becoming familiar with the contract, things like that.

A lot of people come with questions about sick leaves, maternity leave, things which we try to have them look for in the contract themselves. Then there are workload problems and personality clashes between people and their supervisors. I've had quite a few of those. We try to do things informally and not file formal grievances, because this means you have to go through each supervisor, each step . . .

I think all of this has really helped me to develop myself, my personality. I've become a lot more vocal and aggressive, too, and I'm not as gullible as I used to be. Now, you can tell me something, and I want it proven to me. Sometimes it's kind of rough when you do that to your husband! "Give me the facts," you know. "Prove what you just said."

The first time I had to speak in front of a group I was really shaky and nervous. Maybe glad that I did it, but wondering how I sounded to other people, still worrying about that. That takes a long time, to forget about what they think, you know. It's easier for me now, but I've always had trouble getting up in front of people. I still really get shook. It's better if I do it spontaneously and not have to think about it for a long time. That just makes it even worse.

When I first started going to the organizing meetings, I felt for the first time that maybe I could really do something to change things somehow. Before, I never even thought about trying to. So it was a big change in my whole attitude. Also, I think being recognized as a valuable worker helps, too. I was able to do more than my share of work and do it accurately, and I think they kind of recognized me for that and started listening to my ideas about changing things.

Also, being a shop steward, it helps to be able to keep up your end of it, or else they won't listen to you at all. Some of the supervisors really expect a lot of you. They'll do things like use our ideas, saying that they're their own, and then if we come in late or something, they'll say, "What kind of example is this that you're setting for everybody else?" That happens to me because I'm always late!

I've always wanted to work with people in some way that I could help them. And I think this organizing has kind of given me the attitude that you just can't give up, even more so, and that things don't happen overnight. For me, that's been the hardest thing to learn. I can see people becoming more aware of themselves and their rights. These changes are happening. But sometimes you're just so involved that you don't see how much. And you just cannot change a whole structure of a union overnight, which is what we're trying to do!

The Real "Norma Rae" Tells Her Story

Crystal Lee Sutton

The working lives of southern women, black and white, are often cut from a different cloth than their northern and western sisters. The cloth metaphor is appropriate because of the importance of textile manufacturing to the southern economy. Originally textile factories had been located in places such as Lowell, Massachusetts, or Manchester, New Hampshire, but by the early 20th century, many had moved south, especially to the Piedmont region of North Carolina. The reason was simple: southern towns offered a cheap and plentiful labor supply and a conservative political climate hostile to unions. From the beginning, women and children were crucial to the textile work force in the South, that is, white women and white children. Not until the 1960s did blacks win entry into the mills.

The common denominators of the lives of southern textile workers were poverty, long hours, low pay, isolation, and lack of union protection. The

Source: From Victoria Byerly, *Hard Times Cotton Mill Girls: Personal Histories of Womanhood and Poverty in the South,* pp. 205–211. Copyright © 1986. Reprinted by permission of Cornell University Press.

South was noted for its violent and contentious pattern of labor relations, with unionization attempts almost always unsuccessful. This provides the backdrop for Crystal Lee Sutton's story, which is set in Graham, North Carolina.

Married at 18 and then widowed with a three-year-old child, Sutton remarried, had another child, and began to work at the mills. She was fired in 1973 for the union activity described in this excerpt and was not reinstated until 1978. Even though the union won an election at the plant in 1974 (a necessary step toward representation and collective bargaining under the 1935 Wagner Act), J. P. Stevens managed to delay signing a union contract until 1980.

Sutton's story was later made into the successful Hollywood movie, *Norma Rae,* for which Sally Field won an Oscar. The debt that the movie owed to Crystal Lee Sutton's life story is unmistakable in this excerpt, but she never received a penny from the project.

Nobody really approached me about the union. I had been out on sick leave. I had hurt my foot. My sister worked right down from me and she came up and said, "Lee, somebody was handing out union cards but don't you take one 'cause if you do you'll be fired." I said, "Who's handing them out?" She said, "I don't know but don't you take one." Then she went on back there to her job. So I started asking different ones around and nobody would say nothing. So I asked this older woman, "Do you know anything about this union stuff?" And she said, "Lee, all I know is there's a notice about this meeting on the bulletin board." So I took a piece of paper and wrote down the place, it was going to be at a church, and the time. So I started to talk to different ones about if they were going and nobody said nothing, so I asked my friend Liz. I said, "Liz, how about going with me to that union meeting?" She had three little girls. She said, "Lee, I don't have nobody to keep the kids." I said, "Oh, Cookie [her husband] will keep the children."

I never will forget, I went to Burlington that Saturday on Mother's Day, and Mama got mad with me 'cause I left early to go to that union meeting. She didn't think I ought to go. But I went over to JB Younts, he had been a real close friend, and I knew he knew about unions and all because I remember he tried to get Daddy to join the union at Cone Mills. He told me, "Lee, you do everything you can to try to get that union in." He said, "You get home in time to go to that union meeting." So I did. I never will forget it. Liz and I pulled up at this church—it was a black church—and I had never seen so many blacks in all my life. Liz said, "You sure you want to do this?" and I said, "Well, we're here. We might as well go on in." So we went in and there were maybe four or five other white people there. We went down and sat on the front row 'cause I didn't want to miss out on nothing. After the meeting, I agreed to go into the mill wearing a union button to try to get the union in. We were real strong with the blacks but we were weak with the whites. So I knew a lot of people I was going to talk with.

Eli Zivkovitch was the organizer. He was from Fairfield, Virginia, an ex-coal miner. He and his family were so poor that at one time they lived in a tent. He was a very handsome man, and I really loved my daddy more than anything in this world, but Eli was like what I wish my daddy had 'a been as far as being more modern, like realizing that women had more worth in this world than just being a sex object. That women had brains and that they should use those brains. It was okay for women to do so-called men's work. The men I had met before had always seemed to be more concerned with a woman's outward appearance. Eli was a good man, a fighter and a survivor. Hours meant nothing to him as far as his work went. He was not a nine-to-five person. He was available when you needed him, and that's the way he taught me to work. Eli said we could talk union and hand out literature on our break time in the canteens. So I got people to join the union real quick like.

Then they started calling me into the office. I had never been called into the office to be talked to about anything. But all of a sudden I couldn't do nothing right. Talking too much, standing in the bathroom too much. Nothing had changed, that was just their agitation trying to get me to quit trying to organize. Eli had give us this book called *What the Company Will Do for You.* It was all blank pages. He told us if they called us in the office for us to write down what they said. Because if they had a right to write us up, we had a right to write them up. I always took my pencil and my little book and I would write down things that was happening. This blew the boss men's mind. They couldn't believe I was doing this.

Then what happened was that the company posted a notice on the bulletin board and it was, in effect, trying to scare people. It stated something like it was going to be an all black union. Eli said he needed a copy of it to send to the National Labor Relations Board. So different people said they would copy the letter, you know, but whenever they tried they were told they would be fired. So one day, Eli said, "Crystal, I've got to have a copy of that letter." I said, "Okay." So I went up to the bulletin board and I was trying to copy the letter and the boss man came up and said, "You can't copy that, if you do you'll be fired." I went back to Eli that night and said, "Man, they said they'll fire us." He said, "I'm telling you it's your constitutional right," and he said, "I need a copy of that letter." I said, "I'll get a copy of that letter today." So I went on into work and, lo and behold, they had tables set up with tablecloths on them. They were having a safety dinner for us.

When the company claimed that they had no lost time for accidents they'd give us a little old dinner. But I've actually seen people with an arm in a cast sitting in the office. Prior to the union, we thought they were doing us a favor by letting us come in, sit in the office, and pay us. We didn't know nothing about workmen's compensation.

So I went to the pay phone which the company had conveniently installed to keep us out of the office. They had said we could use it any time we wanted to and I had done so. If there had been a storm, I'd call home to make sure the kids were all right and all. So I called Eli and said, "Look man, I can't copy that letter tonight because we're having a safety supper." 'Course he had to know what that was, so I quickly explained it to him. So I said, "Anyway, Eli, I'm hungry and I want to eat my supper." But he said, "Look, Crystal, you can afford to lose a few pounds and I need that letter." He knew he had made me mad then, so I said, "I'll get that damn letter."

So I started talking around and I came up with this idea. I went over to the ones that were in the union and I said, "Look, Eli needs that letter so I'll tell you what let's do. I'll memorize the first two lines of it and go in the bathroom and write it down. Mary, you memorize the next two" and I told all of them the lines of the paragraph to remember. Well, it got to be a big joke because we were pretending like we were getting water, you know, and trying to read the letter too. But we couldn't remember what we had read by the time we got to the bathroom. So we all got to laughing about it. So I said, "Hell, I got to get that letter." So I said to my sister, she was a service person, I said, "Seretha, I need a clipboard." She said, "What you going to do?" I said, "I'm going to get that letter." We didn't have no set time for a break, they said they would motion for us when it was our turn to go eat. Seretha said, "Oh God," but she gave me a clipboard.

As soon as they motioned for us, I took the clipboard and went immediately to the bulletin board and started to write. Because of the supper, everyone from management was at this dinner. So they took turns coming up to me telling me that I couldn't copy that letter. If I did, I'd be fired. Then the big man come up and he called me Lee. His name was Mason Lee. I said, "Mr. Lee, I didn't know you knew my name." And he said, "Yeah, I know who you are." He told me that if I didn't leave he was going to call the police to come in there and take me out. I said, "Mr. Lee, sir, you do what you want on your break time, you even get to go out for supper, and we can't even sit on the steps. This is my break time and I'm telling you I'm going to copy this letter. It's my constitutional right." So I continued to write and my knees were shaking like I was going to collapse any minute. I said, "If you do call the cops, you're going to have to call the Chief of Police because my husband is a jealous man and he won't let me ride home with just anybody." I thought to myself I'm going to put him to the test. I'm just going to push him and see what he does do.

So I copied the letter and folded it up and stuck it down my bra figuring, well, nobody will get it down there. I went on down there and got me a plate and went to this special canteen that the company had installed within the last month. They no longer let the ones in my department go to the old canteen. As soon as we got into work we had to report to the new canteen. Right there within twenty steps of my job they built this canteen. They went to that much trouble to separate me from the rest of the workers. And I went in there and everybody said, "God, you got more guts, what did they say?" I gave my dinner to some man in there and said, "Well as soon as they blow the whistle, they'll come and get me. Mr. Lee said they were going to fire me and call the police. So y'all can expect anything."

I went back out there when I figured break was about up, put on my lipstick, and was acting real cool, calm and collected, when we all started back to work. Then here they come. Three of them. "Mr. Lee wants to see you in the office." So I said, "Seretha don't you let nobody mess with my pocketbook, I'll be back shortly." "All right," she said. So they took me up to the door of the main office and pushed a button and the door came open and they took me in there where they were all sitting at a big table and Mason Lee was sitting at the head. He started talking to me and I said, "Mr. Lee, sir," I had me a pencil and a piece of paper, I said, "Before you tell me anything you going to have to tell me all your names and how to spell them." So he started to spell his name and then he stopped and said, "I don't have to do that."

Then he started telling me all the things that I had done wrong. Said I had stayed in the bathroom too long, used the pay phone when I wasn't supposed to, and, you know, all different kinds of reasons. He was talking so much I remember putting my hands on my ears and thinking, here is all these people in here that I have served at the restaurant, a couple of them I'd danced with, and my floorlady who had had me call my husband and get him to bring chicken up to the mill for us. All these people knew he was lying but didn't a one of them have the guts to say so. None of them said, "Mr. Lee you're lying, she used that phone on her break time, she was told she could use it." Nobody said nothing. I said, "I don't have anything to say. There is nobody in here on my side. Y'all are all company people and no matter what I say, y'all are going to be right and I'm going to be wrong." So then he said, "You going to have to leave the plant." And I said, "I don't have no way to go home, I didn't drive the car today, I got a ride with my sister." He said, "You call your husband to come and get you." And I said, "My husband's at work." So he said, "You call you a taxi." I said, "I don't have any money. You got to let me go back out there and get my pocketbook." Then he told Tommy Gardner, he said, "You go out there and get her pocketbook." I said, "If anybody touches my pocketbook, I'm going to have a warrant taken out on them for stealing." Finally, he said, "Let her back out there to get her pocketbook."

They went through the door with me and I went on around there and this black woman, Mary Moses, said, "What happened?" I said, "He fired me." Then I said, "Mary, give me your magic marker." So I grabbed it and I took a piece of pasteboard and I wrote the word UNION on it and, for some reason, I don't know why I did it, I climbed on the table and I just slowly turned the sign around. Everybody was in a state of shock and the machines started shutting down and everything got quiet. People started giving me the V sign. Then different ones from management came down there and tried to get me down off the table. Even my sister came down there. She said, "Lee, get down off that table and let me call Cookie to come and get you." Then I said to the boss man, "It's not their break time. Y'all gonna have to fire all of them too." Then sure enough here comes the chief of police. I got off the table and walked over there and he said, "Lee, what's wrong?" I said, "The man fired me and he fired me because I been trying to get the union in." He said, "Come on, let me take you home." I said, "You gonna take me home?" and he said, "Yeah." I said, "I want you to put that in writing." And I handed him a piece of paper and he started to write, and then he balled it up and said, "I don't have to do that." Then he grabbed me and literally forced me out of the gate and I was trying to get back in. I was fighting. It was a damn good thing I didn't know karate or he would have had to shoot me, and would have probably gotten away with it. They forced me in the car and took me to jail and locked me up.

Hard-Hatted Women

Susan Eisenberg

Until the 1970s, occupations such as electricians, plumbers, machinists, welders, and carpenters were almost 100 percent male and 100 percent white. But because of the civil rights and women's movements, the barriers began to fall, albeit slowly. Federal action played an important role. For example, a 1978 executive order amended the 1964 Civil Rights Act to set goals and timetables for promoting women's access to jobs in construction. It also made the employer responsible for a harassment-free workplace. Even with such federal mandates, the number of women on construction jobs remains distressingly low—less than 2 percent.

Women wanted jobs in the construction trades for a variety of reasons. Even as young girls, some had wanted the chance to build things or work in nontraditional settings. Many women hated the options for work available to women in the "pink collar ghetto"—wasn't there more to work than typing and filing? But mainly it was the money; work in the building trades often paid two to three times what women could earn in traditional female jobs.

The experience of Boston electrician Susan Eisenberg suggests the rewards and challenges facing hard-hatted women in the 1970s and 1980s. Like most other women in nontraditional jobs, she was the beneficiary of affirmative action guidelines; given the crudeness and hostility that these newcomers often faced on the jobs, it is hard to imagine co-workers voluntarily hiring women. Her story of being pregnant on a blue-collar job gives a new perspective on the challenge of combining childbearing with work. (Another construction worker tells the story of returning to work while still nursing and trying to find semi-private places—like the cab of her loader—to express her breast milk with a pump.) But what comes through most of all is Susan Eisenberg's pride in her work and her young daughter's corresponding pride in her mother who builds things.

Being an electrician has become just another part of who I am—shaping the strengths and weaknesses of my body, the ways I express myself and solve problems, and what I notice. After ten years, both the honeymoon bliss and those first rude shock waves of reality are only strong memories. I find myself both looking back at my decision to become a union electrician without regrets and looking ahead to a life in the trades with a good deal of ambivalence.

Like many of the first women in their locals I've met across the country, I started in 1978, when affirmative action guidelines were mandated. I graduated four years later in the first apprenticeship class of IBEW Local 103 (Boston), to include women. Of the six women who started together, five of us graduated, a higher percentage than the men in our class. We owed that largely to the support, information-sharing and prodding we gave each other. Four of us carpooled

Source: "Susan Eisenberg—Electrician," from *Hard-Hatted Women: Stories of Struggle and Success in the Trades,* ed. Molly Martin (Seattle: The Seal Press, 1988), pp. 216–224. Reprinted by permission of the author.

together to our two-nights-a-week of school for four years. Our carpool conversations made up somewhat for the isolation of usually being the only woman—of any trade—on our jobs. As more women entered, we formed a group, meeting together for personal support and to identify and address the common problems we faced as women in our union.

Entering construction in the late 1970s was a little like falling in love with someone you weren't supposed to. The initial honeymoon was powerful. Enormous pride as I gained agility with tools I hadn't even known the names of when I began. Amazement as I watched new muscles pop out in the mirror almost daily. Fierce loyalty toward the older mechanics who took me under their wing and taught me their special techniques. Everywhere I would go—movies, airports, restaurants—immediately, I would notice the wiring: where fixtures were placed and how they were fed; whether receptacles were two-prong or three-; suddenly imagining what was behind ceilings and walls.

I remember, particularly in those first years, the enormous encouragement I felt from women on the outside, as though I represented them as well. Not only friends, but strangers, too. Women driving past my jobsite who would notice me and honk and give me a raised fist. The neighbor who rode to work on the same early morning bus and always cheered me on. The older black woman I met once in the bathroom of a remodel job, who had noticed my tool pouch on the sink and told me about her own unfulfilled ambitions of a job in the skilled trades, and how she had taught herself radio electronics from books. I felt indebted and privileged that I was able to live out a dream of generations of women who had been locked out. This magnified each success and failure, and kept me from following the urge I sometimes had to just walk away.

My initial experience in union construction was my worst. In the first shop that I worked for the journeymen were extremely hostile and unwilling to train me. There was even a foreman I worked under who tried to get me injured. Fortunately, I was laid off, and went to work for another shop where my experience was just the opposite. I was able to work on small jobs with some good mechanics who took me seriously and gave me a chance to learn the trade. They taught me how to mount boxes, pull and connect wires, and lay out the circuitry from a panel in an electric closet to the receptacles and lights in a room. After a lot of insisting, I got a chance to do the bigger and heavier work: wiring motors; cutting, threading and bending pipe; mounting equipment. I learned how to climb and carry ladders, use power tools, and maneuver myself around the debris and dangers on a construction site.

Even though the work and its newness were exhilarating, I also found myself often overcome with anger, depression or the feeling that I was in over my head. Working outside in a New England winter, or even by the water in the fall, is *cold*. And there were a lot of times I just had to grit my teeth and plunge across fear to do what I was asked: climb a crane, walk across a beam, work on scaffolding.

The hardest part of the job for me to get used to, though, was the talk on a construction site. Not the swearing—which guys often apologized for when I hadn't even noticed it—but jokes about beating up wives, racist and anti-Semitic slurs, degrading remarks about each other's girlfriends or some woman who happened to pass by, and comments about each others' personal lives that I found incredibly cruel. Sometimes I was grateful to be an apprentice, the one designated to go for coffee, so I could have the chance to walk outside and cry without being seen. On one remodel job, a residence for elders, one of the electricians joked about pulling the fire alarm and raping all the women residents—mostly in their eighties and nineties, many of whom I had gotten to know in the months working there. When I tried to say why a comment like that wasn't funny, he suggested that I could rape all the men. It was the casualness of the conversation for him, the assumptions underneath, and everyone else's silence that broke right through my armor. Conversations like that would eat away at me for weeks. I had to learn to harden myself, to expect little support from co-workers in group conversations, and to be selective about who and what was worth responding to. It quickly became clear that responding to all the comments I found offensive would guarantee not being heard. It would also mean being set up for entertainment, like anyone on a construction job who is too predictable—that is, things would be said just to get a rise out of you. So, I learned to let most offensive remarks pass by unchallenged, except in one-on-one situations, and often wondered whether or not I had made the right choice.

I had both my children after I became a journeywoman. As the second woman in my local to give birth, I found I had to do a lot of ground-breaking. Our union's disability and health and welfare policies were written only for the pregnancies of a member's wife. A group of women in the local met for several months, doing research and asking a lot of questions, and then wrote a pamphlet explaining how these benefits applied to a pregnant union member. Unfortunately, like many of the changes women have brought to the union, the pamphlet was only in circulation as long as the women members passed it around themselves.

I worked into the sixth month of my first pregnancy without telling anyone except the general foreman and a woman elevator installer that I was pregnant. I told most people on the day I stopped working. Even my foreman and partner only thought I had gained a little weight (thirty pounds!).

To my friends who saw me after work in maternity clothes, it seemed inconceivable that my pregnancy was anything but obvious. But since I wore baggy clothes to work (what I called my maternity overalls) and since no one *expected* to see a pregnant woman on a construction sight—they didn't. I presented myself as I always had—as an electrician there to work and earn a paycheck.

For me, deciding whether, when and whom to tell I was pregnant raised issues of privacy, safety, emotional vulnerability and confidence as a mechanic. I handled the choice differently in two pregnancies that followed, but for my first pregnancy, not telling felt like the right choice for several reasons:

Safety. During the first trimester, when danger to the fetus from chemical hazards is greatest, I was—by good luck—on a job where there were none. It was the finish stage of a new hotel and there were—a pregnant woman's dream!—twenty-eight new bathrooms on each floor. If safety had been an issue, I probably would have made a different choice.

Insecurity as a mechanic. I was a new journeywoman, out of my time (finished with my apprenticeship) only a year. As one of the first women to graduate in our local, my work performance had always been scrutinized closely. I felt I had worked very hard for years, proving I could do the job. I didn't want to call attention to what had become harder and more tiring.

Gaging limits. Pregnancy lasts a while, and it's not something you can untell someone. I wanted to come to my own decisions (from talking with my doctor, reading the little I could find, and listening to my body) about what I could and could not do as a pregnant electrician. I didn't want to have to deal with everyone else's perceptions of my capabilities or their reactions, which I suspected would be overprotecting, followed by resentment.

Gossip, jokes, careless talk. When I am feeling emotionally raw and vulnerable, a construction site is never where I want to be. Pregnant, I felt very raw. Knowing there is a big risk of miscarriage, particularly in the first trimester (one out of five pregnancies ends in miscarriage)—I did not want that to be everybody's business. But even in the second trimester, I found that I wanted the pregnancy to be quietly personal, that I didn't want to risk being the object of crude remarks. Pregnancy was new for me and for the local: I was the second member, the first journeywoman, to be pregnant. It represented big changes in my homelife and in my relationship with my partner. There *were* men on the job who were friends, whom I would have liked to tell, but it was a very big job (fifty electricians), and there were a number of guys who were pretty hostile toward me. It didn't feel possible to tell a few people without everyone knowing fairly quickly.

Not talking about my pregnancy exaggerated the feeling I often have in construction of feeling split in two. At coffee break, I would be intently aware of the kicking in my womb while having a conversation about the Red Sox. It also meant making a clear pact with myself to ask for help when I needed it or refuse to do things I felt I shouldn't do—that I *would* put health and safety ahead of ego.

My second pregnancy—on another job, with another company—began to miscarry on the job. I began bleeding, called my doctor, who told me to come in immediately, and then told my foreman that I was leaving. When he asked why, I just said, "I have to leave." A few days later I did miscarry. When I called to say I would be out another day, the foreman again said he was concerned, did I need help, what was wrong. At that point, I told him what had happened. He said the other guys on the crew were concerned, too, and asked if he could tell them. He said it wouldn't go beyond the electricians (we were a crew of about six). I said that was fine, and I was very impressed and moved to find that that really was what happened. Aside from one bad joke, the crew was incredibly supportive and respectful.

My third pregnancy began a few months later on that same job. This time I decided to tell people once the first trimester was past. I had been out of my time for a few years and felt more confident. It was the same small crew that had been through the miscarriage with me, so I felt a certain level of safety and intimacy. People already saw me as a wife and mother, so this time around, being pregnant again was no big leap in how I was perceived. I had already had a baby and returned to work once. People expected that this is what I would do again (not, as I'd heard so often when I started: why waste this training on women when they'll only have families and quit). And I was more comfortable with being pregnant. I knew what would happen. I could predict what I could and could not do, how I would feel, making it easier to include other people without feeling like I was losing control.

Driving around Boston, I love pointing out to my daughter and son "the jobs we worked together." It brings back the times when I felt like I carried a delicious secret: lying on a plank across an open airshaft on the roof of a building, tying in a fan motor, talking to the baby-in-utero. It gave me a powerful appreciation for the changes we have brought about. "We built that, Susie?" my daughter asks as we drive by a big hotel. "You bet!" I tell her.

Organizing the Farm Workers

Jessie Lopez De La Cruz

Farmwork has been a way of life for many Mexican-Americans in the Southwest and California since early in the 20th century. Conditions of life have always been hard: toiling long hours in the fields for incredibly low pay, constantly moving around while families follow the crops, being more susceptible to disease and dying young, being unable to break out of the cycle. Huge corporations such as the Bank of America, Safeway, and the Southern Pacific Company owned much of the land in the West; agribusiness wanted, and usually got, a docile and cheap migrant labor force. That is, until Cesar Chavez and the United Farmworkers began organizing in the fields of the San Joaquin valley in 1962.

Jessie Lopez De La Cruz was very much part of Chavez's organizing drive—what participants called simply *La Causa* (the cause). At the time, De La Cruz was 42 years old, married and the mother of six children, and had been a farmworker all her life. Breaking out of traditional Mexican-American gender roles to become a union organizer was not easy, but she drew on her personal history: "I'd been trained as a child that the woman just walked behind the husband and kept quiet, no matter what the husband does. But in work I've been equal to men since I was a child, working alongside men, doing the same hard work and earning the same wages." Jessie Lopez De La Cruz put that determination to use as she built support for the farmworkers' union and eventually became a paid union official. Her oral history traces the roots of her union activity and conveys her belief that poor people must stick together to improve their lives. And her story confirms the vital role that women play in this struggle.

The words of Maria Varela, a Latina from the Southwest, suggest the common struggle that unites people of color and women's role in it: "When

Source: From *Moving the Mountain: Women Working for Social Change* by Ellen Cantarow with Susan Gushee O'Malley and Sharon Hartman Strom. Copyright 1980 by The Feminist Press at The City University of New York, www.feministpress.org.

your race is fighting for survival—to eat, to be clothed, to be housed, to be left in peace—as a woman, you know who you are. You are a principle of life, of survival and endurance . . . This is even more true when, as a woman, you are involved in battling the forces of oppression against your race."

Growing up, I could see all the injustices and I would think, "If only I could do something about it! If only there was somebody who could do something about it!" That was always in the back of my mind. And after I was married, I cared about what was going on, but I felt I couldn't do anything. So I went to work, and I came home to clean the house, and I fixed the food for the next day, took care of the children and the next day went back to work. The whole thing over and over again. Politics to me was something foreign, something I didn't know about. I didn't even listen to the news. I didn't read the newspapers hardly at all. *True Romance* was my thing!

But then late one night in 1962, there was a knock at the door and there were three men. One of them was Cesar Chavez. And the next thing I knew, they were sitting around our table talking about a union. I made coffee. Arnold had already told me about a union for the farmworkers. He was attending their meetings in Fresno, but I didn't. I'd either stay home or stay outside in the car. But then Cesar said, "The women have to be involved. They're the ones working out in the fields with their husbands. If you can take the women out to the fields, you can certainly take them to meetings." So I sat up straight and said to myself, *"That's* what I want!"

When I became involved with the union, I felt I had to get other women involved. Women have been behind men all the time, always. Just waiting to see what the men decide to do, and tell us what to do. In my sister-in-law and brother-in-law's families, the women do a lot of shouting and cussing and they get slapped around. But that's not standing up for what you believe in. It's just trying to boss and not knowing how. I'd hear them scolding their kids and fighting their husbands and I'd say, "Gosh! Why don't you go after the people that have you living like this? Why don't you go after the growers that have you tired from working out in the fields at low wages and keep us poor all the time? Let's go after them! *They're* the cause of our misery!" Then I would say we had to take a part in the things going on around us. "Women can no longer be taken for granted—that we're just going to stay home and do the cooking and cleaning. It's way past the time when our husbands could say, 'You stay home! You have to take care of the children! You have to do as I say!'"

Then some women I spoke to started attending the union meetings, and later they were out on the picket lines.

I think I was made an organizer because in the first place I could relate to the farmworkers, being a lifelong farmworker. I was well-known in the small towns around Fresno. Wherever I went to speak to them, they listened. I told them about how we were excluded from the NLRB in 1935, how we had no benefits, no minimum wage, nothing out in the fields—no restrooms, nothing. I would talk about how we were paid what the grower wanted to pay us, and how we couldn't set a price on our work. I explained that we could do something about these things by joining a union, by working together. I'd ask people how they felt about these many years they had been working out in the fields, how they had been treated. And then we'd all talk about it. They would say, "I was working for so-and-so, and when I complained about something that happened there, I was fired." I said, "Well! Do you think we should be putting up with this in this modern age? You know, we're not back in the twenties. We can stand up! We can talk back! It's not like when I was a little kid and my grandmother used to say, 'You have to especially respect the Anglos,' 'Yessir,' 'Yes, Ma'am!' That's over. This country is very rich, and we want a share of the money these growers make of our sweat and our work by exploiting us and our children!" I'd have my sign-up book and I'd say, "If anyone wants to become a member of the union, I can make you a member right now." And they'd agree!

So I found out that I could organize them and make members of them. Then I offered to help them, like taking them to the doctor's and translating for them, filling out papers that they needed to fill out, writing their letters for those that couldn't write. A lot of people confided in me. Through the letter-writing, I knew a lot of the problems they were having back home, and they knew they could trust me, that I wouldn't tell anyone else about what I had written or read. So that's why they came to me.

There was a migrant camp in Parlier. And these people, the migrants, were being used as strikebreakers. I had something to do with building that camp. By that time, I had been put on the board of the Fresno County Economic Opportunity Commission, and I was supporting migrant housing for farmworkers. But I had no idea it was going to be turned almost into a concentration camp or prison. The houses were just like matchboxes—square, a room for living, a room for cooking, a bathroom that didn't have a door, just a curtain. The houses are so close together that if one catches fire, the next one does, too, and children have burned in them. It happened in Parlier.

So I went to the camp office and said I wanted to go in and visit. By this time, I was well-known as a radical, an educator, and a troublemaker! The man in the office asked what I wanted to talk about. I just wanted to visit, I said.

"Well, you have to sign your name here." I said, "I also would like to know when I can use the hall for a meeting."

"What kind of meeting?"

"An organizing meeting." You see, when it was built, they told us there was supposed to be a hall built for parties and whatever. I felt we could use it for a meeting to talk to the people. But he said, "We can't authorize you to come in here and talk to the people about a union, but you can write Governor Reagan and ask for permission." I left.

I met a nurse who had to go to this camp. She said, "Why don't you come with me as my translator?" Even though she spoke perfect Spanish! So both of us went in, and she said she was from the Health Department and I was her translator. I got in there and talked to the people and told them about our union meetings, and at our next meeting they were there. I had to do things like that in order to organize.

It was very hard being a woman organizer. Many of our people my age and older were raised with the old customs in Mexico: where the husband rules, he is king of his house. The wife obeys, and the children, too. So when we first started it was very, very hard. Men gave us the most trouble—neighbors there in Parlier! They were for the union, but they were not taking orders from women, they said. When they formed the ranch committee at Christian Brothers—that's a big wine company, part of it is in Parlier—the ranch committee was all men. We were working under our first contract in Fresno County. The ranch committee had to enforce the contract. If there are any grievances they meet with us and the supervisors. But there were no women on the first committee.

That year, we'd have a union meeting every week. Men, women, and children would come. Women would ask questions and the men would just stand back. I guess they'd say to themselves, "I'll wait for someone to say something before I do." The women were more aggressive than the men. And I'd get up and say, "Let's go on, let's do it!"

When the first contract was up, we talked about there being no women on the ranch committee. I suggested they be on it, and the men went along with this. And so women were elected.

The women took the lead for picketing, and we would talk to the people. It got to the point that we would have to find them, because the men just wouldn't go and they wouldn't take their wives. So we would say, "We're having our picket line at the Safeway in Fresno, and those that don't show up are going to have to pay a five-dollar fine." We couldn't have four or five come to a picket line and have the rest stay home and watch TV. In the end, we had everybody out there . . .

Sometimes I'd just stop to think: what if our parents had done what we were doing now? My grandparents were poor. They were humble. They never learned to speak English. They felt God meant them to be poor. It was against their religion to fight. I remember there was a huge policeman named Marcos, when I was a child, who used to go around on a horse. My grandmother would say, "Here comes Marcos," and we just grew up thinking, "He's law and order." But during the strikes I stood up to them. They'd come up to arrest me and I'd say, "O.K., here I come if you want. Arrest me!" . . .

It doesn't take courage. All it takes is standing up for what you believe in, talking about things that you know are true, things that should be happening, instead of what is happening. That's all it takes. The way I see it, there's more poor people than rich people. We're trying to get together, organize, stick together. Say I'm outside, and something is happening inside my house. I need help, and I shout. They'll probably hear me a couple of houses down. But then other people come with me and I say, "Help me shout so they can hear me downtown." It'll take quite a few people. But if we can get a hundred people together and we all shout at the same time, we'll be heard further, and that's what we're talking about!

Women on Welfare

Johnnie Tillmon

What if women want to work and cannot find jobs? What if these women are the sole support of their families? Many women are just one man away from welfare, the saying goes. Women do not always live near available jobs (this is especially true of inner-city residents) and if they have children, long commutes are not feasible; the pay for women's jobs is sometimes so low that working full time still leaves women below the poverty line. So this vicious circle often pushes women onto the welfare rolls.

This testimonial by Johnnie Tillmon, published in 1972, forcefully points out that welfare is a women's issue. Tillmon was born in 1928 in Arkansas and started to organize welfare mothers in Los Angeles in 1963 when her health forced her to quit working and go on welfare. She later served as the first chairwoman of the National Welfare Rights Organization (NWRO), an advocacy group founded by George Wiley that lobbied for a guaranteed annual income by arguing that welfare was a basic right of citizenship. Her testimony accentuates the demeaning aspects of going on welfare (the requirement that in order to receive aid, there must not be a man in the house was later modified) and how marginal an existence it provides. She reminds us that the majority of poor families are white, not black, and mocks the idea of "the dignity of work" when the only work available keeps families stuck in poverty. And she punctures the commonly held view that black women have more babies in order to get more welfare money: "Having babies for profit is a lie that only men could make up, and only men could believe." More than anything else, she argues for treating women's work, both paid and unpaid, as worthy of support and respect.

Johnnie Tillmon Blackston died in 1995 at the age of 69. In 1996 President Bill Clinton fulfilled his campaign pledge to "end welfare as we know it" by signing into law the Personal Responsibility and Work Opportunity Act, mandating a historic (and controversial) overhaul of the federal system of welfare entitlements. The law ended the federal guarantee of cash assistance to poor children by abolishing Aid to Families with Dependent Children (ADFC), required most adult recipients to find work within two years, set a five-year limit on payments to any family, and gave states wide discretion in running their welfare programs. Johnnie Tillmon Blackston was a strong critic of the welfare system, but she would certainly have been appalled at new national priorities that, in essence, left mothers and children needing assistance to fend for themselves.

I'm a woman. I'm a black woman. I'm a poor woman. I'm a fat woman. I'm a middle-aged woman. And I'm on welfare.

In this country, if you're any one of those things—poor, black, fat, female, middle-aged, on welfare—you count less as a human being. If you're all those things, you don't count at all. Except as a statistic.

Source: From *America's Working Women* by Rosalyn Baxandall, Linda Gordon, and Susan Reverby. Used by permission of Random House, Inc.

I am a statistic.

I am 45 years old. I have raised six children.

I grew up in Arkansas, and I worked there for fifteen years in a laundry, making about $20 or $30 a week, picking cotton on the side for carfare. I moved to California in 1959 and worked in a laundry there for nearly four years. In 1963 I got too sick to work anymore. Friends helped me to go on welfare.

They didn't call it welfare. They called it A.F.D.C.—Aid to Families with Dependent Children. Each month I get $363 for my kids and me. I pay $128 a month rent; $30 for utilities, which include gas, electricity, and water; $120 for food and non-edible household essentials; $50 for school lunches for the three children in junior and senior high school who are not eligible for reduced-cost meal programs.

There are millions of statistics like me. Some on welfare. Some not. And some, really poor, who don't even know they're entitled to welfare. Not all of them are black. Not at all. In fact, the majority—about two-thirds—of all the poor families in the country are white.

Welfare's like a traffic accident. It can happen to anybody, but especially it happens to women.

And that is why welfare is a women's issue. For a lot of middle-class women in this country, Women's Liberation is a matter of concern. For women on welfare it's a matter of survival.

Forty-four percent of all poor families are headed by women. That's bad enough. But the *families* on A.F.D.C. aren't really families. Because 99 per cent of them are headed by women. That means there is no man around. In half the states there really can't be men around because A.F.D.C. says if there is an "able-bodied" man around, then you can't be on welfare. If the kids are going to eat, and the man can't get a job, then he's got to go. So his kids can eat.

The truth is that A.F.D.C. is like a supersexist marriage. You trade in *a* man for *the* man. But you can't divorce him if he treats you bad. He can divorce you, of course, cut you off anytime he wants. But in that case, *he* keeps the kids, not you.

The man runs everything. In ordinary marriage, sex is supposed to be for your husband. On A.F.D.C. you're not supposed to have any sex at all. You give up control of your own body. It's a condition of aid. You may even have to agree to get your tubes tied so you can never have more children just to avoid being cut off welfare.

The man, the welfare system, controls your money. He tells you what to buy, what not to buy, where to buy it, and how much things cost. If things—rent, for instance—really cost more than he says they do, it's just too bad for you.

There are other welfare programs, other kinds of people on welfare—the blind, the disabled, the aged. (Many of them are women, too, especially the aged.) Those others make up just over a third of all the welfare caseloads. We A.F.D.C.s are two-thirds.

But when the politicians talk about the "welfare cancer eating at our vitals," they're not talking about the aged, blind, and disabled. Nobody minds them. They're the "deserving poor." Politicians are talking about A.F.D.C. Politicians are talking about us—the women who head up 99 per cent of the A.F.D.C. families—and our kids. We're the "cancer," the "undeserving poor." Mothers and children.

In this country we believe in something called the "work ethic." That means that your work is what gives you human worth. But the work ethic itself is a double standard. It applies to men and to women on welfare. It doesn't apply to all women. If you're a society lady from Scarsdale and you spend all your time sitting on your prosperity paring your nails, well, that's okay.

The truth is a job doesn't necessarily mean an adequate income. A woman with three kids—not twelve kids, mind you, just three kids—that woman earning the full federal minimum wage of $2.00 an hour, is still stuck in poverty. She is below the Government's own official poverty line. There are some ten million jobs that now pay less than the minimum wage, and if you're a woman, you've got the best chance of getting one.

The President keeps repeating the "dignity of work" idea. What dignity? Wages are the measure of dignity that society puts on a job. Wages and nothing else. There is no dignity in starvation. Nobody denies, least of all poor women, that there is dignity and satisfaction in being able to support your kids through honest labor.

We wish we could do it.

The problem is that our country's economic policies deny the dignity and satisfaction of self-sufficiency to millions of people—the millions who suffer everyday in underpaid dirty jobs—and still don't have enough to survive.

People still believe that old lie that A.F.D.C. mothers keep on having kids just to get a bigger welfare check. On the average, another baby means another $35 a month—barely enough for food and clothing. Having babies for profit is a lie that only men could make up, and only men could believe. Men, who never have to bear the babies or have to raise them and maybe send them to war.

There are a lot of other lies that male society tells about welfare mothers; that A.F.D.C. mothers are immoral, that A.F.D.C. mothers are lazy, misuse their welfare checks, spend it all on booze and are stupid and incompetent.

If people are willing to believe these lies, it's partly because they're just special versions of the lies that society tells about *all* women.

For instance, the notion that all A.F.D.C. mothers are lazy: that's just a negative version of the idea that women don't work and don't want to. It's a way of rationalizing the male policy of keeping women as domestic slaves.

The notion that A.F.D.C. mothers are immoral is another way of saying that all women are likely to become whores unless they're kept under control by men and marriage. Even many of my own sisters on welfare believe these things about themselves.

On TV, a woman learns that human worth means beauty and that beauty means being thin, white, young and rich.

She learns that her body is really disgusting the way it is, and that she needs all kinds of expensive cosmetics to cover it up.

She learns that a "real woman" spends her time worrying about how her bathroom bowl smells; that being important means being middle class, having two cars, a house in the suburbs, and a minidress under your maxicoat. In other words, an A.F.D.C. mother learns that being a "real woman" means being all the things she isn't and having all the things she can't have.

Either it breaks you, and you start hating yourself, or you break it.

There's one good thing about welfare. It kills your illusions about yourself, and about where this society is really at. It's laid out for you straight. You have to learn to fight, to be aggressive, or you just don't make it. If you can survive being on welfare, you can survive anything. It gives you a kind of freedom, a sense of your own power and togetherness with other women.

Maybe it is we poor welfare women who will really liberate women in this country. We've already started on our welfare plan.

Along with other welfare recipients, we have organized together so we can have some voice. Our group is called the National Welfare Rights Organization (N.W.R.O.). We put together our own welfare plan, called Guaranteed Adequate Income (G.A.I.), which would eliminate sexism from welfare.

There would be no "categories"—men, women, children, single, married, kids, no kids—just poor people who need aid. You'd get paid according to need and family size only—$6,500 for a family of four (which is the Department of Labor's estimate of what's adequate), and that would be upped as the cost of living goes up.

If I were president, I would solve this so-called welfare crisis in a minute and go a long way toward liberating every woman. I'd just issue a proclamation that "women's" work is *real* work.

In other words, I'd start paying women a living wage for doing the work we are already doing—child-raising and housekeeping. And the welfare crisis would be over, just like that. Housewives would be getting wages, too—a legally determined percentage of their husband's salary—instead of having to ask for and account for money they've already earned.

For me, Women's Liberation is simple. No woman in this country can feel dignified, no woman can be liberated, until all women get off their knees. That's what N.W.R.O. is all about—women standing together, on their feet.

Photo Essay

MUCH IN DEMAND IN 1963

After the publication of *The Feminine Mystique* in 1963, Betty Friedan lectured widely across the country about the controversial findings of her best-selling book. (Note in the picture that she is referred to as Mrs. Friedan; the term *Ms.* had not yet been invented.) But Friedan soon came to believe that the problem of the trapped housewife was being "talked to death," even though she herself had been unable to write her projected next book on the new directions that would allow women to move beyond the feminine mystique. The revival of feminism in the 1960s helped to supply some of the answers, although it also raised new questions.
(Credit: Courtesy of the Schlesinger Library, Radcliffe College)

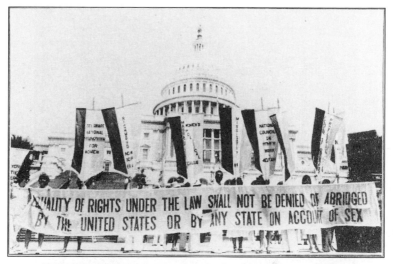

EQUAL RIGHTS DEMONSTRATION AT THE CAPITOL

When the ERA was sent to the states for ratification in 1972, supporters predicted an easy victory. When progress had stalled by 1975, feminists were galvanized into new strategies such as boycotts and mass demonstrations to try to break the stalemate. This 1978 march brought more than 100,000 ERA supporters to Washington to lobby successfully for a three-year extension of the ratification deadline to June 30, 1982. In a conscious evocation of the woman suffrage movement, ERA supporters prominently displayed the suffrage colors of purple, green, and gold in their banners.
(Credit: Courtesy of Bettye Lane)

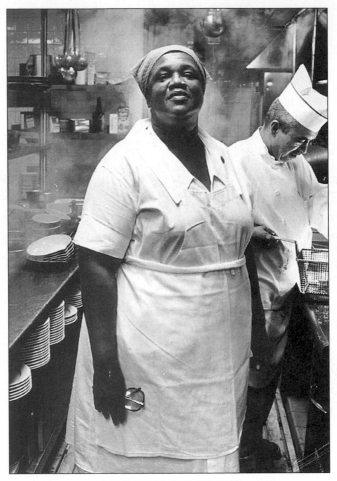

A DAY IN THE KITCHEN

Paid employment has more consistently been a part of black
women's lives than whites' because few black families could
survive on the wages paid to black men alone. But until recently
black women faced circumscribed employment opportunities
limited both by racism and by the segmentation of the work force
into dead-end women's jobs. This 1976 photograph introduces
Velma James, head chef of the Roosevelt Hotel in New York City.
(Credit: Coreen Simpson)

WOMEN AND THE LABOR MOVEMENT

Labor unions have only reluctantly recognized the roles that women workers
can play in the labor movement. At this Labor Day parade in New York City,
the most prominent marchers are Chinese-American garment workers
represented by the International Ladies Garment Workers Union (ILGWU).
The signs, in English, Chinese, and Spanish, reflect the heterogeneity of the
modern labor movement.
(Credit: Earl Dotter Archive Pictures Inc.)

PROTESTS IN HIGHER EDUCATION

Women made strides in higher education as a result of the women's movement, but it took demonstrations like the one these Harvard-Radcliffe graduating seniors staged in 1971 to protest Harvard's admission policy that admitted four men for every woman. The women's banners combine the symbols for women and equality, and the middle one incorporates the student protest sign of the clenched fist, along with a dig at Harvard (the richest university in the country) by spelling its motto VERITA$. Harvard soon instituted a sex-blind admissions policy; in the nation as a whole, women now make up a majority of undergraduates.
(Credit: Courtesy of Radcliffe College Archives)

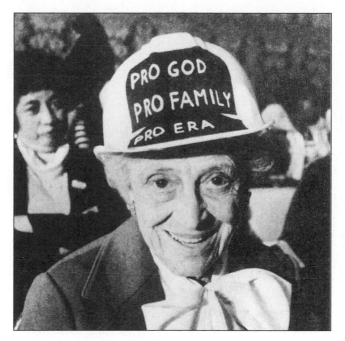

HOUSTON, 1977

Betty K. Hamburger, a delegate from Maryland Advocates for the Aging, captured a lot of attention at the 1977 National Women's Conference in Houston with her "Pro God, Pro Family, Pro ERA" hat, which also had "Free Choice" on the back. Hamburger was 73 years old at the time of the convention and had been active in the Gray Panthers, an advocacy group for senior citizens. Speaking for older Americans, Hamburger recalled, "Houston helped us feel that we were not alone, that younger women had the same feelings we had . . . So many of us have so much to give; we have lots of knowledge and know-how, and we ought to be able to use it."
(Credit: Courtesy of Bettye Lane)

ANITA HILL

Accusations by University of Oklahoma professor Anita Hill
that Supreme Court nominee Clarence Thomas had sexually
harassed her at the Department of Education and Equal
Employment Opportunity Commission in the early 1980s
sparked fierce political debate during his confirmation hearings
in 1991. Many felt that if there had been more women in the
Senate, Professor Hill's charges would have been treated more
seriously. In the wake of the hearings, national polls confirmed
the pervasiveness of sexual harassment on the job: 4 of 10
women said they had been the object of unwanted sexual
advances from men at work. Clarence Thomas won his seat on
the Supreme Court, and Anita Hill became a heroine for the
feminist movement.
(Credit: Reuters/Corbis-Bettmann)

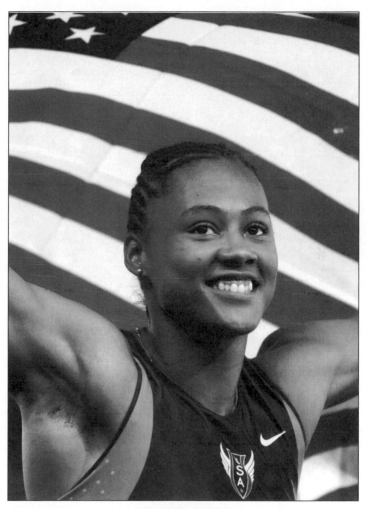

MARION JONES

Marion Jones was born in Los Angeles in 1975, and sports have always been part of her life. At the University of North Carolina, she played basketball and competed in track and field. At the 2000 Summer Olympics in Sydney, Australia, she had a shot at gold medals in five separate events; in the end, she won three gold and two bronze. She is shown here after winning the women's 200 meters before a crowd of more than 100,000 spectators. Marion Jones represents the opportunities for talented women athletes to forge professional careers that bring them national recognition and financial success on a par with male athletes. (Credit: Corbis Images.)

CHAPTER 12

Sexuality and the Body

By the 1960s, American society seemed to be in the grip of a new openness about sexuality, symbolized in many minds by such women's fashions as the miniskirt. Books, movies, and self-help manuals promoted an ethos of casual yet fun sexual relationships. The widespread availability of more effective contraception such as the birth control pill and the intrauterine device (IUD) by the mid-1960s helped to separate sexuality from procreation.

The simultaneous appearance of the so-called sexual revolution and the revival of feminism suggested a link between the two, but in fact they were often at odds. In order for women's sexuality to be freely realized, many of the structures of relationships, such as the double standard, the view of women as sex objects, and the validation of the norms of male dominance and female passivity would have to be changed. Ironically, the wider access to birth control put more pressure on women to engage in sexual relationships with men now that fear of pregnancy was removed. As *Ms.* magazine noted in 1972, "The Sexual Revolution and the Women's Movement are at polar opposites. Women have been liberated only from the right to say 'no.'"

The women's movement did have a significant impact, however, on a variety of issues relating to women's sexuality and health. The 1973 publication of *Our Bodies, Ourselves* by the Boston Women's Health Collective encouraged women to be active participants, not passive patients, in health care issues. Susan Brownmiller's powerful *Against Our Will* (1975) argued that rape was not an issue of sexuality, but of violence and dominance of men over women; feminists organized rape crisis centers that offered counseling and tried to dispel the prevalent tendency to blame the victim for her attack. Women also tried to limit the spread of pornography, which, they argued, encouraged male aggression toward women with its explicitly violent content. Battered-women shelters offered protection to the victims of domestic violence, and the legal system recognized the concept of sexual harassment.

Reproductive freedom continued to be a central tenet of the women's movement, but the legalization of abortion sparked a powerful Right to Life movement and continued legal challenges to *Roe* v. *Wade*. In 1980 the Supreme Court upheld a congressional amendment denying Medicaid funds for abortions for poor women. The 1989 *Webster* v. *Reproductive Health Services* decision permitted states to restrict abortion, and in 1990 the court upheld a federal regulation that forbade personnel at federally funded health clinics from discussing abortion with their clients. In 1992, a 5–4 decision upheld provisions of a Pennsylvania law mandating a 24-hour waiting period and informed-consent requirements. The Court also reaffirmed what it called the "essential holding" of *Roe* v. *Wade*—that women have a constitutional right to abortion—but that right remains hotly contested.

Not all issues of sexuality raised by the women's movement concerned heterosexual women: to paraphrase a popular slogan, "How dare you presume I am heterosexual?" The concerns of lesbians were part of the new attention to sexual issues in the 1960s and 1970s, intersecting both the rising movement for gay pride and the developing feminist analysis of women's situation. As lesbian writer Jill Johnston stated, "Feminism at heart is a massive complaint. Lesbianism is the solution."

The gay liberation movement is usually dated to the 1969 Stonewall riot in New York City, where male patrons of a gay bar fought back when busted by the police. The movement brought new pride and a collective sense to the nation's homosexual men and women who had been forced to live hidden lives "in the closet" by a society that would not tolerate what it defined as deviance. (Not until 1973 did the American Psychiatric Association agree that homosexuality should no longer be listed as a "mental disorder.") Women as well as men were ennobled by this new movement, but lesbians found it difficult to work with gay men, who seemed often to embody the same chauvinistic values shared by the society as a whole. For the most part, lesbians carried on their struggle separately.

The emerging lesbian consciousness was also closely related to the rise of the feminist movement, which gave both gay and straight women a political context for their personal oppression. But this partnership was also troubled, especially in the early 1970s, when lesbianism was seen as a potential embarrassment to feminism. For example, Betty Friedan and the New York chapter of NOW led a purge of the "lavender menace" in 1970. Too many straight feminists were afraid to let go of what Charlotte Bunch called their "heterosexual privilege" (the "actual or promised benefits for the woman who stays in line") and speak out for the concerns of lesbians. In response, a strand of lesbian separatism celebrated biological differences and women's culture within a nationalist framework. Since the mid-1970s there has been less separation between gay and straight women in the movement, in part because lesbians face many of the same problems in employment, housing, credit, and parenting rights as other women. Civil rights laws, however, have not uniformly been extended to protect gay people from discrimination based on sexual preference.

One issue of sexuality that affects both gay and straight women is Acquired Immune Deficiency Syndrome (AIDS), which was first recognized in 1981. Although its earliest victims were predominantly homosexual men, by mid-decade the epidemic was spreading among heterosexuals, especially intravenous drug addicts and their sexual partners, as well as bisexuals. In the early 1990s, the fastest growing category of new AIDS cases was women. Fears about AIDS and other sexually transmitted diseases made the casual experimentation of the 1960s and 1970s less attractive. Widespread public education about safe-sex methods, such as the use of condoms during every sexual act, cut the spread of the disease, but with no cure or vaccine in sight, sexually active men and women will live under the dark threat of AIDS for the foreseeable future.

Sex and the Single Girl

Helen Gurley Brown

The *Playboy* image of swinging bachelors (who were so secure in their heterosexuality that they could never be confused with homosexuals) took root in the 1950s. Women had to wait until the 1960s for their own version of the swinging single life. Not surprisingly, liberated female sexuality proved a much tamer, paler version than the male variety.

This swinging single of the 1960s was in some ways the spiritual granddaughter of the 1920s flapper. She was economically independent (a job was a good place to meet men, and she needed the income to afford her own apartment), fashion conscious (the women's magazines showed her how to dress, and that too took money), and sexually experimental (the birth control pill helped here). Instead of being pitied as a spinster if she had not married by her 20s, these young women with their sophisticated urban lifestyles were seen as desirable and glamorous. In some ways, they served as a deliberate snub to the child-centered lives of suburban housewives, whose lives were anything but glamorous and sexy.

Cosmopolitan editor Helen Gurley Brown played a large role in creating this new image for single women, or as they were called then, girls. Brown used her own example of waiting until age 37 to marry as proof that women could catch the man of their dreams if they pursued the proper strategies. She breathlessly shared her advice in her best-selling *Sex and the Single Girl* (1962), from which these excerpts are drawn. Helen Gurley Brown unabashedly supports the right of a single woman to have an active sex life and does not condemn affairs with married men: "While they are using you to varnish their egos, you're using them to add spice to your life." She offers personality and beauty tips that define women totally in relation to men, all the while bucking up the single woman's spirits by telling her that she has chosen this life because it is where the action is. But despite her disclaimer that the book is about how to stay single in style, *Sex and the Single Girl* is most definitely about how to get married, for the main goal, indeed reward, held out to women for all their efforts is still a wedding ring.

Theoretically a "nice" single woman has no sex life. What nonsense! She has a better sex life than most of her married friends. She need never be bored with one man per lifetime. Her choice of partners is endless and they seek *her*. They never come to her bed duty-bound. Her married friends refer to her pursuers as wolves, but actually many of them turn out to be lambs—to be shorn and worn by her.

Sex of course is more than the act of coitus. It begins with the delicious feeling of attraction between two people. It may never go further, but sex it is. And a single woman may promote the attraction, bask in the sensation, drink it like wine and pour it over her like blossoms, with never a guilty twinge. She can promise with a look, a touch, a letter or a kiss—and she doesn't have to deliver. She can be maddeningly hypocritical and, after arousing desire, insist that it be shut off by stating she wants to be chaste for the man she marries. Her pursuer may strangle her with his necktie, but he can't *argue* with her. A flirtatious married woman is expected to Go Through With Things.

Since for a female getting there is at *least* half the fun, a single woman has reason to prize the luxury of taking long, gossamer, attenuated, pulsating trips before finally arriving in bed. A married woman and her husband have precious little time and energy for romance after they've put the house, animals and children to bed. A married woman with her lover is on an even tighter schedule.

During and after an affair, a single woman suffers emotional stress. Do you think a married woman can bring one off more blissfully free of strain? (One of my close friends, married, committed suicide over a feckless lover. Another is currently in a state of fingernail-biting hysteria.) And I would rather be the other woman than the woman who watches a man *stray* from her.

Yet, while indulging her libido, which she has plenty of if she is young and healthy, it is still possible for the single woman to be a lady, to be highly respected and even envied if she is successful in her work.

I did it. So have many of my friends.

Perhaps this all sounds like bragging. I do not mean to suggest for a moment that being single is not often hell. But I do mean to suggest that it can also be quite heavenly, whether you choose *it* or it chooses *you.*

There is a catch to achieving single bliss. You have to work like a son of a bitch.

But show me the married woman who can loll about and eat cherry bonbons! Hourly she is told by every magazine she reads what she must do to keep her marriage from bursting at the seams. There is no peace for anybody married *or* single unless you do your chores. Frankly, I wouldn't want to make the choice between a married hell or a single hell. They're both hell.

However, serving time as a single woman can give you the foundation for a better marriage if you finally go that route. Funnily enough it also gives you the choice.

What then does it take for a single woman to lead the rich, full life?

Here is what it *doesn't* take.

Great beauty. A man seems not so much attracted to overwhelming beauty as he is just overwhelmed by it—at first. Then he grows accustomed to the face, fabulous as it is, and starts to explore the personality. Now the hidden assets of an *attractive* girl can be as fascinating as the dark side of the moon. Plumbing the depths of a raving beauty may be like plumbing the depths of Saran Wrap.

What it also doesn't take to collect men is money. Have you ever noticed the birds who circle around rich girls? Strictly for the aviary.

You also don't have to be Auntie Mame and electrify everybody with your high-voltage personality. Do *you* like the girl who always grabs the floor to tell what happened to *her* in the elevator? Well neither does anybody else.

And you don't have to be the fireball who organizes bowling teams, gets out the chain letters and makes certain *somebody* gives a shower for the latest bride.

What you do have to do is work with the raw material you have, namely you, and never let up.

If you would like the good single life—since the married life is not just now forthcoming—you can't afford to leave any facet of you unpolished.

You don't have to do anything brassy or show-offy or against your nature. Your most prodigious work will be on *you*—at home. (When I got married, I moved in with six-pound dumbbells, slant board, an electronic device for erasing wrinkles, several pounds of soy lecithin, powdered calcium and yeast-liver concentrate for Serenity Cocktails and enough high-powered vitamins to generate life in a statue.)

Unlike Madame Bovary you don't chase the glittering life, you lay a trap for it. You tunnel up from the bottom.

You *do* need a quiet, private, personal aggression . . . a refusal to take singleness lying down. A sweetly smiling drop-dead attitude for the marrying Sams, and that means *you too.*

You must develop style. Every girl has one . . . it's just a case of getting it out in the open, caring for it and feeding it like an orchid until it leafs out. (One girl is a long-legged, tennis-playing whiz by day, a serene pool at night for friends to drown their tensions in. Wholesomeness is her trademark. A petite brunette is gamine but serious-minded. A knockout in black jersey, she is forever promoting discussions on Stendhal or diminishing colonialism. An intellectual charmer.)

Brains are an asset but it doesn't take brainy brains like a nuclear physicist's. Whatever it is that keeps you from saying anything unkind and keeps you asking bright questions even when you don't quite understand the answers will do nicely. A lively interest in people and things (even if you aren't *that* interested) is why bosses trust you with new assignments, why men talk to you at parties . . . and sometimes ask you on to dinner.

Fashion is your powerful ally. Let the "secure" married girls eschew shortening their skirts (or lengthening them) and wear their classic cashmeres and tweeds until everybody could throw up. You be the girl other girls look at to see what America has copied from Paris.

Roommates are for sorority girls. You need an apartment alone even if it's over a garage.

Your figure can't harbor an ounce of baby fat. It never looked good on anybody but babies.

You must cook well. It will serve you faithfully.

You must have a job that interests you, at which you work hard.

I say "must" about all these things as though you were under orders. You don't have to do anything. I'm just telling you what worked for me.

I'm sure of this. You're not too fat, too thin, too tall, too small, too dumb, or too myopic to have married women gazing at you wistfully.

This then is not a study on how to get married but how to stay single—in superlative style.

Coming Out

Margaret Cruikshank

Gay liberation developed in the supportive climate of the 1960s and 1970s. Because many gay Americans still find it necessary to conceal their sexual preference, there are no totally reliable figures on the numbers of homosexuals and lesbians in the population at large. Figures from the late 1970s suggested that 13.95 percent of males and 4.25 percent of females had extensive homosexual experience; one out of five women had had some overt lesbian experience since puberty. The Kinsey Institute for Sex Research thus concluded in 1977 that "a significant percentage of the American population is predominantly homosexual in its sexual and affectional preference."

The late 1960s and early 1970s did not create an increase in homosexuality: What the period did was to provide a personal and political climate for many gay men and women to recognize and accept their sexual orientation. This process is known as *coming out*. It encompasses the struggle to tell your friends and parents about your sexual orientation and to challenge the homophobia that discriminates against gays in our society. On a more personal level, it means the end of silence, both personal and political, an acceptance of one's self. As one woman asserted, "Coming out to me is much more than expressing another sexual preference. It is finding and developing a whole self-identity and then becoming comfortable with it."

For women, it made a big difference whether they came out before or after the advent of the women's movement. Women who identified as lesbians before the mid-1960s often conceptualized their sexual preference in terms of women physically loving women; after 1970, lesbianism could be seen in the wider political context of feminist ideology. This autobiographical story by Margaret Cruikshank entitled "Is This the Reward of a Catholic Girlhood?" describes her own growing awareness of her sexual preference. As she reminds us, there is not always a "happy" or simple or even feminist ending to these personal and political journeys.

My coming out story is unexciting. If I were to fictionalize it, I would make it sexier and funnier, and assign myself a younger age than 26 and a less staid personality. The other woman, Mary, could keep her real age of 23; that's a good age for coming out.

I met her a few months before her 23rd birthday in a literary criticism class at the midwestern Jesuit school where we were both graduate students who had

Source: Margaret Cruikshank, "Is This the Reward of a Catholic Girlhood?" from *The Coming Out Stories,* edited by Julia Stanley and Susan Wolfe (Watertown: Persephone Press, 1980), pp. 31–35. Reprinted by permission of the author.

National Defense Education Act grants to get Ph.D.'s. Our educations contributed nothing to the national defense, of course; and it was certainly not the intention of the male bureaucrats at H.E.W. to bring young lesbians out of the provinces and into big cities, where they could meet, fall in love, and oppose the Vietnam war together. Left in the small towns where we grew up and dependent only on private enterprise, Mary and I might never have felt free enough to love each other, or any other woman. From my failures to care deeply about a man, I would have concluded that I was not a caring person or someone who belonged in an intimate relationship.

That at least was my suspicion after an experience with a man in 1965, several months before I met Mary and got her to stop sitting in the front row of lit. crit. class like a pious Catholic schoolgirl and to sit with sloppy indifference next to me in the last row. A male friend from my hometown, whom I had met at the Graduate Record Exam (I hope young lesbians are finding each other these days at the GRE), called to announce that he had that day passed his doctoral comprehensives and could now attend to other business—would I marry him? Confused as I was about love, men, and my future, I saw at once that there was something ludicrous about putting emotional life second to intellectual life. But what to say? I didn't love him, but I knew women were supposed to want marriage. Why didn't I? Awkwardness was the main emotion I felt. As potential mates, John and I had lumbered along in a way that reminded me of the Herbert Spencer-George Eliot romance; and, ironically, his dissertation was to be on Spencer, mine on Eliot. I said on the phone that I would send my answer by mail. I remember going to the library to do the letter, probably because I felt safe in libraries and no doubt also because the letter would be like an assignment. With a directness and honesty I hardly ever attained in those days, I told John that I couldn't marry him because I was not physically attracted to him. Thinking of the letter today I feel frustrated because, although I had correctly diagnosed the problem with that relationship, I was blind to the implications of the letter, which seem so obvious now: 1) no man would be sexually attractive to me, except in a casual/temporary way; and 2) I was attracted to women.

Not understanding these crucial facts about myself in 1965, I had no expectation at all, when I began to spend time with Mary, that I could love her. How could I have been so ignorant of this possibility, I wonder now, when two years before the call from John, one of my roommates had fallen in love with me. I obviously couldn't connect one experience with a woman to another. I was attracted to Karla, the roommate, an Irish Catholic from Iowa with a background much like mine. I remember walking by myself one day and getting a thunderous message from my brain *she loves me* which made me stop suddenly as I was crossing the street. But my attention was focused so much on her dilemma (poor Karla—what a rotten thing to happen to her) that I never asked myself what *my* response might be or thought in any general way about women loving women. Soon I had persuaded myself that I was crazed from studying too much—Karla didn't love me. But one night she came to my room late at night, sat on my floor, and looking very embarrassed she said that Marge, the third woman in our apartment, had been making fun of her for loving me. She hoped I would not be angry with her. I wasn't, but I couldn't have been very sensitive, either. All I remember is that our conversation was short and awkward. In the days that followed, although I did not feel love for Karla, I did want some physical contact with her, but I was too inhibited to touch her. One night we got a little drunk together and sat next to each other on the living room couch with our arms around each other. Marge, who was with us but sober, said: "Goddamned lesbians!" I remember thinking, smugly, No, absurd, if we were goddamned lesbians we would have to be doing this in some secret place; we couldn't be hugging right out here in the living room in the presence of another person. This spectacularly false assumption was one I suppose I had to accept: to question it would have led me to uncomfortable thoughts about the significance of all my attachments to women.

The early weeks of close friendship with Mary gave me no clues about what was to follow. We tossed a football around in the park, hung upside down from the jungle gym, and studied hard. After our long talks late at night, I'd walk her back to her apartment and then she'd walk me back to mine. That pattern should have been a clue. The first Superbowl was also her birthday. We watched together in high spirits and then our friends came for a surprise party. I had never liked a woman well enough to plan a party for her, and no one had ever given a party for Mary. Those clues were lost on us, too. Although she asked me to move in with her when her roommate left, we were so far from knowing what was happening between us that we invited a third woman to share the small apartment with us.

Within a month after the move, I realized I cared for Mary very much, but had no idea that my feelings were the appropriate ones for the beginning of a love relationship. I took my two new roommates to a Clancy brothers' concert on St. Patrick's Day, and during the concert I held Mary's hand in the dark. I had never had that experience before. The raucous Clancy's must have loosened me up. Later that evening as Mary and I were taking off our coats in our big walk-in closet, we stood for a long time with our arms around each other. I felt scared and excited at the same time. Hugging a woman through her winter coat is not very satisfying, I now realize, but for someone like me who had hardly ever been able to touch another woman (or a man or a child), this closet cuddling was a great step forward. One night not long after St. Pat's I was sick in bed. Mary sat for a long time on the edge of my bed and then kissed me on the neck (I think she was aiming for my cheek) and ran out of my bedroom. I was overwhelmed. This was even more exciting than holding her hand or feeling her coat. I wanted to be kissed again but was too shy to say so or to kiss her. But one night when she was reading I sat on the floor at her feet and leaned against the chair she was sitting in. She lifted me into the chair with her and we kissed and laughed for about four hours. That we both liked prolonged physical contact was a great discovery. We must have known vaguely that we were doing a forbidden thing, but whatever guilt we bore did not keep us from doing what felt good. We had both had such repulsively successful careers as Catholic schoolgirls and devout young women that we ought to have been guilt-ridden, but somehow we escaped the tortures of a bad conscience. In all their vivid descriptions of the sinful, secular, atheistical world into which they were reluctantly sending us, those of us not good enough to want to imitate them and become nuns, our teachers never mentioned that feeling sexual attraction for another woman was an abomination. At Mary's college, the "mulier fortis" was much lauded (the valiant woman), and at my school, her counterpart was the "dynamic Christian woman." But we were never told that a mulier fortis must refrain from passionately kissing a dynamic Christian woman. Maybe that's why the *sin* button didn't flash red the night I sat in Mary's lap kissing her and knowing that I loved her.

The rest came only gradually. Once when we were doing our Beowulf lesson together, while sitting on the floor not too close to each other, we began to kiss and somehow got wound around each other on the couch, neither of us sure what to do with our bodies. Mary knew enough the next time to touch me with her hand, and I was amazed by the pleasure she could give me. But I was too frightened and self-conscious to touch her until two weeks later when she came home late one night and demanded that pleasure for herself. I was too surprised to refuse (she was not at all a demanding person). After that, our love-making was less inhibited, although often furtive, because of the third woman in our one-bedroom apartment. Luckily she taught an early morning class. As soon as she walked out the door, I would bounce on her bed on my way into Mary's bed. Those were exuberant mornings, and it pleases me to recall that we got the highest grades on the Beowulf exam, too.

We lived together very happily for three years, the last two in our own apartment. During summer vacations we had wonderful times traveling in Mary's Volkswagen. We saw the iron mines in northern Minnesota and walked around on Isle Royale, and watched the Little League world series in Pennsylvania. We got thrown out of a pet cemetery for laughing at the inscriptions on the tombstones, and another time we were stranded in a small town in Scotland and had to sleep in the local jail.

During the school terms we helped each other with teaching (we had the same classes) and with studying. I might not have been able to write a dissertation without Mary's constant reassurances and good suggestions. And for six terrible weeks in 1969 when I was fighting with my department over my dissertation, she plotted my strategy with great cunning, helped me figure out the moves against me, and once when I cracked and decided to go right to the chairman's office and curse him, she literally barred the door and kept me home. She even stood at my side for 2-1/2 hours while I xeroxed the required number of copies of my dissertation for the men who were to sit in judgment of it.

Those days were idyllic. Neither of us pretended to be looking for men to fulfill us. And yet we did not see ourselves as lesbians—the word had vile connotations—as women who had made a conscious choice of a woman to love. I told myself that the person I loved happened to be a woman, and she must have said the same thing to herself. In any case, we had no conversations about lesbians or lesbianism. Perhaps in our happy state we felt no need to reflect on our coming together. As survivors of unhappy families, we must have been relieved and constantly delighted to find ourselves always happy. It would have seemed unnatural, surely, to live together for three years and never mention that we were English teachers or that we loved literature. But a far more basic fact about ourselves (or at least about me), emotional and sexual identity, went unmentioned.

I wish I could end this story on a good lesbian feminist note—perhaps this can't be a *real* coming out story without a good lesbian feminist conclusion. Such as: Peg and Mary discover that they are lesbians, rejoice in the discovery, drive off into the setting sun in the little blue VW, certain to grow more deeply attached to each other, thanks to their raised consciousnesses, and to continue their relationship for many years. Before the discovery and the rejoicing, unfortunately, we separated, without pain, partly because we could not get jobs in the same town and partly because we were ready for a change. But I'm afraid that we separated not really knowing that a female couple could stay together indefinitely, or even that we had in fact been a couple. We had experienced something for which we had no room in our imaginations—an alternative to marriage, a way of living ideally suited to us.

Sex and Sports

Mariah Burton Nelson

Basketball, softball, swimming, tennis, golf—you name the sport, and women love to play it, and play it well. But in very few sports is there gender parity, either on the collegiate or professional level, despite federal laws like the 1972 Title IX of the Civil Rights Act, which forbids gender discrimination in federally funded educational institutions. In 1977 Title IX was extended to cover discrimination in intercollegiate sports. While there have been important breakthroughs for women and girls in organized athletics, they still lag behind men and boys. In 1991 women made up more than half the student population but only one-third of college athletes; women received less than a quarter of athletic budgets and even less for scholarships and recruitment.

Sports may be an American obsession, but once again the focus is on men. One study found that 92 percent of televised sports coverage focused on men, with only 5 percent on women. In newspapers, 81 percent of the coverage was of men's sports and only 3.5 percent of women. Nationwide only 8 percent of sportscasters and broadcasters are female.

One of the most pernicious ways of discouraging women from participating in sports is by implying that there is something unfeminine or sexually deviant about women athletes. Of course, some athletes are gay, but many are not. This stigma of lesbianism is so strong that many female athletes who are gay, especially professionals, remain in the closet for fear of losing sponsors or damaging the image of their sport with the public.

Source: Mariah Burton Nelson, "Paid to Play a Game," which first appeared in *Sportsdykes: Stories from On and Off the Field,* ed. Susan Fox Rogers (New York: St. Martin's Press, 1994), pp. 87–94. Maria Burton Nelson is the author of *The Stronger Women Get, the More Men Love Football.* Reprinted by permission of the author.

Mariah Burton Nelson's story of being fired from the Women's Pro Basketball League for being a lesbian shows the intersection of sexuality and sports. Unlike male college stars who can plan on careers in professional sports, the former captain of Stanford's women's basketball team had a hard time making a living at the sport she loved. Her openness about her sexual orientation made it even tougher. After her basketball career was summarily ended by homophobia, she wrote several hard-hitting books about gender and sports, including *The Stronger Women Get, The More Men Love Football* (1994).

The story of how I got fired from the Women's Pro Basketball League for being a lesbian—which is akin to being fired from the National Basketball League for being black—is the most lucrative and least known story of my athletic career. Lucrative because an earlier version of it was purchased twice: first by what was then called *Women's Sports* magazine, then by *Ms.* magazine. Least known because both magazines "killed" it, citing fears that advertisers would jump ship if the magazines deigned to mention lesbians.

I'll begin the story at the end, or near the end, of my brief stint as a pro basketball player. At San Francisco's Civic Center Plaza, in the summer of 1979, I felt the binocular burn of two eyes staring at me and turned to see who it might be.

There were a lot of possibilities. I was standing among 200,000 other people. The Gay Pride Parade had just marched peacefully through San Francisco, and now we were gathered at Civic Center Plaza to listen to music, hear speeches, and express sorrow and outrage at the recent murder of supervisor Harvey Milk. I was standing to the left of the stage, swaying happily to the music of Linda Tillery. Turning, I scanned the crowd for familiar faces. Finally, I saw on a raised media platform, a television reporter who knew me, and waved weakly. My career as a professional athlete flashed before my eyes.

Just a week or two before, the reporter had interviewed me for a television spot about professional women. In 1979, even female lawyers and bankers were newsworthy, but as a female pro basketball player I was a particular anomaly. During the interview, the reporter posed some antagonistic questions typical of that era (and, unfortunately, still typical of this era): Does playing basketball threaten your femininity? Do you have a boyfriend? Do the men in your life approve of your playing basketball?

"No, basketball doesn't threaten my femininity," I told him, adding pointedly, "but it does seem to threaten some men." I was young (twenty-three), angry, and emboldened by the lesbian and feminist environment in which I had come of age. To the question about male approval I said curtly, "All of my friends approve of my playing basketball or they wouldn't be my friends."

I didn't come out to him because I hadn't come out to my coach on the San Francisco Pioneers, and didn't intend to. The coach had clued me in by telling me our uniforms were made by "a bunch of faggots." He also insisted on calling us girls, though we asked to be called women. "This is a business, not a women's lib thing," he said bluntly. Later in the season, at a home game, a group from Berkeley unfurled a large banner reading "Lesbians Against Police Violence"; the security guards made them take it down. All of the owners and coaches in the Women's Pro Basketball League were men. Evidently it was *not* a women's lib thing.

But Gay Day had become a four-year tradition I was not willing to forego. When, at nineteen, I came out of the closet, I came roaring out, waving banners and carrying torches and making a spectacle of myself. Within months of beginning a relationship with Stephanie, a basketball teammate, I was speaking to high school classes about the joys of being a lesbian. Stephanie founded a Gay Counseling Center on campus. None of this seemed to bother our Stanford coaches, who let us room together on road trips, or our teammates, many of whom, one-by-one and two-by-two, came out themselves.

The gay liberation movement was in its pre-AIDS, giddy, innocent infancy. Anita Bryant had lambasted homosexuals but we lambasted back until the orange juice company dropped her as a spokesperson and she retracted her homophobic comments. The Briggs Initiative proposed firing all of California's gay teachers as well as straight teachers who publicly supported gay colleagues; voters defeated the bill.

I devoured books: *Rubyfruit Jungle, Sappho Was a Right-On Woman.* I discovered, preserved on microfilm at the Stanford library, issues of *The Ladder,* the lesbian newspaper from the fifties, and made it the subject of a paper for a women's history class.

Feminism, even more than the gay movement, validated my life-long observations and my rage. With great glee I read books by Robin Morgan, Toni Morrison, Marge Piercy, and Susan Brownmiller. I joined a consciousness-raising group. I helped organize a women's film festival and taught a course called Women and Body Image.

On my embroidered jeans jacket one button proclaimed, "A Woman Without a Man Is Like a Fish Without a Bicycle," another said, "Teenage Lesbian," and a third, a small red one, announced: "I'm menstruating."

In these heady days it seemed natural to me that sports teams—groups of strong women who enjoy their own bodies and each other's—would provide an outlet for my feelings of empowerment and love for women. In high school, I had played on a predominantly lesbian basketball team that traveled throughout the southwest. During one car caravan from Phoenix to Gallup, New Mexico, the VW bug I was riding in repeatedly played just one cassette tape: Helen Reddy's "I Am Woman."

For three years at Stanford I was the team captain, and its leading scorer and rebounder. I felt loved and respected, almost revered. In my bedroom I hung a poster that showed women swimming, running, and cycling. "Women in Sports," it said: "We Can."

Yet even before that fateful Gay Pride Day, I had been rudely awakened to the fact that women's sports were not always the lesbian/feminist mecca I wanted them to be. At a summer basketball camp during college I had been the victim of a witch hunt. A group of fourteen-year-old campers accused dozens of counselors of lesbian atrocities, primarily public kissing and fondling. My alleged crime was showering with another counselor. There were details: I had supposedly spread soap suds all over her body. It sounded like fun, but inappropriate, and I didn't do it. I was horrified at having to explain to the camp directors that, though I was gay, I had not committed the crime. To their credit, the directors—themselves closeted lesbians—ultimately gathered all the campers and counselors and lectured them sternly: "If you're going to be in sports, you're going to have to learn to get along with lesbians."

After Stanford I was drafted by the New Jersey Gems of the fledgling (and short-lived) Women's Pro Basketball League, and also by le C.U.C. (pronounced "Le Kook"), a French pro team that traveled throughout Europe. Let's see: France or New Jersey? The decision was not difficult.

But in France I discovered, much to my horror, that I was not the best basketball player in the world. The fall from Stanford star to foreign sub was a steep, miserable descent. Because of a quirk in the French rules, once I was designated backup center I was not even allowed to dress for about half of the games. I'd watch glumly from the bleachers, adding a sad, self-pitying voice to the singsong cheers: *"Allez, les filles."* (Go, girls.) My teammates began to resent my relatively high paycheck, and told me so. I further offended them by not shaving my legs, not eating meat, and not drinking wine. To make matters worse, the woman I fell in love with—the starting center—informed me that she was in love with me too, but Jesus would not approve. She then refused to speak to me.

Eight months later, when I arrived back in the States, the New Jersey Gems still "owned the rights" to me—meaning I could not play for any other pro team until they sold those rights. I agreed to play the last third of the season with them on the condition that I be traded to San Francisco the following year.

In New Jersey I began to recover my athletic self-esteem. Yet my last paycheck—for $1000—bounced. And the gay players would not talk openly. When I asked, two specifically denied their relationship, making me feel slightly crazy as well as angry and isolated.

So it had dawned on me that the "real world" was not going to embrace me as lovingly as idyllic Stanford had. When I saw the television reporter, and saw that he'd seen me, it occurred to me to call him up and ask him not to tell my coach that I'd been at Gay Pride Day. But the contradiction of showing up at Gay Pride Day, then diving into the closet was too great, so I didn't call.

Three weeks into the regular season, I was fired. (They call it being put on waivers, which means that another team is free to buy your contract, but basically you're out of a job.)

"Why?" I asked the coach. I was shocked. I had been playing with confidence, and had expected to start at center.

He looked surprised. "You're not tall enough," he said after a moment's thought.

I stared at him incredulously. "I'm the tallest person on the team!" I protested. Two teammates were exactly my height; no one on the team was taller.

"Oh. Then you're not quick enough," he said lamely.

I learned from a teammate who was close to the coach that the reporter had indeed told the owner of the Pioneers (I never quite got used to calling him "my owner") about my appearance at Gay Pride Day. I had not mentioned the incident to the player, and she had no other way of knowing about it. She responded to me sympathetically but made a mad dash for the closet herself, immediately introducing a "fiancé" to the team.

About half of my teammates, I estimate (including the two tall ones), and at least half of the players in the league were gay. But no others were politically active.

One gay friend was fired along with me; I think they thought we were lovers. When the two of us walked out of the gym that day, into the unusually bright San Francisco sunshine, I was in a stupor. My friend led me to a cafe, where she alternately told chatty, cheerful stories and ranted against the stupidity of our coach. She was already in graduate school, and was to some extent relieved at the prospect of not spending so much time in gyms. She hadn't been enjoying the serious, stifling atmosphere of the professional sports scene. She didn't particularly mind an early departure.

I was devastated. I had thought I'd play in the U.S. pros for at least a year or two, and had given up a shot at the Olympic team with that in mind. I clung to the same dream that led so many naive young women to postpone other careers and to accept bad coaching and bounced checks during that three-year life of the WBL: continuing to play the game we so loved. France had been a disappointment, New Jersey a brief redemption. I wanted more. A Stanford graduate with a psychology degree, I nevertheless had no other career plans.

For three days, I lay in my bed in shock. I was unable to move, unable to feel. I didn't cry. I just lay there. Teammates kindly came by to visit, and for them I lugubriously hauled myself out of bed and into the living room, where I thudded into a beanbag chair. They treated me as if somebody had died.

Two local feminist newspapers learned of the firing but I refused to talk to them, fearing further repercussions. Though I hated the idea of being closeted, my passion for basketball temporarily won out.

Finally my agent called: the California Dreams, of Los Angeles, had invited me to try out. I didn't feel particularly excited. Still depressed, I did not want to move to smoggy L.A. After almost a year in France and New Jersey, I wanted to be home, and because of Stanford, home had become the San Francisco Bay Area. Nevertheless, this opportunity was knocking, and no one else was at the door.

Relinquishing a then-precious symbol of feminism, I bought a razor and shaved my legs. This token attempt at conformity failed when, at the first day of practice with the Dreams, an old friend called across the gym: "I can't believe you shaved your legs!"

Almost immediately, the Dreams sent us to John Robert Powers Charm School. Their intention, of course, was to teach us to portray a feminine (that is, heterosexual) image. Leg-shaving I could do; charm school I could not, so I quietly boycotted, but my teammates reported that they learned such useful skills as how to walk upstairs sideways.

Then, just when I was getting used to the idea of living in L.A., the coach arrived at my door and asked to speak to me alone. I was sharing the apartment with
other players, so I invited him into my bedroom. There we sat stiffly on the twin
beds, facing each other. "I'm sorry to tell you this," he said kindly, "but we've
traded you to the Dallas Diamonds."

"Why?" I asked.

He explained that they needed to let go of one center, and the others had no-
cut, no-trade contracts. "I'm sorry," he said again.

I stared at him dumbly. I did not want to go to Dallas. With no warning, all
the tears I'd held back in France, and New Jersey, and San Francisco, came pour-
ing out. Great, heaving sobs shook my body, and when I tried to speak, the words
were muffled through uncontrollable gasps. Uncomfortable, naturally, the coach
stayed with me, not touching me or trying to comfort me, which would have only
heightened my embarrassment, but simply sitting on the opposite bed, listening.
Thankful for his kindness, I tried to explain that my tears weren't really about
these particular California Dreams—they were about a larger dream, and larger
losses, and a simple desire to be home. I wanted to tell him more—about the
woman I'd loved in France, the Gay Pride Day, the "faggot" remark. This desire
to talk to someone—even a man I'd only known for a few weeks—made me realize that I was terribly lonely.

But once I regained my composure, I agreed to go to Dallas. Homesickness
and loneliness aside, I still had that dream. "What the heck," I told the coach, drying my face and beginning to laugh at my outburst, "It'll be an adventure."

In Dallas I shared a two-bedroom apartment with Michelle and Valerie, who
knitted, watched a lot of television, ate Spaghetti-O's, and carried Bibles in their
gym bags. One of them generously offered me what had been her bedroom. "Valerie and I will sleep together until you find your own place," she told me.

I believed that ruse until I woke up in the middle of the first night freezing. It
was November in Dallas—cold—and the bed was made with just one thin blanket. Clearly no one had slept in it for months.

The Diamonds wanted me to stay but didn't want to pay my moving expenses. Instead of sending me to San Francisco to get my things, they wanted me
to wait until we flew there for a game two months hence. I was still living out of
the gym bag I'd brought to Los Angeles nearly a month before. Rather than turn
the matter over to my agent, I pointed out to the owner that under the terms of the
contract, the Diamonds were obligated to pay the expenses. He then put me on
waivers, explaining that I was "too aggressive off the court."

And so it was that my life as a professional athlete ignominiously came to an
end. This time there were no tears. I felt as if I had been released from bondage.
My agent soon informed me that the New Orleans team was interested, but I told
her that I wasn't. I had run out of tolerance for men who called us girls, for ignorant reporters, for gay teammates who hid behind Bibles, for coaches and owners
who seemed threatened by outspoken women. Also, after years of jumping, running, and pivoting, my knees were very sore and, as it turns out, permanently
damaged. On the flight home to San Francisco from Dallas, I promised my knees

I would quit. Then, as I began to imagine life beyond basketball, my spirits began to lift.

For one season I coached the junior varsity at a local high school, a job I enjoyed tremendously, but the varsity coach, herself a lesbian, made it a condition of employment that I not come out to the girls. A college coach—yet another closeted lesbian—invited me to interview with her after that, but I declined.

I turned instead to writing—a lifelong dream predating basketball—where, as in the case of the two "killed" versions of this story, I still sometimes feel stifled by homophobes. But publishers are increasingly making way for the voices of openly lesbian authors, and in my books I've been able to integrate my passions for women's sports, for women's rights, and for women. I was also recently hired to coach high school girls basketball, which makes me one of the first openly lesbian coaches in the country. I hope to write a book about that too. It's become clear to me that sport, with its physical empowerment and lesbian potential, is an inherently feminist act. Another feminist act is telling the truth. I'm doing my best to combine the two.

Becoming La Mujer

Marissa Navarro

For many Mexican-American young women, growing up means trying to live up to familial and community ideals of being a good *hijita,* or good daughter. In addition to working hard, respecting one's elders, and doing well in school, young Chicanas and Tejanas have to navigate the minefield of sexuality. Influenced by the strong cultural dichotomy that divides women into Madonnas and whores, young women struggle to find ways to express their sexuality that do not make them a slut in the eyes of their families and communities or, alternatively, deny them sexual experience entirely. As Marissa Navarro says in this piece about her own sexual coming of age in a middle-class Mexican-American family from Los Angeles, "I needed only to keep my legs tightly locked, and everything would be all right."

Issues of Chicana sexuality grow more complex when lesbianism is introduced into the equation. Coming out often meant initially being estranged from Chicanos and Chicana heterosexuals. As noted writer Cherrie Moraga revealed, "My lesbianism is the avenue through which I have learned the most about silence and oppression." In the 1980s and 1990s, the increased acceptance of noted Chicana lesbian writers such as Moraga, Gloria Anzaldúa (see Chapter 13), Emma Perez, and Ana Castillo brought more cultural acceptance for different sexual orientations within Mexican-American communities and helped to create public and private spaces where Chicanas could affirmatively embrace this choice. Political organizing and caucusing followed as well, such as the 1987 founding of LLEGO, The National Latina

Source: © 1998, 2000 by Marisa Navarro. Excerpted from her essay "Becoming *La Mujer,*" reprinted from *Body Outlaws: Young Women Write About Body Image and Identity,* edited by Ophira Edut and reprinted by permission of Seal Press.

and Latino Lesbian and Gay Organization. But as noted Chicana scholar Vicki Ruiz observes, "The stories of Mexicana/Chicana lesbians have only begun to be told."

Marisa Navarro's story is only in small part a coming out story. It also deals with issues central to women's complicated relationship to their bodies, issues of color consciousness within the Mexican-American community, standards of dress and appearance, and relationships. When she went away to college, she finally came to accept who she had become: *la mujer.*

I used to dream that Superwoman would fly into my life, her legs unshaven and her hair cropped short. She would swoop me up and take me somewhere that made me feel safe and beautiful—a place far from the hell I knew as public high school. In this distant place, I would feel sensual for the first time ever, without feeling dirty. No one would assume I was destined to be a teenage mom, or that my brown skin marked me as a criminal. I wouldn't be "too dark" or "too fat," and my intelligence would never be compromised.

Those were ambitious goals for a Mexican-American girl growing up near East Los Angeles. Every year, the drill team girl had a kid, then the prom queen. Pregnancy was so common it was almost a game to guess who the next teenage mother would be. Still, East L.A. is the only place I've lived where the scent of Aqua Net and overprocessed hair mingles with the sounds of English, Spanish, Chinese, Korean and Armenian. There was comfort in being surrounded by hundreds of other brown people. I missed that when I went away to college and found my skin color and dark hair made me stand out in class.

I was one of the fortunate at my high school, shielded from some of Los Angeles's harshness by college prep classes. My parents stressed education all my life, so I focused on earning good grades, hoping they would be my ticket to a better life. But there was a price to pay. Since many of my female classmates wouldn't make it to graduation (pregnancy or lack of interest leading them to drop out), girls' actions became dichotomized into right and wrong. There were "good girls" (those who went to college) and "bad girls" (teenage mothers on welfare).

Early on, my parents reinforced that message, and there could be no margin of error. "It's out of love we tell you this, *mijita,*" they'd say. "Be quiet. Study hard. Don't have sex. Go to college, and then get married. A good daughter doesn't dress like a slut. A good daughter doesn't pierce or tattoo herself. A good daughter doesn't rock the boat." If I messed up, my whole future would be over. I must be a good *hijita.*

My parents also grew up in East L.A. I never told them what I faced at school, but I'm sure they knew. That made the parental leash even tighter. As an immigrant (my dad) and a first-generation American (my mom), they stressed hard work and success at any cost. It's a drive I don't think any person who is fourth-generation American or beyond can fully understand. Perhaps it's the stigma of the accent fresh in the memory, the blunter racism and the hard labor not even a distant memory. Either way, it fuels parents' determination that their children will not be like them.

In my family, being a good *hijita* meant more than simply being an obedient daughter. It also meant being desexualized. Being of mind but not of body. Wrapped in that word were my parents hopes for me—and for themselves. I was to transcend the racism they'd experienced and to surpass society's low expectations.

My father was the success story in the family, and he was proud of it. He came from a small town in Mexico, graduated from college in the United States and made lots of money. Somehow, my sister and I had to do even better than he had. On top of being supernaturally smart, we had to fulfill his macho idea of sensuality, a classic Madonna/whore tightrope that demanded we be attractive yet pure. We were expected to be skinny, have long hair and wear clothes that showed our womanliness. Yet, we had to carry this off in a way that let men know we were unavailable for sex.

Sex was the biggest threat to my parents' carefully laid plans. Having sex meant I'd impede my chances to succeed, to achieve an American dream greater than the one offered to my parents. It meant I'd inevitably get pregnant and become a statistic, trapped in a community that was slowly falling apart. My body (and what I did with it) could make or break our family's future. The concept of the body as a battleground had much more meaning than even the most radical feminist could conceive. I needed only to keep my legs tightly locked, and everything would be all right.

Eventually, the word *hijita* left a sour taste in my mouth. It meant I was my parents' daughter. I didn't belong to me . . .

I left Los Angeles for Smith College in Northampton, Massachusetts, knowing the distance of a thousand miles had to release the parental leash. I wanted the power to create my identity, a power that I didn't have before. I purposely chose a women's college because I knew I needed time away from men.

School saved my mind and body. In college, I wasn't anyone's *hijita,* and I wouldn't be anyone's slut. I was able to come out of the closet, first to myself and a year later to everyone else. Women told me I was smart and beautiful; neither quality was ever questioned. When I took up smoking and drinking, I wasn't a bad *hijita.* Good and bad vanished, and I was *la mujer.* That phrase sounded beautiful and empowering to me . . .

In the end, no Superfeminist ever flew in from the sky to save me. It took me years to realize that nobody else could rescue me. I didn't have to be a superhero. I just had to allow myself to become *la mujer.*

Women and Disabilities

Nancy Mairs

Until recently, very few people—and even fewer women—talked openly about the issue of disability. But that silence began to change in the 1980s, led in part by groundbreaking anthologies such as Marsha Saxton and Florence Howe's edited anthology *With Wings* (1987), which was devoted to literature by and about women living with disabilities or other physical limitations. The disability rights movement, itself a product of the same forces that had spawned the civil rights movement, second-wave feminism, gay rights, and other movements of identity politics since the 1960s, counted a major legislative victory in 1990 with the passage of the Americans with Disabilities Act, which barred discrimination against people with physical or mental disabilities.

All people coping with disabilities suffer widespread discrimination in employment, housing, access, and personal relationships, but women with disabilities face the additional burdens associated with discrimination based on sex. Disabled women earn only 52 percent of what nondisabled women earn, which puts them even further behind able-bodied men. Just like women's contributions in general, disabled women's skills are often minimized or overlooked; disabled women often suffer serious self-esteem problems as they deal with stigma and stereotypes, like the supposed asexuality of all disabled people, despite evidence of those who have been able to maintain relationships and bear and raise children. And yet when many women reflect on their diseases or disabilities, they find that they feel strong, capable, and proud of the lives they are leading. In other words, they don't feel like victims.

In this selection, Nancy Mairs discusses with both insight and humor what it is like to have multiple sclerosis (MS), a chronic degenerative disease of the central nervous system for which there is not yet a cure. The title of her essay, "On Being a Cripple," shows how she identifies herself—she enjoys the shock, the slap in the face, that the word conveys, as opposed to more neutral terms like disabled, handicapped, or the hated "differently abled." Her essay conveys both the normality of the life that she leads and the special challenges that she faces every day. Nancy Mairs has taught women's studies and writing at the University of Arizona and UCLA and is the author of *Plaintext* (1986) and *Voice Lessons: Becoming a (Woman) Writer* (1994).

The other day I was thinking of writing an essay on being a cripple. I was thinking hard in one of the stalls of the women's room in my office building, as I was shoving my shirt into my jeans and tugging up my zipper. Preoccupied, I flushed, picked up my book bag, took my cane down from the hook, and unlatched the door. So many movements unbalanced me, and as I pulled the door open I fell over backward, landing fully clothed on the toilet seat with my legs splayed in front of me: the old beetle-on-its-back routine. Saturday afternoon, the building deserted, I was free to laugh aloud as I wriggled back to my feet, my voice bouncing off the yellowish tiles from all directions. Had anyone been there with me, I'd have been still and faint and hot with chagrin.

I decided that it was high time to write the essay.

Source: Excerpt from *Plaintext* by Nancy Mairs. Copyright © 1986 The Arizona Board of Regents. Reprinted by permission of the University of Arizona Press.

First, the matter of semantics. I am a cripple. I choose this word to name me. I choose from among several possibilities, the most common of which are *handicapped* and *disabled*. I made the choice a number of years ago, without thinking, unaware of my motives for doing so. Even now, I'm not sure what those motives are, but I recognize that they are complex and not entirely flattering. People— crippled or not—wince at the word *cripple,* as they do not at *handicapped* or *disabled*. Perhaps I want them to wince. I want them to see me as a tough customer, one to whom the fates/gods/viruses have not been kind, but who can face the brutal truth of her existence squarely. As a cripple, I swagger.

But, to be fair to myself, a certain amount of honesty underlies my choice. *Cripple* seems to me a clean word, straightforward and precise. It has an honorable history, having made its first appearance in the Lindisfarne Gospel in the tenth century. As a lover of words, I like the accuracy with which it describes my condition: I have lost the full use of my limbs. *Disabled,* by contrast, suggests any incapacity, physical or mental. And I certainly don't like *handicapped,* which implies that I have deliberately been put at a disadvantage, by whom I can't imagine (my God is not a Handicapper General), in order to equalize chances in the great race of life. These words seem to me to be moving away from my condition, to be widening the gap between word and reality. Most remote is the recently coined euphemism *differently abled,* which partakes of the same semantic hopefulness that transformed countries from *undeveloped* to *underdeveloped,* then to *less developed,* and finally to *developing* nations. People have continued to starve in those countries during the shift. Some realities do not obey the dictates of language.

Mine is one of them. Whatever you call me, I remain crippled. But I don't care what I am called, as long as it isn't *differently abled,* which strikes me as pure verbal garbage designed, by its ability to describe anyone, to describe no one. I subscribe to George Orwell's thesis that "the sloppiness of our language makes it easier for us to have foolish thoughts." And I refuse to participate in the degeneration of the language to the extent that I deny that I have lost anything in the course of this calamitous disease; I refuse to pretend that the only differences between you and me are the various ordinary ones that distinguish any one person from another. But call me *disabled* or *handicapped* if you like. I have long since grown accustomed to them; and if they are vague, at least they hint at the truth. Moreover, I use them myself. Society is no readier to accept crippledness than to accept death, war, sex, sweat, or wrinkles. I would never refer to another person as a cripple. It is the word I use to name only myself.

I haven't always been crippled, a fact for which I am soundly grateful. To be whole of limb is, I know from experience, infinitely more pleasant and useful than to be crippled; and if that knowledge leaves me open to bitterness at my loss, the physical soundness I once enjoyed (though I did not enjoy it half enough) is well worth the occasional stab of regret. Though never any good at sports, I was a normally active child and young adult. I climbed trees, played hopscotch, jumped rope, skated, swam, rode my bicycle, sailed. I despised team sports, spending some of the most wretched afternoons of my life, sweaty and humiliated, behind a field-hockey stick and under a basketball hoop. I tramped alone for miles along the bridle paths that webbed the woods behind the house I grew up in. I swayed through countless dim hours in the arms of one man or another under the scattered shot of light from mirrored balls, and gyrated through countless more as Tab Hunter and Johnny Mathis gave way to the Rolling Stones, Creedence Clearwater Revival, Cream. I walked down the aisle. I pushed baby carriages, changed tires in the rain, marched for peace.

When I was twenty-nine, I started to trip and drop things. What at first seemed my natural clumsiness soon became too pronounced to shrug off. I consulted a neurologist, who told me that I had a brain tumor. A battery of tests, increasingly disagreeable, revealed no tumor. About a year and a half later I developed a blurred spot in one eye. I had, at last, the episodes "disseminated in space and time" requisite for a diagnosis: multiple sclerosis. I have never been sorry for the doctor's initial misdiagnosis, however. For almost a week, until the negative results of the tests were in, I thought that I was going to die right away. Every day for the past nearly ten years, then, has been a kind of gift. I accept all gifts . . .

I lead, on the whole, an ordinary life, probably rather like the one I would have led had I not had MS. I am lucky that my predilections were already solitary, sedentary, and bookish—unlike the world-famous French cellist I have read about, or the young woman I talked with one long afternoon who wanted only to be a jockey. I had just begun graduate school when I found out something was wrong with me, and I have remained—interminably—a graduate student. Perhaps I would not have if I'd thought I had the stamina to return to a full-time job as a technical editor; but I've enjoyed my studies.

In addition to studying, I teach writing courses. I also teach medical students how to give neurological examinations. I pick up free-lance editing jobs here and there. I have raised a foster son and sent him into the world, where he has made me two grandbabies, and I am still escorting my daughter and son through adolescence. I go to mass every Saturday. I am a superb, if messy, cook. I am also an enthusiastic laundress, capable of sorting a hamper full of clothes into five subtly differentiated piles, but a terrible housekeeper. I can do italic writing and, in an emergency, bathe an oil-soaked cat. I play a fiendish game of Scrabble. When I have the time and the money, I like to sit on my front steps with my husband, drinking Amaretto and smoking a cigar, as we imagine our counterparts in Leningrad and make sure that the sun gets down once more behind the sharp childish scrawl of the Tucson mountains.

This lively plenty has its bleak complement, of course, in all the things I can no longer do. I will never run again, except in dreams, and one day I may have to write that I will never walk again. I like to go camping, but I can't follow George and the children along the trails that wander out of a campsite through the desert or into the mountains. In fact, even on the level I've learned never to check the weather or try to hold a coherent conversation: I need all my attention for my wayward feet. Of late, I have begun to catch myself wondering how people can propel themselves without canes. With only one usable hand, I have to select my clothing with care not so much for style as for ease of ingress and egress, and even so, dressing can be laborious. I can no longer do fine stitchery, pick up babies, play the piano, braid my hair. I am immobilized by acute attacks of depression, which may or may not be physiologically related to MS but are certainly its logical concomitant . . .

Like many women I know, I have always had an uneasy relationship with my body. I was not a popular child, largely, I think now, because I was peculiar: intelligent, intense, moody, shy, given to unexpected actions and inexplicable notions and emotions. But as I entered adolescence, I believed myself unpopular because I was homely: my breasts too flat, my mouth too wide, my hips too narrow, my clothing never quite right in fit or style. I was not, in fact, particularly ugly, old photographs inform me, though I was well off the ideal; but I carried this sense of self-alienation with me into adulthood, where it regenerated in response to the depredations of MS. Even with my brace I walk with a limp so pronounced that, seeing myself on the videotape of a television program on the disabled, I couldn't believe that anything but an inchworm could make progress humping along like that. My shoulders droop and my pelvis thrusts forward as I try to balance myself upright, throwing my frame into a bony S. As a result of contractures, one shoulder is higher than the other and I carry one arm bent in front of me, the fingers curled into a claw. My left arm and leg have wasted into pipe-stems, and I try always to keep them covered. When I think about how my body must look to others, especially to men, to whom I have been trained to display myself, I feel ludicrous, even loathsome.

At my age, however, I don't spend much time thinking about my appearance. The burning egocentricity of adolescence, which assures one that all the world is looking all the time, has passed, thank God, and I'm generally too caught up in what I'm doing to step back, as I used to, and watch myself as though upon a stage. I'm also too old to believe in the accuracy of self-image. I know that I'm not a hideous crone, that in fact, when I'm rested, well dressed, and well made up, I look fine. The self-loathing I feel is neither physically nor intellectually substantial. What I hate is not me but a disease.

I am not a disease . . .

All the same, if a cure were found, would I take it? In a minute. I may be cripple, but I'm only occasionally a loony and never a saint. Anyway, in my brand of theology God doesn't give bonus points for a limp. I'd take a cure; I just don't need one. A friend who also has MS startled me once by asking, "Do you ever say to yourself, 'Why me, Lord?'" "No, Michael, I don't," I told him, "because whenever I try, the only response I can think of is 'Why not?'" If I could make a cosmic deal, who would I put in my place? What in my life would I give up in exchange for sound limbs and a thrilling rush of energy? No one. Nothing. I might as well do the job myself. Now that I'm getting the hang of it.

The Voice of an Anorexic

Abra Fortune Chernik

In the 1980s and 1990s, excessive dieting and an obsession with thinness seemed so prevalent on college campuses that the media talked about an epidemic of eating disorders and how young American women were literally "at risk." As historian Joan Jacobs Brumberg has shown in *Fasting Girls: The Emergence of Anorexia Nervosa as a Modern Disease* (1988), anorexia had its cultural roots in Victorian America, long before the current cultural obsession with thinness. But broad social pressures, such as widespread dieting and widely dispersed media images of what women are supposed to look like, have made the disease much more prevalent today.

Public awareness of eating disorders, often first called the "starving disease," began to rise in the 1970s; when popular singer Karen Carpenter died of complications from the disease in 1983 at the age of 32, images of her emaciated body were widely disseminated in magazines such as *People.* The media often lumped together *anorexia nervosa* (literally "loss of appetite," or self-starving) and *bulimia* (binging on huge amounts of calories, then purging the body through vomiting or laxatives). Like the AIDS epidemic, it is a rare American family that does not know someone who has been touched by an eating disorder.

Abra Fortune Chernik's description of her battle against anorexia confirms the uneasy relationship that many women today have with their bodies. Her whole life was defined by what she ate and how much she weighed, and while she thought that she was gaining control over her body, in fact her eating disorder was taking control of her. Only after three months of hospitalization and two years of outpatient psychotherapy did she learn to accept her body as it was; she now shares her insights with audiences on college campuses, lecture tours, and in a screenplay she has written on the subject. But what about young women who can't afford treatment or don't respond? And what about the rest of us, who while not technically suffering from an eating disorder, still hate our bodies and believe that life would be better if we weighed 10 pounds less? Abra Fortune Chernik is one of the lucky ones.

Growing up in New York City, I did not care about the feminist movement. Although I attended an all-girls high school, we read mostly male authors and studied the history of men. Embracing mainstream culture without question, I learned about womanhood from fashion magazines, Madison Avenue and Hollywood. I dismissed feminist alternatives as foreign and offensive, swathed as they were in stereotypes that threatened my adolescent need for conformity.

Puberty hit late; I did not complain. I enjoyed living in the lanky body of a tall child and insisted on the title of "girl." If anyone referred to me as a "young woman," I would cry out, horrified, "Do not call me the *W* word!" But at sixteen

years old, I could no longer deny my fate. My stomach and breasts rounded. Curly
black hair sprouted in the most embarrassing places. Hips swelled from a once-
flat plane. Interpreting maturation as an unacceptable lapse into fleshiness, I resolved to eradicate the physical symptoms of my impending womanhood.

Magazine articles, television commercials, lunchroom conversation, gym-
nastics coaches and write-ups on models had saturated me with diet savvy. Once
I decided to lose weight, I quickly turned expert. I dropped hot chocolate from my
regular breakfast order at the Skyline Diner. I replaced lunches of peanut butter
and Marshmallow Fluff sandwiches with small platters of cottage cheese and can-
taloupe. I eliminated dinner altogether and blunted my appetite with Tab, Camel
Lights, and Carefree bubble gum. When furious craving overwhelmed my resolve
and I swallowed an extra something, I would flee to the nearest bathroom to purge
my mistake.

Within three months, I had returned my body to its preadolescent proportions
and had manipulated my monthly period into drying up. Over the next five years,
I devoted my life to losing my weight. I came to resent the body in which I lived,
the body that threatened to develop, the body whose hunger I despised but could
not extinguish. If I neglected a workout or added a pound or ate a bite too many, I
would stare in the mirror and drown myself in a tidal wave of criticism. Hatred of
my body generalized to hatred of myself as a person, and self-referential labels
such as "pig," "failure" and "glutton" allowed me to believe that I deserved punishment. My self-hatred became fuel for the self-mutilating behaviors of the eating disorder.

As my body shrank, so did my world. I starved away my power and vision,
my energy and inclinations. Obsessed with dieting, I allowed relationships, passions and identity to wither. I pulled back from the world, off of the beach, out of
the sand. The waves of my existence ceased to roll beyond the inside of my skin.

And society applauded my shrinking. Pound after pound the applause continued, like the pounding ocean outside the door of my beach house.

The word "anorexia" literally means "loss of appetite." But as an anorexic, I
felt hunger thrashing inside my body. I denied my appetite, ignored it, but never
lost it. Sometimes the pangs twisted so sharply, I feared they would consume the
meat of my heart. On desperate nights I rose in a flannel nightgown and allowed
myself to eat an unplanned something.

No matter how much I ate, I could not soothe the pangs. Standing in the
kitchen at midnight, spotlighted by the blue-white light of the open refrigerator, I
would frantically feed my neglected appetite: the Chinese food I had not touched
at dinner; ice cream and whipped cream; microwaved bread; cereal and chocolate
milk; doughnuts and bananas. Then, solid sadness inside my gut, swelling agitation, a too-big meal I would not digest. In the bathroom I would rip off my shirt,
tie up my hair, and prepare to execute the desperate ritual, again. I would ram the
back of my throat with a toothbrush handle, crying, impatient, until the food
rushed up. I would vomit until the toilet filled and I emptied, until I forgave myself, until I felt ready to try my life again. Standing up from my position over the
toilet, wiping my mouth, I would believe that I was safe. Looking in the mirror

through puffy eyes in a tumescent face, I would promise to take care of myself. Kept awake by the fast, confused beating of my heart and the ache in my chest, I would swear I did not miss the world outside. Lost within myself, I almost died.

By the time I entered the hospital, a mess of protruding bones defined my body, and the bones of my emaciated life rattled me crazy. I carried a pillow around because it hurt to sit down, and I shivered with cold in sultry July. Clumps of brittle hair clogged the drain when I showered, and blackened eyes appeared to sink into my head. My vision of reality wrinkled and my disposition turned mercurial as I slipped into starvation psychosis, a condition associated with severe malnutrition. People told me that I resembled a concentration camp prisoner, a chemotherapy patient, a famine victim or a fashion model.

In the hospital, I examined my eating disorder under the lenses of various therapies. I dissected my childhood, my family structure, my intimate relationships, my belief systems. I participated in experiential therapies of movement, art and psychodrama. I learned to use words instead of eating patterns to communicate my feelings. And still I refused to gain more than a minimal amount of weight.

I felt powerful as an anorexic. Controlling my body yielded an illusion of control over my life; I received incessant praise for my figure despite my sickly mien, and my frailty manipulated family and friends into protecting me from conflict. I had reduced my world to a plate of steamed carrots, and over this tiny kingdom I proudly crowned myself queen.

I sat cross-legged on my hospital bed for nearly two months before I earned an afternoon pass to go to the mall with my mother. The privilege came just in time; I felt unbearably large and desperately wanted a new outfit under which to hide gained weight. At the mall, I searched for two hours before finally discovering, in the maternity section at Macy's, a shirt large enough to cover what I perceived as my enormous body.

With an hour left on my pass, I spotted a sign on a shop window: "Body Fat Testing, $3.00." I suggested to my mother that we split up for ten minutes; she headed to Barnes & Noble, and I snuck into the fitness store.

I sat down in front of a machine hooked up to a computer, and a burly young body builder fired questions at me:

"Age?"

"Twenty-one."

"Height?"

"Five nine."

"Weight?"

"Ninety-nine."

The young man punched my statistics into his keyboard and pinched my arm with clippers wired to the testing machine. In a moment, the computer spit out my results. "Only ten percent body fat! Unbelievably healthy. The average for a woman your age is twenty-five percent. Fantastic! You're this week's blue ribbon winner."

I stared at him in disbelief. *Winner? Healthy? Fantastic?* I glanced around at the other customers in the store, some of whom had congregated to watch my testing, and I felt embarrassed by his praise. And then I felt furious. Furious at this man and at the society that programmed him for their ignorant approbation of my illness and my suffering.

"I am dying of anorexia," I whispered. "Don't congratulate me."

I spent my remaining month in the hospital supplementing psychotherapy with an independent examination of eating disorders from a social and political point of view. I needed to understand why society would reward my starvation and encourage my vanishing. In the bathroom, a mirror on the open door behind me reflected my backside in a mirror over the sink. Vertebrae poked at my skin, ribs hung like wings over chiseled hip bones, the two sides of my buttocks did not touch. I had not seen this view of myself before.

In writing, I recorded instances in which my eating disorder had tangled the progress of my life and thwarted my relationships. I filled three and a half Mead marble notebooks. Five years' worth of: *I wouldn't sit with Daddy when he was alone in the hospital because I needed to go jogging; I told Derek not to visit me because I couldn't throw up when he was there; I almost failed my comprehensive exams because I was so hungry; I spent my year at Oxford with my head in the toilet bowl; I wouldn't eat the dinner my friends cooked me for my nineteenth birthday because I knew they had used oil in the recipe; I told my family not to come to my college graduation because I didn't want to miss a day at the gym or have to eat a restaurant meal.* And on and on for hundreds of pages.

This honest account of my life dissolved the illusion of anorexic power. I saw myself naked in the truth of my pain, my loneliness, my obsessions, my craziness, my selfishness, my defeat. I also recognized the social and political implications of consuming myself with the trivialities of calories and weight. At college, I had watched as classmates involved themselves in extracurricular clubs, volunteer work, politics and applications for jobs and graduate schools. Obsessed with exercising and exhausted by starvation, I did not even consider joining in such pursuits. Despite my love of writing and painting and literature, despite ranking at the top of my class, I wanted only to teach aerobics. Despite my adolescent days as a loud-mouthed, rambunctious class leader, I had grown into a silent, hungry young woman.

And society preferred me this way: hungry, fragile, crazy. *Winner! Healthy! Fantastic!* I began reading feminist literature to further understand the disempowerment of women in our culture. I digested the connection between a nation of starving, self-obsessed women and the continued success of the patriarchy. I also cultivated an awareness of alternative models of womanhood. In the stillness of the hospital library, new voices in my life rose from printed pages to echo my rage and provide the conception of my feminist consciousness.

I had been willing to accept self-sabotage, but now I refused to sacrifice myself to a society that profited from my pain. I finally understood that my eating disorder symbolized more than "personal psychodynamic trauma." Gazing in the mirror at my emaciated body, I observed a woman held up by her culture as the physical ideal because she was starving, self-obsessed and powerless, a woman called beautiful because she threatened no one except herself. Despite my intelligence, my education, and my supposed Manhattan sophistication, I had believed all of the lies; I had almost given my life in order to achieve the sickly impotence that this culture aggressively links with female happiness, love and success. And everything I had to offer to the world, every tumbling wave, every thought and every passion, nearly died inside me.

As long as society resists female power, fashion will call healthy women physically flawed. As long as society accepts the physical, sexual and economic abuse of women, popular culture will prefer women who resemble little girls. Sitting in the hospital the summer after my college graduation, I grasped the absurdity of a nation of adult women dying to grow small.

Armed with this insight, I loosened the grip of the starvation disease on my body. I determined to recreate myself based on an image of a woman warrior. I remembered my ocean, and I took my first bite.

Gaining weight and getting my head out of the toilet bowl was the most political act I have ever committed.

The Vagina Monologues

Eve Ensler

There I've said it, even put it in the title (and the publisher went along). Why does the word *vagina* still have such power to shock today in the sex-saturated world of popular culture, literature, and film? That is one of the questions that propelled Eve Ensler to conduct more than 200 interviews with women and then turn their reflections and stories into a theatrical performance, *The Vagina Monologues,* whose off-Broadway production in New York won a 1997 Obie Award and which has toured extensively in the United States, as well as Jerusalem, London, and Zagreb. As an icebreaker, Ensler often asked women, "If your vagina got dressed up, what would it wear?" and she got hilarious answers that ranged from blue jeans to emeralds to a leather jacket. She talked with activist Betty Dodson, who runs a vagina workshop, and, in one of the most compelling sections, with women who were raped in Bosnia in the early 1990s. The following riff on the v-word opens the play and also serves as the introduction to the published version of the text, which appeared in 1998.

One trademark of contemporary feminism, especially among younger women, is an outspokenness on matters of sex, a willingness to really talk about women's bodies, especially where pleasure, reproduction, and body image are concerned. Previous discussions about birth control or access to abortion have morphed into debates about body piercing, bulimia, and tattoos. The old gay/straight split has been supplanted by a more fluid understanding of sexuality, including transgendered individuals, bisexuals, and male-to-female and (less often) female-to-male transvestites. This is in contrast to what Gloria Steinem refers to as the "down there" generation, a linguistic dodge for not specifically naming the female genitalia and more generally for not talking about, let alone celebrating, the pleasure and sensuality of women's bodies. Eve Ensler realizes that many women today, and not just older women, are still in the "down there" frame of mind, and the mission of her theatrical performance is to engender pride, self-knowledge, and truth-telling.

Eve Ensler is a playwright, poet, activist, and screenwriter. She lives in New York City with her partner, Ariel Orr Jordan.

"Vagina." There, I've said it. "Vagina"—said it again. I've been saying that word over and over for the last three years. I've been saying it in the theaters, at colleges, in living rooms, in cafés, at dinner parties, on radio programs all over the country. I would be saying it on TV if someone would let me. I say it one hundred and twenty-eight times every evening I perform my show, *The Vagina Monologues,* which is based on interviews with a diverse group of over two hundred women about their vaginas. I say it in my sleep. I say it because I'm not supposed to say it. I say it because it's an invisible word—a word that stirs up anxiety, awkwardness, contempt, and disgust.

I say it because I believe that what we don't say we don't see, acknowledge, or remember. What we don't say becomes a secret, and secrets often create shame and fear and myths. I say it because I want to someday feel comfortable saying it, and not ashamed and guilty.

I say it because we haven't come up with a word that's more inclusive, that really describes the entire area and all its parts. "Pussy" is probably a better word, but it has so much baggage connected with it. And besides, I don't think most of us have a clear idea of what we're talking about when we say "pussy." "Vulva" is a good word; it speaks more specifically, but I don't think most of us are clear what the vulva includes.

I say "vagina" because when I started saying it I discovered how fragmented I was, how disconnected my body was from my mind. My vagina was something over there, away in the distance. I rarely lived inside it, or even visited. I was busy working, writing; being a mother, a friend. I did not see my vagina as my primary resource, a place of sustenance, humor, and creativity. It was fraught there, full of fear. I'd been raped as a little girl, and although I'd grown up, and done all the adult things one does with one's vagina, I had never really reentered that part of my body after I'd been violated. I had essentially lived most of my life without my motor, my center, my second heart.

I say "vagina" because I want people to respond, and they have. They have tried to censor the word wherever *The Vagina Monologues* has traveled and in every form of communication: in ads in major newspapers, on tickets sold in department stores, on banners that hang in front of theaters, on box-office phone machines where the voice says only "Monologues" or "V. Monologues."

"Why is this?" I ask. "'Vagina' is not a pornographic word; it's actually a medical word, a term for a body part, like 'elbow,' 'hand,' or 'rib.'"

"It may not be pornographic," people say, "but it's dirty. What if our little daughters were to hear it, what would we tell them?"

"Maybe you could tell them that they have a vagina," I say. "If they don't already know it. Maybe you could celebrate that."

"But we don't call their vaginas 'vagina,'" they say.

"What do you call them?" I ask.

And they tell me: "pooki," "poochie," "poope," "peepe poopelu" . . . and the list goes on and on.

I say "vagina" because I have read the statistics, and bad things are happening to women's vaginas everywhere: 500,000 women are raped every year in the United States; 100 million women have been genitally mutilated worldwide; and the list goes on and on. I say "vagina" because I want these bad things to stop. I know they will not stop until we acknowledge that they're going on, and the only way to make that possible is to enable women to talk without fear of punishment or retribution.

It's scary saying the word. "Vagina." At first it feels like you're crashing through an invisible wall. "Vagina." You feel guilty and wrong, as if someone's going to strike you down. Then, after you say the word the hundredth time or the thousandth time, it occurs to you that it's *your* word, *your* body, *your* most essential place. You suddenly realize that all the shame and embarrassment you've previously felt saying the word has been a form of silencing your desire, eroding your ambition.

Then you begin to say the word more and more. You say it with a kind of passion, a kind of urgency, because you sense that if you stop saying it, the fear will overcome you again and you will fall back into an embarrassed whisper. So you say it everywhere you can, bring it up in every conversation.

You're excited about your vagina; you want to study it and explore it and introduce yourself to it, and find out how to listen to it, and give it pleasure, and keep it healthy and wise and strong. You learn how to satisfy yourself and teach your lover how to satisfy you.

You're aware of your vagina all day, wherever you are—in your car, at the supermarket, at the gym, in the office. You're aware of this precious, gorgeous, life-bearing part of you between your legs, and it makes you smile; it makes you proud.

And as more women say the word, saying it becomes less of a big deal; it becomes part of our language, part of our lives. Our vaginas become integrated and respected and sacred. They become part of our bodies, connected to our minds, fueling our spirits. And the shame leaves and the violation stops, because vaginas are visible and real, and they are connected to powerful, wise, vagina-talking women.

We have a huge journey in front of us.

This is the beginning. Here's the place to think about our vaginas, to learn about other women's vaginas, to hear stories and interviews, to answer questions and to ask them. Here's the place to release the myths, shame, and fear. Here's the place to practice saying the word, because, as we know, the word is what propels us and sets us free. "VAGINA."

CHAPTER *13*

Backlash and Progress

Although the women's movement maintained the momentum associated with the 60s longer than any other group, it too had stalled by the mid-1970s. The fate of the Equal Rights Amendment was an early indication of the changing social and political climate.

After passing Congress in 1972, the proposed amendment was expected by most activists to win quick acceptance, and in fact 34 states ratified it between 1972 and 1974, just 4 short of the 38 necessary for ratification. But then the momentum stopped; only one state (Indiana) ratified after 1974. Even with a three-year extension on the ratification deadline, the ERA went down to defeat on June 30, 1982. Although most of the holdouts were in the South, a notable exception was Illinois, where massive organizational efforts by feminists failed to sway the state legislature. While some states have passed their own equal rights amendments, efforts since the 1980s to revive the amendment on the national level have gone nowhere.

Although the suffrage amendment was successful (thank goodness) while the ERA was not, there are still many parallels between the two political mobilizations and their aftermaths. After 1982, the women's movement, like suffragists, no longer had a single goal or issue around which to rally, and it now directed its still enormous energy to a variety of issues, such as workplace conditions, sexual harassment, battered women, pay equity, reproductive rights, and pornography. But some of these issues, especially pornography, revealed deep divisions within the women's movement itself about issues of censorship and violence against women.

In another parallel to the 1920s, the political and social climate of the 1980s and 1990s was far less hospitable to social change and reform, and this profoundly affected the fortunes of feminism. The media and popular culture went out of their way to proclaim that feminism was either dead or no longer necessary. (The term *postfeminist* was often accompanied by a smirk or sigh of relief, implying the country was lucky it did not have to deal with that pesky women's movement anymore.) Journalist Susan Faludi documented this backlash in a very influential 1991 book of the same name.

A final parallel to the 1920s was the generational and ideological fault lines that appeared within feminism itself. Many younger women see no need to identify with the feminist movement at all, and those who do (the so-called "third wave feminists") are often at odds with their elders over whether current agendas overemphasize women's oppression and paint women too much as victims (of date rape, pay inequity, the beauty myth, and so forth). Instead some young feminists want to mobilize around issues of empowerment and self-actualization to counter what they see as the passivity of "victim" feminism. Another internal battle concerns those who want to promote equality between men and women versus those who celebrate women's essential differences from men (so-called *cultural feminists,* not to be confused with right-wing followers of Phyllis Schlafly who promote their own version of highly stratified gender roles). Feminism also struggled mightily in the 1980s and 1990s with the awareness that differences among women, especially by race, class, and sexual orientation, were often as profound as the common bonds that tie women together. How to promote gender consciousness (getting women to say "we") while at the same time acknowledging difference is essential to the continued viability of feminism as a political and ideological movement.

In the 1990s public opinion polls suggested widespread popular acceptance for women's equality with men in the workplace and at home. But as sociologist Alice Rossi pointed out several decades ago, "Many people. . . espouse belief in sex equality but resist its manifestations in their personal lives," an observation that is still true today. And those who profess a commitment to equality still sometimes shun identification with feminism. The many women, young, old, and in between, who say, "I'm not a feminist, but. . ." capture this tension.

Basically, the movement for women's equality has entered a different stage. It is strong testimony to the major changes that have occurred since the 1960s that they have become so quickly accepted as normal. Young women coming of age today have access to sports programs and women's studies courses at school, have the option of being called *Ms.,* and can contemplate careers as doctors, lawyers, engineers, or carpenters. Today's women can build on the political and legislative victories won by previous generations (that is, when they are not defending them from attack from the right) and move on to new concerns. For women of all ages, many of these issues center on the balance between work and family life and relationships, especially how to combine satisfying work with the demands and joys of parenting and still get more than four hours of sleep a night.

While younger women may or may not identify with feminism, their lives, indeed the lives of most Americans, have been profoundly influenced by this far-reaching social movement. More than any other legacy, the revival of feminism in the 1960s and 1970s gave women greater freedom of choice in most aspects of their lives and removed many of the artificial barriers that prevented the realization of women's full capabilities. Even when a powerful conservative backlash stalled further breakthroughs in the 1980s, women's lives were in little danger of reverting to the patterns of the 1950s and early 1960s. Continuing the generational analogy, those of us whose consciousnesses were raised in the 1960s and 1970s are going to be around for a long time, joined by new recruits who are proud to embrace the feminist label. Therefore, to paraphrase Mark Twain, reports of the death of feminism are greatly exaggerated.

The Backlash against Feminism

Susan Faludi

In a widely read 1991 book titled *Backlash: The Undeclared War Against American Women,* Pulitzer Prize-winning journalist Susan Faludi described a powerful counterattack, or backlash, against the gains American women had won in the 1960s and 1970s. In compelling detail, she showed how the media consistently and inaccurately held the women's movement responsible for every ill afflicting modern women—from infertility to eating disorders to rising divorce rates to the "man shortage." For example, Faludi picked apart the statistics put forward by the media showing a drastic decline in the chances for college-educated, unwed women over 30 to marry. (In *Newsweek*'s inflammatory—and inaccurate—headline, women over 40 were "more likely to be killed by a terrorist" than make it to the altar.) She also demolished widely reported stories about an "infertility epidemic" among professional women who postpone childbearing or supposed trends of widespread emotional "burnout" among career women. But in a backlash climate, such accusations, even when untrue, seemed plausible.

Faludi proposed a different interpretation. It was a myth that the women's movement and feminism were women's own worst enemy; it was a myth that women were unhappy precisely because they had achieved equality. Instead, many of contemporary women's problems were traceable to the fact that they did not have *enough* equality, not that they had too much. Certainly the current debates about reproductive rights, pay equity, the "glass ceiling," and the "mommy track" suggest that the issues of modern feminism are far from accepted. And very few would argue that women had achieved equality based on how women are portrayed in the media and popular culture, especially in television, film, popular music, and advertising.

As a journalist, Faludi realized the power of the media and popular culture to shape public attitudes and affect public policy. Her agenda was to expose the campaign that was attempting to thwart women's progress in the 1980s and 1990s, to show that women still have many battles to fight before equality would be achieved, and to reaffirm that many women were consciously resisting the backlash message, both individually and collectively. This selection from the introduction, titled "Blame It on Feminism," shows the passion and conviction with which she argues her case.

To be a woman in America at the close of the 20th century—what good fortune. That's what we keep hearing, anyway. The barricades have fallen, politicians assure us. Women have "made it," Madison Avenue cheers. Women's fight for equality has "largely been won," *Time* magazine announces. Enroll at any university, join any law firm, apply for credit at any bank. Women have so many opportunities now, corporate leaders say, that we don't really need equal opportunity policies. Women are so equal now, lawmakers say, that we no longer need an Equal Rights Amendment. Women have "so much," former President Ronald

Reagan says, that the White House no longer needs to appoint them to higher office. Even American Express ads are saluting a woman's freedom to charge it. At last, women have received their full citizenship papers.

And yet . . .

Behind this celebration of the American woman's victory, behind the news, cheerfully and endlessly repeated, that the struggle for women's rights is won, another message flashes. You may be free and equal now, it says to women, but you have never been more miserable.

This bulletin of despair is posted everywhere—at the newsstand, on the TV set, at the movies, in advertisements and doctors' offices and academic journals. Professional women are suffering "burnout" and succumbing to an "infertility epidemic." Single women are grieving from a "man shortage." The *New York Times* reports: Childless women are "depressed and confused" and their ranks are swelling. *Newsweek* says: Unwed women are "hysterical" and crumbling under a "profound crisis of confidence." The health advice manuals inform: High-powered career women are stricken with unprecedented outbreaks of "stress-induced disorders," hair loss, bad nerves, alcoholism, and even heart attacks. The psychology books advise: Independent women's loneliness represents "a major mental health problem today." Even founding feminist Betty Friedan has been spreading the word: she warns that women now suffer from a new identity crisis and "new 'problems that have no name.'"

How can American women be in so much trouble at the same time that they are supposed to be so blessed? If the status of women has never been higher, why is their emotional state so low? If women got what they asked for, what could possibly be the matter now?

The prevailing wisdom of the past decade has supported one, and only one, answer to this riddle: it must be all that equality that's causing all that pain. Women are unhappy precisely *because* they are free. Women are enslaved by their own liberation. They have grabbed at the gold ring of independence, only to miss the one ring that really matters. They have gained control of their fertility, only to destroy it. They have pursued their own professional dreams—and lost out on the greatest female adventure. The women's movement, as we are told time and again, has proved women's own worst enemy.

"In dispensing its spoils, women's liberation has given my generation high incomes, our own cigarette, the option of single parenthood, rape crisis centers, personal lines of credit, free love, and female gynecologists," Mona Charen, a young law student, writes in the *National Review,* in an article titled "The Feminist Mistake." "In return it has effectively robbed us of one thing upon which the happiness of most women rests—men." The *National Review* is a conservative publication, but such charges against the women's movement are not confined to its pages. "Our generation was the human sacrifice" to the women's movement, *Los Angeles Times* feature writer Elizabeth Mehren contends in a *Time* cover story. Baby-boom women like her, she says, have been duped by feminism: "We believed the rhetoric." In *Newsweek,* writer Kay Ebeling dubs feminism "the Great Experiment That Failed" and asserts "women in my generation, its perpetrators, are the casualties." Even the beauty magazines are saying it: *Harper's Bazaar* accuses the women's movement of having "lost us [women] ground instead of gaining it."

The truth is that the last decade has seen a powerful counterassault on women's rights, a backlash, an attempt to retract the handful of small and hard-won victories that the feminist movement did manage to win for women. This counterassault is largely insidious: in a kind of pop-culture version of the Big Lie, it stands the truth boldly on its head and proclaims that the very steps that have elevated women's position have actually led to their downfall.

The backlash is at once sophisticated and banal, deceptively "progressive" and proudly backward. It deploys both the "new" findings of "scientific research" and the dime-store moralism of yesteryear; it turns into media sound bites both the glib pronouncements of pop-psych trend-watchers and the frenzied rhetoric of New Right preachers. The backlash has succeeded in framing virtually the whole issue of women's rights in its own language. Just as Reaganism shifted political discourse far to the right and demonized liberalism, so the backlash convinced the public that women's "liberation" was the true contemporary American scourge—the source of an endless laundry list of personal, social, and economic problems.

But what has made women unhappy in the last decade is not their "equality"—which they don't yet have—but the rising pressure to halt, and even reverse, women's quest for that equality. The "man shortage" and the "infertility epidemic" are not the price of liberation; in fact, they do not even exist. But these chimeras are the chisels of a society-wide backlash. They are part of a relentless whittling-down process—much of it amounting to outright propaganda—that has served to stir women's private anxieties and break their political wills. Identifying feminism as women's enemy only furthers the ends of a backlash against women's equality, simultaneously deflecting attention from the backlash's central role and recruiting women to attack their own cause . . .

Women's advances and retreats are generally described in military terms: battles won, battles lost, points and territory gained and surrendered. The metaphor of combat is not without its merits in this context and, clearly, the same sort of martial accounting and vocabulary is already surfacing here. But by imagining the conflict as two battalions neatly arrayed on either side of the line, we miss the entangled nature, the locked embrace, of a "war" between women and the male culture they inhabit. We miss the reactive nature of a backlash, which, by definition, can exist only in response to another force.

In times when feminism is at a low ebb, women assume the reactive role—privately and most often covertly struggling to assert themselves against the dominant cultural tide. But when feminism itself becomes the tide, the opposition doesn't simply go along with the reversal: it digs in its heels, brandishes its fists, builds walls and dams. And its resistance creates countercurrents and treacherous undertows.

The force and furor of the backlash churn beneath the surface, largely invisible to the public eye. On occasion in the last decade, they have burst into view. We have seen New Right politicians condemn women's independence, antiabortion protesters firebomb women's clinics, fundamentalist preachers damn feminists as "whores" and "witches." Other signs of the backlash's wrath, by their sheer brutality, can push their way into public consciousness for a time—the sharp increase in rape, for example, or the rise in pornography that depicts extreme violence against women.

More subtle indicators in popular culture may receive momentary, and often bemused, media notice, then quickly slip from social awareness: A report, for instance, that the image of women on prime-time TV shows has suddenly degenerated. A survey of mystery fiction finding the numbers of female characters tortured and mutilated mysteriously multiplying. The puzzling news that, as one commentator put it, "So many hit songs have the B-word [bitch] to refer to women that some rap music seems to be veering toward rape music." The ascendancy of virulently misogynist comics like Andrew Dice Clay—who called women "pigs" and "sluts" and strutted in films in which women were beaten, tortured, and blown up—or radio hosts like Rush Limbaugh, whose broadsides against "femi-Nazi" feminists made his syndicated program the most popular radio talk show in the nation. Or word that in 1987, the American Women in Radio & Television couldn't award its annual prize for ads that feature women positively: it could find no ad that qualified.

These phenomena are all related, but that doesn't mean they are somehow coordinated. The backlash is not a conspiracy, with a council dispatching agents from some central control room, nor are the people who serve its ends often aware of their role; some even consider themselves feminists. For the most part, its workings are encoded and internalized, diffuse and chameleonic. Not all of the manifestations of the backlash are of equal weight or significance either; some are mere ephemera, generated by a culture machine that is always scrounging for a "fresh" angle. Taken as a whole, however, these codes and cajolings, these whispers and threats and myths, move overwhelmingly in one direction: they try to push women back into their "acceptable" roles—whether as Daddy's girl or fluttery romantic, active nester or passive love object.

Although the backlash is not an organized movement, that doesn't make it any less destructive. In fact, the lack of orchestration, the absence of a single string-puller, only makes it harder to see—and perhaps more effective. A backlash against women's rights succeeds to the degree that it appears *not* to be political, that it appears not to be a struggle at all. It is most powerful when it goes private, when it lodges inside a woman's mind and turns her vision inward, until she imagines the pressure is all in her head, until she begins to enforce the backlash, too—on herself.

In the last decade, the backlash has moved through the culture's secret chambers, traveling through passageways of flattery and fear. Along the way, it has adopted disguises: a mask of mild derision or the painted face of deep "concern." Its lips profess pity for any woman who won't fit the mold, while it tries to clamp the mold around her ears. It pursues a divide-and-conquer strategy: single versus married women, working women versus homemakers, middle- versus working-class.

It manipulates a system of rewards and punishments, elevating women who follow its rules, isolating those who don't. The backlash remarkets old myths about women as new facts and ignores all appeals to reason. Cornered, it denies its own existence, points an accusatory finger at feminism, and burrows deeper underground.

Backlash happens to be the title of a 1947 Hollywood movie in which a man frames his wife for a murder he's committed. The backlash against women's rights works in much the same way: its rhetoric charges feminists with all the crimes it perpetrates. The backlash line blames the women's movement for the "feminization of poverty"—while the backlash's own instigators in Washington pushed through the budget cuts that helped impoverish millions of women, fought pay equity proposals, and undermined equal opportunity laws. The backlash line claims the women's movement cares nothing for children's rights—while its own representatives in the capital and state legislatures have blocked one bill after another to improve child care, slashed billions of dollars in federal aid for children, and relaxed state licensing standards for day care centers. The backlash line accuses the women's movement of creating a generation of unhappy single and childless women—but its purveyors in the media are the ones guilty of making single and childless women feel like circus freaks.

To blame feminism for women's "lesser life" is to miss entirely the point of feminism, which is to win women a wider range of experience. Feminism remains a pretty simple concept, despite repeated—and enormously effective—efforts to dress it up in greasepaint and turn its proponents into gargoyles. As Rebecca West wrote sardonically in 1913, "I myself have never been able to find out precisely what feminism is: I only know that people call me a feminist whenever I express sentiments that differentiate me from a doormat."

The meaning of the word "feminist" has not really changed since it first appeared in a book review in the *Athenaeum* of April 27, 1895, describing a woman who "has in her the capacity of fighting her way back to independence." It is the basic proposition that, as Nora put it in Ibsen's *A Doll's House* a century ago, "Before everything else I'm a human being." It is the simply worded sign hoisted by a little girl in the 1970 Women's Strike for Equality: I AM NOT A BARBIE DOLL. Feminism asks the world to recognize at long last that women aren't decorative ornaments, worthy vessels, members of a "special-interest group." They are half (in fact, now more than half) of the national population, and just as deserving of rights and opportunities, just as capable of participating in the world's events, as the other half. Feminism's agenda is basic: It asks that women not be forced to "choose" between public justice and private happiness. It asks that women be free to define themselves—instead of having their identity defined for them, time and again, by their culture and their men.

The fact that these are still such incendiary notions should tell us that American women have a way to go before they enter the promised land of equality.

A Woman of Conscience

Anita Hill

In 1991, the same year that Susan Faludi published *Backlash,* the confirmation hearings of Supreme Court nominee Clarence Thomas brought the issue
of sexual harassment in the workplace forcefully to the nation's attention,
with decidedly mixed results. Allegations by University of Oklahoma law
professor Anita Hill that she had been sexually harassed by Thomas when he
was her boss at the Department of Education and the Equal Employment Opportunity Commission (ironically, the very governmental body delegated to
deal with the issue of sexual harassment) almost derailed the confirmation of
the conservative African-American Thomas. Hill's forceful and measured
accusations, broadcast to a national television audience riveted by this unexpected turn in the hearings, were denied by Thomas himself, who called the
event "a high-tech lynching." The Senate narrowly confirmed Thomas by a
vote of 52–48.

Opinion polls at the time showed wide divergence in whether people
believed Clarence Thomas or Anita Hill. Support did not break down along
race or gender lines, with many women (49 percent in one poll) believing
Thomas. In an attempt to discredit the allegations, supporters of the nomina-
tion viciously attacked Anita Hill's personal integrity. Feminists rallied
around Hill, rebutting the attacks and pointing out that her experience of sexual harassment on the job was unfortunately a far too typical experience for
American women. In 1992, Hillary Rodham Clinton stated forcefully, "All
women who care about equality of opportunity, about integrity in the workplace, are in Anita Hill's debt."

"They just don't get it," was the refrain of many women as the all-male
Senate Judiciary Committee dismissed Hill's charges. The Thomas-Hill
hearings spurred the number of women running for political office, with dramatic results in the 1992 elections. When Senator Robert Packwood of Oregon was forced to resign in 1995 after allegations of sexual harassment of
staff and campaign workers, it seemed that finally, after all, elected public
officials did "get it"—sexual harassment was illegal and devastating to their
political careers.

Statement of Professor Anita F. Hill to the Senate Judiciary Committee, October 11, 1991

Mr. Chairman, Senator Thurmond, members of the committee:

My name is Anita F. Hill, and I am a professor of law at the University of Oklahoma. I was born on a farm in Okmulgee County, Oklahoma, in 1956. I am the
youngest of thirteen children.

I had my early education in Okmulgee County. My mother's name is Irma
Hill. She is also a farmer and a housewife.

My childhood was one of a lot of hard work and not much money, but it was
one of solid family affection as represented by my parents. I was reared in a

Source: "Statement of Professor Anita F. Hill to the Senate Judiciary Committee, October 11, 1991,"
S. Hrg 102–1084, Part 4 (Washington, DC: Government Printing Office, 1993).

religious atmosphere in the Baptist faith, and I have been a member of the Antioch Baptist church in Tulsa, Oklahoma, since 1983. It is a very warm part of my life at the present time.

For my undergraduate work, I went to Oklahoma State University and graduated from there in 1977. I am attaching to this statement a copy of my resume for further details of my education.

Senator Joseph R. Biden, Jr.: It will be included in the record.

Professor Hill: Thank you.

I graduated from the university with academic honors, and proceeded to the Yale Law School, where I received my J.D. degree in 1980.

Upon graduation from law school, I became a practicing lawyer with the Washington, D.C., firm of Wald, Hardraker & Ross. In 1981 I was introduced to now Judge Thomas by a mutual friend.

Judge Thomas told me that he was anticipating a political appointment, and he asked if I would be interested in working with him.

He was in fact appointed as assistant secretary of education for civil rights. After he was—after he had taken that post, he asked if I would become his assistant, and I accepted that position.

In my early period there, I had two major projects. The first was an article I wrote for Judge Thomas's signature on the education of minority students. The second was the organization of a seminar on high-risk students, which was abandoned because Judge Thomas transferred to the E.E.O.C., where he became the chairman of that office.

During this period at the Department of Education my working relationship with Judge Thomas was positive. I had a good deal of responsibility and independence. I thought he respected my work, and that he trusted my judgment.

After approximately three months of working there, he asked me to go out socially with him. What happened next, and telling the world about it, are the two most difficult things—experiences of my life.

It is only after a great deal of agonizing consideration, and . . . great number of sleepless nights, that I am able to talk of these unpleasant matters to anyone but my close friends.

I declined the invitation to go out socially with him, and explained to him that I thought it would jeopardize at—what at the time I considered to be a very good working relationship. I had a normal social life with other men outside the office. I believe then, as now, that having a social relationship with a person who was supervising my work would be ill advised. I was very uncomfortable with the idea and told him so.

I thought that by saying no and explaining my reasons, my employer would abandon his social suggestions. However, to my regret, in the following few weeks, he continued to ask me out on several occasions.

He pressed me to justify my reasons for saying no to him. These incidents took place in his office, or mine. They were in the form of private conversations, which not—would not have been overheard by anyone else.

My working relationship became even more strained when Judge Thomas began to use work situations to discuss sex. On these occasions he would call me into his office for a course on education issues and projects, or he might suggest that because of the time pressures of his schedule we go to lunch to a government cafeteria.

After a brief discussion of work, he would turn the conversation to a discussion of sexual matters. His conversations were very vivid. He spoke about acts that he had seen in pornographic films involving such matters as women having sex with animals, and films showing group sex or rape scenes.

He talked about pornographic materials depicting individuals with large penises or large breasts involving various sex acts.

On several occasions, Thomas told me graphically of his own sexual prowess.

Because I was extremely uncomfortable talking about sex with him at all, and particularly in such a graphic way, I told him that I did not want to talk about this subject. I would also try to change the subject to education matters or to nonsexual personal matters, such as his background or his beliefs.

My efforts to change the subject were rarely successful.

Throughout the period of these conversations, he also from time to time asked me for social engagements. My reaction to these conversations was to avoid them by eliminating opportunities for us to engage in extended conversations.

This was difficult because, at the time, I was his only assistant at the office of education—or office for civil rights. During the latter part of my time at the Department of Education, the social pressures, and any conversation of his offensive behavior, ended. I began both to believe and hope that our working relationship could be a proper, cordial, and professional one.

When Judge Thomas was made chair of the EEOC, I needed to face the question of whether to go with him. I was asked to do so, and I did.

The work itself was interesting, and at that time it appeared that the sexual overtures which had so troubled me had ended.

I also faced the realistic fact that I had no alternative job. While I might have gone back to private practice, perhaps in my old firm or at another, I was dedicated to civil rights work and my first choice was to be in that field. Moreover, at that time, the Department of Education itself was a dubious venture. President Reagan was seeking to abolish the entire department.

For my first months at the EEOC where I continued to be an assistant to Judge Thomas, there were no sexual conversations or overtures. However, during the fall and winter of 1982 these began again. The comments were random and ranged from pressing me about why I didn't go out with him to remarks about my personal appearance. I remember his saying that some day I would have to tell him the real reason that I wouldn't go out with him.

He began to show displeasure in his tone and voice and his demeanor and his continued pressure for an explanation. He commented on what I was wearing in terms of whether it made me more or less sexually attractive. The incidents occurred in his inner office at the EEOC.

One of the oddest episodes I remember was an occasion in which Thomas was drinking a Coke in his office. He got up from the table at which we were working, went over to his desk to get the Coke, looked at the can and asked, "Who has put pubic hair on my Coke?"

On other occasions, he referred to the size of his own penis as being larger than normal and he also spoke on some occasions of the pleasures he had given to women with oral sex. At this point, late 1982, I began to be concerned that Clarence Thomas might take out his anger with me by degrading me or not giving me important assignments. I also thought that he might find an excuse for dismissing me.

In January of 1983, I began looking for another job. I was handicapped because I feared that if he found out, he might make it difficult for me to find other employment and I might be dismissed from the job I had. Another factor that made my search more difficult was that there was a period—this was during a period—of a hiring freeze in the government . . .

In the spring of 1983, an opportunity to teach at Oral Roberts University opened up. I participated in a seminar, taught an afternoon session in a seminar at Oral Roberts University. The dean of the university saw me teaching and inquired as to whether I would be interested in further pursuing a career in teaching beginning at Oral Roberts University.

I agreed to take the job, in large part because of my desire to escape the pressures I felt at the EEOC due to Judge Thomas.

When I informed him that I was leaving in July, I recall that his response was that now I would no longer have an excuse for not going out with him. I told him that I still preferred not to do so. At some time after that meeting, he asked if he could take me to dinner at the end of the term. When I declined, he assured me that the dinner was a professional courtesy only and not a social invitation. I reluctantly agreed to accept that invitation but only if it was at the very end of a working day.

On, as I recall, the last day of my employment at the EEOC in the summer of 1983, I did have dinner with Clarence Thomas. We went directly from work to a restaurant near the office. We talked about the work I had done, both at Education and at the EEOC. He told me that he was pleased with all of it except for an article and speech that I had done for him while we were at the Office for Civil Rights. Finally he made a comment that I will vividly remember. He said that if I ever told anyone of his behavior that it would ruin his career. This was not an apology; nor was it an explanation. That was his last remark about the possibility of our going out or reference to his behavior.

In July of 1983 I left the Washington, D.C., area and I've had minimal contacts with Judge Clarence Thomas since. I am of course aware from the press that some questions have been raised about conversations I had with Judge Clarence Thomas after I left the EEOC. From 1983 until today, I have seen Judge Thomas only twice. On one occasion, I needed to get a reference from him and on another he made a public appearance in Tulsa. On one occasion he called me at home and we had an inconsequential conversation. On one occasion he called me without reaching me and I returned the call without reaching him and nothing came of it . . .

It is only after a great deal of agonizing consideration that I am able to talk of these unpleasant matters to anyone except my closest friends. As I've said before, these last few days have been very trying and very hard for me and it hasn't just been the last few days this week.

It has actually been over a month now that I have been under the strain of this issue.

Telling the world is the most difficult experience of my life, but it is very close to having to live through the experience that occasioned this meeting.

I may have used poor judgment early on in my relationship with this issue. I was aware, however, that telling at any point in my career could adversely affect my future career, and I did not want, early on, to burn all the bridges to the EEOC.

As I said, I may have used poor judgment. Perhaps I should have taken angry or even militant steps, both when I was in the agency or after I left it. But I must confess to the world that the course that I took seemed the better as well as the easier approach.

I declined any comment to newspapers, but later, when Senate staff asked me about these matters, I felt I had a duty to report.

I have no personal vendetta against Clarence Thomas. I seek only to provide the committee with information which it may regard as relevant.

It would have been more comfortable to remain silent. I took no initiative to inform anyone. But when I was asked by a representative of this committee to report my experience, I felt that I had to tell the truth. I could not keep silent.

Date Rape: Hysteria or Epidemic?

Katie Roiphe

Katie Roiphe offers a different take on sexual politics, which she first developed in an op-ed piece for the *New York Times* in 1991 and then expanded into a much-discussed book called *The Morning After: Sex, Fear, and Feminism* (1993). The gist of her argument is that the evidence of date rape on campus has been greatly exaggerated, in part because of an overly broad definition of rape but also because of a campus culture that encourages a sisterhood of victimhood. Instead of women seeing themselves as victims, she urges women to accept themselves as sexual beings and take responsibility for their actions, rather than automatically blaming men.

Roiphe's ideas caused quite a stir. The media were delighted to find a young feminist (she was a graduate student at Princeton when the original essay appeared) who seemed to be critical of her feminist elders, and the *New York Times Magazine* presented her ideas under the sensational headline of "Rape Hype Betrays Feminism." The fact that she was the daughter of Anne Roiphe, whose 1969 *Up The Sandbox* was an early feminist novel, added to her attractiveness. Many older feminists found her arguments glib

Source: Katie Roiphe, "Voices of the New Generation: Date Rape Hysteria," *New York Times,* November 20, 1991, p. 27.

and focused too much on the sexual agenda of feminism at the expense of other priorities; younger feminists were often upset that her ideas were used by the media to fuel the backlash against feminism, even if they admitted that there was more than a grain of truth in her analysis. Unfortunately Roiphe did not seem to realize that you could be both pro-sex and anti-rape, but her willingness to speak up and criticize feminist mainstays such as "Take Back the Night" marches or rape crisis centers on campus is typical of how many younger feminists are striking out on their own and creating a version (or versions) of feminism that speaks to their lives and concerns.

In classrooms and journals, in lectures and coffee shops, academics everywhere are talking about rape. Although it wears a fashionable leftist mask, this is a neo-puritan preoccupation. While real women get battered, while real mothers need day care, certain feminists are busy turning rape into fiction. Every time one Henry James character seizes the hand of another Henry James character, someone is calling it rape.

At a certain point the metaphor gets paranoid. An overused word, like an over-painted sunset, becomes a cliche, drained of specificity and meaning. With every new article on rape imagery, we threaten to confirm the vision of that 18th-century patriarch, Henry Fielding, when he wrote, "These words of exclamation (murder! robbery! rape!) are used by ladies in a fright, as fa la la . . . are in music, only as vehicles of sound and without any fixed idea."

Only now the cry across campuses is "date rape." Those involved frame it as a liberal concern, cut and dry, beyond debate. But they don't stop to consider the fundamentally sexist images lurking beneath their rhetoric. The term "date rape" itself hints at its conservative bent. More than just a polemic against rape, it reveals a desire for dates.

Although not an explicit part of their movement, these feminists are responding, in this time of sexual suspicion, to the need for a more rigid courtship structure. The message represents, in part, a nostalgia for 1950's-style dating. For Johnny picking Susie up for a movie and a Coke.

And the assumption embedded in this movement is our grandmother's assumption: men want sex, women don't. In emphasizing this struggle, him pushing, her resisting, the movement against date rape recycles and promotes an old model of sexuality.

One book, "Avoiding Rape On and Off Campus," by Carol Pritchard, warns young women to "think carefully before you go to a male friend's apartment or dorm . . . Do not expose yourself to any unnecessary risk." When did the possibility of sex become an "unnecessary risk"? Are we really such fragile creatures that we need such an extreme definition of safety? Should we really subject our male friends to scrutiny because after all men want one thing and one thing only?

The definition of date rape stretches beyond acts of physical force. According to pamphlets widely distributed on college campuses, even "verbal coercion" constitutes "date rape." With this expansive version of rape, then, these feminists invent a kinder, gentler sexuality. These pamphlets are clearly intended to protect innocent college women from the insatiable force of male desire. We have been hearing about this for centuries. He is still nearly uncontrollable; she is still the one drawing lines. This so-called feminist movement peddles an image of gender relations that denies female desire and infantilizes women. Once again, our bodies seem to be sacred vessels. We've come a long way, and now it seems, we are going back.

The date rape pamphlets begin to sound like Victorian guides to conduct. The most common date rape guide, published by the American College Health Association, advises its delicate readers to "communicate your limits clearly. If someone starts to offend you, tell them firmly and early."

Sharing these assumptions about female sensibilities, a manners guide from 1853 advises young women, "Do not suffer your hand to be held or squeezed without showing that it displeases you by instantly withdrawing it . . . These and many other little points of refinement will operate as an almost invisible though a very impenetrable fence, keeping off vulgar familiarity, and that desecration of the person which has so often led to vice." And so ideals of female virtue and repression resonate through time.

Let's not chase the same stereotypes our mothers have spent so much energy running away from. Let's not reinforce the images that oppress us, that label us victims, and deny our own agency and intelligence, as strong and sensual, as autonomous, pleasure-seeking, sexual beings.

Who Stole Feminism?

Christina Hoff Sommers

Like Katie Roiphe, Clark University philosophy professor Christina Hoff Sommers considers herself a feminist who is unhappy with the current state of feminism, but there the similarities end. Roiphe's stance is that of a daughter criticizing the feminism of her liberal elders; Sommers attacks feminism from the perspective of the conservative right. According to Sommers, "gender feminists" have taken over American feminism and threaten to destroy free speech in our nation's universities and classrooms by their insistence that "all our institutions, from the state to the family to the grade schools, perpetuate male dominance" and that "contemporary women live in an oppressive 'male hegemony.'" Spinning a conspiracy theory that rivals Susan Faludi's backlash against feminism except that it has been masterminded by feminists themselves, Christina Hoff Sommers paints a picture in *Who Stole Feminism? How Women Have Betrayed Women* (1994) of campuses and classrooms under the domination of feminist professors who will not allow criticism or dissent and perpetuate their own anger and resentment against women's unequal place in contemporary society. Many feminist

Source: From Christina Hoff Sommers, *Who Stole Feminism? How Women Have Betrayed Women* pp. 90–91, 95–96, 98–99, 116. Copyright © 1994. Reprinted by permission of Simon & Schuster.

341

scholars who toil to have their scholarship and teaching taken seriously have been somewhat surprised at this enormous power imputed to them.

In this selection Christina Hoff Sommers analyzes women's studies courses at various institutions across the country. The fact that students might be capable of forming their own opinions about ideologies such as feminism and distancing themselves from their professors' views does not seem to be part of Sommers's view of current academic practice.

For the past few years I have reviewed hundreds of syllabi from women's studies courses, attended more feminist conferences than I care to remember, studied the new "feminist pedagogy," reviewed dozens of texts, journals, newsletters, and done a lot of late-into-the-night reading of e-mail letters that thousands of "networked" women's studies teachers send to one another. I have taught feminist theory. I have debated gender feminists on college campuses around the country, and on national television and radio. My experience with academic feminism and my immersion in the ever-growing gender feminist literature have served to deepen my conviction that the majority of women's studies classes and other classes that teach a "reconceptualized" subject matter are unscholarly, intolerant of dissent, and full of gimmicks. In other words, they are a waste of time. And although they attract female students because of their social ambience, they attract almost no men. They divert the energies of students—especially young women—who sorely need to be learning how to live in a world that demands of them applicable talents and skills, not feminist fervor or ideological rectitude.

Journalist Karen Lehrman visited women's studies programs at Berkeley, the University of Iowa, Smith College, and Dartmouth, audited almost thirty classes, and interviewed many professors and students for a story in *Mother Jones:* "In many classes discussions alternate between the personal and the political, with mere pit stops at the academic. Sometimes they are filled with unintelligible poststructuralist jargon; sometimes they consist of consciousness-raising psychobabble, with the students' feelings and experiences valued as much as anything the professor or texts have to offer." Ms. Lehrman considers this a betrayal: "A hundred years ago, women were fighting for the right to learn math, science, Latin— to be educated like men; today, many women are content to get their feelings heard, their personal problems aired, their instincts and intuition respected."

The feminist classroom does little to prepare students to cope in the world of work and culture. It is an embarrassing scandal that, in the name of feminism, young women in our colleges and universities are taking courses in feminist classrooms that subject them to a lot of bad prose, psychobabble, and "new age" nonsense. What has real feminism to do with sitting around in circles and talking about our feelings on menstruation? To use a phrase much used by resenter feminists, the feminist classroom *shortchanges* women students. It wastes their time and gives them bad intellectual habits. It isolates them, socially and academically. While male students are off studying such "vertical" subjects as engineering and biology, women in feminist classrooms are sitting around being "safe" and "honoring" feelings. In this way, gender feminist pedagogy plays into old sexist stereotypes that extol women's capacity for intuition, emotion, and empathy while denigrating their capacity to think objectively and systematically in the way men can.

A parent should think very carefully before sending a daughter to one of the more gender-feminized colleges. Any school has the freedom to transform itself into a feminist bastion, but because the effect on the students is so powerful it ought to be honest about its attitude. I would like to see Wellesley College, Mount Holyoke, Smith, Mills, and the University of Minnesota—among the more extreme examples—print the following announcement on the first page of their bulletins:

> We will help your daughter discover the extent to which she has been in complicity with the patriarchy. We will encourage her to reconstruct herself through dialogue with us. She may become enraged and chronically offended. She will very likely reject the religious and moral codes you raised her with. She may well distance herself from family and friends. She may change her appearance, and even her sexual orientation. She may end up hating you (her father) and pitying you (her mother). After she has completed her reeducation with us, you will certainly be out tens of thousands of dollars and very possibly be out one daughter as well . . .

This pedagogical philosophy licenses the feminist teacher to lay down "conclusions" or "rules" without feeling the need to argue for them. Consider the "ground rules" developed by the Center for Research on Women at Memphis State University and used at Rutgers University, the University of Minnesota, Penn State, and other schools around the country. The students are asked to accept them as a condition for taking the course:

> For the purposes of this course we agree to these rules:
> 1. Acknowledge that oppression (i.e., racism, sexism, classism) exists.
> 2. Acknowledge that one of the mechanisms of oppression (i.e., racism, sexism, classism, heterosexism) is that we are all systematically taught misinformation about our own groups and about members of both dominant and subordinate groups.
> 3. Assume that people (both the groups we study and the members of the class) always do the best they can.
> 4. If members of the class wish to make comments that they do not want repeated outside the classroom, they can preface their remarks with a request and the class will agree not to repeat the remarks.

First, it should be pointed out that these "rules" are very unusual for a college class. Teachers frequently have rules about absences or late papers, but here the rules demand that the students adopt particular *beliefs,* none of which is self-evident. Consider rule no. 1, which asserts that "oppression exists." Stated in this unqualified way, it cannot be denied. But since the student is meant to understand that oppression exists in the United States in the form of classism and sexism, the matter is not nearly so simple. Is it not at least arguable that one of the good features of American life is that here, in contrast to most other countries, an individual can rise in the socioeconomic scale despite his or her background? Is this not one reason why many outsiders are so eager to come here? Why then speak of class oppression?

The coupling of sexism and racism is also problematic. Are they really that similar? Is sexism a national problem on a par with racism? The rule requires the student to accept that it is. Indeed, it is typical of the structure of many women's studies courses in putting a lot of loaded and controversial questions beyond the pale of discussion. And that is exactly what a college course should not be doing.

Rule no. 2 says: "One of the mechanisms of oppression is that we are all systematically taught misinformation." No doubt on occasion everyone is taught something that is not true. But are we "systematically" being given "misinformation"? When people were of the opinion that the world was flat, one might say they were "systematically" being taught that. But since everyone thought that was true, we shouldn't speak of "misinformation," which connotes more than unintentional error. As the women's studies scholars here use it, "systematically" connotes "deliberately" and with political purposes in mind. This alludes to the insidious workings of patriarchy, the "Hidden Unity" that keeps women in thrall to men. But it is certainly *false* that all of us are being deliberately (systematically) taught untruths.

Rule no. 3 asks students to assume that groups always do the best they can. But why should they be required to make such a plainly false assumption? People, especially in groups, often could do a lot better than they do. Why assume the opposite? This rule, too, is characteristic of the "feel good" spirit of many women's studies courses. Since every group is "doing its best," it is churlish to criticize any given group. (Does this assumption extend to fraternities? And to the football team?) Rule no. 3 serves another, unstated purpose: to preempt criticism that might disrupt the teacher's agenda.

Rule no. 4, which requires absolute confidentiality, is similarly objectionable. Classes should be free and open: anything said in the classroom should be repeatable outside. That an instructor invites or even allows her students to "speak out" about personal affairs is an unfailing sign that the course is unsubstantial and unscholarly. Moreover, the students who are encouraged to speak of painful incidents in their lives not only are being shortchanged scholastically, they are also at risk of being harmed by their disclosures. Even mental health professionals in clinical settings exercise great caution in eliciting traumatic disclosures. Any good school provides professional help to distressed students who need it. The amateur interventions of a teacher are intrusive and potentially harmful . . .

Students are quick to learn that open criticism of the feminist classroom will not win them support from teachers who privately agree with them. The lesson they learn from the cravenness of their teachers is never lost on them: keep clear of controversy. Conformity is safest: practice it. That is a terrible lesson to convey to one's students and the antithesis of what the college experience should be.

In the story "The Emperor's New Clothes," the boy at the parade who dared to declare that the emperor had nothing on was immediately joined by his elders, who were grateful that someone had given voice to that innocent and obvious truth. Sadly, the story is not true to life. In real life the boy is more likely to be shunted aside by parading functionaries for failing to perceive the emperor's finery. In real life, the spectators do not take the boy's side. At Minnesota, Northwestern, Michigan, Wooster, New Hampshire, Harvard, and on campuses across the country, the gender feminists are unchallenged because the faculties have so far found it politic to look the other way.

Equal Protection Under the Law: United States v. Virginia (1996)

Despite a sense of feminism under siege in the 1990s, important progress continued to unfold in many areas of American society. In 1996, the Supreme Court ruled that the equal protection class of the 14th Amendment precluded Virginia Military Institute (VMI), an all-male, state-supported institution, from denying women access to the unique educational opportunities offered by the school.[1] VMI's mission was to produce citizen soldiers—graduates who could be leaders in both civilian and military life—using educational methods that relied on rigorous physical training, mental stress, and absolute equality of treatment. VMI claimed that admitting women would necessitate changing many of its educational and training programs and offered instead to set up a separate Virginia Women's Institute for Leadership, affiliated with Mary Baldwin College. In the majority opinion, delivered by Justice Ruth Bader Ginsburg, the court ruled that the compromise would not provide equal opportunity for women and that women must be admitted to Virginia Military Institute.

The application of the 14th Amendment's equal protection clause to sex was the result of what historian Linda Kerber has called "an extraordinary legal transformation in the situation of women in the United States" between 1971 and 1975. Before 1971, courts had routinely found precedents, legal and social, to justify such unequal treatment as refusing to allow women to work as bartenders (*Goesaert v. Cleary,* 1948) or excluding women from jury service (*Hoyt v. Florida,* 1961). Then in 1971, in the case of *Reed v. Reed,* the Supreme Court used the equal protection clause to rule that an Idaho statute that gave absolute preference to male executors when there were several "equally qualified" persons to administer a dead person's estate was unconstitutional. In 1973, a female Air Force officer successfully challenged a regulation that did not allow her to claim benefits for her husband on the same basis as male officers did for their wives *(Frontiero v. Richardson).* These cases offered precedents for later sex discrimination cases.

There is something wonderfully fitting about Justice Ruth Bader Ginsburg delivering the majority opinion in this case, because she had drafted the original brief in the precedent-setting *Reed v. Reed.* Her career demonstrates

Source: United States v. Virginia, 518 U.S. 515 (1996).
[1]The relevant text of the 14th Amendment reads, "No State shall make or enforce any law which shall abridge the privileges or immunities of citizens of the United States; nor shall any State deprive any person of life, liberty, or property, without due process of law; nor deny to any person within its jurisdiction the equal protection of the laws."

345

the barriers and opportunities open to women in the law. When she graduated from Columbia Law School in 1959, she found most law firms closed
to her because of her sex. So she taught at Rutgers Law School and later Columbia and was a key member of the ACLU's Women's Rights Project,
which litigated test sex discrimination cases in the 1960s and 1970s. In 1980
she was appointed to the U.S. Court of Appeals for Washington, D.C., and in
1993 she was named an associate justice of the U.S. Supreme Court, joining
Justice Sandra Day O'Connor, who had been the first woman, appointed in
1981.

The cross-petitions in this case present two ultimate issues. First, does Virginia's
exclusion of women from the educational opportunities provided by VMI—extraordinary opportunities for military training and civilian leadership development—
deny to women "capable of all of the individual activities required of VMI
cadets," 766 F. Supp., at 1412, the equal protection of the laws guaranteed by the
Fourteenth Amendment? Second, if VMI's "unique" situation, *id.,* at 1413—as
Virginia's sole single-sex public institution of higher education—offends the Constitution's equal protection principle, what is the remedial requirement?

IV

We note, once again, the core instruction of this Court's pathmarking decisions in
J. E. B. v. Alabama ex rel. T. B., 511 U.S. 127, 136–137, 128 L. Ed. 2d 89, 114 S.
Ct. 1419, and n. 6 (1994), and *Mississippi Univ. for Women,* 458 U.S. at 724 (internal quotation marks omitted): Parties who seek to defend gender-based government action must demonstrate an "exceedingly persuasive justification" for
that action.

Today's skeptical scrutiny of official action denying rights or opportunities
based on sex responds to volumes of history. As a plurality of this Court acknowledged a generation ago, "our Nation has had a long and unfortunate history
of sex discrimination." *Frontiero v. Richardson,* 411 U.S. 677, 684, 36 L. Ed. 2d
583, 93 S. Ct. 1764 (1973). Through a century plus three decades and more of that
history, women did not count among voters composing "We the People"; not until 1920 did women gain a constitutional right to the franchise. *Id.,* at 685. And for
a half century thereafter, it remained the prevailing doctrine that government, both
federal and state, could withhold from women opportunities accorded men so long
as any "basis in reason" could be conceived for the discrimination. See, *e. g., Goesaert v. Cleary,* 335 U.S. 464, 467, 93 L. Ed. 163, 69 S. Ct. 198 (1948) (rejecting
challenge of female tavern owner and her daughter to Michigan law denying bar-
tender licenses to females—except for wives and daughters of male tavern owners; Court would not "give ear" to the contention that "an unchivalrous desire of
male bartenders to . . . monopolize the calling" prompted the legislation).

In 1971, for the first time in our Nation's history, this Court ruled in favor of
a woman who complained that her State had denied her the equal protection of its

laws. *Reed v. Reed,* 404 U.S. 71, 73, 30 L. Ed. 2d 225, 92 S. Ct. 251 (holding unconstitutional Idaho Code prescription that, among "'several persons claiming
and equally entitled to administer [a decedent's estate], males must be preferred to
females'"). Since *Reed,* the Court has repeatedly recognized that neither federal
nor state government acts compatibly with the equal protection principle when a
law or official policy denies to women, simply because they are women, full citizenship stature—equal opportunity to aspire, achieve, participate in and contribute to society based on their individual talents and capacities. See, *e. g.,*
Kirchberg v. Feenstra, 450 U.S. 455, 462–463, 67 L. Ed. 2d 428, 101 S. Ct. 1195
(1981) (affirming invalidity of Louisiana law that made husband "head and master" of property jointly owned with his wife, giving him unilateral right to dispose
of such property without his wife's consent); *Stanton v. Stanton,* 421 U.S. 7, 43 L.
Ed. 2d 688, 95 S. Ct. 1373 (1975) (invalidating Utah requirement that parents support boys until age 21, girls only until age 18).

Without equating gender classifications, for all purposes, to classifications
based on race or national origin, the Court, in post-*Reed* decisions, has carefully
inspected official action that closes a door or denies opportunity to women (or to
men). See *J. E. B.,* 511 U.S. at 152 (KENNEDY, J., concurring in judgment) (case
law evolving since 1971 "reveal[s] a strong presumption that gender classifications are invalid"). To summarize the Court's current directions for cases of official classification based on gender: Focusing on the differential treatment or
denial of opportunity for which relief is sought, the reviewing court must determine whether the proffered justification is "exceedingly persuasive." The burden
of justification is demanding and it rests entirely on the State. See *Mississippi
Univ. for Women,* 458 U.S. at 724. The State must show "at least that the [chal-
lenged] classification serves 'important governmental objectives and that the discriminatory means employed' are 'substantially related to the achievement of
those objectives.'" *Ibid.* (quoting *Wengler v. Druggists Mut. Ins. Co.,* 446 U.S.
142, 150, 64 L. Ed. 2d 107, 100 S. Ct. 1540 (1980)). The justification must be
genuine, not hypothesized or invented *post hoc* in response to litigation. And it
must not rely on overbroad generalizations about the different talents, capacities,
or preferences of males and females. See *Weinberger v. Wiesenfeld,* 420 U.S. 636,
643, 648, 43 L. Ed. 2d 514, 95 S. Ct. 1225 (1975); *Califano v. Goldfarb,* 430 U.S.
199, 223-224, 51 L. Ed. 2d 270, 97 S. Ct. 1021 (1977) (STEVENS, J., concurring
in judgment).

The heightened review standard our precedent establishes does not make sex
a proscribed classification. Supposed "inherent differences" are no longer accepted as a ground for race or national origin classifications. See *Loving v. Virginia,* 388 U.S. 1, 18 L. Ed. 2d 1010, 87 S. Ct. 1817 (1967). Physical differences
between men and women, however, are enduring: "The two sexes are not fungi-
ble; a community made up exclusively of one [sex] is different from a community
composed of both." *Ballard v. United States,* 329 U.S. 187, 193, 91 L. Ed. 181, 67
S. Ct. 261 (1946).

"Inherent differences" between men and women, we have come to appreciate, remain cause for celebration, but not for denigration of the members of either

sex or for artificial constraints on an individual's opportunity. Sex classifications may be used to compensate women "for particular economic disabilities [they have] suffered," *Califano v. Webster,* 430 U.S. 313, 320, 51 L. Ed. 2d 360, 97 S. Ct. 1192 (1977) *(per curiam),* to "promote equal employment opportunity," see *California Fed. Sav. & Loan Assn. v. Guerra,* 479 U.S. 272, 289, 93 L. Ed. 2d 613, 107 S. Ct. 683 (1987), to advance full development of the talent and capacities of our Nation's people. But such classifications may not be used, as they once were, see *Goesaert,* 335 U.S. at 467, to create or perpetuate the legal, social, and economic inferiority of women.

Measuring the record in this case against the review standard just described, we conclude that Virginia has shown no "exceedingly persuasive justification" for excluding all women from the citizen-soldier training afforded by VMI. We therefore affirm the Fourth Circuit's initial judgment, which held that Virginia had violated the Fourteenth Amendment's Equal Protection Clause. Because the remedy proffered by Virginia—the Mary Baldwin VWIL program—does not cure the constitutional violation, *i.e.,* it does not provide equal opportunity, we reverse the Fourth Circuit's final judgment in this case . . .

VII

A generation ago, "the authorities controlling Virginia higher education," despite long established tradition, agreed "to innovate and favorably entertained the [then] relatively new idea that there must be no discrimination by sex in offering educational opportunity." *Kirstein,* 309 F. Supp., at 186. Commencing in 1970, Virginia opened to women "educational opportunities at the Charlottesville campus that [were] not afforded in other [state-operated] institutions." *Id.,* at 187; see *supra,* at 538. A federal court approved the Commonwealth's innovation, emphasizing that the University of Virginia "offered courses of instruction . . . not available elsewhere." 309 F. Supp., at 187. The court further noted: "There exists at Charlottesville a 'prestige' factor [not paralleled in] other Virginia educational institutions." *Ibid.*

VMI, too, offers an educational opportunity no other Virginia institution provides, and the school's "prestige"—associated with its success in developing "citizen-soldiers"—is unequaled. Virginia has closed this facility to its daughters and, instead, has devised for them a "parallel program," with a faculty less impressively credentialed and less well paid, more limited course offerings, fewer opportunities for military training and for scientific specialization. Cf. *Sweatt,* 339 U.S. at 633. VMI, beyond question, "possesses to a far greater degree" than the VWIL program "those qualities which are incapable of objective measurement but which make for greatness in a . . . school," including "position and influence of the alumni, standing in the community, traditions and prestige." *Id.,* at 634. Women seeking and fit for a VMI-quality education cannot be offered anything less, under the Commonwealth's obligation to afford them genuinely equal protection.

A prime part of the history of our Constitution, historian Richard Morris re-counted, is the story of the extension of constitutional rights and protections to people once ignored or excluded. VMI's story continued as our comprehension of "We the People" expanded. See *supra,* at 546, n. 16. There is no reason to believe that the admission of women capable of all the activities required of VMI cadets would destroy the Institute rather than enhance its capacity to serve the "more perfect Union."

A Third Wave Feminist Manifesta

Jennifer Baumgardner and Amy Richards

Here is a great definition of third wave feminism:

No, it's not the techno-crazy theory put forth by Alvin and Heidi Toffler, the couple who were unfortunately picked to be Newt Gingrich's gurus. Third Wave means the core mass of the current women's movement in their late teens through their thirties, roughly speaking—the ones who grew up with Judy Blume books, *Free to Be . . . You and Me,* and *Sesame Street.* Another way of looking at Third Wave is as the "daughters," both real and metaphor-ical, of the Second Wave, the women who read *Ms.* magazine, *Our Bodies, Ourselves,* and lobbied for *Roe v. Wade* and the ERA.

What kind of smart, sassy writers could capture the contemporary scene so well? Two friends, each born in 1970, met while working at *Ms.* magazine in the mid-1990s and decided to write a book about contemporary feminism that was published in 2000 as *Manifesta: Young Women, Feminism, and the Future.*

Their names are Jennifer Baumgardner and Amy Richards, and while no two individuals can stand in for a movement (for example, they are both white and based in New York), they fearlessly explain and explore history, politics, and popular culture through the eyes of their feminist generation. Activists as well as writers, their book is a call to action. "When in the course of thirty years of uninterrupted feminism it becomes evident that a single generation can only go so far, it behooves the next generation to pick up the reins and articulate the plot that will move their cause forward." Second wave feminists had Houston in 1977. Here is the feminist agenda that Baumgardner and Richards drafted for third wave feminism.

THIRD WAVE MANIFESTA: A THIRTEEN-POINT AGENDA

1. To out unacknowledged feminists, specifically those who are younger, so that Generation X can become a visible movement and, further, a voting block of eighteen- to forty-year-olds.

2. To safeguard a woman's right to bear or not to bear a child, regardless of circumstances, including women who are younger than eighteen or impoverished. To preserve this right throughout her life and support the choice to be childless.

3. To make explicit that the fight for reproductive rights must include birth control; the right for poor women and lesbians to have children; partner adoption for gay couples; subsidized fertility treatments for all women who choose them; and freedom from sterilization abuse. Furthermore, to support the idea that sex can be—and usually is—for pleasure, not procreation

4. To bring down the double standard in sex and sexual health, and foster male responsibility and assertiveness in the following areas: achieving freedom from STDs; more fairly dividing the burden of family planning as well as responsibilities such as child care; and eliminating violence against women.

5. To tap into and raise awareness of our revolutionary history, and the fact that almost all movements began as youth movements. To have access to our intellectual feminist legacy and women's history; for the classics of radical feminism, womanism, *mujeristas,* women's liberation, and all our roots to remain in print; and to have women's history taught to men as well as women as a part of all curricula.

6. To support and increase the visibility and power of lesbians and bisexual women in the feminist movement, in high schools, colleges, and the workplace. To recognize that queer women have always been at the forefront of the feminist movement, and that there is nothing to be gained—and much to be lost—by downplaying their history, whether inadvertently or actively.

7. To practice "autokeonony" ("self in community"): to see activism not as a choice between self and community but as a link between them that creates balance.

8. To have equal access to health care, regardless of income, which includes coverage equivalent to men's and keeping in mind that women use the system more often than men do because of our reproductive capacity.

9. For women who so desire to participate in all reaches of the military, including combat, and to enjoy all the benefits (loans, health care, pensions) offered to its members for as long as we continue to have an active military. The largest expenditure of our national budget goes toward maintaining this welfare system, and feminists have a duty to make sure women have access to every echelon.

10. To liberate adolescents from slut-bashing, listless educators, sexual harassment, and bullying at school, as well as violence in all walks of life, and the silence that hangs over adolescents' heads, often keeping them isolated, lonely, and indifferent to the world.

11. To make the workplace responsive to an individual's wants, needs, and talents. This includes valuing (monetarily) stay-at-home parents, aiding employees who want to spend more time with family and continue to work, equalizing pay for jobs of comparable worth, enacting a minimum wage that would bring a full-time worker with two children over the poverty line, and providing employee benefits for freelance and part-time workers.

12. To acknowledge that, although feminists may have disparate values, we share the same goal of equality, and of supporting one another in our efforts to gain the power to make our own choices.
13. To pass the Equal Rights Amendment so that we can have a constitutional foundation of righteousness and equality upon which future women's rights conventions will stand.

Global Feminism

Charlotte Bunch

As third wave feminists readily admit, feminism is a global phenomenon whose essence is "looking at the world through women's eyes." Nothing has done more to advance global feminism than the United Nations World Conferences on Women, starting with Mexico City in 1975 (see Chapter 10). More than 6,000 women attended the second conference in Copenhagen in 1980, 14,000 came to Nairobi in 1985, and more than 30,000 journeyed to Beijing in 1995. Each of these conferences followed a similar structure of two parallel meetings: delegates representing their countries met in one, representatives of nongovernmental organizations (NGOs) met in a second. Activist Charlotte Bunch, whose speech to the opening NGO plenary in 1995 is excerpted here, called them "global town meetings."

Obviously any forum that brings together women from all over the world, from first and third world countries, from different religions, even from countries at war will find it difficult to find common ground, but the Beijing Women's Conference adopted a platform that set three preconditions for women's global advancement: equality, development, and peace. Underlying the platform was the insistence that human rights, which had traditionally been applied to such concepts as freedom of religion and speech, be expanded (in Bunch's words) "to seek a redefinition of human rights that acknowledges that the first fundamental of all human rights is the right to exist, the right to life itself." First Lady Hillary Rodham Clinton, who also addressed the conference, noted that women were often the ones whose human rights were most violated—as rape victims during military conflicts, as the majority (with their children) of the world's refugees, as those most likely to be excluded from the political process. "If there is one message that echoes forth from this conference," she concluded forcefully, "it is that human rights are women's rights . . . And women's rights are human rights."

Charlotte Bunch has devoted her life to feminism. Born in 1944, she was a veteran activist and organizer in the civil rights and antiwar movements before she embraced radical feminism. She also came out as a lesbian and in the early 1970s was a member of the Furies, an influential Washington, D.C., lesbian separatist group. Her books include *Passionate Politics: Essays, 1968–1986* (1987) and (with Niamh Reilly) *Demanding Account-*

Source: Charlotte Bunch, "Through Women's Eyes: Global Forces Facing Women in the 21st Century," speech delivered to the Opening Plenary, NGO Forum '95, Huairou, China, August 31, 1995. Reprinted by permission of Charlotte Bunch.

ability: The Global Campaign and Vienna Tribunal for Women's Human Rights (1994). She is currently the director of the Center for Women's Global Leadership at Rutgers University. In 1999 she received the Eleanor Roosevelt Award for Human Rights at the White House.

This Conference is occurring at a critical juncture in time throughout the world because it is a time of transition—a time when the ways of governing, the ways of living and of doing business, the ways of interacting amongst people and nations are in flux. In my region, Europe and North America, which has a long history of war and domination that has affected the entire globe, we see this transition in what is called the end of the cold war. We have now what I call the hot peace. Rather than a truly peaceful era, we are seeing a shift in power blocs in which the anticipated peace dividend has turned instead into increased racial, ethnic, religious and gender-based conflicts and violence. In this escalation, the role of women—questions of women's human rights and the violation of women as a symbol of their cultures and peoples—has become central.

These global changes are offering both opportunity and danger for women, as in any time of crisis. The opportunity is there for women to offer new solutions, to enter the public policy debate in a way that we have never been able to do before. And the danger is that even those advances we have made in this century will be reversed if we are not able to take this opportunity to move forward. When I talk about women entering the global policy debates and influencing those discussions, I don't see this as totally separate from, but rather building on, the work that women are already doing. Women are usually the leaders at the local community level. Women are the leaders who have held families and communities together in times of crisis. Women have managed budgets that were inadequate to raise children and have managed to keep people together in times of war and other conflicts. And yet, as power moves up the ladder from that local community to national and international policy making, women's voices and women themselves disappear. It is precisely a movement to change this that women have begun in the last two decades—we have begun to demand a place at the table of global policy making as well as at the table in the kitchen. The incredible failures of international policy in this century make it clear that women's expertise and experience must be brought to the global agenda if we are to see change in the 21st century . . .

When I look at the list of the global forces that we are to speak about today, I realize the one most important to me is the global force of women in movement around the world today. This global force of women around the world has many different names, call it feminist, call it womanist, call it women in development, call it women's rights or women's human rights. Call it many different things because each of us has found different terms that describe best for us that reality of domination and change. Women are the most important new global force on the horizon in the world today with the potential to create a more humane future and a humane global governance.

For women to be such a force, however, carries great responsibility. We can not be a movement that thinks and speaks only from our own experiences. We began our movement in this past few decades with the concept that the personal is political and with the need to put women's experiences on the agenda because these were missing. Women's issues, women's perspectives, women's experiences were and still often are left out of policy deliberations. But if we don't want to be simply an added on dimension, we must also bring in all those whose voices are not heard—all the diverse women and men whose voices have been muted—so that we show it is possible for this world to hear from all its peoples. There will be conflicts, but we must seek non-violent ways to resolve them that move toward the future and away from the militaristic models of domination that the world operates from today.

This Beijing conference comes at a critical time in the process of women becoming a global force in the world and has become in many ways a referendum on the role that women will play in the twenty-first century. In that regard, it is also a referendum on the human rights of women. It is about how far we have come in being recognized as full and equal citizens of the world, with equal human rights and with full responsibility for the future direction of the globe. Whether addressing poverty, education, health, violence, etc. all of these are issues of women's access to full humanity, to full human rights, to the conditions necessary to exercise political rights and to take responsibility for enacting visions of where we want to go in the world. This is what it takes for us to become a global political force involved in shaping the twenty-first century.

In this process of empowering women to become greater actors in shaping our societies, women's human rights are key in many ways. Perhaps the simplest way to put this is, how can leaders talk about creating a democratic, sustainable development or a culture of peace and respect for human rights in public life if there is still pervasive denial of development and violation of the human rights of half of humanity in private life? The violence and domination of women that prevails at the core of society in the family undermines any talk of such goals. I believe that it is this connection that women have understood. The public and the private are not separate spheres. As long as we teach violence and domination at the core in our homes and allow them to permeate children's lives from the beginning, we are never going to be able to end the militarism and violence that dominates other relations around differences of race or religion or nationality. Children are taught very early to accept domination based on differences and to see violence as an acceptable solution to conflict and to believe that they have to be either victims or the conquerors. To alter such a dynamic and this violence in public life requires eliminating it in private life as well.

I want to add that I think the United States has a severe problem in its cultural tradition of violence. We often refer to cultural traditions as if they only existed in the third world. One of the traditions of the United States is a tradition of violence. This violence extends from the family to the media to our sport stars to our militarization around the world. And it is this cultural tradition that we must counter in our region just as women from other regions challenge the domination of women in their cultural traditions. So I ask that we never again make the mistake of talking about culture and tradition as if they did not apply to every country and every region of the world when we speak of the changes necessary for the achievement of women's human rights.

Finally, at this conference, we must take one step further into the global arenas of this decade. I think of these UN world conferences as global town meetings. They are opportunities where we meet and talk to each other across the lines of nationality, across lines that we don't often have other opportunities to cross. But as global town meetings, they are also occasions for us to show the world our visions. Looking at the world through women's eyes is an excellent slogan for this forum because this is the place where we can demonstrate the visions of possibility that come from women. In this week at the NGO Forum, we must send forward to that UN conference next week in Beijing the idea that we believe the world can be transformed by looking at it through women's eyes. In so doing, we are opening ever wider the horizon so that what gets onto the global stage, into the internet, and onto that CNN television screen reflects more of reality and more of what women believe can be done for change. So we put the UN and the governments on trial not only this week, but this year and this decade. We are participating now, we are watching, we are demanding, and we are here to see if this can become the arena of real participation where global governance and policies can be created with a human face that is both male and female and where all the diversity of both male and female can emerge. And if this does not prove possible, women must say to the United Nations and to all of our governments, that we have a vision for the future and that is where we are going. We hope that they will allow us to participate and to lead. If they don't, we will take leadership anyway and show that the world can be better for all in the twenty-first century.

The Borderlands

Gloria Anzaldúa

Having opened this anthology with visions of the New Woman at the end of the 19th century, it seems appropriate to close it with a piece pointing toward a new consciousness for the 21st century. A borderlands consciousness arises wherever two (or more) cultures meet. The most vibrant contemporary examples of this new consciousness come from Latina writers. More than just a combination of English and Spanish, Latina literature reflects the realities of women who live in two cultures, affected by both but often feeling an outsider or alien in each.

Chicana *tejana* lesbian-feminist poet and writer Gloria Anzaldúa is one of the most powerful of these voices. Born and raised along the border between Texas and Mexico, she has been active in the migrant farmworkers movement (her father was a sharecropper) as well as teaching Chicano studies, feminist studies, and creative writing at various universities. Anzaldúa

Source: From *Borderlands/La Frontera: The New Mestiza*, © 1987 by Gloria Anzaldúa. Reprinted by permission from Aunt Lute Books.

was a coeditor of *This Bridge Called My Back: Writing by Radical Women of Color* (1981), an enormously influential anthology that brought together prose, poetry, personal narrative, and analysis from African-American, Asian-American, Latina, and Native American women. Her memoir, *Borderlands/La Frontera: The New Mestiza,* from which the final selection was excerpted, was published in 1987.

The term *mestizo/mestiza* refers to a person of mixed Indian and Spanish blood. The new consciousness that Anzaldúa is talking about is very much women's consciouness, *una conciencia de mujer,* as well as a consciousness of ambiguity, constant flux, multiple identities, and divided loyalties. Most fundamentally it is a highly political consciousness, deeply aware of past injustices and looking to a future where we see reality and ourselves within a collective struggle that, as Anzaldúa hopes, could "bring us to the end of rape, of violence, of war."

Una lucha de fronteras / A STRUGGLE OF BORDERS

Because I, a *mestiza,*
    continually walk out of one culture
and into another,
    because I am in all cultures at the same time,
alma entre dos mundos, tres, cuatro,
    me zumba la cabeza con lo contradictorio.
Estoy norteada por todas las voces que me hablan
    simultáneamente.

The ambivalence from the clash of voices results in mental and emotional states of perplexity. Internal strife results in insecurity and indecisiveness. The mestiza's dual or multiple personality is plagued by psychic restlessness.

In a constant state of mental nepantilism, an Aztec word meaning torn between ways, *la mestiza* is a product of the transfer of the cultural and spiritual values of one group to another. Being tricultural, monolingual, bilingual, or multilingual, speaking a patois, and in a state of perpetual transition, the *mestiza* faces the dilemma of the mixed breed: which collectivity does the daughter of a darkskinned mother listen to?

El choque de un alma atrapado entre el mundo del espíritu y el mundo de la técnica a veces la deja entullada. Cradled in one culture, sandwiched between two cultures, straddling all three cultures and their value systems, *la mestiza* undergoes a struggle of flesh, a struggle of borders, an inner war. Like all people, we perceive the version of reality that our culture communicates. Like others having or living in more than one culture, we get multiple, often opposing messages. The coming together of two self-consistent but habitually incompatible frames of reference[3] causes *un choque,* a cultural collision.

---

[3] Arthur Koestler termed this "bisociation." Albert Rothenberg, *The Creative Process in Art, Science, and Other Fields* (Chicago, IL: University of Chicago Press, 1979), 12.

Within us and within *la cultura chicana,* commonly held beliefs of the white culture attack commonly held beliefs of the Mexican culture, and both attack commonly held beliefs of the indigenous culture. Subconsciously, we see an attack on ourselves and our beliefs as a threat and we attempt to block with a counterstance.

But it is not enough to stand on the opposite river bank, shouting questions, challenging patriarchal, white conventions. A counterstance locks one into a duel of oppressor and oppressed; locked in mortal combat, like the cop and the criminal, both are reduced to a common denominator of violence. The counterstance refutes the dominant culture's views and beliefs, and, for this, it is proudly defiant. All reaction is limited by, and dependent on, what it is reacting against. Because the counterstance stems from a problem with authority—outer as well as inner—it's a step towards liberation from cultural domination. But it is not a way of life. At some point, on our way to a new consciousness, we will have to leave the opposite bank, the split between the two mortal combatants somehow healed so that we are on both shores at once and, at once, see through serpent and eagle eyes. Or perhaps we will decide to disengage from the dominant culture, write it off altogether as a lost cause, and cross the border into a wholly new and separate territory. Or we might go another route. The possibilities are numerous once we decide to act and not react.

A TOLERANCE FOR AMBIGUITY

These numerous possibilities leave *la mestiza* floundering in uncharted seas. In perceiving conflicting information and points of view, she is subjected to a swamping of her psychological borders. She has discovered that she can't hold concepts or ideas in rigid boundaries. The borders and walls that are supposed to keep the undesirable ideas out are entrenched habits and patterns of behavior; these habits and patterns are the enemy within. Rigidity means death. Only by remaining flexible is she able to stretch the psyche horizontally and vertically. *La mestiza* constantly has to shift out of habitual formations; from convergent thinking, analytical reasoning that tends to use rationality to move toward a single goal (a Western mode), to divergent thinking,[4] characterized by movement away from set patterns and goals and toward a more whole perspective, one that includes rather than excludes.

The new *mestiza* copes by developing a tolerance for contradictions, a tolerance for ambiguity. She learns to be an Indian in Mexican culture, to be Mexican from an Anglo point of view. She learns to juggle cultures. She has a plural personality, she operates in a pluralistic mode—nothing is thrust out, the good the bad and the ugly, nothing rejected, nothing abandoned. Not only does she sustain contradictions, she turns the ambivalence into something else.

She can be jarred out of ambivalence by an intense, and often painful, emotional event which inverts or resolves the ambivalence. I'm not sure exactly how.

---

[4]In part, I derive my definitions for "convergent" and "divergent" thinking from Rothenberg, 12–13.

The work takes place underground—subconsciously. It is work that the soul performs. That focal point or fulcrum, that juncture where the mestiza stands, is where phenomena tend to collide. It is where the possibility of uniting all that is separate occurs. This assembly is not one where severed or separated pieces merely come together. Nor is it a balancing of opposing powers. In attempting to work out a synthesis, the self has added a third element which is greater than the sum of its severed parts. That third element is a new consciousness—a mestiza consciousness—and though it is a source of intense pain, its energy comes from continual creative motion that keeps breaking down the unitary aspect of each new paradigm.

En unas pocas centurias, the future will belong to the mestiza. Because the future depends on the breaking down of paradigms, it depends on the straddling of two or more cultures. By creating a new mythos—that is, a change in the way we perceive reality, the way we see ourselves, and the ways we behave—*la mestiza* creates a new consciousness.

The work of *mestiza* consciousness is to break down the subject-object duality that keeps her a prisoner and to show in the flesh and through the images in her work how duality is transcended. The answer to the problem between the white race and the colored, between males and females, lies in healing the split that originates in the very foundation of our lives, our culture, our languages, our thoughts. A massive uprooting of dualistic thinking in the individual and collective consciousness is the beginning of a long struggle, but one that could, in our best hopes, bring us to the end of rape, of violence, of war.

La encrucijada / THE CROSSROADS

A chicken is being sacrificed
    at a crossroads, a simple mound of earth
a mud shrine for *Eshu,*
    Yoruba god of indeterminacy,
who blesses her choice of path.
    She begins her journey.

Su cuerpo es una bocacalle. La mestiza has gone from being the sacrificial goat to becoming the officiating priestess at the crossroads.

As a *mestiza* I have no country, my homeland cast me out; yet all countries are mine because I am every woman's sister or potential lover. (As a lesbian I have no race, my own people disclaim me; but I am all races because there is the queer of me in all races.) I am cultureless because, as a feminist, I challenge the collective cultural/religious male-derived beliefs of Indo-Hispanics and Anglos; yet I am cultured because I am participating in the creation of yet another culture, a new story to explain the world and our participation in it, a new value system with images and symbols that connect us to each other and to the planet. *Soy un amasamiento,* I am an act of kneading, of uniting and joining that not only has produced both a creature of darkness and a creature of light, but also a creature that questions the definitions of light and dark and gives them new meanings.

We are the people who leap in the dark, we are the people on the knees of the gods. In our very flesh, (r)evolution works out the clash of cultures. It makes us crazy constantly, but if the center holds, we've made some kind of evolutionary step forward. *Neustra alma el trabajo,* the opus, the great alchemical work; spiritual *mestizaje,* a "morphogenesis,"[5] an inevitable unfolding. We have become the quickening serpent movement.

Indigenous like corn, like corn, the *mestiza* is a product of crossbreeding, designed for preservation under a variety of conditions. Like an ear of corn—a female seed-bearing organ—the *mestiza* is tenacious, tightly wrapped in the husks of her culture. Like kernels she clings to the cob; with thick stalks and strong brace roots, she holds tight to the earth—she will survive the crossroads . . .

El día de la Chicana

I will not be shamed again
Nor will I shame myself.

I am possessed by a vision: that we Chicanas and Chicanos have taken back or uncovered our true faces, our dignity and self-respect. It's a validation vision.

Seeing the Chicana anew in light of her history. I seek an exoneration, a seeing through the fictions of white supremacy, a seeing of ourselves in our true guises and not as the false racial personality that has been given to us and that we have given to ourselves. I seek our woman's face, our true features, the positive and the negative seen clearly, free of the tainted biases of male dominance. I seek new images of identity, new beliefs about ourselves, our humanity and worth no longer in question.

Estamos viviendo en la noche de la Raza, un tiempo cuando el trabajo se hace a lo quieto, en el oscuro. El día cuando aceptamos tal y como somos y para en donde vamos y porque—ese día será el día de la Raza. Yo tengo el conpromiso de expresar mi visión, mi sensibilidad, mi percepción de la revalidación de la gente mexicana, su mérito, estimación, honra, aprecio, y validez.

On December 2nd when my sun goes into my first house, I celebrate *el día de la Chicana y el Chicano.* On that day I clean my altars, light my *Coatlalopeuh* candle, burn sage and copal, take *el baño para espantar basura,* sweep my house. On that day I bare my soul, make myself vulnerable to friends and family by expressing my feelings. On that day I affirm who we are.

On that day I look inside our conflicts and our basic introverted racial temperament. I identify our needs, voice them. I acknowledge that the self and the

---

[5]To borrow chemist Ilya Prigogine's theory of "dissipative structures." Prigogine discovered that substances interact not in predictable ways as it was taught in science, but in different and fluctuating ways to produce new and more complex structures, a kind of birth he called "morphogenesis," which created unpredictable innovations. Harold Gilliam, "Searching for a New World View," *This World* (January, 1981), 23.

race have been wounded. I recognize the need to take care of our personhood, of our racial self. On that day I gather the splintered and disowned parts of *la gente mexicana* and hold them in my arms. *Todas las partes de nosotros valen.*

On that day I say, "Yes, all you people wound us when you reject us. Rejection strips us of self-worth; our vulnerability exposes us to shame. It is our innate identity you find wanting. We are ashamed that we need your good opinion, that we need your acceptance. We can no longer camouflage our needs, can no longer let defenses and fences sprout around us. We can no longer withdraw. To rage and look upon you with contempt is to rage and be contemptuous of ourselves. We can no longer blame you, nor disown the white parts, the male parts, the pathological parts, the queer parts, the vulnerable parts. Here we are weaponless with open arms, with only our magic. Let's try it our way, the mestiza way, the Chicana way, the woman way.

On that day, I search for our essential dignity as a people, a people with a sense of purpose—to belong and contribute to something greater than our *pueblo.* On that day I seek to recover and reshape my spiritual identity. *¡Anímate! Raza, a celebrar el día 'de la Chicana.*

SUGGESTIONS FOR FURTHER READING

Acosta-Belen, Edna, ed. *The Puerto Rican Woman.* New York, 1986.

Bataille, Gretchen M. and Kathleen Mullen Sands. *American Indian Women: Telling Their Lives.* Lincoln, NE, 1984.

Brownmiller, Susan. *Against Our Will: Men, Women, and Rape.* New York, 1975.

Brumberg, Joan Jacobs. *The Body Project: An Intimate History of American Girls.* New York, 1997.

Cade, Toni, ed. *The Black Woman: An Anthology.* New York, 1970.

Cahn, Susan K. *Coming on Strong: Gender and Sexuality in Twentieth-Century Women's Sport.* New York, 1994.

Castillo-Speed, Lillian, ed. *Latina: Women's Voices from the Borderlands.* New York, 1995.

Cohen, Marcia. *The Sisterhood: The True Story of the Women Who Changed the World.* New York, 1988.

Collins, Patricia. *Black Feminist Thought: Knowledge, Consciousness, and the Politics of Empowerment.* Boston, 1990.

Crow Dog, Mary, and Richard Erdoes. *Lakota Woman.* New York, 1990.

Davis, Angela Y. *Women, Race, and Class.* New York, 1983.

Douglas, Susan J. *Where the Girls Are: Growing Up Female with the Mass Media.* New York, 1994.

Echols, Alice. *Daring to Be Bad: Radical Feminism in America, 1967–1975.* Minneapolis, 1989.

Edut, Ophira, ed. *Adios, Barbie: Young Women Write about Body Image and Identity.* Seattle, 1998.

Eisenberg, Susan. *We'll Call You If We Need You: Experiences of Women Working Construction.* Ithaca, 1998.

Evans, Sara. *Personal Politics: The Roots of Women's Liberation in the Civil Rights Movement and the New Left.* New York, 1979.

Faderman, Lillian. *Odd Girls and Twilight Lovers: A History of Lesbian Life in 20th Century America.* New York, 1991.

Faludi, Susan. *Backlash: The Undeclared War Against American Women.* New York, 1991.

Findlen, Barbara, ed. *Listen Up: Voices from the Next Feminist Generation.* Seattle, 1995.

Freeman, Jo. *The Politics of Women's Liberation.* New York, 1975.

Friedan, Betty. *It Changed My Life.* New York, 1977.

Gabin, Nancy. *Feminism in the Labor Movement: Women and the United Auto Workers, 1935–1975.* Ithaca, 1990.

Garcia, Alma, ed. *Chicana Feminist Thought.* New York, 1997.

Garrow, David. *Liberty and Sexuality: The Right to Privacy and the Making of Roe v. Wade.* New York, 1994.

Gilligan, Carol. *In a Different Voice: Psychological Theory and Women's Development.* Cambridge, 1982.

Ginsburg, Faye. *Contested Lives: The Abortion Debate in an American Community.* Berkeley, 1989.

Harrison, Cynthia. *On Account of Sex: The Politics of Women's Issues, 1945–1968.* Berkeley, 1988.

Hartmann, Susan M. *From Margin to Mainstream: American Women and Politics Since 1960.* New York, 1989.

Hartmann, Susan M. *The Other Feminists: Activists in the Liberal Establishment.* New Haven, 1998.

Hill, Anita. *Speaking Truth to Power.* New York, 1998.

Hochschild, Arlie. *The Second Shift: Working Parents and the Revolution at Home.* New York, 1989.

Hoff-Wilson, Joan, ed. *Rites of Passage: The Past and Future of the ERA.* Bloomington, 1986.

hooks, bell. *Feminist Theory: From Margin to Center.* Boston, 1984.

Howe, Louise Kapp. *Pink Collar Workers: Inside the World of Women's Work.* New York, 1977.

Hull, Gloria, Patricia Bell Scott, and Barbara Smith. *But Some of Us Are Brave: Black Women's Studies.* Old Westbury, 1982.

Kennedy, Elizabeth Lapovsky, and Madeline D. Davis. *Boots of Leather, Slippers of Gold: The History of a Lesbian Community.* New York, 1993.

Klatch, Rebecca E. *Women of the New Right.* Philadelphia, 1987.

Linden-Ward, Blanche, and Carol Hurd Green. *American Women in the 1960s: Changing the Future.* New York, 1993.

Mansbridge, Jane J. *Why We Lost the ERA.* Chicago, 1986.

Mathews, Donald G., and Jane Sherron DeHart. *Sex, Gender, and the Politics of the ERA: A State and the Nation.* New York, 1990.

Mora, Magdalena, and Adelaida Del Castillo. *Mexican-American Women in the United States: Struggles Past and Present.* Los Angeles, 1980.

Moraga, Cherrie, and Gloria Anzaldúa. *This Bridge Called My Back: Writings by Radical Women of Color.* Watertown, MA, 1981.

Morrison, Toni, ed. *Race-ing Justice, En-gendering Power: Essays on Anita Hill, Clarence Thomas, and the Construction of Social Reality.* New York, 1992.

Rosen, Ruth. *The World Split Open: How the Modern Women's Movement Changed America.* New York, 2000.

Rosenberg, Rosalind. *Divided Lives: American Women in the Twentieth Century.* New York, 1992.

Rubin, Lillian. *Worlds of Pain: Life in the Working-Class Family.* New York, 1976.

Seifer, Nancy. *Nobody Speaks for Me! Self-Portraits of American Working Class Women.* New York, 1976.

Smith, Barbara, ed. *Home Girls: A Black Feminist Anthology.* New York, 1983.

Solinger, Rickie. *Wake Up Little Susie: Single Pregnancy and Race Before Roe v. Wade.* New York, 1992.

Steinem, Gloria. *Outrageous Acts and Everyday Rebellions.* New York, 1983.

Walker, Rebecca, ed. *To Be Real: Telling the Truth and Changing the Face of Feminism.* New York, 1995.

Wallace, Michele. *Black Macho and the Myth of the Superwoman.* New York, 1979.

Wandersee, Winifred. *On the Move: American Women in the 1970s.* Boston, 1988.

Williams, Patricia J. *The Alchemy of Race and Rights.* Cambridge, 1991.

Wolf, Naomi. *The Beauty Myth.* New York, 1991.

Zavella, Patricia. *Women's Work and Chicano Families: Cannery Workers of the Santa Clara Valley.* Ithaca, 1987.